Political Authority and Provincial Identity in Thailand

Cornell University

Yoshinori Nishizaki

Political Authority and Provincial Identity in Thailand
The Making of Banharn-buri

SOUTHEAST ASIA PROGRAM PUBLICATIONS
Southeast Asia Program
Cornell University
Ithaca, New York
2011

Cornell Southeast Asia Program Publications
640 Stewart Avenue, Ithaca, NY 14850-3857

Studies on Southeast Asia No. 53

Printed in the United States of America

ISBN: hc 978-087727-783-5
ISBN: pb 978-087727-753-8

Cover: designed by Kat Dalton; photograph by Yoshinori Nishizaki

Index: compiled by Paula Douglass

TABLE OF CONTENTS

LIST OF TABLES, FIGURES, AND MAPS

LIST OF TABLES

LIST OF FIGURES AND MAPS

Unless otherwise indicated in the text, all photographs are by the author.

LIST OF RESPONDENTS

- The number that appears in a bracket after each respondent in the text, e.g., (#1), corresponds to the number in the first column below.
- "Age group" and "Occupation" were applicable at the time of interviews.
- "Place of residence" refers to the district where each respondent resided in Suphanburi at the time of the interview. In the cases of respondents who lived outside Suphanburi, the names of provinces where they were born and resided are indicated (marked with *).
- Bangkok-based civil servants are not included on the list. Also excluded are the people who requested absolute confidentiality. Interview dates for these people are given in the text.

#	Age Group	Sex	Occupation	Place of Residence	Date of Interview(s)	Remark
1	15–19	M	student	Muang	Oct 99	son of #34
2	15–19	M	student	Phayao *	Feb 07	studies at Chiang Mai Univ
3	20–29	M	janitor	Muang	Nov 99	from farmer's family
4	20–29	F	college student	Sam Chuk	Feb 00, Apr 00	from farmer's family, friend of #14
5	20–29	M	barber	U-Thong	Oct 99	from farmer's family
6	20–29	F	housemaid	Muang	Mar 00	husband is an electric appliances repairman
7	20–29	F	photocopier	Song Phi Nong	Jul 99	from farmer's family; works in Bangkok
8	20–29	M	restaurant waiter	Bang Pla Ma	Feb 02	from shrimp farmer's family; boyfriend of #10
9	20–29	M	college student	Muang	Feb 02	civil service intern
10	20–29	F	hotel employee	U-Thong	Apr 02	college graduate
11	20–29	M	unemployed	Muang	Feb 02	BA from Ramkhamhaeng Univ, Bangkok
12	20–29	M	security guard	Muang	Jan 02	from farmer's family; formerly construction worker
13	20–29	F	waitress	Sri Prachan	May 04	husband is a trader in general merchandise
14	20–29	F	college student	Sri Prachan	Feb 00	friend of #4
15	20–29	F	gas station clerk	Bang Pla Ma	May 02	parents are shrimp farmers

16	20–29	F	hotel receptionist	Mukdaharn *	Apr 02	college graduate
17	20–29	F	clerk	Nakhon Pathom *	Feb 00	college graduate worked in Bangkok
18	20–29	F	student	Kanchan-aburi *	Mar 00	brother works in Suphanburi
19	20–29	F	college student	Phayao *	Feb 02	lived in Suphanburi for 3 years
20	30–39	M	contractor/village head	Muang	Dec 99	MA from Florida International Univ
21	30–39	M	construction worker	Muang	Oct 99, Mar 02	from farmer's family; born in Song Phi Nong
22	30–39	F	petty merchant	Song Phi Nong	Mar 02	husband is a farmer; neighbor of #52
23	30–39	M	unemployed	Song Phi Nong	May 02	formerly wage worker in Bangkok
24	30–39	M	petty merchant	Don Chedi	Dec 99	family grows rice; son attends technical college
25	30–39	F	petty merchant	Muang	Apr 02	long-distance university student
26	30–39	F	food stall owner	U-Thong	Jan 00, Apr 2000	12 years of education; married to company employee
27	30–39	F	civil servant	Muang	Jan 00, May 02	from farmer's family
28	30–39	F	civil servant	Muang	Mar 02	husband is from Kampheng Phet Province
29	30–39	M	noodle vendor	Nong Ya Sai	Dec 99	from farmer's family
30	30–39	M	motorcyclist for hire	Dan Chang	Dec 99	from farmer's family
31	30–39	M	schoolteacher	Muang	Feb 02	has lived in Buriram Province for 1 year
32	30–39	M	policeman	Sam Chuk	Dec 99	daughter attends university in Bangkok
33	30–39	M	internet café manager	Muang	Apr 02	BA from Ramkhamhaeng Univ, Bangkok
34	30–39	M	clerk	Muang	Oct 99	from a farmer's family; father of #1
35	30–39	M	security guard	Muang	Mar 02	from farmer's family; 9 years of education
36	30–40	M	security guard	Muang	Apr 02	from farmer's family; 6 years of education
37	30–39	F	civil servant	Muang	Apr 00	secretly hates Banharn
38	30–39	M	civil servant	Saraburi *	Dec 99	works in Provincial Office of Public Works
39	30–39	F	factory worker	Saraburi *	Feb 00	works as a motorcyclist for hire on weekends
40	30–39	F	janitor	Saraburi *	Feb 00	husband is long-distance truck driver
41	30–39	M	merchant	Phayao *	Dec 07	deals in shoes & accessories; 9 years of education
42	30–39	M	civil servant	Ayutthaya*	Mar 00	from farmer's family in Ayutthaya

43	40–49	M	security guard	Bang Pla Ma	Oct 99, Dec 99, Jan 00, Apr 00	from farmer's family; lost job after 1997 economic crisis
44	40–49	F	farmer	Muang	May 02	niece of respondent #104
45	40–50	F	farmer	Muang	May 02	sister of #44
46	40–49	F	civil servant	Muang	Jan 02	niece runs a restaurant in California
47	40–49	M	noodle vendor	Song Phi Nong	Mar 00	family grows corn and vegetables
48	40–49	F	lottery ticket seller	Muang	Jan 00	from farmer's family
49	40–49	M	car mechanic	Muang	Sep 99	son attends university in Nakhon Pathom
50	40–49	M	bank teller	Dan Chang	Jan 00	from farmer's family; graduate of technical college
51	40–49	M	drinks vendor	Sam Chuk	Jun 04	from farmer's family in Derm Bang Nang Buat
52	40–49	F	farmer	Song Phi Nong	Mar 02	4 years of education; neighbor of #22
53	40–49	F	farmer/street cleaner	Muang	Jun 02	5 years of education
54	40–49	F	farmer	Sri Prachan	May 02	husband is a farmer; does odd jobs on the side
55	40–49	F	car dealer	Muang	Mar 00, Mar 02	uncle is a well-known local Sino-Thai capitalist
56	40–49	F	farmer	Song Phi Nong	Apr 02	7 years of education
57	40–49	M	primary school master	Muang	Dec 99	thinks Banharn is authoritarian
58	40–49	F	civil servant	Muang	Dec 99	MA from Mahidol Univ
59	40–49	F	civil servant	Song Phi Nong	May 02	close friend of #58
60	40–49	M	civil servant	Don Chedi	Dec 99	parents couldn't afford his university education
61	40–49	F	farmer	Song Phi Nong	Apr 02	neighbor of #91
62	40–49	M	security guard	Sri Prachan	Nov 99	works at Provincial Court
63	40–49	M	food stall owner	Muang	Mar 00	wife from Chainat Province
64	40–49	M	drinks vendor	Muang	Jan 00	wife from Kampheng Phet Province
65	40–49	M	former contractor	Muang	Mar 00	went bankrupt after economic crisis of 1997
66	40–49	M	schoolteacher	Sam Chuk	Feb 02	from farmer's family
67	40–49	F	schoolteacher	Muang	Feb, Mar 00	husband runs a stationery shop
68	40–49	M	civil servant	U-Thong	Jan 00	from farmer's family in Dan Chang
69	40–49	M	civil servant	Nong Ya Sai	Mar 00	family owns a local contracting co.
70	40–49	M	chauffeur	Phetchaburi *	Feb 00	now works in Suphanburi

71	40–49	M	civil servant	Kancha-naburi *	Mar 00	works in Provincial Office of Highways
72	40–49	F	merchant	Lopburi *	Oct 99	deals in general merchandise
73	50–59	F	drinks vendor	Sri Prachan	Dec 01	husband is a farmer
74	50–59	M	car mechanic	Song Phi Nong	Apr 00	graduated from technical college
75	50–59	F	civil servant	Muang	Jan 02	born in Lopburi; has lived in Suphanburi for 30 years
76	50–59	M	policeman	U-Thong	Feb 00	from farmer's family
77	50–59	F	farmer	Bang Pla Ma	Mar 00	neighbor & friend of #96
78	50–59	F	farmer	Song Phi Nong	Jun 02	originally from Bang Pla Ma; 4 years of education
79	50–59	M	schoolteacher	Muang	Feb 00	teaches at the largest primary school in Suphanburi
80	50–59	M	newspaper reporter	Muang	Apr 02	used to work for *Thai Rath* newspaper
81	50–59	F	civil servant clerk	Muang	Dec 99, Jan 2000	4 years of education; daughter is BA holder
82	50–59	F	civil servant	Muang	Apr 02	born in Ayutthaya; anti-Banharn
83	50–59	M	civil servant	Muang	Jan 02	anti-Banharn
84	50–59	M	petty merchant	Muang	Feb 00	son attends the best secondary school in Suphanburi
85	50–59	F	schoolteacher	Muang	Nov 99, Mar 00	born in Sam Chuk; has relatives in Ayutthaya Province
86	50–59	M	farmer	Derm Bang Nang Buat	Dec 99	daughters live in Singburi and Chainat Provinces
87	50–59	M	farmer	Dan Chang	Feb 02	sister and daughter live in surrounding provinces
88	50–59	M	schoolteacher	Muang	Jan 02	from farmer's family
89	50–59	F	civil servant	Muang	Mar 02	works in the Provincial Office of Education
90	50–59	M	noodle vendor	Song Phi Nong	Dec 99	formerly a farmer
91	50–59	F	farmer	Song Phi Nong	Apr 02	neighbor of #61
92	50–59	M	civil servant	Phayao *	Jan 07	once assigned to work in Ayutthaya Province
93	60–69	M	merchant	Bangkok *	May 04	Sino-Thai who came to know Banharn in the 1950s
94	60–69	F	retired schoolteacher	Muang	Nov 99, Dec 00	taught at a primary school in central Suphanburi
95	60–69	M	retired civil servant	Muang	Jan 00	worked in Provincial Office of Public Health
96	60–69	F	farmer	Bang Pla Ma	Mar 00	neighbor & friend of #77

97	60–69	M	retired college teacher	Muang	Nov, Dec 99	Chart Thai Party branch manager
98	60–69	M	merchant	Muang	May 04	deals in electric appliances
99	70–79	M	farmer	Muang	Feb 02	neighbor of #105
100	70–79	F	pharmacist	Muang	Sep 99	Sino-Thai who knows Banharn and his wife personally
101	70–79	M	retired civil servant	Muang	Jan 00	knows Banharn personally
102	70–79	M	retired doctor	Muang	Nov 1999, Jan 2000	has known Banharn since 1950s
103	70–79	M	merchant	Muang	Sep, Nov 99	Sino-Thai
104	70–79	M	farmer	Muang	Mar 02	related to respondents #44 and #45
105	80–89	M	farmer	Muang	Feb 02	former village head

ACKNOWLEDGMENTS

I owe the completion of this book manuscript to numerous people. First and foremost, I thank literally hundreds of people in Suphanburi and elsewhere in Thailand for sharing their insightful views and/or valuable data with me. Their hospitality made my long and otherwise lonely fieldwork an enjoyable experience, memories of which will always remain in my heart. Mrs. "C," in particular, deserves special thanks. From the beginning, she treated me as her de facto son, making sure that I was well fed and also letting me use her motorcycle and, sometimes, even her car (BMW!), for free, as long as I stayed in Suphanburi. Despite the fact that she did not like Banharn, she showed an interest in my project and gave me lots of "leads" on the politician. I am enormously fortunate to have met her, by chance, shortly after I arrived in Suphanburi. I could not have done my fieldwork without her marvelously unstinting support. She and all other Thais I met did not simply contribute to the ideas I present in this volume; much more than that, their stories and viewpoints have broadened my horizons in life.

Over the years, many scholars have shaped my ideas in profound ways. My teachers at the University of Washington offered critical feedback as well as words of encouragement on my PhD dissertation, out of which this book has grown. Charles Keyes took pains to teach me much about rural Thailand. I cannot remember how many times I appreciated his truly warm-hearted mentorship. Mary Callahan earned my heartfelt gratitude for commenting on many horrendously long drafts with much humor, despite her busy schedule of watching the Los Angeles Lakers games (besides regular teaching and researching). The late Dan Lev eagerly took me in as his student, and with his characteristically wry sarcasm, cautioned me against doing pretentious research on "Third World democratization"—a piece of advice I have taken to heart to date. I am proud that I was his last student in his long, distinguished academic career. Ellis Goldberg, whose immense knowledge of comparative politics, anthropology, history, and discourse analysis never failed to inspire (and scare!) me, played a pivotal part in what little intellectual development I achieved. I learned much about state–society relations from Joel Migdal, as is readily apparent in the pages that follow. It was a constant challenge for me to try to meet the high scholarly and stylistic standards he set for his students. Also, his skepticism of "the narrowly constructed world of rigor" assured me that there was much more to political science than numbers, hypotheses, and tests. I am indebted to Jonathan Mercer and Karen Litfin for having directed my interest toward the ideational and psychological dimensions of politics.

At the Australian National University, where I spent a brief stint as a doctoral fellow and as a research fellow, I benefited much from my interactions with noted scholars of Southeast Asia. Craig Reynolds reeducated me about everything, ranging from Thai studies to the use of commas and semicolons. His firm insistence that I base my research on local language sources saved me from becoming a shallow political "scientist," for which I am eternally grateful. Ben Kerkvliet, whose works on rural Filipino politics I had always admired, offered timely and constructive criticisms. Quite apart from this, I am simply thankful to him and his wife, Melinda, for their genuine friendship. Edward Aspinall, Andrew Brown, Nankyung Choi, Harold Crouch, Ardeth Maung, and Andrew Walker were valuable sounding boards for many ideas that were floating around in my mind. Thanks are also due Penny Oakes, a distinguished social psychologist, for making available several dozens of her and her colleagues' published works and works-in-progress in just one day, and for listening to my still inchoate ideas with patience. At Waseda University in Japan, I had the fortune to meet Professor Eiji Murashima, a Thai specialist whose meticulous scholarship I hope to emulate someday, and to present part of my research at his graduate school seminar. To Jojo Abinales of Kyoto University, I owe much for his encouragement and support.

At the National University of Singapore, Jamie Davidson, Erik Mobrand, Michael Montesano, and Vatthana Pholsena read various versions or parts of this manuscript, including the book proposal. Irving Johnson and Goh Beng Lan introduced me to the relevant anthropology literature of which I was unaware. I also owe a deep debt to Reynaldo Ileto, former head of the Southeast Asian Studies Department, for recruiting me to NUS shortly after I finished my PhD studies. In the Department of Political Science, where I am currently based, I have received consistent support from its head, Terry Nardin, for which I am much obliged. Lee Li Kheng of the Cartography Department drew numerous maps for me on short notice.

Special mention must be made of two wonderful people I had the pleasure of meeting during my student years at NUS. My personal debt to Professor Hajime Shimizu, formerly of the Institute of Developing Economies and now of Waseda University, knows no bounds for reasons that are too numerous to list here. The late Dr. Benjamin Batson, who let me stay at his house for free for three months, piqued my serious interest in Thailand. If only he were alive, he might be gratified to know that he did not waste all his time talking to me, in Singapore, Bangkok, and Tokyo, about Thailand. After all these years, I still fondly remember the ritualistic yet uproarious outings I had with him and Professor Shimizu every week to the Singapore River, the Newton Circus, and the Holland Village.

At the Cornell University Southeast Asia Program, I thank my two reviewers for carefully reading my manuscript. I would like to extend my deep thanks to one of the reviewers, in particular, for offering many detailed and thought-provoking points that pushed me to rethink my ideas. The editorial board members also made useful comments that helped refine my argument. It would be utterly remiss of me not to thank Deborah Homsher and Fred Conner for their meticulous copyediting work and encouragement.

I have received generous and timely financial support for my fieldwork in Thailand from the Ford Foundation, the Luce Foundation, the Australian National University, and the National University of Singapore.

Last but not least, I could not have completed this project (and many others) if not for the boundless moral support I have received from my family, particularly my parents. Words simply fail to describe how grateful I am to them. They have not simply encouraged me to pursue my various interests over the years, as I have moved across continents to Singapore, Thailand, the United States, Australia, and then back to Singapore. Most of all, they have taught me, by such fine example, how much happiness and emotional fulfillment human beings can get simply from working hard, helping other people in need, and leading unpretentious and humorous lives every day. Finally, millions of thanks to my wife for standing by me and for just being her always. This work is dedicated to her and my parents.

Yoshinori Nishizaki
Singapore

Map of Thailand, Showing Suphanburi

PREFACE

In countries ranging from the Philippines and Indonesia to Brazil and Russia, democratization has failed to resolve, and actually has exacerbated, a host of preexisting political, economic, and social problems. Thailand is no exception. It has made a transition to democracy since 1973, when a student-led mass uprising toppled long-standing military rule. There has been a serious question, however, about the *substance*, as opposed to the form, of democracy in the country. The recent rule and ouster of Prime Minister Thaksin Shinawatra (in office: 2001–06), a "parliamentary dictator" who suppressed human rights and media freedom, offer one good case in point.

Thaksin is not the first politician who jeopardized substantive democratization in Thailand, however. Long before he came to power, scholars had deplored the political ascendance of allegedly corrupt rural-based strongmen as one of the seemly consequences of the post-1973 democratization. These strongmen were held responsible for many of the ills that plagued Thailand, including the high incidence of ghastly murders, the resilient underground economy, fiscal mismanagement, rampant electoral fraud, and political instability. The dominance of these rural-based politicians supplied urban-based elites, including King Bhumibol, with a powerful rationale or pretext for reforming Thailand's political system in the 1990s. These reforms have resulted, unexpectedly and ironically, in a greater social divide between the city and the countryside, in the context of which Thaksin came to power and exacerbated many of the problems that the urban-based elites had sought to resolve by changing the political system in the first place.

Thus, the rural-based politicians have shaped the nature of contemporary Thai politics and society in profound ways. To gain a deep understanding of why or how Thailand has become the way it is now, we need to understand how those politicians came to power and stay in power in the countryside, where the preponderant majority of Thais reside. "All politics is local," as the maxim in American politics goes. Yet, despite the obvious importance of Thailand's rural-based politicians, no scholar, to my knowledge, has ever studied any one of them in depth, as an individual. The existing literature focuses on national-level political figures who did not have to be elected in the countryside, such as Sarit Thanarat, Chamlong Srimuang, Thaksin Shinawatra, and Prem Tinsulanonda. Some scholars, to be sure, have shed some light on a handful of rural-based politicians, but their analyses, based as they are mainly or even exclusively on Bangkok-based secondary sources, give a frustratingly cursory and one-sided account of the mechanism or pattern of rural Thai politics. These scholars, moreover, offer their analyses by using their own normative and value-ridden yardsticks of what kind of people make good politicians. The voices of local people remain hidden or suppressed in these top-down scholarly accounts; we seldom reach the "local," the intended destination. As a result, we still know relatively little about what ordinary rural folks actually think and say about their politicians. Rectifying this shortcoming was the primary motive behind my fieldwork on which this study is based.

The fieldwork began in 1999, when I went to the mountainous northern province of Phrae to study its nationally well-known boss, Narong Wongwan, a suspected drug trafficker whose assumption of power as prime minister in 1992 was sensationally blocked by the United States government. My purpose was to investigate why Narong suddenly lost the general election of 1995 after having dominated politics in Phrae for nearly two decades. To my disappointment, however, most people in the province seemed to treat this erstwhile leader as a "washed-up" politician of the distant past or a man not worth talking about. They showed little interest in discussing him, or simply remembered so little about him that they had few things to say.

After staying in Phrae for a few months, I went to my second fieldwork site, Suphanburi Province in the rice-growing Chao Phraya delta of the central region. I wanted to compare Narong to the powerful don of Suphanburi, Banharn Silpa-archa, whose domination remained—and still remains—unshaken. What I saw and heard in this province was quite different from my experiences in Phrae. On arriving in Suphanburi, I got a ride in an old minibus and struck up a casual conversation with a fellow passenger, a construction worker in his late thirties (#21).[1] Several minutes later, we passed the modern provincial stadium, which Banharn had renovated with state funds in the early 1990s. Totally unprompted, the worker mentioned Banharn's name in praising the stadium's size and beauty. To encourage him to talk more, I feigned ignorance of Banharn. Showing surprise at my ignorance, the worker went on at length about Banharn's history as Suphanburi's member of parliament (MP) and his contributions to Suphanburi's development. Then I asked: "You seem to like him a lot. Is that right?" He answered immediately: "Of course, I like him! You don't have to ask that kind of question here. Anyone who was born in Suphan [an abbreviation for Suphanburi] must like him. If there's anyone who doesn't, that person is not a Suphanburian." This worker was the first Suphanburian I talked to at length, and I was struck by his ardent support for Banharn and his eagerness to talk about him. Scholars and journalists typically disdain Banharn as an unscrupulous, despicable provincial boss who buys his way into parliament and exchanges unsavory pork-barrel projects for votes. The worker's account flew in the face of such negative images. I could sense that Banharn's local domination runs much deeper than is commonly assumed. I had almost no hesitation in changing the focus of my fieldwork from Narong to Banharn.

Over the next seven years, I lived in Suphanburi on and off for varying periods of time, trying to find out the why and how of Banharn's political authority. A fan of political anthropology, I was initially going to stay in a particular agrarian village of Banharn's electoral constituency to investigate this question. It was not long, however, before I changed my mind. Suphanburians' support for Banharn, I realized, is not confined to any one particular social class in one small village community; it encompasses all social classes all over Suphanburi, including the areas that lie *outside* his electoral constituency. While I knew the benefits of anthropological research, I thought—correctly, I hope—that I could learn even more about Banharn by widening the geographical scope of my research. Therefore, except

---

[1] The number given in parentheses after each respondent corresponds with the number in the "List of Respondents."

when I was cooped up in the provincial archives and library, I spent almost every day visiting various places in Suphanburi on a motorcycle, sometimes covering three-hundred kilometers in one day. By the end of my fieldwork, I had visited all the 111 subdistricts in the province; I visited many of them repeatedly.

Along the way, I met and talked to literally hundreds of Suphanburians, both pro-Banharn and anti-Banharn, from all walks of life and age groups. I adopted the methodology similar to the one that my mentor, Benedict Kerkvliet, had partially adopted in the Philippine countryside. I never set up an appointment to meet anybody. I talked to anyone who had the time and willingness to talk to me. I rarely had any trouble finding such a person. Once I found one person to talk to, the circle of my informants expanded in all sorts of directions. That person typically introduced me to his or her friends, neighbors, family members, colleagues, and so on, who in turn introduced me to more people. Most people were initially surprised at my appearance as a total stranger, but they turned out to be quite eager to talk to a "bizarre alien" who wanted to know about their province, of all things on earth. Many invited me to their homes and treated me to lunch, dinner, or a boisterous (and ribald) beer-drinking session. Because my "interviews" were open-ended and informal (I never used structured interviews or questionnaires), we did not always talk about Banharn or politics. When it seemed awkward to mention his name, I did not do so. We talked about many silly, frivolous things (e.g., soccer, Japanese actresses), which I believe helped establish mutual rapport. The fact that I am, and look like, a typical short Asian man with black hair may have helped lower the psychological barrier that might otherwise have existed. For these reasons, I believe that when my interviewees did talk about Banharn (and they did so quite often), they were speaking their minds candidly, irrespective of whether they were praising or criticizing him. While this methodology may leave some room for questioning whether my respondents were generally representative of Suphanburi's whole population, I maintain that my "sample" is sufficiently large so that the following portraits of Banharn do not merely capture the anomalous views of a numerical minority.

The initial approach I took was to examine the extent to which Suphanburians' perceptions of Banharn reflected the "reality." I sought to reveal the clear disjuncture between the two, so as to argue that Suphanburians were under an ideological spell and to use this case to question Professor James Scott's "Lilliputians are not mystified" argument, presented in his widely read *Weapons of the Weak*.[2] The approach frustrated me, however. It soon became clear to me that, while some of the Suphanburians' narratives about Banharn were patently false or dubious, some others were based on objectively true facts. Still others were simply impossible or very difficult to verify conclusively. Gradually, it dawned on me that a much more fruitful and interesting line of inquiry would be to let Suphanburians explain in their own terms why they support Banharn in the way they do, and to examine why or how they have come to hold the beliefs they do. This is the objective of the empirical chapters that follow.

Banharn's (or any other politician's) dominance is admittedly a very complex phenomenon, and I found several different "faces" of him in the course of doing research. To construct a holistic explanation that spotlights all those faces would

---

[2] James C. Scott, *Weapons of the Weak: Everyday Forms of Peasant Resistance* (New Haven, CT: Yale University Press, 1985).

have its own distinctive merit as one sort of analysis. Instead of doing so, however, I have decided, for the sake of "parsimony" and due to space constraints, to zero in on one element of his rule that few scholars have taken sufficient account of thus far—Suphanburians' positive identification with Banharn as the heroic developer of their formerly "backward" province. Banharn has cultivated this collective pride by projecting himself as the antithesis to the inefficient central state, which had neglected Suphanburi's development in the past. This projected image is a hitherto overlooked yet enormously important—if not the only—reason for the Suphanburians' strong support for Banharn. The readers interested in a biography of Banharn, a chronological analysis of his political career, his (alleged) local-level corruption, his electoral campaign strategies, and so on might be disappointed at the analysis that follows. I will talk about these issues only insofar as they are pertinent to the Suphanburians' provincial pride, which underpins his political authority at the local level.

The account I offer defies much of the standard literature on rural politics and society in Thailand and other democratizing countries of Southeast Asia. This literature tends to describe farmers and other ordinary people in the countryside in a litany of negative and pessimistic ways. Scholars influenced by modernization theory portray these rural constituents as poor, uneducated, naïve, and venal. Many scholars of Thai politics belong to this camp and argue—rather tritely, in my view—that improving the economic and educational standards of rural dwellers will lead to Thailand's "progress" (whatever that means). On the other hand, scholars working in the Marxist or moral economy traditions view and construct agricultural producers—ominously called "peasants" rather than farmers—as helpless, powerless, downtrodden, and perennially indignant victims of exploitative capitalism. These producers, therefore, are depicted as resisting and rebelling against capitalist encroachment, overtly or covertly, to protect their subsistence rights. A study that does not bring out these conflictual aspects of class-based rural life would be considered naïve, uncritical, or even surreal. Such a tendency, I believe, reflects, and stems from, the hegemonic individual-centered materialist paradigm that many social scientists, especially those influenced by Marxism, seem to have adopted.

I do not repudiate these depictions outright. The Marxist school of thought, in particular, is extremely insightful, and I owe an enormous intellectual debt to it. Nonetheless, I believe that the *sum* of existing works contributes, if inadvertently, to perpetuating unbalanced and stereotyped images of the countryside by subsuming rural folks under a negative category that is essentially different from "us"—the people who live in more "modern" societies. I admit that the economic and educational standards of Suphanburians are relatively low, and that these people embrace many traditional values, but I believe that it is a terrible—and condescending—mistake to attribute their political behavior wholly and crudely to these sociological factors. Likewise, I concede that the capitalist economy enforced by the modern coercive state has not been particularly kind to the majority of lower-class Suphanburians, and I will pay due attention to some of the individual and collective hardships that these people have suffered at the hands of the state. But hardship is not all there is to their lives. These people do not simply or always worry and grumble about how to make both ends meet. While the means of economic survival available to them are severely limited, many Suphanburians lead quite normal—and even "happy"—lives within such constraints, in the same way that their counterparts in more developed countries do. It is from such perspectives that I present this study, in the hope that it will contribute, empirically and theoretically, to providing a more balanced, complex, and nuanced picture of rural politics and state-society relations in democratizing Thailand.

Perhaps, there could not be a more opportune time to offer this kind of study, with all the urban-centric news stories and reports flying around concerning the supposedly unbridgeable urban–rural schism in Thailand—a schism based on many reporters' unexamined, facile assumption that rural voters support the likes of Banharn because they are poorly educated. The overwhelming support that the ousted Thaksin continues to receive in rural areas, as manifested by the growth of the so-called "red-shirt" movement, has only corroborated and perpetuated that negative image for many observers of Thailand. Only recently have a handful of scholars come to take issue with this widely held image. If this book invites "anti-rural" scholars and non-scholars alike to revisit their stereotyped views of the Thai countryside and its people, it will have served its modest purpose.

CHAPTER ONE

RETHINKING DOMINATION IN THE THAI COUNTRYSIDE

Politicians, like any other human beings, have different public "faces," which can be radically different from each other. The late Ferdinand Marcos is widely regarded as a corrupt dictator who plundered the Philippine state, but the people in his home region of Ilocos still fondly remember him as "the best leader the Philippines ever had,"[1] a person who "approximated their concept of a true leader."[2] Similarly, the Burmese military leaders, whose repressive policies are universally condemned in the international media, actually enjoy pockets of legitimacy in some villages of the country.[3] Beyond Southeast Asia, President Trujillo of the Dominican Republic, a tyrant notorious for his repressive rule, was a hero of his country's peasants.[4] These accounts indicate the difficulties and dangers of pigeonholing politicians in one way or the other. Depending on the types, interests, and ideologies of the audience, politicians can be "good" or "bad." As with physical beauty, the legitimacy of any politician resides in the subjective eye of the beholder. This book sheds light on one such politician in rural Thailand.

The specific politician I consider is Banharn Silpa-archa (b. 1932) from Suphanburi, an agrarian province located some one hundred kilometers north of Bangkok (see figure 1.1).[5] Banharn served as Suphanburi's member of parliament (hereafter MP) from 1976 to 2008. Between 1995 and 1996, he even served as prime minister of Thailand. His long-standing and seemingly distinguished political career, however, has been marred by numerous well-publicized corruption scandals. His (and other politicians') misuse of office was allegedly so egregious that the military used it as a pretext for ousting the elected civilian government in 1991. Banharn's short-lived, self-serving administration and its bungled financial policies are also believed to have contributed to the devastating economic crisis that hit Thailand in 1997. He is accordingly called all sorts of pejorative names, such as "a walking ATM" that indiscriminately dispenses money under the table to anyone who needs it. Similarly, his cabinet was likened to a "7-Eleven Store," open for dirty-money

---

[1] *Asiaweek*, June 2, 1995, p. 80.

[2] Fernando Zialcita, "Perspectives on Legitimacy in Ilocos Norte," in *From Marcos to Aquino: Local Perspectives on Political Transition in the Philippines*, ed. Benedict Kerkvliet and Resil Mojares (Manila: Ateneo de Manila University Press, 1991), p. 274.

[3] Ardeth Maung Thawnghmung, *Behind the Teak Curtain: Authoritarianism, Agricultural Policies, and Political Legitimacy in Rural Burma* (London: Kegan & Paul, 2003).

[4] Richard Turits, *Foundations of Despotism: Peasants, the Trujillo Regime, and Modernity in Dominican History* (Stanford, CA: Stanford University Press, 2003).

[5] Suphanburi comprises an area of 5,358 square kilometers and a population of nearly 860,000 at present. Delaware, the second smallest state in the United States, is almost equivalent to Suphanburi in area and population.

transactions twenty-four hours a day. The Chart Thai (CT) Party, of which he was deputy secretary-general (1976–79), secretary-general (1979–94), and leader (1994–2008), was also regarded as one of the most money-tainted parties in Thailand.[6] By 2008, Banharn had become one of the wealthiest politicians in Thailand, having amassed assets of nearly 3,369 million baht (along with his wife),[7] although we cannot determine how much of this was made through dishonest means. Banharn, in short, is one of the many allegedly crooked rural-based politicians whose rise to power has accompanied the process of democratization in post-1973 Thailand. Many

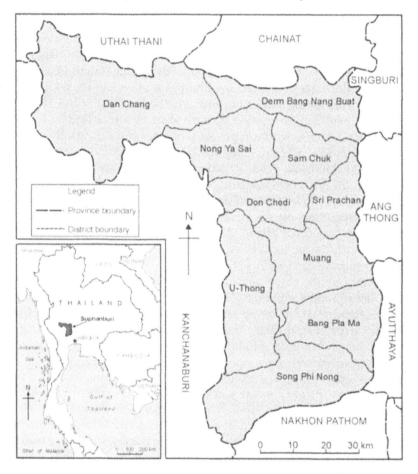

Figure 1.1 Map of Suphanburi and its Districts[8]

---

[6] In December 2008, the Constitutional Court banned the CT Party on the grounds that one of its executive members committed electoral fraud. The court also stripped Banharn (and many other MPs) of his political power (see chapter 8 for details).

[7] National Counter-Corruption Committee, MP File no. 343. More than 60 percent of this wealth derives from landownership. Banharn and his wife own 243 plots of land (nearly 1,895 *rai*; 1 *rai* = 1,600 square meters) in Bangkok and seven Central Region provinces, including Suphanburi. By way of contrast, the declared assets of Kanlaya Sophonpanich and her husband, Chote, son of the founder of the powerful Bangkok Bank Group, were 544,221,367 baht in 2008. National Counter Corruption Committee, MP File no. 25.

[8] Drawn by the Cartography Department, National University of Singapore.

urban-based, well-educated Thais deride him as the personification of "dirty-money politics," a brand of politics that impedes the institutionalization of transparent democratic governance.[9] In contemporary Thailand, where the discourse of political reforms has gained much ground, Banharn finds it increasingly difficult to occupy legitimate political space.

Even the revered King Bhumibol has repeatedly made public his disapproval of "ambitious, corrupt politicians" in general, of whom Banharn is a prime example. Thus, when the Banharn government took office in July 1995, the king was "visibly distraught," and his unhappiness was perhaps not entirely due to the fact that his mother had just passed away. Subsequently, by using unusually harsh language that was "unbecoming" for him, the king denounced the Banharn government and its politicians for being "incompetent" and "unconcerned for the people." The king thus contributed to "discrediting ... the Banharn administration" from the start.[10] In the face of this severe legitimacy crisis, Banharn was forced to resign just over a year after becoming prime minister. Thus, the monarchy was complicit in "colluding in the ouster" of Banharn (and several other elected prime ministers), "of whom it disapproved."[11]

Despite all this negative publicity, Banharn has commanded a great deal of support and respect in Suphanburi. As but one reflection of this support, he has won a landslide victory in all the elections he has contested since 1976, receiving 63 to 94 percent of the vote. The interviews that I conducted in Suphanburi at various times from 1999 to 2006 supported these seemingly suspicious election results. I asked 171 Suphanburians of all ages and social classes to rate the strength of their support for Banharn on a scale of 1 to 5. They gave him an average of 4.1 points. Seventy-nine people (46 percent) rated him at five points, while only nineteen people gave him less than three points. Neither age, social class, nor the level of educational attainment caused significant variation in the level of my respondents' support for him. Some respondents couched their support in quite strong, emotion-laden language. According to one noodle vendor, "Every Suphanburian must give him five points. Anybody who gives him less than five doesn't deserve to be a Suphanburian." Interestingly, even the Suphanburians who live *outside* Banharn's electoral constituency expressed similarly positive sentiments. This does not mean, of course, that every Suphanburian likes Banharn; he has his share of inveterate detractors who criticize him on many grounds. The presence of these detractors, however, does not diminish the fact that the sizable majority of Suphanburians support and respect him—so much so that they refer to their own province, with a mixture of humor and pride, as "Banharn-buri."[12] Although Bangkokians cite this nickname to sneer at Banharn for turning Suphanburi into his personal turf, the label carries a far more positive and affectionate connotation when used by

---

[9] David Murray, "The 1995 National Elections in Thailand: A Step Backward for Democracy," *Asian Survey* 36,4 (1996): 361–75; and Philip Robertson, Jr., "The Rise of the Rural Network Politician: Will Thailand's New Elite Endure?" *Asian Survey* 36,9 (1996): 924–41.

[10] Paul Handley, *The King Never Smiles: A Biography of Thailand's Bhumibol Adulyadej* (New Haven, CT: Yale University Press, 2006), pp. 370, 371.

[11] Duncan McCargo, "Network Monarchy and Legitimacy Crises in Thailand," *Pacific Review* 18,4 (2005): 509.

[12] The suffix, *buri*, means "town" in Thai. "Banharn-buri" thus means "Banharn's Town."

Suphanburians. It is the crystallized expression of their support for, and their identification with, Banharn as the legitimate leader of Suphanburi.

Banharn contrasts sharply with many other rural-based MPs who once seemed "invincible," yet suffered humiliating electoral losses in the last decade or so. Examples include (but are not limited to): Narong Wongwan, a suspected drug lord in the northern province of Phrae; Vatthana Asavaheme, another suspected drug trafficker, in Samut Prakan Province; Piya Angkinan from Phetchaburi Province; Yingphan Manasikan from Phisanulok Province; and members of the Khamprakorp clan in Nakhon Sawan Province. While these rural-based politicians have come and gone, Banharn remains firmly in the saddle of power, having won one resounding victory after another at the polls since 1976. Even after the Constitutional Court ruling of 2008 that barred him from politics for five years, he remains the well-respected "shadow" ruler of Suphanburi. Why?

The puzzle becomes even more curious when we consider that Banharn has done a relatively poor job of raising Suphanburians' living standards. Although Suphanburi's per capita Gross Provincial Product (GPP) has recorded a quite respectable 470 percent increase since 1974, the provinces adjacent to Suphanburi have achieved far more impressive growth. The contrast between Suphanburi and Ayutthaya, a province situated east of Suphanburi, is particularly striking. In 1974, Ayutthaya's GPP per capita was lower than Suphanburi's; since then, it has risen by nearly 3,900 percent, thanks to the infusion of foreign manufacturing capital. Ayutthaya's GPP is now nearly six times higher than Suphanburi's. Over 80 percent of Ayutthaya's GPP comes from manufacturing, and only 2.5 percent from agriculture. In contrast, agriculture still remains the largest economic sector in Suphanburi, accounting for 27 percent of the GPP, while the share of manufacturing is only 16 percent. Of the seventy-five provinces in Thailand, Suphanburi is among the most reliant on agriculture.[13] Thus, ordinary Suphanburians have reaped relatively few benefits from Thailand's recent industrial growth. This is not to say that Suphanburians are impoverished. All Suphanburians actually enjoy minimum living standards; everyone has a place to live, food to eat, and clothes to wear. Banharn certainly has not created a huge landless class of abjectly poor peasants. The majority of Suphanburians, however, are comparatively less well off than their counterparts in many other provinces that have achieved a fundamental structural change to their economies.

If individual Suphanburians are rational in the utilitarian or instrumentalist sense, they should be dissatisfied with, and even vote out of office, an allegedly corrupt MP like Banharn, who has done relatively little to enhance their individual material interests. Yet, their strong, steadfast support for him runs directly counter to such expectations. How, then, has he won their ready and enthusiastic support?

THE DOMINANT PLOT IN RURAL THAI POLITICS

The historian Hayden White has stirred up a controversy by denying the existence of "objective" history, which mainstream historians all aspire to write.

---

[13] http://www.nesdb.go.th/econSocial/macro/gpp_data/index.html, accessed in October 2004; Provincial Office of Suphanburi, *Phaen Long Thun Changwat Suphanburi* (Suphanburi: 1994), pp. 43, 48; Provincial Statistical Office of Suphanburi, *Samut Rai-ngan Sathiti Changwat: Suphanburi 2539* (Suphanburi: Provincial Statistical Office, 1997), p. 13.

According to White, no social phenomenon has an ontologically absolute quality. Given this condition, what historians, or social scientists in general, can do, White argues, is to engage in "emplotment"—to invent or reconstruct the past by imputing a certain "plot" or a structure of meanings to it. The "plot" is not based on objectively accurate evidence, but on social scientists' subjective, selective, and creative interpretations of the available evidence—interpretations that reflect their respective (subconscious) worldviews or ideological stances.[14]

Illuminating and liberating as it may be to some historians, this polemical postmodernist or deconstructivist argument has come under heavy fire from positivist social scientists. One of their main criticisms is that White's historiography condones or encourages unbridled relativism. His critics argue that denying the possibility of writing objective history is tantamount to saying that a particular social phenomenon can be interpreted from any perspective.[15] As Kuisma Korhonen has argued, summing up these critiques, White advances the untenable notion that "nothing matters and everything is permitted."[16]

Such relativism, however, has failed to emerge in some areas of research in Southeast Asian studies. Instead, a more or less uniform "plot" continues to predominate, overshadowing or marginalizing alternative interpretations. Research on rural politics in Thailand is one case in point, although the situation is slowly changing. As the country has made a steady move to democratization during the last three decades or so, scholars have turned their attention to the political dynamics in the countryside, where the vast majority of politicians are elected. This is a wholesome trend that marks a departure from the past capital-city-centric scholarship.[17] Many of these scholars, however, portray the processes and effects of democratization in overwhelmingly negative terms, highlighting the electoral successes of corrupt capitalists-cum-politicians, including violent gangsters. As a consequence of the rise to power of these dishonest politicians, a plethora of seamy problems—murders, coercion, vote-buying, pork-barreling, patronage, and skullduggery—have allegedly reached endemic proportions in rural Thailand.[18]

---

[14] Hayden White, *Metahistory: The Historical Imagination in Nineteenth-century Europe* (Baltimore, MD: Johns Hopkins University Press, 1973); Hayden White, *Tropics of Discourse: Essays in Cultural Criticism* (Baltimore, MD: Johns Hopkins University Press, 1978); and Hayden White, *The Content of the Form: Narrative Discourse and Historical Representation* (Baltimore, MD: Johns Hopkins University Press, 1987). For an application of White to interpretations of Thai history, see Craig Reynolds, "The Plot of Thai History: Theory and Practice," in *Patterns and Illusions: Thai History and Thought*, ed. Gehan Wijeyewardene and E. C. Chapman (Canberra: Australian National University, 1992), pp. 313–32.

[15] Keith Windschuttle, *The Killing of History: How Literary Critics and Social Theorists are Murdering our Past* (New York, NY: Free Press, 1997).

[16] Kuisma Korhonen, "General Introduction: The History/Literature Debate," in *Tropes for the Past: Hayden White and the History/Literature Debate*, ed. Kusima Korhonen (New York, NY: Rodopi, 2006), p. 15.

[17] Allen Hicken, "Developing Democracies," in *Southeast Asia in Political Science: Theory, Region, and Qualitative Analysis*, ed. Erik Kuhonta, Dan Slater, and Tuong Vu (Stanford, CA: Stanford University Press, 2008), pp. 85–86.

[18] See, among others, Benedict Anderson, "Murder and Progress in Modern Siam," *New Left Review* 181 (1990): 33–48; Daniel Arghiros, *Democracy, Development, and Decentralization in Provincial Thailand* (Richmond, UK: Curzon, 2001); William Callahan and Duncan McCargo, "Vote-buying in Thailand's Northeast: The July 1995 General Election," *Asian Survey* 36,4 (1996): 376–92; Ruth McVey, ed., *Money and Power in Provincial Thailand* (Honolulu, HI: University of Hawai'i Press, 2000), pp. 1–122; Michael Nelson, *Central Authority and Local*

To elaborate, much of the literature on Thailand attributes the rise of rural-based politicians to a vast network of their clients. Given the insufficient rule of law in the countryside, ordinary people, especially economically vulnerable farmers, need to cultivate strong local patrons who have enough material and coercive resources to protect their lives and property from exploitative state officials. Oftentimes, such local patrons are violent gangsters with entrenched interests in profitable underground businesses (e.g., the drug trade, smuggling, gambling, and prostitution). For the rural poor, however, such seemingly despicable patrons are actually considered quite desirable, because their illegal wealth constitutes an enormous "tax-free" source of personal largesse, and also because they can offer protection by using force, if necessary. If the poorly enforced rule of law renders poor villagers' lives precarious, then they look for a powerful local leader who can turn that institutional defect to their advantage. Hence we see the rise of Janus-faced *nakleng*-type leaders beyond the gaze and reach of the central state—that is, the leaders who are cruel, belligerent, and fearless toward their enemies, yet at the same time generous and compassionate towards their supporters.[19] Such people, who take on the character of what Eric Hobsbawm and Oliver Wolters respectively called "social bandits" and "men of prowess," endowed with "soul stuff,"[20] are presumed to have been the most favored types of leaders in the Thai countryside.

According to the standard literature on rural Thai rural politics, these strongmen rely on their patron–client networks to mobilize votes for them come election time. They win elections hands down. All they have to do is to ask for votes from their clients. These clients, consisting mostly of uneducated, tradition-bound, and submissive farmers, who comply unquestioningly out of gratitude for all the benevolent patronage they had received.[21] As electoral competition has increased over the years, many politicians have come to rely also on money and other material inducements to drum up votes for them—a phenomenon typically labeled "vote-buying." If any formidable political rival emerges, the strongmen simply resort to intimidation or murder, for which they easily escape punishment, thanks to the weak legal apparatus of the state. Local policemen, who are supposed to crack down on such crimes, look the other way in exchange for bribes, which they eagerly grab to supplement their meager official incomes.

Elected to parliament through these means, local strongmen make "legitimate" use of their official power to channel scarce state resources, such as infrastructure projects, into their respective constituencies. These pork-barrel projects—the

---

Administration in Thailand (Bangkok: White Lotus, 1998); James Ockey, *Making Democracy: Leadership, Class, Gender, and Political Participation in Thailand* (Honolulu, HI: University of Hawai'i Press, 2004), pp. 81–123; Somrudee Nicro, "Thailand's NIC Democracy: Studying from General Elections," *Pacific Affairs* 66,2 (1993): 167–82; and Pasuk Phongpaichit and Sungsidh Piriyarangsan, *Corruption and Democracy in Thailand* (Chiang Mai: Silkworm, 1996), pp. 57–107.

[19] David Johnston, "Bandit, Nakleng, and Peasant in Rural Thai Society," *Contributions to Asian Studies* 15 (1980): 90–101.

[20] Eric Hobsbawm, *Bandits* (Harmondsworth: Penguin, 1972); Oliver W. Wolters, *History, Culture, and Region in Southeast Asian Perspectives* (Ithaca, NY: Cornell Southeast Asia Program Publications, 1999), pp. 18, 94.

[21] This analysis of rural Thai politics has scarcely changed since 1958, when Herbert Phillips published his classic study of election rituals in Ayutthaya Province. Herbert Phillips, "The Election Ritual in a Thai Village," *Journal of Social Issues* 14,4 (1958): 36–50.

"collective political patronage," as Daniel Arghiros calls it—further strengthen and widen the unscrupulous leaders' local base of support by attracting a growing number of contractors and bureaucrats as *hua khanaen* (vote canvassers).[22] The domination of these leaders is so solid that many of them are called "godfathers" (*chaopho*) or, more euphemistically, "men of influence" (*phu mii itthiphon*).

Minor differences aside, most existing scholarly works conform essentially to this "plot" when describing the characteristic dynamics of rural Thai politics. I do not dispute the scholarly contributions of these works. Taken *individually*, each study has done enormous academic service by uncovering the unwholesome effects of democratization on rural politics. Rather, what I find disturbing is the *cumulative*, if unintended, effect of the extant works *as a whole* on the general image of the Thai countryside. The countryside emerges uncannily from the sum of these works as a socially inferior and changeless "other"—a perennially problematic and incorrigible entity inhabited by a hopelessly docile and venal people. The scholars who expose the "problems" of local Thai politics and society, no matter how well intentioned they may be, are (unknowingly) complicit in reproducing and perpetuating this uniformly adverse "Orientalist" image.[23]

This is not to say that alternative interpretations are wholly nonexistent. In recent years, a small number of scholars have questioned or challenged the dominant view. Anek Laothamatas, for one, has drawn our attention to the two conflicting meanings of democracy that urban middle-class people and rural dwellers have come to embrace in the historical context of Thailand's uneven socioeconomic development. While economically well-off Bangkok residents (can afford to) define democracy as a set of high-sounding principles, such as freedom and transparency, rural voters, whose socioeconomic interests have long been neglected by the central state, regard democracy as a mechanism that brings them concrete material benefits. Accordingly, for rural voters, honest politicians who promote the abstract "national interests" of Thailand do not necessarily make good politicians; instead, the rural voters' ideal politicians are "those who visit them often, address their immediate grievances effectively, and bring numerous public works to their communities."[24] Anek thus makes a simple yet important point that rural-based politicians do not (always) buy their way into corridors of power; they get elected because they have the voters' support.[25] Andrew Walker provides valuable empirical support to Anek's (unsubstantiated) generalization by highlighting the unwritten, time-honored "rural constitution"—a set of locally embedded moral values, norms, expectations, and

---

[22] Daniel Arghiros, *Political Structures and Strategies: A Study of Electoral Politics in Central Rural Thailand* (Hull: University of Hull, Center for South-East Asian Studies, 1995), p. 2; and Arghiros, *Democracy, Development, and Decentralization in Provincial Thailand*, p. 167.

[23] Reynaldo Ileto uses the case of the Philippines to present a similar critique of the discursive or scholarly construction of the inferior "other," although I do not agree with his extreme conclusion that Western scholars are motivated by an insidious neocolonial project. Reynaldo Ileto, *Knowing America's Colony: A Hundred Years from the Philippine War* (Honolulu, HI: University of Hawai'i, Center for Philippine Studies, 1999), chapter 3.

[24] Anek Laothamatas, "A Tale of Two Democracies: Conflicting Perceptions of Elections and Democracy in Thailand," in *The Politics of Elections in Southeast Asia*, ed. Robert Taylor (New York, NY: Woodrow Wilson Center Press, 1996), p. 202.

[25] Ibid., p. 207.

aspirations—in Chiang Mai Province.[26] William Callahan also scrutinizes the allegedly rampant vote-buying in rural Thailand, suggesting that it is not so much an actual phenomenon as a biased discursive concept that is utilized, problematized, and perpetuated by urban elites to maintain their self-righteous sense of moral superiority over the countryside.[27] Most recently, Marc Askew has shown that the virtual hegemony of the Democrat Party in southern Thailand is based on the party's successful invention and manipulation of the voters' regional identity as "virtuous southerners" (although he accords due attention to the use of money and party machines in the region).[28] Valuable and refreshing as they are, however, these kinds of interpretations are still few and far between, with the deplorable result that the negative image of the Thai countryside remains widely accepted in much of the scholarly and journalistic discourse, as exemplified by popular characterizations of former Prime Minister Thaksin as a politician who had the support of the uneducated rural poor.

By using the case of Banharn, this study seeks to breathe some more fresh air into the generally stifling discourse on rural Thai politics. Banharn is a particularly intriguing case in this respect because the mainstream literature on Thai politics portrays him as the prototype of debased rural bosses, yet most Suphanburians see a quite different politician in him.

Misfits

According to the prevailing "plot" that guides most studies of rural Thai politics, politicians employ four specific means of domination in combination or in isolation: (1) violence or the threat thereof, (2) electoral fraud, especially vote-buying, (3) private patronage, including the holding of charities, and (4) pork-barrel projects. Banharn's domination in Suphanburi, however, does not fit this emplotment well.

"Violence" is a clear misfit, simply because Banharn has never used it. He has also never been involved in the sorts of underground businesses that murderous strongmen maintain as economic bases for recruiting "professional gunmen" (*mue puen*). Politics in Suphanburi, therefore, has been remarkably free of the sort of gruesome murders committed in some other provinces of Thailand at election time. Some local-level politicians, including those connected to Banharn, have been killed, but these murders arose not from electoral politics, but from business conflicts among those individual politicians. On May 4, 1997, for example, Anant Rueangsuk-udom, a provincial councilor of U-Thong District and the owner of a construction

---

[26] Andrew Walker, "The Rural Constitution and the Everyday Politics of Elections in Northern Thailand," *Journal of Contemporary Asia* 38,1 (2008): 84–105. For a historical account of the localist discourse on vote-buying in Chiang Mai, see Katherine Bowie, "Vote Buying and Village Outrage in an Election in Northern Thailand: Recent Legal Reforms in Historical Context," *Journal of Asian Studies* 67,2 (2008): 469–511.

[27] William Callahan, "The Discourse of Vote Buying and Political Reform in Thailand," *Pacific Affairs* 78,1 (2005): 95–113. For similar, if brief, critiques, see Thongchai Winichakul, "The Others Within: Travel and Ethno–Spatial Differentiation of Siamese Subjects 1885–1910," in *Civility and Savagery: Social Identity in Tai States*, ed. Andrew Turton (Richmond, UK: Curzon), pp. 55–56; and Thongchai Winichakul, "Toppling Democracy," *Journal of Contemporary Asia* 38,1 (2008): 24–26.

[28] Marc Askew, *Performing Political Identity: The Democrat Party in Southern Thailand* (Chiang Mai: Silkworm, 2008).

company (Tancharoen), was shot dead. The suspected mastermind of this murder was Khiang Matrasri, a village head in U-Thong, whose construction company (Matrasri Jakrakon) had business conflicts with Anant's firm. Six days later, Khiang himself was killed in retaliation.[29] Banharn, however, did not have any reason to be involved in either murder case, because both Anant and Khiang had long acted as his vote canvassers in U-Thong. He actually lost two of his key supporters because of their "petty" business rivalry, which had little to do with him. Contrary to the image conjured up in much of the extant literature, politically motivated violence is not rife in all rural provinces of Thailand, and Suphanburi is a prime example. Many Suphanburians praise Banharn on this account. They believe that, thanks to Banharn, Suphanburi has not degenerated into a "gangster province" in the way some other provinces, such as Chonburi, have. If he had ever resorted to violence in attaining and maintaining power, it is likely that he would be enjoying much less popular support now.[30]

Vote-buying does not explain Banharn's electoral success well, either. Many Suphanburians I talked to claimed that they had never received any money from Banharn or the CT Party's vote canvassers. I established good rapport with these respondents, so I have little reason to suspect that they misled me in any way. Some other people admitted, quite openly, that they had received money, but we cannot jump to the conclusion that money solely determined their support for Banharn. This is because he was not the only candidate who dispensed money; other candidates did the same. Some of them actually offered more money than Banharn did, yet the overwhelming majority of my respondents ended up voting for Barnharn. His rival candidates only wasted their money; the cash pay-outs were ineffective in winning over voters. One respondent, a rice farmer's son (#43), gave a typical reply: "We are poor, so we grab all the money we can lay our hands on. But when we vote, we vote for the person we like ... Banharn doesn't actually have to use money. We fully support him, regardless of whether we are given money or how much we are given." Voters in Suphanburi, as elsewhere in provincial Thailand, simply regard money-giving as "a custom" (*prapheni*), which all candidates must observe to demonstrate their generosity or to avoid being branded as stingy.[31] Given this view, the dispensing of cash gifts is not an *active* attempt to buy votes. It is rather a *defensive* ritualistic act on the part of candidates who do not wish to deviate from the unwritten social norms or etiquette in rural society. Voters, therefore, have little compunction about accepting money to supplement their incomes. But when they cast their votes, they do so according to their own preferences.

In other words, contrary to what the standard literature would have us believe, voters in Suphanburi have an autonomous choice. At the time of receiving money,

---

[29] *Khon Suphan*, May 16, 1997, pp. 1, 10; *Thai Rat*, May 5, 1997, pp. 1, 18.

[30] Even in the provinces where violence is presumed to be common, it cannot explain election results very well. A good example is Chonburi Province, the fiefdom of Kamnan Po, who is reputedly the most violent gangster in Thailand. Since 1983, he has extended electoral support to his henchmen in the province, but some of them, including his relatives, have occasionally suffered humiliating electoral losses. Scholars who view violence as the decisive instrument of domination would be stumped to explain this phenomenon.

[31] See also Walker, "The Rural Constitution and the Everyday Politics of Elections in Northern Thailand," p. 90; Anek, "A Tale of Two Democracies," p. 207; Arghiros, *Political Structures and Strategies*, p. 38; and Arghiros, *Democracy, Development, and Decentralization in Provincial Thailand*, p. 216.

they may promise, almost always verbally, to vote for a particular candidate, but we cannot assume that they will actually keep their word. If they do not like the candidate for some reason—they may simply dislike the way he or she looks—they will vote for somebody else. In the absence of an effective mechanism for finding out who votes for whom in the closed (i.e., secret) voting booths, voters have ample room to defect at the last minute without having to fear subsequent reprisal or punishment. We should not take their verbal promises in public at face value; they are not totally compliant and unquestioning slaves to money.[32] Dispensing money alone, therefore, does not translate automatically into *effective* vote-buying. Instead of facilely assuming that Banharn buys Suphanburians' support, we should be asking why they do not defect from him when they have so much leeway to do so. If vote-buying were really as effective as it is assumed to be by many analysts of Thai politics, it would have been quite easy for a billionaire like Thaksin to defeat Banharn. In the parliamentary elections of 2001 and 2005, however, Suphanburi was one of the few provinces in Thailand where even Thaksin's cash-rich Thai Rak Thai Party could not win a single seat.

Private patronage is an equally inadequate explanation for Barnham's successes at the polls. As will be shown in chapter three, Banharn organized a number of charities for the poor in the 1960s and 1970s. The beneficiaries of these charities regarded, and still regard, Banharn as a bighearted man, and this is certainly one important element of his moral authority. One of many such beneficiaries was a rice farmer in Muang District, who received a notebook and pencils at a charity organized by Banharn in the late 1960s. The farmer has been an ardent supporter of Banharn for years. It would be simplistic, however, to establish a strong causal link between this farmer's unwavering support and Banharn's charity. The problem is that the farmer benefited from Banharn's largesse only *once*, and that was four decades ago. The goods he received, moreover, were worth no more than a few dozen baht. We would be hard put to explain why the farmer continues to support Banharn as fervently and consistently as he does in return for the small material benefits that he once received such a long time ago.

A more telling piece of evidence is the fact that the majority of Suphanburians have *never* received any kind of patronage from Banharn and his party. He has certainly organized numerous charities over the decades, but their benefits have not filtered down even to half of the provincial population.[33] It is worth noting, further, that, apart from his contributions to occasional charities, Banharn does not provide for the social welfare of any individual Suphanburian on a regular basis. He does not sponsor any funeral, for example, nor does he extend any emergency loan or pay medical and school expenses for anybody, nor does he mediate in any local dispute. Suphanburi has a population of more than 800,000 people at present (as of 2010) and

---

[32] For similar accounts of voters' autonomous choice, see Anek, "A Tale of Two Democracies," pp. 207–8; Somchai Phatharathananunth, "The Thai Rak Thai Party and Elections in North-eastern Thailand," *Journal of Contemporary Asia* 38,1 (2008): 119; Arghiros, *Political Structures and Strategies*, pp. 69–80; and Callahan and McCargo, "Vote-buying in Thailand's Northeast," pp. 387, 391. Instead of elaborating the implications of voters' autonomy, the last two of these works unfortunately end up emphasizing vote-buying as the ultimate determinant of voters' behavior.

[33] For a similar point on the Philippines, see Benedict Kerkvliet, "Toward a More Comprehensive Analysis of Philippine Politics: Beyond the Patron–Client, Factional Framework," *Journal of Southeast Asian Studies* 26,2 (1995): 401–19.

it would be utterly impossible for Banharn (or anybody) to look after the individual welfare of all these people. If he were to do that, he would be inundated with requests for help from hundreds of people every day. He has neither time nor material resources to accommodate such requests.

Thus, Banharn does not, or cannot, render the kinds of patronage that a bighearted patron is supposed to provide according to the orthodox literature on rural Thai politics. Yet, many non-recipients of Banharn's patronage still support him eagerly. Their support is not conditionally tied to the actual or expected acquisition of any particular short-term material benefit; it is based instead on what Howard Wechsler would call "a reservoir of generalized goodwill" toward Banharn.[34] In the language of David Easton, Suphanburians' support is not "specific" and "direct," but "diffuse" and "indirect."[35] Thus, it would be insufficient to attribute Banharn's domination to his paternalism and munificence on the basis of the patron–client model.

The concept of "pork-barrel politics" has a little more explanatory value. Since becoming Suphanburi's MP in 1976, Banharn has channeled a multitude of public development projects into the province to the benefit of villagers (see chapter 4). These projects have also enriched many local contractors and bureaucrats, who constitute his extensive patron–client network in Suphanburi. Banharn is surely a consummate pork-barrel politician. At a glance, all this appears to support the prevailing transactional view that the likes of Banharn exchange tangible pork-barrel projects for votes.[36] However, this explanation runs into a few serious empirical snags, too.

First, if the instrumentalist explanation were correct, we would expect Suphanburians' support for Banharn to vary, depending on the number of development projects they have received. In actuality, however, that is not the case. Even the villagers who have not benefited directly from Banharn's pork-barrel projects have consistently supported him. An example is a group of rice farmers in Don Tarl of Muang District, whose old wooden houses are linked to the outer communities by a single bumpy, unpaved road. Yet none of these farmers holds any grudge against Banharn; far from it, they all remain staunch supporters of him. When I asked about the unsurfaced road in the village, one farmer (#44) replied, "It is not that Banharn wants to keep our village like this forever. We must keep in mind that he can't develop every part of Suphanburi at the same time. He has to do it bit by bit. We must be patient." Her elder sister (#45) chipped in with a comment: "Sooner or later, Banharn will renovate the road. Come back here next year, and you might see a brand-new road." Based as it is on a utilitarian simplification of human interests, the literature that identifies pork-barrel projects as key elements of rural

---

[34] Howard Wechsler, *Offerings of Jade and Silk: Ritual and Symbol in the Legitimation of the T'ang Dynasty* (New Haven, CT: Yale University Press, 1985), p. 224.

[35] David Easton, *A Systems Analysis of Political Life* (Chicago, IL: University of Chicago Press, 1965).

[36] Anek, "A Tale of Two Democracies," pp. 206, 222; Daniel King, "Thailand in 1995: Open Society, Dynamic Economies, and Troubled Politics," *Asian Survey* 36,2 (1996): 136; James Ockey, "Thai Society and Patterns of Political Leadership," *Asian Survey* 36,4 (1996): 353; Pasuk Phongpaichit and Chris Baker, *Thailand's Boom and Bust* (Chiang Mai: Silkworm, 1998), p. 263; Pasuk Phongpaichit and Chris Baker, *Thailand: Economy and Politics* (New York, NY: Oxford University Press, 2002), p. 421; Murray, "The 1995 National Elections in Thailand," pp. 371, 373; and Robertson, "The Rise of the Rural Network Politician," pp. 924–25.

Thai politics is too limited to explain why these Suphanburians support Banharn the way they do.

Second, contrary to what the literature leads us to expect, the contractors and bureaucrats who have benefited handsomely from Banharn's pork-barrel projects do not act as his vote canvassers. A good case in point is a subdistrict chief (#20) in Muang District, who is well known for his personal closeness to Banharn.[37] Thanks to this connection, his construction company, Nakphanit, won public bids for undertaking renovation projects worth 18.4 million baht at five of the nine primary schools in his subdistrict in the late 1990s.[38] Despite all this, however, the subdistrict head always stays at home at election time without ever trying to mobilize votes for Banharn. He explained his inaction to me plainly: "Banharn doesn't need my help to win an election. Why should I waste my time and energy to help him when so many people already support him?" Several villagers confirmed this account, saying that the subdistrict head pays a visit to their homes shortly before each election, only to remind them of the date of election and the need to bring their ID cards.

Just as revealing is the same subdistrict head's inaction in the well-publicized and fiercely contested senate election of March 2000, in which Manas Rung-ruang, Banharn's protégé and the former mayor of Muang municipality, ran for office against Pridi Charoensil, a former provincial police colonel who defected from Banharn's camp. Three days before the election, the subdistrict head "happened" to be traveling in Hong Kong with his college classmates, instead of canvassing for votes on Manas's behalf. On that day, I asked the subdistrict head's close friend if he should not be helping Banharn get Manas elected. She replied with a wry smile: "Well, he [the subdistrict head] doesn't really care. If he doesn't want to help, he doesn't have to." Manas lost the election despite Banharn's support.[39] The existing literature would have us believe that a powerful provincial boss like Banharn can get anyone elected by activating his huge electoral "machine," but that was not the case here. Banharn's machine malfunctioned because its cogs did not work. The voters, for their part, cast their ballots for Pridi because they considered him a better candidate than Manas, who had done little for their community when he was mayor. As one voter explained, "In the general election, we vote for Mr. Banharn ... But the senate election was different. We had to pick candidates who could function independently... We [had] our own choice of senators. Is it wrong for us to vote for our favorites to be senators?"[40] Even Banharn's support for Manas did not sway the decision of this voter and other Suphanburians. This episode underscores the point I noted above: Rural-based voters, just like their counterparts in Bangkok, exercise their choices autonomously by acting on their own preferences. The typical "pork-

---

[37] Until his death in 1990, the father of this subdistrict head (b. 1962) had been a subdistrict head himself and Banharn's close friend. Thus, Banharn has known the present subdistrict head since he was a little boy and has treated him well for many years. Banharn helped him get into the Bangkok Christian College, and when he got married in 2001, Banharn attended the wedding ceremony as the main guest of honor. Interview with the subdistrict head, December 7, 1999; and *Khon Suphan*, March 16, 2001, p. 4.

[38] Department of Business Development, Ministry of Commerce, Suphanburi Company File no. 177.

[39] See chapter 8 for more details on this election and the candidate Pridi.

[40] *Bangkok Post*, March 21, 2000, p. 2.

barrel" explanation is not entirely wrong, but it is insufficient to accommodate these anomalies.[41]

In brief, the widely accepted narratives of rural politics cannot fully or accurately explain Banharn's political dominance in Suphanburi. There is more to his domination than the prevailing explanations would have us believe. To understand why he commands the Suphanburians' strong support and respect the way he does, I present a different narrative or interpretation that highlights the little-studied social-psychological basis of his political authority: the provincial pride shared by Suphanburians. I will show the historical and social process through which this collective pride has emerged and the effects it has had on Banharn's strong hold on politics in Suphanburi.

TOWARD ANOTHER PLOT

Broadly speaking, I will argue that Banharn's domination is the product of a series of heroic actions that he has taken over the decades to develop Suphanburi within the national and global ideological milieu that stigmatizes "backwardness." Suphanburi was once a typical "backward" province in Thailand, owing to the negligence of the central state. Since the 1960s, however, Banharn has rectified this condition by using a combination of his personal funds and institutional power in the state, to a point where Suphanburi now boasts many roads, schools, and other development works of superior quality. The reason why many Suphanburians support Banharn is because all the developmental initiatives he has taken visually represent his valiant efforts to enhance the image, prestige, reputation, or social status of their province. For these people, Banharn is a benevolent and efficient "Robin Hood" who has developed the formerly backward Suphanburi on behalf of, or in contrast to, the callous, inept, and lackadaisical central state. The result is a strong and positive provincial identity, of which Banharn and his many initiatives are an integral part. In a nutshell, Banharn has boosted the Suphanburians' pride in being Suphanburians; they are no longer ashamed of the backwardness of their province. This collective pride underlies Banharn's legitimate authority in Suphanburi.

Let me elaborate.

An Imagined New Social Geography of Thailand

The reason why many Suphanburians hold favorable beliefs about Banharn, or why those beliefs hold enormous emotional appeal the way they do, can be better understood if we consider the broad historical context, in which a deep social stigma has been attached to the people living in "backwardness." In the post-Enlightenment global system of visual and verbal representations, a handful of national and subnational groups have been upheld as superior models of development, while the rest have been despised or degraded as "backward" or "uncivilized." As the whole world has been mapped physically through the means of impersonal cartographic technology, another kind of geography—"the imaginary *social* geography," in which

---

[41] See Yoshinori Nishizaki, "The Weapon of the Strong: Identity, Community, and Domination in Provincial Thailand" (PhD dissertation, University of Washington, Seattle, WA, 2004), chapter 1, for details.

some territorial-based social groups enjoy (putatively) higher social status than others—has been symbolically and discursively constructed.[42] This nonmaterial dimension of intergroup relations is often overlooked by most political scientists or economists, who view the value of modernization in terms of socioeconomic material benefits alone (e.g., income distribution, employment, literacy rate, and access to education and public healthcare).

At the international level, the imagined social geography has been reflected in "a prestige hierarchy of nations."[43] Possessing the products of industrial technology—perceived metaphysically as things big, new, tall, bright, wide, clean, fast, beautiful, neat, convenient, fragrant, safe, orderly, and so on—has been represented, through various modes of discourses and practices (e.g., colonial officials' documents, world fairs), as the mark of civilization, and the small number of Western nations that possess such things have been able to colonize, scorn, and humiliate non-Western have-nots.[44] The end of colonialism did not put an end to this status hierarchy. The former colonies are now lumped under the newly invented rubric of the "Third World" (or its synonyms), which needs to emulate the models of development offered by the "First World."[45] As Eric Hobsbawm put it aptly, "... only political euphemism separates the various synonyms of 'backwardness.'"[46] A second-level tier of status hierarchy has existed within the "uncivilized" camp itself. The more "civilized" groups within this camp have been in a position to despise the less civilized. An example is Meiji Japan, which positioned itself as the only "civilized" nation in Asia, compared to its "barbarous" neighbors.[47] Similarly, Thailand has traditionally regarded Laos as its defacto "less-than-human" colony, "needful of the civilizing influences the Siamese can provide."[48] In both these cases, Japan and Thailand, which were or are still relegated to inferior status in relation to the West, assume the superior position of "modern metropolises" vis-à-vis their immediate neighbors.

The third tier of status hierarchy—the most relevant one for my argument—has existed within each "Third World" country. Many Indians, for example, consider Bihar to be "the most impoverished, backward, and crime-ridden state in the

---

[42] Edward Said, *Orientalism* (New York, NY: Vintage Books, 1979), pp. 53–54, emphasis mine.

[43] R. P. Dore, "The Prestige Factor in International Affairs," *International Affairs* 51,2 (1975): 190–207.

[44] Michael Adas, *Machines as the Measure of Men: Science, Technology, and Ideologies of Western Dominance* (Ithaca, NY: Cornell University Press, 1989); and Robert Rydell, *All the World's a Fair: Visions of Empire at America International Expositions, 1876–1916* (Chicago, IL: University of Chicago Press, 1984).

[45] Arturo Escobar, *Encountering Development: The Making and Unmaking of the Third World* (Princeton, NJ: Princeton University Press, 1995); and Gustavo Lagos, *International Stratification and Underdeveloped Countries* (Chapel Hill, NC: University of North Carolina Press, 1963), p. 24.

[46] Eric Hobsbawm, *Age of Extremes: The Short Twentieth Century, 1914–1991* (London: Abacus, 1995), p. 200.

[47] Daikichi Irokawa, *The Culture of the Meiji Period*, trans. Marius Jansen (Princeton, NJ: Princeton University Press, 1985), pp. 59–60, 213.

[48] Charles F. Keyes, "A Princess in a People's Republic: A New Phase in the Construction of the Lao Nation," in *Civility and Savagery: Social Identity in Tai States*, ed. Andrew Turton (Richmond, UK: Curzon, 2000), pp. 206, 222.

nation."[49] Similarly, in the "geographical imaginings" of South Korea, the poor agriculture-based southwestern region of Cholla "has long suffered the stigma of social discrimination."[50] The same holds true for several less developed prefectures of Japan, which are located across the sea from Korea. Lumped under the derogatory category of *Ura-Nihon* (backside Japan), these prefectures have been regarded in post-Meiji Japan as inferior to the more prosperous *Omote-Nihon* (front-side Japan) region along the Pacific coast.[51] *Ura-Nihon* is considered as "somehow an alien region" and "Japan's domestic 'other.'"[52] Similar domestic status hierarchies exist in other countries as diverse as Indonesia, China, Sri Lanka, Nepal, and the Philippines.[53]

Thailand is no exception. The seventy-five rural provinces of Thailand are categorized by the sweeping label of *ban nork*, a pejorative word for the countryside. As in many other late-developing countries, the Thai state has long pursued the skewed pattern of development that favors the capital city of Bangkok and its vicinity. The *ban nork* has consequently lagged far behind economically and socially. Although a few provinces, such as Chiang Mai, have fared relatively well, most provinces have not. Thais living in the huge area outside Bangkok have been represented and marginalized as socially inferior, backward "others." For example, since the late nineteenth century, Siamese kings and court officials have traveled through the countryside to observe, describe, and document the living conditions of "uncivilized" people—the "others within" Siam—from "a superior, gazing position."[54] In the 1960s and 1970s, the negative image of the countryside deepened, thanks to the propaganda of the military regime that played up the causal connection between backwardness and communist insurgency.[55] Drawing on the title of Michael Lewis's insightful study, we might say that, as the Thai state has endeavored to achieve national integration, the countryside has become physically "a part" of Thailand, while at the same time paradoxically growing "apart" from urban Thailand in the imaginary domestic social geography of the country.[56] This explains

---

[49] Peter Gottschalk, *Beyond Hindu and Muslim: Multiple Identity in Narratives from Village India* (New York, NY: Oxford University Press, 2000), p. 57.

[50] Sallie Yea, "Maps of Resistance and Geographies of Dissent in the Cholla Region of South Korea," *Korean Studies* 24 (2000): 69.

[51] Tadao Furumaya, *Ura Nippon: Kindai Nippon wo Toinaosu* [Backside Japan: Reappraising Contemporary Japan] (Tokyo: Iwanami Shinsho, 1997); and Jacob Schlesinger, *Shadow Shoguns: The Rise and Fall of Japan's Postwar Political Machine* (New York, NY: Simon & Schuster, 1997), pp. 37–38.

[52] Michael Lewis, *Becoming Apart: National Power and Local Politics in Toyama, 1868–1945* (Cambridge, MA: Harvard East Asian Studies, 2000), p. 10.

[53] See James Brow, "The Incorporation of a Marginal Community within the Sinhalese Nation," *Anthropological Quarterly* 63,1 (1990): 7–17; Arjun Guneratne, "Modernization, the State, and the Construction of a Tharu Identity in Nepal," *Journal of Asian Studies* 57,3 (1998): 749–73; Tim Oakes, "China's Provincial Identities: Reviving Regionalism and Reinventing 'Chineseness,'" *Journal of Asian Studies* 59,3 (2000): 667–92; Jonathan Rigg, Anna Allott, Rachel Harrison, and Ulrich Kratz, "Understanding Languages of Modernization: A Southeast Asian View," *Modern Asian Studies* 33,3 (1999): 586; and Zialcita, "Perspectives on Legitimacy in Ilocos Norte," p. 283.

[54] Thongchai, "The Others Within," pp. 50–52.

[55] Kasian Techapira, *Commodifying Marxism: The Formation of Modern Thai Radical Culture, 1927–1958* (Kyoto: Kyoto University Press, 2001).

[56] Lewis, *Becoming Apart*.

why rural folks, as several anthropologists have observed, regard development as a zero-sum "competition" for escaping the label of backwardness.[57] Development has this nonmaterial social value.

As will be shown in chapter 2, Suphanburi was once branded and looked down upon as a typical "backward" province in *ban nork*. As such, it did not have a high social status. Suphanburians blamed this situation on the inattentive and irresponsible central state that failed to meet their needs for development. In the national and global discursive milieu that deeply stigmatized (and still stigmatizes) those who live in "backward" and "uncivilized" places,[58] many Suphanburians felt ashamed or socially inferior.[59] They accordingly felt a strong desire to overcome such conditions and to attain signs of "development" or "modernity."

Against this background, Banharn appeared in the 1960s as a heroic developer of Suphanburi, in contradistinction to the negligent central state. His perceived heroism involved, first of all, his generous donations to the cause of local development. Once an ordinary migrant worker in Bangkok, Banharn "hit the jackpot" in the construction business that he launched in the 1950s. In the mid-1960s, he started using his attendant personal wealth to perform a series of deeds that symbolized Suphanburi's development and prestige. These donations won Banharn a landslide victory in the parliamentary election of 1976.

Since becoming an MP, Banharn has contributed even more to Suphanburi's development by supplementing his personal largesse with huge portions of state funds. He has been able to tap those state monies thanks to the institutional context of Thailand, in which an outwardly democratic state displays a fundamental, historical continuity of patrimonial features—the weak public–private division. A person adept in patronage politics, Banharn has harnessed his personal connections in this state (which I call the "patrimonial democratic state") to channel an unprecedented number of state-funded development projects, both large and small, into various parts of the formerly backward Suphanburi. This pattern reached its peak during his premiership in 1995–96. Suphanburi's development has thus accelerated to such an extent that the province now boasts a wide range of development projects that are unmatched in quality in rural Thailand and have, accordingly, won admiration and even envy from many Thais living outside the province.

---

[57] Arghiros, *Democracy, Development, and Decentralization in Provincial Thailand*, p. 213; Philip Hirsch, "What is the Thai Village?" in *National Identity and its Defenders, 1939–1989*, ed. Craig Reynolds (Clayton: Monash University Center of Southeast Asian Studies, 1991), p. 332; and Ratana Boonmathya, "Contested Concepts of Development in Rural Northeastern Thailand" (PhD dissertation, University of Washington, Seattle, WA, 1997), pp. 131, 145.

[58] Michael Rhum, "'Modernity' and 'Tradition' in 'Thailand,'" *Modern Asian Studies* 30,2 (1996): 325–55.

[59] Such negative sentiments were not limited to Suphanburians; their counterparts in the rest of *ban nork* felt much the same way. See Charles F. Keyes, *Isan: Regionalism in Northeastern Thailand* (Ithaca, NY: Cornell Southeast Asia Program, 1967), pp. 38, 39; and Thak Chaloemtiarana, *Thailand: The Politics of Despotic Paternalism* (Bangkok: Social Science Association of Thailand, 1979), p. 205. Bangkok residents' contemptuous attitude toward rural folks has become the emotion-laden motif in many country pop music songs (*luuk-thung*), such as "Value as Low as the Ground," "The Poor Stink," and "The Smell of Mud and Buffaloes." *Bangkok Post*, "Outlook," January 3, 1996, p. 13. Interestingly, Suphanburi has produced some of the most famous *luuk-thung* singers (see below for more details).

The influx of state funds has not been the only factor fueling Suphanburi's impressive development since 1976. Another major contributing factor has been Banharn's "fussy" personality, amply demonstrated by his strict and meticulous supervision of local civil servants. Because of this supervision, local civil servants, who might otherwise be slothful and predatory, are forced or disciplined to make efficient use of the massive state funds supplied by Banharn. They cannot afford to do otherwise, since Banharn controls their promotions in the patrimonial democratic state. Thus, many ordinary Suphanburians hail Banharn as a leader who has minimized corruption at the local level—a far cry from his usual image as an avaricious politician who plunders state funds.

As a result of all these actions by Banharn—personal donations, the allocation of state funds, and the close supervision of local bureaucrats—a wide array of high-quality development projects has come to fill public space in Suphanburi. But there is more to these projects. Once they have been completed, Banharn's local clients—civil servants and contractors—erect ubiquitous signboards and organize numerous ceremonies to advertise these newest accomplishments to the public as his *personal* benevolent and efficient contributions to local development. To live in Suphanburi is to live in this symbolic universe, which produces and reproduces highly positive images of Banharn "here and there." Out of constant exposure to this symbolic universe emerges a distinct form of ordinary Suphanburians' provincialist imagining at the village level. Plainly stated, the people who see one of Banharn's personal development projects in a particular village come to gradually imagine that village as just one of the many, many villages that he has similarly developed in the broader and invisible provincial community of Suphanburi. Thus, a large number of villagers scattered over wide geographical distances come to identify strongly and positively with Banharn as the developer of Suphanburi *as a whole*, to a point where they call their province "Banharn-buri," or Banharn's Town. Contrary to what the standard literature on rural Thai politics would lead us to believe, Banharn's local-level clients do not play the role of vote canvassers at election time. Instead, they function as his essential "political entrepreneurs" who (sometimes grudgingly) assist in the symbolic construction of "Banharn-buri," an imagined community into which the provincial population of Suphanburi is incrementally integrated.

The strongest form of this pride finds verbal expression in a variety of social narratives that many Suphanburians tell in order to categorize their province as more "developed" than many or all others in Thailand. These accounts are highly subjective, however; they are not based on any objective assessment of Suphanburi's development in relation to other provinces. Objectively speaking, Suphanburi is still underdeveloped in many ways, as exemplified by its lack of industrialization. Many Suphanburians themselves are well aware of these persistent signs of backwardness, but they selectively emphasize the areas of development in which Banharn has made his most outstanding contributions (e.g., "The roads in Suphanburi are the best in the country"). At the same time, they arbitrarily discount, rationalize, or even justify his relatively poor contributions in the other areas of development (e.g., "If Suphanburi is not industrialized, we should be thankful because we still have unpolluted air"). I contend that this subjectivity is the very manifestation and source of Suphanburians' strong provincial pride. They acquire, maintain, and bolster this pride by embracing a variety of subjective views that (exaggeratedly) accentuate Banharn's legendary contributions to provincial development. Constructing and maintaining such views allows Suphanburians to imagine the emergence of a "new social geography" of

Thailand, in which their province has now shed the humiliating label or stigma of "backwardness" and has attained a good measure of respectability or even a position of superiority. Banharn's authority hinges, in large part, on this "imagined"—but not wholly illusionary—national development hierarchy, from which Suphanburians from all walks of life derive their provincial pride. The seemingly simple and lighthearted designation, "Banharn-buri," reflects and condenses this subjective provincialist pride.

It comes as little surprise, then, that many Suphanburians subjectively deflect, spurn, or rationalize a variety of criticisms that scholars and journalists commonly level against Banharn (e.g., his graft). These outsiders' criticisms threaten and impair their cherished image of Banharn as a hero who has rectified the unjust and inequitable relationship between the Bangkok-centric central state and socially marginalized Suphanburi. Because this shining image of Banharn is such an essential part of Suphanburians' provincial pride, they seek to preserve and enshrine him in it. We can make better sense of their unwavering support for him if we take into account this localized system of beliefs and values.

Banharn, in short, has enhanced a highly subjective sense of Suphanburians' pride in their province. While the Thai state may have created "Suphanburi" as an impersonal administrative unit, it failed to create "proud" Suphanburians. This is what Banharn has succeeded in doing. The resultant positive collective identity, as manifested by the popular moniker "Banharn-buri," has enabled this politician to establish and maintain his unrivaled dominance in Suphanburi without recourse to unscrupulous means of social control, such as violence and vote-buying.

To sum up, I weave the following four factors into my social-psychological explanation of how Suphanburians' provincial identity has emerged as an essential component of Banharn's domination within the wider ideological context that extols "development" and stigmatizes "backwardness" (see also figure 1.2):

1) *history*: legacies of state neglect and memories of the backward past
2) *social actions*: Banharn's generous donations, state funds allocation, and strict local-level leadership that reflects his meticulous personality
3) *institutions*: the patrimonial democratic state in the post-1973 period, which has made his social actions possible
4) *political entrepreneurs*: a huge clientelist network that advertises various development projects in Banharn's name

The rise of Suphanburians' provincial pride has been contingent on a combination of these factors. If any of them were missing, the pride would not have emerged or would have taken a less strong form.

In Thai and Southeast Asian studies, collective identity has received much scholarly attention. To date, however, the existing literature has focused, by and large, on nationalism and regionalism only, without paying comparable attention to the historical and social process through which provincialism—another form of collective identity that exists below the level of nation and region—emerges.[60]

---

[60] On nationalism, see Benedict Anderson, *Imagined Communities: Reflections on the Origin and the Spread of Nationalism* (London: Verso, 1991); Katherine Bowie, *Rituals of National Loyalty: An Anthropology of the State and the Village Scout Movement in Thailand* (New York, NY: Columbia University Press, 1997); Craig Reynolds, ed., *National Identity and its Defenders, 1939–1989* (Clayton: Monash University Center of Southeast Asian Studies, 1991); and Thongchai

Moreover, none of the extant literature, except Askew's recent study of regionalism in southern Thailand, discusses the *political* effects of collective identity on why or how a particular politician or party attains and maintains power. I make one attempt to remedy this deficiency by shedding light on the close relationship between Suphanburians' provincial identity and Banharn's political domination.

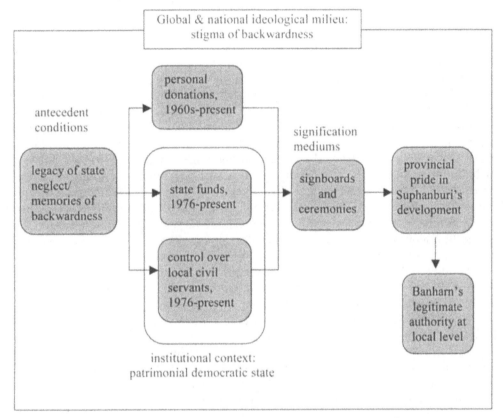

Figure 1.2 Causal Mechanism of Banharn's Domination

Addressing Potential Critiques

One might notice that some parts of my argument outlined above are similar to those discussed in the recent literature on rural Thai politics. For example, Anek has argued that successful candidates in the countryside are those who "make donations to local charities," "bring ... large budget allocations and public infrastructure projects," or "stay close to the electorate."[61] I admit that Banharn has done all these. In this respect, my argument might appear to offer nothing new. However, the kind

---

Winichakul, *Siam Mapped: A History of the Geo-Body of Siam* (Honolulu, HI: University of Hawai'i Press, 1994). On regionalism, see Keyes, *Isan*; and Askew, *Performing Political Identity*.

[61] Anek, "A Tale of Two Democracies," pp. 208, 222. See also Walker, "The Rural Constitution and the Everyday Politics of Elections in Northern Thailand," p. 92.

of explanation advanced by Anek and others is rooted mainly or solely in the materialist realm: Politicians get elected because of the material benefits they provide for voters and their communities. I do not reject the relevance of such interpretations for Banharn's case at all, but I go one step further, shedding light on the *non*-material dimension or outcome of Banharn's material contributions to local development, by which I mean the rise of provincial pride. I highlight the change in Suphanburians' provincial identity, which he has fostered by positioning and establishing himself as a compassionate and efficient developer who stands in sharp contrast to unfeeling and inefficient state officials.

This is not to argue, however, that Banharn and his actions are the only source of Suphanburians' provincial identity. Supanburians are proud of other individuals and/or events concerning about their province. For example, they take intense pride in the fact that the famous historic battle in which King Naresuan defeated the invading Burmese army in the late sixteenth century—an event extolled in Thai historiography—was fought in what is now Don Chedi District of Suphanburi. To commemorate this victory in honor of Suphanburians' ancient hero, Field Marshal Phibun Songkhram constructed a large monument in Don Chedi in 1953. Completed in 1959, the monument was officially made public in a ceremony attended by King Bhumibol.[62] The so-called Don Chedi Festival, held in front of this monument every January, draws a huge crowd of Suphanburians (and non-Suphanburians) and serves as an occasion for reaffirming provincial identity. In 2007, a multi-million-baht movie that featured King Naresuan (entitled *Tamnan somdet phra Naresuan maharat*) became a box-office hit in Thailand, further enhancing Suphanburians' pride.

Another claim to fame for Suphanburians is that their province has produced some of the most famous singers of Thai country pop songs (*luuk-thung*)—songs that are enormously popular with rural Thais in general for upholding the pristine qualities of the countryside vis-à-vis materially developed, yet morally decadent, Bangkok. These singers include Suraphon Sombatcharoen (the king of *luuk-thung*), Waiphot Phetsuphan, and Phumphuan Duangchan (the queen of *luuk-thung*). Many Suphanburians claim that their distinctive accent (called *neur*)—"the real Thai accent dating back to the Ayutthaya period"[63]—is particularly suitable for singing Thai *luuk-thung* songs. Moreover, Khamron Sambunnanon, the first person to compose and sing the so-called "songs for life" (*phlaeng phuea cheewit*) in opposition to military rule in the late 1950s, as well as another extremely popular "songs-for-life" singer, Ad Carabao, are also Suphanburians. These singers are the pride of the province.[64]

While these sources of provincial pride are certainly important, most Thais living outside Suphanburi show no keen interest in them. Few non-Suphanburians really care about what happened in Suphanburi nearly five hundred years ago, and, in any case, Thai historiography and the media have constructed King Naresuan as a hero for Thais in general, not for Suphanburians alone. Similarly, few non-Suphanburians care deeply about the birthplaces of *luuk-thung* singers. In fact, to the extent that *luuk-thung* songs are regarded by upper-class Bangkok residents as cheap entertainment for unsophisticated rural rednecks, the very popularity of Suphanburi-born *luuk-*

---

[62] National Archives, *Phra Rachakaraniyakit 2502*, jo/2502/3; and *Khon Suphan*, July 16, 1997, p. 1. See also chapters 2 and 3 for more details.

[63] *Bangkok Post*, January 5, 2006, H3.

[64] *Nation Sutsabda*, July 14, 1995, p. 12; and Osamu Oh-uchi, *Tai: Enka no Ohkoku* (Tokyo: Gendai Shokan, 1999).

thung singers has probably perpetuated Suphanburi's negative image as a rural backwater. In brief, while Suphanburians may be proud of King Naresuan's time-honored victory over Burma and the successes of many Suphanburi-born *luuk-thung* singers, neither is an issue that appeals strongly to, or sparks envy in, most people who live outside the province. To draw a (hopefully not too-far-fetched) analogy, it is as if students at some small university in Idaho were bragging about their strong badminton team when the vast majority of Americans are far more interested in football or basketball.

In this regard, Suphanburians' provincial pride in Banharn is different, because it revolves around a point of major interest that concerns most people in rural Thailand: development (*kan phattana*). Rural Thais are intensely conscious of the questions: "To what extent is our province developed, compared to other provinces?" and "How much has our MP done to develop our province?" Politicians are expected to meet the paramount collective concerns of their constituents. This is why every electoral candidate's campaign and slogan promise "development"; no candidate can expect to win and remain in office without at least some reference, whether sincere or token, to this elusive yet enormously appealing concept.[65] In this wider ideological context, Banharn's conspicuous contributions to provincial development have become the socially resonant objects or symbols of many non-Suphanburians' admiration, envy, and resentment. As such, they have become the most important—but not the only—sources of Suphanburians' provincial identity. They allow Suphanburians to assert a strong sense of provincial identity on an overarching theme or issue that so many rural Thais care about.

Similarly, I do not make the patently spurious argument that the provincial identity, whether derived from Banharn or not, is the only or the most important form of collective identity embraced by Suphanburians. Residents of Suphanburi, like any human beings, adopt multiple identities based on their locations, ethnicity, religion, gender, and so forth. They identify themselves simultaneously as Asians, Thais, Buddhists, men or women, and residents of a particular district, subdistrict, and village, for example. Their identity as Suphanburians is just one of these (and other) kinds of collective identities. Without denying this complexity, what I want to argue is that Banharn has heightened Suphanburians' identification with their province by undertaking an array of development projects that conjure up the image of "Banharn-buri"—a broad provincial community that has developed more rapidly than many or all other rural provinces, thanks to his donations, allocation of state funds, and strict governing style over the decades. He has done so, moreover, without threatening or impinging on any of Suphanburians' preexisting collective identities. In this respect, he is markedly different from Thaksin, whose insolent CEO style of leadership posed a direct challenge to the Thais' traditional national identity, which had been carefully fashioned around the monarchy. Thaksin was "punished" for trying to create this competing national identity in the royal-sanctioned coup of 2006.[66] Banharn has refrained from committing Thaksin's political error. In fact, as the succeeding chapters will show, he has constructed his local-level authority by

---

[65] See Askew, *Performing Political Identity*; Arghiros, *Democracy, Development, and Decentralization in Provincial Thailand*; and Ratana "Contested Concepts of Development in Rural Northeastern Thailand."

[66] Ukrist Pathmanand, "A Different *Coup d'Etat?" Journal of Contemporary Asia* 38,1 (2008): 124–42.

relying on the prestige of the royal family and by emulating the king's leadership style. That is why the Suphanburians' national and provincial identities, which revolve around the monarchy and Banharn, respectively, coexist comfortably with each other.

Another question that might be raised concerns Banharn's intentionality: Has he developed Suphanburi in the way he has, knowing that it would raise Suphanburi's social status and thereby foster Suphanburians' provincial pride? Put differently, this line of critique would see my argument as a crudely functionalist one: Suphanburians did not have a positive provincial identity before, and Banharn has simply and purposely given it to them to legitimize his rule. Everything he has done has been clearly *intended* to create and heighten his constituents' provincial pride, which was lacking before. I equivocate somewhat in response to these questions. In some cases, evidence suggests that Banharn intentionally took his actions as a way to enhance Suphanburians' pride. In other cases, however, it is hard to demonstrate his intentions. In the latter cases, it would appear that he sought to initiate development projects as an end in themselves, rather than as a means to an end. With this duly noted, however, I would defend myself by saying that, at least for the purpose of my argument, his intentions are not particularly important. Far more important to my argument is the cumulative *effect* of his actions.[67] He has implemented a number of development projects, which, irrespective of his true intentions, have had the *effect* of nurturing Suphanburians' positive provincial identity. This is not a thinly veiled attempt to sidestep my critics' difficult questions; rather, I simply want to acknowledge that politically significant effects can sometimes be brought about independently of clear human intentions. That is what ultimately matters to my argument.

Last but not least, to the extent that the overall image of Banharn that emerges from this study is positive, some readers might mistakenly conclude that I am uncritically reconstructing an unabashedly corrupt villain as "a nice guy," or that I am naïve enough to have been fooled by Suphanburians' stories. Banharn, according to this line of critique, is essentially a despicable politician, and any other interpretation constitutes an absurd deviation from that "truth" and is therefore "wrong." I disavow such an essentialist position, either "for" or "against" Banharn. That sort of essentialist argument is predicated on an epistemologically untenable assumption that Banharn has one absolute or objectively true quality as a politician, when he actually has no such ontological quality. Following White and others,[68] I take the view that "truth" (beyond indisputable basic facts) is a socially constructed artifact. One and the same person or phenomenon is subject to competing interpretations. While Bangkok-based scholars and journalists use their control over the ideological apparatus to construct the seemingly indubitable "truth" that Banharn is a crook, many Suphanburians, in their own historical, social, and cultural contexts, construct an equally powerful and valid "truth" that he is a good, morally

---

[67] Here I follow the line of defense given in Lisa Wedeen, *Ambiguities of Domination: Politics, Rhetoric, and Symbols in Contemporary Syria* (Chicago, IL: University of Chicago Press, 1999), pp. 25, 153.

[68] H. White, *Tropics of Discourse*; H. White, *The Content of the Form*; Michel Foucault, *The Archaeology of Knowledge*, trans. Sheridan Smith (New York, NY: Pantheon, 1972); Michel Foucault, *Power/Knowledge*, ed. and trans. Colin Gordon (New York, NY: Pantheon, 1980); and John Searle, *The Construction of Social Reality* (New York, NY: Free Press, 1995).

upright politician. Put another way, Banharn is an "objectively" good politician in the "subjective" eyes of Suphanburians.

What this volume aims to do is to spotlight the Suphanburians' version of "truth" or "reality," which has been hidden, stifled, or expunged from the prevailing media and academic accounts. To paraphrase Clifford Geertz,[69] I attempt to "construct" the way Suphanburians "construct" Banharn as a good politician. This is one modest step we should take to "know more about the character and persistence of indigenous value systems, about the changing nature of the relationship between political center and periphery, and about how ordinary people [have] perceived and experienced their world."[70] To this end, I hope to explore what might be called the "autonomous local history" of Suphanburi as viewed by ordinary Suphanburians.[71] My ultimate goal is not to analyze the objective accuracy of this history, although I will try to highlight its spurious nature wherever relevant. What interests me most is the phenomenology of many Suphanburians' support for Banharn and its implications for broader issues of power, domination, and obedience in Thailand and other late-developing societies. I describe and explain Banharn's dominance from Suphanburians' viewpoints, not because I am a beguiled "pro-Banharn" supporter who wants to write a hagiography about him, but because I believe that this case teaches us an important lesson about how a seemingly illegitimate politician can enjoy legitimate political authority.

CHAPTER OVERVIEW AND SOURCES

The empirical chapters that follow will flesh out the argument sketched above. Chapter 2 traces the historical origin of Banharn's dominance. I show what kind of "backward" past Suphanburians had lived through before Banharn's appearance in the 1960s, and how they apprehended, and continue to apprehend, that past. This sets a historical context for Chapter 3, which details a range of high-profile donations made by Banharn before becoming an MP in 1976. Chapters 4 and 5 describe his actions as an MP in the post-1976 period. Using the construction of roads and schools as illustrative examples, chapter 4 highlights his allocation of state funds for the formerly disadvantaged Suphanburi. Chapter 5 details two modes of surveillance that Banharn has devised to enforce his meticulous supervision of local development projects: regular inspection tours and meetings with local civil servants. Chapter 6 then takes an ethnographic approach to show how Banharn's contributions to local development, as trumpeted via the mediums of ubiquitous signboards and frequent ceremonies, help nuture Suphanburians' sense of identification with "Banharn-buri" at the grassroots level. Chapters 7 casts light on the strongest forms of this provincial pride, as reflected in numerous everyday social narratives—stories, jokes, and gossip—which hold up Suphanburi as "developed" and put down other provinces as "backward." Chapter 8 then examines the variety of ways in which Suphanburians subjectively fend off, minimize, dismiss, or rationalize outsiders'

---

[69] Clifford Geertz, *The Interpretation of Cultures* (New York, NY: Basic Books, 1973), p. 9.

[70] Ruth McVey, "Introduction: Local Voices, Central Power," in *Southeast Asian Transitions: Approaches through Local History*, ed. Ruth McVey (New Haven, CT: Yale University Press, 1978), pp. 2–3.

[71] Cf. John Smail, "On the Possibility of an Autonomous History of Southeast Asia," *Journal of Southeast Asian History* 1,2 (1961): 72–102.

criticisms regarding Banharn's incompetence as a politician. This analysis will be followed by a brief discussion of why the counter-hegemonic anti-Banharn movement in Suphanburi remains feeble and what might lie in store for the future of Banharn's provincial dynasty. Chapter 9, the final chapter, situates my case study in theoretical and comparative perspectives. By drawing on the literature on social narratives and social identity theory, I will recast my argument and restate the importance of collective pride as a social-psychological foundation of domination and compliance. I will then compare Banharn to four other politicians in Thailand and elsewhere in Asia to suggest the wider applicability of my argument. I will conclude by teasing out the broad implications of this case study for ongoing political debates and conflicts in Thailand.

Unless otherwise noted, all the accounts I cite in the empirical chapters are based on my open-ended informal "interviews" or casual conversations with more than 400 Suphanburians—farmers, (petty) merchants, blue-collar and white-collar workers, the jobless, street vendors, civil servants, teachers, students, and others— who represent all age groups and social classes, and who come from all the ten districts of the province. In chapter 7, I also base my analysis on the accounts given by more than 170 Thais who live outside Suphanburi. All these interviews were conducted in Thai in and outside Suphanburi at various times between 1999 and 2007—mostly in 1999–2000, 2001–02, and 2004 (see "List of Respondents," given at the outset). Although it is simply impossible for me to introduce the accounts of all the interviewees in full, I will recount some of the most representative to show what kind of beliefs are held by both Suphanburians and non-Suphanburians about Banharn and his contributions to provincial development.

I supplement the interview data with the information culled from two kinds of written Thai-language materials: (1) provincial newspapers, and (2) official documents compiled by Thai government ministries and departments. To the extent that local newspapers reflect and shape local discourse, including rumors and gossip, I draw on the newspapers published in Suphanburi as useful and vital sources of information on how ordinary Suphanburians felt about the backward conditions in the pre-Banharn past, and how they evaluate the various actions that Banharn has taken to ameliorate those conditions. These issues are not dealt with in any other written source. *Khon Suphan* (*Suphan People*)—the oldest provincial newspaper, in print since 1957—has been particularly valuable in this respect. Even during the heyday of authoritarian rule in the 1960s, the newspaper enjoyed a good measure of autonomy (as is the case with the Thai press in general) without becoming a mouthpiece for the state; in fact, I found much critical analysis of the state in it. I also draw on a few other Thai-language provincial newspapers that are no longer in print, such as *Suphanburi Sarn* (*Suphanburi News*), *Thin Thai* (*Thai Land*), and *Suphan Post*.[72]

Government documents, especially those issued by the Budget Bureau, have enabled me to stand back from Suphanburians' views and to scrutinize them from a detached, neutral perspective. On the basis of these documents, I will demonstrate empirically that many issues that Suphanburians raise in their narratives—notably the state's failure to promote Suphanburi's development in the past and the quality of state-funded projects channeled by Banharn as an MP—are actually based on objective facts, although they may be sometimes exaggerated. At the same time, I

---

[72] These three newspapers were in print in 1985–89, 1975–92, and 1999–2006, respectively.

will use the government documents to point out the speciousness of some Suphanburians' accounts, wherever applicable.

At times, the amount of empirical data I provide might strike readers as "too much." I plead "guilty" in mitigation here. I want to buck one increasingly dominant tendency in (American) political science—a tendency to aim for (grand) theory-building on the basis of skin-deep empirical data derived from secondary sources and/or superficial fieldwork. Area-studies specialists, who value solid empirical details, find this trend disturbing or even offensive, while political scientists tend to write off area studies as too descriptive to make any theoretical contribution. The result is a widening gap between the two fields, to the point where they seem mutually irreconcilable. As a person trained both in area studies and political science, I find this a pity, because the two fields actually have enormous potential to enrich each other; they are complimentary.[73] Holding this belief, I want to do my share, no matter how small it may be, to bridge the gap between the two. To this end, I will provide many descriptive details, but I will make every effort to present them in ways that illustrate and support my broad conceptual argument.

---

[73] See also Kuhonta, Slater, and Vu, eds., *Southeast Asia in Political Science.*

CHAPTER TWO

RECALLING AND REPRESENTING THE BACKWARD PAST

Like Rome, Banharn's dominance was not built in a day. It is the historical product of what he has done for Suphanburi's development since the mid-1960s, more than a decade before he was first elected to parliament in 1976. In explaining their support for Banharn, many Suphanburians begin by recalling and describing this period.

These people do not give positive accounts of what their province used to be like. Their narratives typically deplore the "perennial" conditions of Suphanburi's backwardness. Many elderly people who lived through the pre-Banharn period commonly use one expression to depict and belittle the past: "There was nothing but jungles" (*mii tae pa*) in Suphanburi. This terse statement captures the Suphanburians' negative apprehension of the not-so-distant past, since the word *pa* (jungles) is closely associated in the Thai discourse with socially stigmatized wilderness or lack of civilization.[1] One middle-ranking civil servant (#46) offered an amusing analogy: "Suphan was to Thailand what Kansas is to America now. It had nothing at all. If you had shown a map of Thailand to any Thai and asked, 'Where is Suphan?,' you would have gotten an answer, 'I don't know.' How many Americans know exactly where Kansas is? Not many. Suphan was like that." So, why was Suphan like that, I asked. The civil servant replied, "The government wasn't interested in developing Suphan." A sense of resentment was palpable. Suphanburi, according to this respondent and many others, was backward and socially obscure because of the central state. This is the recent past of Suphanburi that they evoke, reflect on, and deplore as a temporal contrast to, or a foil for, the present that Banharn has constructed.

This chapter first describes the socioeconomic conditions that Suphanburians experienced before the 1960s—the conditions that have shaped their negative characterizations and memories of the past. I will then show how Suphanburians blamed, and still blame, those conditions squarely on the failure of the central "developmental" state.

FROM (PUTATIVE) GLORY TO BACKWARDNESS

Suphanburi occupies a pride of place in the national historiography of pre-eighteenth-century Siam. That is, at least, what Suphanburians (or Thais in general) believe or have been taught to believe. U-Thong, which corresponds roughly to one of the districts in present-day Suphanburi, is said to have been a major principality in

---

[1] Philip Stott, "Mu'ang and Pa: Elite Views of Nature in a Changing Thailand," in *Thai Constructions of Knowledge*, ed. Manas Chitakasem and Andrew Turton (London: School of Oriental and African Studies, University of London, 1991), pp. 142–54.

the Buddhist Dvaravati civilization that flourished in the lower Chao Phraya delta between the sixth and tenth centuries. Over the next few centuries, the adjacent Suphanburi became a new major principality in the area. Although Suphanburi was subsequently incorporated into the Kingdom of Sukhothai that emerged in the upper Chao Phraya delta in the mid-thirteenth century, this subordination was nominal. When King Ramkhamhaeng, a powerful warrior king who had held the Sukhothai Kingdom together, died in 1298, Suphanburi asserted its virtual independence. Then, in 1351, Prince U-Thong, who was married to a daughter of Suphanburi's ruler, united several towns and principalities to establish the Kingdom of Ayutthaya. After U-Thong's death in 1369, an internal conflict arose between Suphanburi and another principality, Lopburi, but the ruling family of Suphanburi succeeded in achieving dominance over Lopburi in 1409. Over the next century or so, the Ayutthaya Kingdom expanded its domain to include not only Nakhon Si Thammarat in the south but also Sukhothai and Angkor to the north and east.[2] Suphanburi was a major principality in this prosperous kingdom.

Suphanburi's supposed glory reached its peak in January 1593, when the legendary King Naresuan (reign: 1590–1605) of the Ayutthaya Kingdom, riding an elephant, valiantly routed and repelled the invading Burmese army. This battle, fought in what is now the Don Chedi District of Suphanburi, is eulogized and romanticized in Thai historical discourse as the laudable manifestation of Siamese bravery and unity, and it has become the subject of numerous well-known nationalist sagas, dramas, and movies, such as Luang Wichit Wathakan's *Blood of Suphan*. As the Ayutthaya Kingdom further prospered after the battle, Suphanburi, as one well-respected "amateur" local historian, Manas Ophakul (1919–), puts it, enjoyed "more glory [*run rueng*] and splendor [*or ar*] than any other town" in the kingdom.[3] This invented, mythical image of Suphanburi's glorious past continues to hold much emotional appeal for Suphanburians today, as exemplified by the officially endorsed provincial slogan that upholds Suphanburi as "the town of heroic elephant-riding battles" (*muang yutthahatthi*).

Suphanburi's "golden age," however, did not last too long. In 1767, Burma attacked Ayutthaya again, this time successfully, and set it on fire. During and after the war, "people left Suphanburi to live elsewhere," causing it to lapse into a desolate town. Suphanburi thus "lost its old glory" and was left "in ruins" (*rok rang*), as Manas lamented in his newspaper account.[4] If "Burma" conjures up negative images for many Thais at present, it is all the more so for Suphanburians. "If not for

---

[2] See Charnvit Kasetsiri, *The Rise of Ayudhya: A History of Siam in the Fourteenth and Fifteenth Centuries* (Kuala Lumpur: Oxford University Press, 1976), pp. 16–25, 52–53; David Wyatt, *Thailand: A Short History* (New Haven, CT: Yale University Press, 1984), pp. 25–26, 64–65; and Waruni Osatharom, *Muang Suphan bon Sen Thang kan Plian Plaeng Thang Prawatisat: Phuthasatawat thi 8 — Ton Phuthasatawat thi 25* (Bangkok: Thammasat University Press, 2004), pp. 69–144.

[3] *Suphanburi Sarn*, December 25, 1987, p. 6. Although many Suphanburians refer to Manas as an historian, he has never received advanced training to practice the profession. Nonetheless, he has contributed many commentaries on Suphanburi's history to local newspapers. He might be considered a spokesperson for ordinary Suphanburians whose views he shares, or as a local intellectual who has shaped their views. As an aside, Manas is the father of Ad Carabao, a nationally famous Thai singer of the so-called "songs for life" (*phlaeng phuea cheewit*)—songs that critically address a myriad of social and political problems in Thailand, such as corruption, military rule, and farmers' poverty.

[4] Ibid.

Burma," one college student (#4) said with a straight face, "Suphanburi might be the capital of Thailand now."

Suphanburi's decline continued after the new dynasty, the present-day Chakri dynasty, was established in Bangkok in 1782. When King Chulalongkorn (reign: 1868–1910) and Minister of the Interior Prince Damrong reorganized Siam into eighteen new administrative units, called *monthon*, in 1892, Suphanburi, due to its sparse population, was simply incorporated into the Nakhon Chaisri *monthon* along with a few other towns. It was only in 1910 that Suphanburi was upgraded to provincial status. The Chakri dynasty spent far more of its resources on Bangkok and the court than on rural development. The royal expenditures, which amounted to nearly 11 percent of the national budget, were "four times the amount spent on education and five times the amount spent on roads."[5] The development of the countryside, including Suphanburi, took a back seat. The 1932 coup, which abolished absolute monarchy, did not alter this pattern of uneven development. In subsequent years, the urban–rural disparity widened further.[6] As a result, by the middle of the twentieth century, Suphanburi, a thriving town in the mythical past, had become typical of neglected provinces in the Thai countryside. In several respects, Suphanburi was actually worse off than many other provinces. Even the rise of the much-touted "developmental" authoritarian state in 1957 did little to improve such conditions in Suphanburi (as explained below). This gave rise to the negative, politicized perceptions of the past that many Suphanburians share today.

Those perceptions are not groundless. Suphanburi's relative backwardness was reflected, first of all, in its preponderantly agriculture-based economy. In 1974, for instance, agriculture accounted for 60.5 percent of Suphanburi's GPP (Gross Provincial Product). Of the seventy provinces in Thailand at that time, only twelve relied more heavily on agriculture. In contrast, the wholesale and retail trade sector constituted a mere 5.3 percent of Suphanburi's GPP—the second lowest figure among all the provinces in the country.[7] Suphanburi's skewed reliance on agriculture was also reflected in the minuscule size of its urban population. In 1968, only 4.2 percent of Suphanburians lived in commercialized municipal areas. This figure was the eighteenth lowest in the country.[8]

Another indication of Suphanburi's backwardness was the scarcity of public health facilities. In 1960, Suphanburi had only one public hospital, Chaophraya Yommarat Hospital (built in 1926), for a population of nearly 500,000. Professional medical care was deficient. Although rural Thailand in general had difficulty stemming the outer migration of qualified doctors into Bangkok, this was "a problem especially for Suphanburi," as one local newspaper commented. As of 1963, only three Suphanburi-born doctors had returned home after finishing their studies in

---

[5] Benjamin Batson, *The End of the Absolute Monarchy in Siam* (Singapore: Oxford University Press, 1984), pp. 17–18.

[6] See John Girling, *Thailand: Politics and Society* (Ithaca, NY: Cornell University Press, 1981); James Ingram, *Economic Change in Thailand, 1850–1970* (Stanford, CA: Stanford University Press, 1971).

[7] National Economic and Social Development Board, *Phalitaphan Phak lae Changwat 2521* (Bangkok: NESDB, 1979).

[8] Wilai Wongserbchart, Darawan Jiampermpoon, and Mayuree Nokyoonthong, *Prachakon khong Prathet Thai: Satiti nai Chuang 25 pii (2511–2535)* (Bangkok: Institute of Population Studies, Chulalongkorn University, 1993), pp. 11–15.

Bangkok.[9] Consequently, in 1963, there were only twelve doctors and ten nurses in Suphanburi.[10] The ratio of doctors and nurses to the provincial population (1: 8,356) was the second worst among the central-region provinces.[11]

Evidence suggests that insufficient state funds were responsible for poor public health conditions. In 1963, the Ministry of Public Health allocated more than 35 million baht (US$1 equaled approximately 21 baht at the time) for 120 public health facilities nationwide but only one health center in Suphanburi received 50,000 baht, or 0.14 percent of the total budget. In contrast, the provinces adjacent to Suphanburi—Nakhon Pathom, Ayutthaya, Ang Thong, Singburi, and Uthai Thani— obtained 900,000, 160,000, 230,000, 120,000, and 800,000 baht, respectively.[12] The contrast becomes even more striking when we factor in the provinces' populations to compute their respective per capita funding: 0.085 baht (Suphanburi), 2.05 baht (Nakhon Pathom), 0.3 baht (Ayutthaya), 1.03 baht (Ang Thong), 0.7 baht (Singburi), and 4.85 baht (Uthai Thani). Even this disproportionately small share of public funds was actually a vast improvement over 1962, when the health ministry expended over 25.7 million baht nationwide without channeling any of it to Suphanburi.[13] Apparently, state resources were diverted to other provinces at the expense of Suphanburi.

Schools, too, were in short supply. In 1967, of all the provinces in Thailand, Suphanburi had the ninth worst ratio of primary ($n = 406$) and secondary ($n = 8$) schools combined to the provincial population (1: 1,433). Again, all the other central region provinces had a much better ratio. The number of students, especially secondary school students, was correspondingly low. In 1967, there were only 2,466 secondary school students in Suphanburi. Comparable figures for Ayutthaya, Ratchaburi, and Lopburi—the provinces with a smaller population than Suphanburi—were much higher.[14] In addition, the eight secondary schools in Suphanburi were concentrated in the central district of Muang. The extremely poor road system in Suphanburi (see below) made it time-consuming and costly for students living far from the central district to commute to school.[15] Thus, many children living in remote villages had to give up on pursuing secondary school education.

As in the case of public health, inadequate state funding was to blame for the relative lack of schools. In 1964, for example, the Ministry of Education (MOE) allocated over 82.4 million baht for building or expanding two hundred schools nationwide, but only one school in Suphanburi received any money—just 130,000

---

[9] *Khon Suphan*, October 30, 1963, p. 5.

[10] See *Khon Suphan*, October 20, 1963, p. 5; and National Statistical Office (NSO), *Statistical Yearbook Thailand 1970–1971* (Bangkok: NSO, 1972), p. 42.

[11] Uraiwan Kanungsukkasem, *Comparative Population and Health Statistics for Thailand: Regional and Provincial Levels* (Bangkok: Mahidol University Institute for Population and Social Research, 1983).

[12] Budget Bureau, *Ekasarn Ngop-pramarn 2506*, 3,3 (1962): 485–527, 541–72.

[13] Budget Bureau, *Ekasarn Ngop-pramarn 2505*, 3,3 (1961): 425–56, 467–504.

[14] NSO, *Statistical Yearbook Thailand 1970–1971*, pp. 115, 118–20.

[15] Chart Thai (CT) Party, *Chart Thai Samphan* 13 (May–June 2001), p. 5. See also the editorials titled "Aren't the Schools in the Countryside Good?" in *Khon Suphan*, December 30, 1969, p. 5; and *Khon Suphan*, January 10, 1970, p. 5.

baht, or 0.16 percent of the budget.[16] Suphanburi was the most disadvantaged central region province in the allocation of MOE funds (figure 2.1).

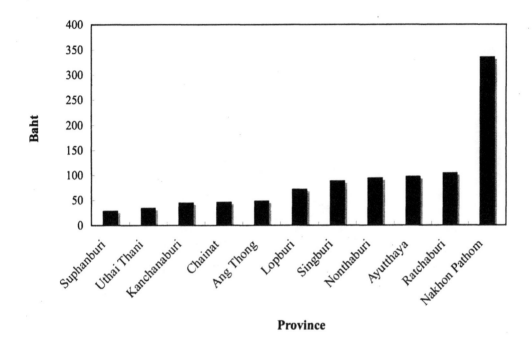

Figure 2.1 Per Capita Construction Funds Allocated by the Ministry of Education: A Comparison of Suphanburi and its Neighboring Provinces, 1961–72[17]

Roads were inadequate and of poor quality, too. This was, in fact, what most Suphanburians cite as the most notorious mark of Suphanburi's backwardness in the recent past. After the Chakri dynasty was founded in Bangkok, the strategic importance of Suphanburi declined in relative terms. To protect the new capital from future attacks by Burma, the new ruling court devoted resources to building roads in the provinces situated directly between Bangkok and Burma. Located off this vital strategic route, Suphanburi's benefited little from the court's expenditures on road construction.[18] This "benign neglect" by the state continued well into the twentieth century, even after Suphanburi was upgraded to provincial status in 1910.

Before 1956, for example, there was no road connecting Suphanburi to Bangkok, or even to its neighboring provinces. Suphanburi was effectively isolated from the outside world. In 1936, the government formulated an ambitious eighteen-year road construction project, under which all provinces, including Suphanburi, were to be

[16] See Budget Bureau, *Ekasarn Ngop-pramarn 2508*, 3,3 (1964): 890–92; and National Economic Development Board (NEDB), *The National Economic Development Plan, 1961–1966: Second Phase, 1964–1966* (Bangkok: NEDB, 1964), p. 140.

[17] *Sources*: Compiled from Budget Bureau, *Ekasarn Ngop-pramarn* 3,6, various years (1960, 1970–71); Budget Bureau, *Ekasarn Ngop-pramarn* 3,3, various years (1961–66); Budget Bureau, *Ekasarn Ngop-pramarn 2511* 3,4 (1967); Budget Bureau, *Ekasarn Ngop-pramarn 2512* 3,8 (1968); Budget Bureau, *Ekasarn Ngop-pramarn 2513* 4 (1969).

[18] Waruni, *Muang Suphan*, p. 190.

linked by roadways to Bangkok, but the project came to a standstill with the outbreak of the Pacific War.[19] Many elderly people I talked to deplored the shortage of roads, saying forcefully that it made Suphanburi a veritable "closed town" (*muang pit*).[20]

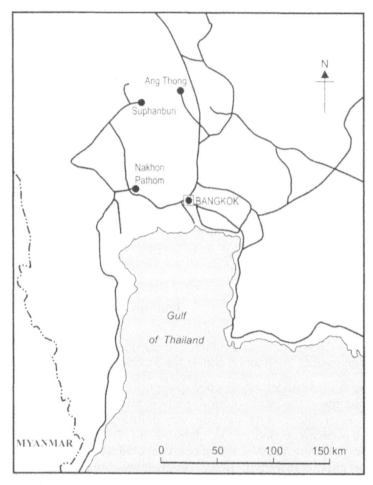

Figure 2.2 Road Networks in Suphanburi and Neighboring Provinces, 1967[21]

In the absence of roads, the only way to get to Bangkok was to row a boat along the Tha Chin River (which flows through Suphanburi)—a means of transport that

---

[19] See Ichiro Kakizaki, "Rikken Kakumeigo no Tai ni okeru Douroseibi (1932–1941): Saisho no Douro Kensetsukeikaku no Sakutei," *Tonan Ajia Kenkyu* 39,4 (2002): 488, 490; and Ichiro Kakizaki, "Sengo Hukkouki Tai ni okeru Douro Setsubi (1945–1957): Teikikaku Douro kara Kokikaku Douro he," *Asia Keizai* 48,3 (2002): 6.

[20] See also *Khon Suphan*, April 1, 2003, p. 4, where the same expression is used to describe Suphanburi's past.

[21] *Source*: Drawn by the Cartography Department, National University of Singapore. This is a simplified version of the map in NEDB, The Second National Economic and Social Development Plan, 1967–71 (Bangkok: NEDB, 1967), page number unspecified.

was available only during the rainy season.[22] The trip would take two to three days—a condition that had changed little since 1843, when a French missionary had to spend four days traveling from Suphanburi to Bangkok.[23] In the mid-1920s, Suphan Phanit, a local company run by two brothers of the tenth governor of Suphanburi, Yi Kanasoot (term: 1911–23), started operating a motor-powered boat, which made the trip to Bangkok more convenient and gave many Suphanburians a chance to "see civilization of the capital city" for the first time.[24] Nonetheless, the trip still took some fifteen hours. One Sino–Thai merchant (b. 1929; #103) jokingly recalled his childhood boat trip to and from Bangkok: "I was exposed to intense sunrays for so many hours that my head and face got scorched brown, like a roasted duck. When I came back home, nobody could recognize me. Even my mother asked me, 'Who are you?'"

To remedy such conditions, the postwar government, led by Field Marshal Phibun Songkhram, set out to build a highway between Suphanburi and Bangkok in 1950.[25] The construction was finally completed in 1956.[26] The new highway, however, did not link Suphanburi to Bangkok directly. The route was via Nakhon Pathom, a province situated west of Bangkok. Therefore, Suphanburians had to take the long way around to this province first before reaching Bangkok (figure 2.2), a trip that took seven to eight hours. To travel to neighboring Ang Thong, a province situated fewer than thirty kilometers east of Suphanburi, involved an even worse ordeal. The only "modern" way to get to Ang Thong was to take what many Suphanburians viewed as a ludicrous detour: go first to Bangkok via Nakhon Pathom, and then travel north to Ang Thong. This route was some 250 kilometers long. Thus, it was extremely inconvenient to venture anywhere outside Suphanburi.

Furthermore, the new highway was of inferior quality. It was made of gravel or laterite (*luuk rang*), a construction material of the poorest quality. When it rained, the road would turn muddy and slippery, hampering the movement of vehicles.[27] This highway was therefore one of the many roads that the National Economic Development Board (NEDB) admitted was "poor in quality" and "cause[d] many districts to be cut off from communication with the rest of the country, especially during the rainy season."[28] It was only in 1966 that the highway was paved with asphalt.[29]

---

[22] Manas Ophakul, *Prawat Luang Phor Tor Wat Jampa* (Suphanburi: n.p., 1995), p. 26. It was because water transport was available that the government had accorded low priority to road construction in Suphanburi. Kakizaki, "Rikken Kakumeigo no Tai ni okeru Douroseibi," p. 497.

[23] Jean-Baptiste Pallegoix, *Description of the Thai Kingdom or Siam: Thailand under King Mongkut*, trans. Walter Tips (Bangkok: White Lotus, 2000), p. 51.

[24] See *Suphanburi Sarn*, December 25, 1987, p. 6; and Manas, *Prawat Luang Phor Tor Wat Jampa*, pp. 9, 13–14.

[25] See *Khon Suphan*, April 1, 2003, p. 4; and Kakizaki, "Sengo Hukkouki Tai ni okeru Douro Setsubi," pp. 9, 16.

[26] *Khon Suphan*, January 18, 1966, p. 1.

[27] *Khon Suphan*, October 25, 1963, p. 5.

[28] NEDB, *The National Economic Development Plan, 1961–1966*, p. 107.

[29] See *Khon Suphan*, January 18, 1966, p. 1; Budget Bureau, *Ekasarn Ngop-pramarn 2504*, 3,2 (1960): 693; Budget Bureau, *Ekasarn Ngop-pramarn 2506*, 3,2 (1962): 923, 932, 935; Budget Bureau, *Ekasarn Ngop-pramarn 2507*, 3,3 (1963): 355; Budget Bureau, *Ekasarn Ngop-pramarn 2508*, 3,2 (1964): 392–393; and Budget Bureau, *Ekasarn Ngop-pramarn 2509*, 3,3 (1965): 455, 460.

In reviewing its own performance in 1965, the NEDB proudly announced that 60 percent of all the highways nationwide (9,492 kilometers) had been paved with asphalt or concrete.[30] Suphanburi, however, accounted for only 1.2 percent of those surfaced roads. This condition hardly improved in subsequent years, thanks to the inequitable distribution of state funds. Between 1966 and 1971, for instance, Suphanburi accounted for a mere 0.9 percent of road construction funds dispensed by the Department of Highways (DOH) nationwide.[31] By 1976, the DOH had surfaced 16,244 kilometers of roads nationwide with asphalt or concrete, but Suphanburi had only four asphalted roads, with a combined length of less than 170 kilometers.[32] If the presence of roads is a yardstick of "civilization,"[33] there is good reason to believe that Suphanburi was one of the least civilized provinces in Thailand. It was a province in which over nine hundred villages existed in physical isolation from each other, and residents of those villages had relatively weak emotional bonds with each other.

Because good roads were scarce, communist and other illicit activities were rife. Inaccessibility by road meant ineffective state penetration and surveillance, and thus plenty of space existed in which outlaws could operate with impunity. Despite the often-touted administrative reforms initiated by King Chulalongkorn in the late nineteenth century, the power of the central state had not reached the far-flung corners of Suphanburi. To the extent that road density is an indicator of the state's ability to extend its authority over distance,[34] Suphanburi was one of the least effectively governed provinces. The Communist Party of Thailand (CPT) capitalized on the attendant "breathing space" in Suphanburi to plot armed uprisings, prompting provincial police to make a total of thirty-eight well-publicized arrests of local CPT leaders (including nationally famous Ruam Wongphan) in the province in the 1960s.[35] Despite the state's massive counter-insurgency operations, however, the CPT managed to expand. In 1969, the CPT announced, to the chagrin of state officials, that it had successfully infiltrated thirty-four Thai provinces, including Suphanburi.[36]

---

[30] NEDB, *Performance Evaluation of Development in Thailand for 1965 under National Economic Development Plan, 1961–1966* (Bangkok: NEDB, 1966), p. 42.

[31] Yoshinori Nishizaki, "Suphanburi in the Fast Lane: Roads, Prestige, and Domination in Provincial Thailand," *Journal of Asian Studies* 67,2 (2008): 442.

[32] See *Khon Suphan*, January 18, 1966, p. 1; Budget Bureau, *Ekasarn Ngop-pramarn 2513*, 3 (1969): 50; Budget Bureau, *Ekasarn Ngop-pramarn 2514*, 3,4 (1970): 387; Budget Bureau, *Ekasarn Ngop-pramarn 2515*, 3,4 (1971): 382; DOH, *Rai-ngan Prachampii 2519* (Bangkok: DOH, 1977), p. 116; and DOH, *Rai-ngan Prachampii 2528* (Bangkok: DOH, 1986), p. 79.

[33] Eugen Weber, *Peasants into Frenchmen: The Modernization of Rural France, 1870–1914* (Stanford, CA: Stanford University Press, 1976), p. 208.

[34] Jeffrey Herbst, *States and Power in Africa: Comparative Lessons in Authority and Control* (Princeton, NJ: Princeton University Press, 2000), pp. 84–87, 161–63.

[35] See *Khon Suphan* (February 25, 1962, p. 1; February 28, 1962, p. 1; March 25, 1962, pp. 1, 8; March 30, 1962, p. 1; January 24, 1967, p. 1; October 20, 1967, pp. 1, 8; and February 19, 1968, p. 1); David Wilson, "Thailand: Old Leaders and New Directions," *Asian Survey* 3,2 (1963): 83; and Donald Weatherbee, *The United Front in Thailand* (Columbia, SC: University of South Carolina, Institute of International Studies, 1970), p. 24.

[36] See David Morell and Chai-anan Samudavanija, *Political Conflict in Thailand: Reform, Reaction, Revolution* (Cambridge, MA: Oelgeschlager, 1981), p. 83; and Weatherbee, *The United Front in Thailand*, p. 5.

The CPT's announcement severely tarnished the image of Suphanburi (as well as the other thirty-three provinces), given the fact that the military regime had effectively played up communism as "the epitome of un-Thainess" or an evil that jeopardized the revered monarchy and the existence of Thailand.[37] Consider, for example, the implications of the following public statement made in 1967 by Phat Bunyaratphan, former governor of Suphanburi (1957–66) and then-director of the Board of Communist Suppression in the Northeast Region. He explained the cause of the growing communist insurgency in rural Thailand as follows:

> Those who are easily deceived into joining the communists are mostly the people in remote backward areas or in places far away from developed societies. They are too stupid [*khlao*] to perceive imminent dangers around them. They don't feel all the changes taking place in the present world. Therefore, if somebody [a communist] lures them into doing something bad, they drift away [to that person], just as wax melts away with fire [*samuen khi phueng thi thuuk ron duay fai*].[38]

Although not targeted specifically at Suphanburi, Phat's comment was based on his long, previous experience in the province. His logic served, by implication, to project Suphanburi in a negative light: Only backward provinces inhabited by "stupid" people were falling prey to communism, and Suphanburi was one of those provinces. Living in a backward province was thus problematized and socially stigmatized via association with communism, the enemy of the Thai nation. Accordingly, many villages in Suphanburi became the objects of frequent visits and inspections by state officials and development "experts" from abroad, who were all a mission to ameliorate Suphanburi's "backwardness."[39]

The absence of roads made conditions ripe for other illegal activities, such as drug-dealing, illegal distilling of alcohol, and gambling, as evidenced by numerous police raids in the 1960s and 1970s.[40] Armed robbery was the most rampant crime. It was "an everyday occurrence in town, and Suphanburians in general felt even inured to it."[41] Indeed, Suphanburi had long been notorious as "the town of bandits." In a major campaign conducted in the 1880s, the military arrested as many as 300 bandits in Suphanburi, but the campaign failed to root out banditry. In the late 1890s, a notorious bandit named Aisua Thuam emerged to control much of Suphanburi. From 1941 to 1945, three major bandits—Suea Fai, Suea Mahesuan, and Suea Bai—exploited wartime economic chaos to rise to positions of dominance, and they

---

[37] Kasian Techapira, *Commodifying Marxism: The Formation of Modern Thai Radical Culture, 1927–1958* (Kyoto: Kyoto University Press, 2001), p. 190.

[38] *Khon Suphan*, February 14, 1967, p. 4.

[39] See various reports in *Khon Suphan* (March 30, 1969; October 10, 1970; April 10, 1972; March 20, 1975; June 20, 1975; November 1, 1980; and December 30, 1980).

[40] See the reports in *Khon Suphan* (November 25, 1961; December 15 and 20, 1961; February 25, 1962; April 10, 1962; December 5, 1962; March 25 and 30, 1963; August 15, 1963; September 15, 1963; October 25, 1963; November 5 and 15, 1963; April 25, 1964; June 10, 1964; September 1, 1964; August 30, 1966; April 25, 1967; July 30, 1967; June 20, 1968; July 10, 20, and 30, 1968; September 20, 1968; March 20, 1970; May 30, 1970; April 10, 1971; August 10, 1971; November 10, 1971; July 10 and 20, 1974; August 30, 1974; September 20, 1974; October 20, 1974; April 10, 1975; May 30, 1975; July 20, 1975; August 10, 1975; September 20, 1975; and June 10, 1976).

[41] *Suphanburi Sarn*, December 25, 1987, p. 12.

reigned supreme for the next two or three decades.[42] One newspaper deplored the high incidence of armed robbery with an exaggerated remark: "When it comes to bandits [*jon phu rai*], Suphanburi is No. 1."[43]

Suphanburians, therefore, had to take unusual care to protect themselves. As one elderly man ruefully recalled, "Anybody who went outside home without arming himself was considered as a show-off [for demonstrating reckless bravery]. Everybody had to carry a truncheon or a knife, or he was considered as foolhardy."[44] A former member of parliament (MP) from Suphanburi, Dr. Bun-uea Prasertsuwan (b. 1919), similarly recollected: "Civil servants who were assigned to Suphanburi had to learn how to shoot guns because it was swarming with notorious gangs."[45] The local historian, Manas, recalled that many Suphanburians made it a point to carry "earthenware pots" with them as protective weapons whenever they went outside.[46] Thus, ordinary Suphanburians lived their daily lives in fear of banditry, according to one newspaper editorial published in 1987. On the other hand, "people in other provinces," the editorial continued, "never felt the same way as Suphanburians, because their provinces did not have robbery cases. Only in Suphanburi were there robberies."[47] Overstated as that may be, these recollections reveal the unruly and even lawless impressions that Suphanburians had, and continue to have, of their province.

Thus, by the mid-twentieth century, Suphanburi had become what might be called a stagnant and rough backwater. The so-called golden days of the Ayutthaya period, in which Suphanburi supposedly enjoyed "more glory and splendor than any other town,"[48] were a thing of the distant past. In absolute or objective terms, Suphanburi may not have been the most disadvantaged or backward Thai province, but it was one of the worst off.

According to the many Suphanburians I talked to, this condition was not the result of natural historical evolution; instead, they attributed—and still attribute—it to the discriminatory "developmental" central state, as the accounts in the next section indicate. In other words, the Thai state was the alleged culprit behind Suphanburi's backwardness.

TAKING THE "DEVELOPMENTAL" STATE TO TASK

The "state" is a concept reified by social scientists to refer to the locus of political and economic power. In the minds of ordinary people living at the geographical

---

[42] See *Khon Suphan*, August 1, 1993, p. 3; Manas, *Prawat Luang Phor Tor Wat Jampa*, p. 28; Pasuk Phongpaichit and Chris Baker, *Thailand: Economy and Politics* (New York, NY: Oxford University Press, 1995), pp. 218–19; and Tej Bunnag, *The Provincial Administration of Siam, 1892–1915* (Kuala Lumpur: Oxford University Press, 1977), p. 102. A Thai movie in 2000, "Tears of the Black Tiger," featured Suea Fai's right-hand man.

[43] *Khon Suphan*, October 20, 1963, p. 5.

[44] *Khon Suphan*, December 1, 2002, p. 4.

[45] Association of Suphanburians, *Hoksip Pii Samakhom Chao Suphanburi* (Suphanburi: Association of Suphanburians, 1996), p. 123; CT Party, *Chart Thai Samphan* 13 (May–June 2001), p. 5.

[46] Manas, *Prawat Luang Phor Tor Wat Jampa*, p. 28.

[47] *Suphanburi Sarn*, December 25, 1987, p. 12.

[48] Ibid., p. 6.

periphery of any country, however, the "state" is little more than a distant, abstract, amorphous, and invisible Goliath located in, and associated with, the capital city, where faceless "big shots" make important decisions. Yet, somewhat paradoxically, at the same time the "state" exists vividly in the eyes, ears, and bodies of these ordinary people. Local people construct or imagine the "state" on the basis of what they hear, see, and (are made to) do firsthand in the course of their daily lives and interactions with rank-and-file agents of the state. The otherwise intangible "state" thus consists of various images created by the concrete behavior, practices, and words of local-level officials.[49] As James Scott aptly put it, "No abstract force, collectivity, or system ever arrives at the door of human experience, except as it is mediated by concrete, particular human 'carriers.'"[50] The state is a prime example of such collective entities.

In provincial Thailand, the images of the state have not been positive. Ordinary villagers have traditionally regarded local-level state officials as undesirable characters—arrogant, insensitive, dishonest, inefficient, unresponsive, lazy, slow, irresponsible, insincere, haphazard, untrustworthy, and so on. Suphanburians are among the many rural-based Thais who have held civil servants in such low regard.

Such negative perceptions have deep historical roots, but they were quite likely reinforced during the heyday of the "bureaucratic polity" in the 1950s–70s, when civilian and military bureaucrats monopolized power in Thailand.[51] Standard accounts have it that the Thai version of the "developmental" authoritarian state emerged in 1957, when Field Marshal Sarit Thanarat assumed power. In subsequent years, Sarit (prime minister, 1958–63) and his successor, Field Marshal Thanom Kittikachon (prime minister, 1963–73), undertook massive rural infrastructure development by relying on Western-educated technocrats and by receiving hefty financial support from the United States and the World Bank.[52] Thus, during this period, the ideology of "development" spread rapidly throughout rural Thailand.[53] And yet the supposedly "developmental" state was conspicuous for its relative absence in Suphanburi. As one street peddler of soft drinks in Sri Prachan District (b. 1948, #73) recalled, "[Sarit] developed rural areas, mainly in Isan [northeastern Thailand]. He built many things there, such as roads. But Suphan [Suphanburi] got fewer. While he was prime minister, Suphan didn't change much. Yes, he was a rural

---

[49] See Akhil Gupta, "Blurred Boundaries: The Discourse of Corruption, the Culture of Politics, and the Imagined State," *American Ethnologist* 22,2 (1995): 375–402; Joel Migdal, *State in Society: Studying How States and Societies Transform and Constitute One Another* (New York, NY: Cambridge University Press, 2001), pp. 15–23; and Timothy Mitchell, *Colonising Egypt* (Berkeley, CA: University of California Press, 1991).

[50] James C. Scott, "Afterword to 'Moral Economies, State Spaces, and Categorical Violence,'" *American Anthropologist* 107,3 (2005): 398.

[51] Fred Riggs, *Thailand: The Modernization of a Bureaucratic Polity* (Honolulu, HI: East–West Center Press, 1966).

[52] Thak Chaloemtiarana, *Thailand: The Politics of Despotic Paternalism*, rev. ed. (Ithaca, NY: Cornell Southeast Asia Program Publications, 2007), pp. 147–77.

[53] Sarit popularized the word "development" (*phattana*). Many villagers heard the word for the first time while Sarit was prime minister. Ratana Boonmathya, "Contested Concepts of Development in Rural Northeastern Thailand" (PhD dissertation, University of Washington, Seattle, WA, 1997), p., 68. While it sounded alien to most Thais at first, the word soon became widely known, thanks to the sheer frequency with which Sarit used it in public. For example, in his annual state address in 1963, he used the word twenty-six times. Akira Suehiro, *Tai: Kaishatsu to Minshushugi* (Tokyo: Iwanami Shoten, 1993), p. 38.

developer, but only for some provinces." Thus, from the perspective of ordinary Suphanburians, there was a yawning gap between what the state publicly pledged to do and what it actually did. This gap led many Suphanburians to lower their already low opinions of the state.

The Unfeeling State

First and foremost, Suphanburians criticized the supposedly "cash-awash" state for failing to allocate sufficient funds for badly needed local development projects—a perception that had a firm factual basis, given the unfair distribution of state resources, as shown earlier. For example, in the early 1960s, the paving of the seventy-nine-kilometer provincial highway between Suphanburi and Nakhon Pathom—the only road to Bangkok at the time—was a major concern to Suphanburians. Although Prime Minister Sarit approved this surfacing project in mid-1962, it was frozen due to an unexplained "budgetary crunch" before the end of the year. This news caused great disappointment among Suphanburians, leading the local newspaper, *Khon Suphan*, to mourn in a front-page headline: "Suphanburi Has No Hope Yet to Get an Asphalt Road."[54] In mid-1963, *Khon Suphan*'s reporters asked then-Deputy Prime Minister Thanom when the surfacing project would be revived. "Soon" (*nai mai cha*) was the response.[55] Thanom did revive the project, but during the next two years, he allocated only three million baht for it. This sum was enough to surface just a little over one-third of the highway. A *Khon Suphan* reporter bewailed the situation, writing that the requested budget for Suphanburi "was curtailed so much that only three million was left." He concluded with bitter resignation: "Suphanburians must temper their hopes of seeing the entire highway paved with asphalt" and "wait longer."[56]

To compensate for the paucity of state funds, villagers in various parts of Suphanburi had to carry out, literally, dirty and backbreaking development projects by using their own simple tools and money (figures 2.3 and 2.4). One example of such grassroots development projects was the construction of an unsurfaced footpath, 156 meters in length and one meter in width, in Don Tarl, Muang District, in 1974.[57] The villagers had to do this work despite the fact that the state had accorded "top priority" to road construction in the countryside.[58] In his conversation with me, a former village head of Don Tarl (#105), now over eighty years old, used one pithy, resentful sentence to explain the circumstances under which he was compelled to mobilize his villagers, both young and old, male and female, to build the rudimentary road on their own: "*Ngop mai thueng*" (The budget [of the state] didn't reach [us]). He elaborated on the unresponsive and tightfisted nature of the "developmental" state and its officials:

---

[54] *Khon Suphan*, December 10, 1962, p. 1.

[55] *Khon Suphan*, September 30, 1963, p. 1.

[56] See *Khon Suphan*, October 10, 1963, p. 1; and *Khon Suphan*, October 15, 1963, p. 5. For similar accounts, see *Khon Suphan*, January 30, 1964, p. 1; *Khon Suphan*, February 5, 1964, p. 12; *Khon Suphan*, April 15, 1964, pp. 1, 12; and *Khon Suphan*, May 2, 1967, pp. 1, 7.

[57] *Khon Suphan*, June 10, 1974, p. 1.

[58] NEDB, *The National Economic Development Plan, 1961–1966*, p. 107.

At the time, there was no road at all around here. So, the villagers had lots of trouble even just going to the market to buy and sell things. So they asked me again and again to do something about it. I contacted the District Office several times to ask for money [to build a road]. Each time, I was told, "The budget isn't sufficient." I said, "Not sufficient budget? I heard that the province received several million baht for local development. Why not give our village some of it?" Their answer was, "We decide how the money is used." So, in the end I gave up, and I went around the village, asking people: "If they aren't going to build a road for us, why not do it on our own?" Most people agreed because a road was so important to us. So, people around here [mostly farmers] took turns to help build a road together. It was very tiring.

Another elderly man in the same village (#99) gruffly recalled that, while this laborious and protracted work was under way, the local civil servants acted as if they were "gold that does not know hotness" (*thong mai ruu rorn*)—a Thai idiom describing coldhearted indifference to other people's hardships.

Figure 2.3 Villagers building a road on their own with simple tools
Note: The third adult from the left is the former village head I interviewed[59]

Stories of other infrastructure-building works undertaken by Suphanburi's villagers abound. In 1968, some four hundred villagers in Nong Ya Sai subdistrict got together to dig a twenty-kilometer irrigation ditch.[60] In the same year, villagers of another subdistrict, Kho Khok Tao, built a primary school classroom by "depending

---

[59] Source: *Khon Suphan*, June 10, 1974.

[60] *Khon Suphan*, September 10, 1968, p. 1.

on their own labor" and "without any budgetary assistance from the state." The local temple abbot scraped up the construction funds from the villagers.[61] Although the second National Economic Development Plan (1967–71) increased expenditures for education by some 4 percent (relative to the first plan), the state funds apparently failed to reach the people in Suphanburi who needed them.[62]

Figure 2.4 Villagers digging an irrigation ditch in Muang District[63]

These works were truly collective projects involving almost everyone in a given local community. Villagers representing different occupations—farmers, landlords, merchants, schoolteachers, students, and others—all contributed their manual labor. A good case in point was the construction of an unpaved road, three kilometers in length and six meters in width, in Don Kam Yan, Muang District, in May 1968. The subdistrict chief mobilized some one thousand villagers, including women and children, for this work. Landlords and other well-off villagers supplied a grader and three tractors. Those who did not engage in physical labor—presumably the sick and the old—cooked simple lunches and served them to the workers. The construction expense of 20,000 baht came entirely from the villagers' own pockets. "Free riders" were not tolerated; they faced severe village-level sanctions, such as ostracism.[64]

It would be a mistake to interpret all these local development works, as some scholars might do,[65] as cooperative ventures that demonstrate the villagers' time-

---

[61] *Khon Suphan,* June 20, 1968, p. 1. For accounts of other development works by villagers, see various reports in *Khon Suphan* (February 5, 1962; April 5, 10, and 25, 1962; May 10, 1962; June 15, 1962; March 14, 1967; April 4, 1967; June 28, 1968; February 28, 1970; June 10, 1970; June 20, 1972; May 10, 1973; November 30, 1975; December 20, 1975; and August 20, 1976).

[62] NEDB, *The Second National Economic and Social Development Plan 1967–1971* (Bangkok: NEDB, 1967), p. 195.

[63] *Source: Khon Suphan,* June 20, 1968.

[64] *Khon Suphan,* May 20, 1968, pp. 1, 8.

[65] Chatthip Nartsupha, *The Thai Village Economy in the Past* (Chiang Mai: Silkworm, 1997).

honored norms of self-reliance, mutual help, and public-spiritedness, and the consequent superfluity of the modern intrusive state. Such interpretations romanticize or gloss over the sheer amount of time, labor, and material resources that were required of villagers. For example, the construction of one simple, unsurfaced road, 2.5 kilometers long and four meters wide, in Pho Phraya of Muang District, took as many as twenty years (!) to complete.[66]

The villagers who were involved in this kind of work have nothing but bitter memories; they all remember how onerous these grassroots projects were. Out of sympathy, a local newspaper columnist once wrote about the villagers who were building a small bridge in U-Thong District "with their clothes and faces dirtied with mud and sweat," and the columnist sarcastically exhorted the "big shots in Bangkok" to "come and dig together with these villagers to accumulate [Buddhist] merit."[67] The message to central state officials was simple and clear: "Put yourself in our position, and you'll know how arduous this task is." There is little room for romanticism in this kind of poignant account. Villagers toiling together for the benefit of their community under the scorching sun over a long period of time deserve our admiration, but we should not make volunteerism an inherent feature of village life. If villagers in Suphanburi "volunteered" to carry out development works on their own, it is only because the central state failed to make adequate funds available and put the burden of development on their shoulders. Plainly, the villagers were forced to do what the state was unable or unwilling to do.[68] And in the act of undertaking development on behalf of the "developmental" state, the villagers were acutely (through bodily pain) made to realize its impassive and unsympathetic nature.

The Crooked State

One major cause of the shortage of funds at the local level was corruption, which Suphanburians thought pervaded the developmental state. Political corruption was not anything new to Suphanburians; it had been a serious problem in their province since at least the late nineteenth century. When Minister of Interior Prince Damrong visited Suphanburi in 1892, villagers submitted "countless petitions against misgovernment" to him. Damrong subsequently sacked Suphanburi's governor for being corrupt. Damrong also referred to the provincial nobility of Suphanburi as "an assembly of crooks" that hampered effective local administration.[69]

---

[66] *Khon Suphan*, June 10, 1971, pp. 1, 12.

[67] *Khon Suphan*, May 10, 1973, p. 2.

[68] A study conducted in another Thai province, Khon Kaen, lends additional support to my interpretation here. This study found that, while supporting the cause of development in principle, few villagers wanted to sacrifice their own time and money for it. Plainly, they wanted public development works, but not if they had to contribute to them. Ratana, "Contested Concepts of Development in Rural Northeastern Thailand," pp. 69–70, 146–149. Another study found that villagers regard their participation in local development works as a form of corvée labor. See: Jonathan Rigg, Anna Allott, Rachel Harrison, and Ulrich Kratz, "Understanding Languages of Modernization: A Southeast Asian View," *Modern Asian Studies* 33,3 (1999): 585, 593.

[69] Tej, *The Provincial Administration of Siam*, pp. 100, 105, 167, 174.

The tradition of *kin ban kin muang*, or simply *kin muang* ("eating the state," or appropriating public funds) persisted well into the twentieth century.[70] In particular, with the advent of the developmental state under Sarit and Thanom, political corruption reached epic and epidemic proportions. Between 1969 and 1971, when Thanom allowed parliament to exist, Suphanburi's MP, Bun-uea Prasertsuwan, along with MPs from other provinces, exposed embarrassing cases of corruption among local officials, which prompted an irritated Thanom to stage a coup against his own government in November 1971 and to scrap the disobedient parliament.[71]

Ordinary Suphanburians were fed up with rampant corruption. A noodle vendor (#47) in Song Phi Nong District expressed that frustration when he described his deep mistrust of local officials:

> I can't remember exactly when. It was many decades ago, Thanom's days. Our village was isolated, so we asked for state funds for a road. Our village head filed a request. We waited for a year, but we received no reply. We thought, "Oh, they just ignored our request. Our village is so small. It's not important to them." Then we received the news that our request was approved. I can't remember how much, but we got a big fund. We were all happy. I thought, "The government does care about us." But what happened? They built a road all right, but it was not up to standard. Everyone could tell it was sloppy work [*mai pen sapparot*]. ... We should have gotten a much better road. We asked the civil servant in charge, "Why?" He said the budget was slashed. We didn't believe it. He and his superiors must have "eaten" [the budget].

Most dramatically, in 1975, the villagers in Sakaew of Muang District, utterly disgusted at the extent of local-level corruption, sent a letter to then-Governor Sawat Meephian, expressing a strong desire to secede from the municipality in which their village was located. Their complaint was that local state officials had been pocketing land taxes (which had been raised from three baht to five baht per 1,600 square meters) without using them for village development.[72] This localized "secessionist movement" was not a knee-jerk reaction; it was the culmination of the villagers' deep-rooted grievances that had been growing against dishonest local officials.

None of my respondents, of course, knew the exact extent of state corruption. It is simply unknowable. But they all depicted an adverse image of the state, consisting of rapacious officials bent on "devouring" development funds. A common scenario of corruption that most respondents related is that, before state funds were funneled into Suphanburi, "big men" in Bangkok first took a cut from them. As soon as the remaining funds reached Suphanburi, the governor took a second cut, followed by cuts for the deputy governors. When the rest of the funds were transferred to a lower department, its chief took an additional cut, followed by his subordinates. As the funds went down the bureaucratic ladder, they were thus "eaten" at each rung. By

---

[70] For an historical analysis of *kin muang*, see Pasuk Phongpaichit and Sungsidh Piriyarangsan, *Corruption and Democracy in Thailand* (Chiang Mai: Silkworm, 1996), pp. 7, 110–12; and Katherine Bowie, "Vote Buying and Village Outrage in an Election in Northern Thailand: Recent Legal Reforms in Historical Context," *Journal of Asian Studies* 67,2 (2008): 476–77.

[71] David Morell, "Power and Parliament in Thailand: The Futile Challenge, 1968–1971" (PhD dissertation, Princeton University, 1974), pp. 638–68.

[72] *Khon Suphan*, September 10, 1975, pp. 1, 2.

the time they reached the lowest village level, practically nothing was left. My respondents did not have any concrete evidence for this system of vertical "bureaucratic eating"; it is, essentially, an image they had constructed in their heads to explain the "missing" state funds earmarked for the villages. Yet, for these people, it is a powerful image that fits the "reality" so well, for the image explains perfectly why villagers were chronically suffering from a dearth of state monies and why they had to carry out local improvements on their own.

The Ineffectual State

When the state did allocate development funds to Suphanburi, the villagers found local state agents inefficient and desultory in fulfilling their duties. For example, in the early 1960s, the Department of Public Works built a fifteen-kilometer road from the market of Don Chedi District to the nearby Sa Krajom subdistrict. Within a few years, however, the road developed many potholes and bumps due to its shoddy quality. Some potholes were "even a meter deep." A local newspaper reporter complained that the road—the "artery (*sen lueat*) for the Sa Krajom community"—could hardly be called "a real road" and urged that the Provincial Office repair it immediately, without being "inactive and indifferent."[73] More than a year later, however, the Provincial Office had not done the repair work.[74] It was not until July 1969 that the state allocated 500,000 baht for repairing the road. This amount was only enough to repair less than half the road.[75]

Another case in point concerns the maintenance of the provincial athletic field, which the Department of Physical Education built in mid-1973 at a cost of 200,000 baht. At first, the Provincial Office took good care to maintain this field in preparation for a provincial-level sports competition to be held there at the end of 1973. This maintenance work led a local newspaper to predict with pride: "We believe that from now on, the level of athletics in Suphanburi will get better and better."[76] This expectation turned out to be premature, however. Once the scheduled competition was called off due to the October 1973 student-led "revolution" in Bangkok, the Provincial Office completely neglected its duty to maintain the field, leaving the lawn and weeds to grow "thick and wild" (*benja phan*). When a provincial newspaper reporter went to see the conditions in person, he had to "spend a long time figuring out even where the field tracks were," because the weeds had covered the whole field. The reporter expressed his disappointment that the Provincial Office had "abandoned" the field for such a long time. He lamented: "It never occurred to me that our province would fail to take good care of its own athletic field like this."[77]

A more telling example of the state's negligence and sloppiness concerned the DOH's construction of a 110-kilometer highway linking Suphanburi to Chainat, a province situated north of Suphanburi. During his visit to Suphanburi in 1967, then-Prime Minister Thanom recognized the importance of building this highway. He subsequently included it in the five-year highway development plan (1965-69) by

---

[73] *Khon Suphan*, December 28, 1965, p. 8.

[74] *Khon Suphan*, January 3, 1967, p. 1.

[75] *Khon Suphan*, July 20, 1969, pp. 1, 12; *Khon Suphan*, August 30, 1969, pp. 1, 12.

[76] *Khon Suphan*, June 20, 1973, p. 1; *Khon Suphan*, July 30, 1973, pp, 1, 2.

[77] *Khon Suphan*, October 30, 1974, p. 1, 2.

allocating 2.66 million baht, nearly 50 percent of which came from the World Bank.[78] The highway was completed in 1970, but it was a substandard road made of gravel. Within a year, the road became impassable due to severe damage caused by heavy trucks. Therefore, Bun-uea, then-MP from Suphanburi, submitted a petition to Thanom that the highway be asphalted. Thanom approved the request and announced that the surfacing would take place in 1971, using another World Bank loan of nearly 70 million baht.[79] In mid-1971, however, the project had not even begun, leading Suphanburians to regard the state as too "capricious" (*lorlee*) to be trusted.[80]

To make matters even worse, following the coup of November 1971, Thanom froze the project for no good reason. It was only in early 1973 that the project got under way with another World Bank loan of 21.4 million baht.[81] The government announced that the construction would be completed in 1974. In mid-1974, however, the DOH announced that the construction would be delayed due to the rising prices of raw materials, which forced the state and the contractor, Hyundai of South Korea, to renegotiate the original budget. The negotiation fell through.[82] As a result, Hyundai withdrew from the project in 1975, abandoning its ongoing construction work. Then the government announced that it would choose a new contractor via a public bidding process, but that the selection process would "take another eight to ten months." Clearly, the state displayed little sense of urgency in implementing the project.[83] The patience of Suphanburians wore thin. Local officials indicated that the construction might be completed by the end of 1975, but Suphanburians brushed off that prediction as disingenuous, as "a placebo [*ya horm*] aimed to make them happy [temporarily]." That placebo, far from allaying Suphanburians' disaffection, only exacerbated it. Therefore, a local newspaper urged:

> State officials in charge should not be sitting idle, showing no concern [*ning duu daai*] for this project. Suphanburians have felt like this for a long time, but they just don't speak up. ... If Hyundai has abandoned this work, let it be. We'd better get another company to undertake the work. [The state should] do it quickly without dragging its feet [*oi ying*] like this forever.[84]

These accounts show how the negative images of state officials were produced and reproduced in the impressions of many Suphanburians. The "developmental" leviathan state, when seen through the concrete actions (or lack thereof) and practices of its agents at the local level, fell far short of doing what it had publicly

---

[78] *Khon Suphan*, May 30, 1968, p. 1; NEDB, *Development Projects Requiring Financial Assistance under the Second Plan (1967–1971)* (Bangkok: NEDB, 1968), p. 35.

[79] *Khon Suphan*, October 30, 1970, p. 1; *Khon Suphan*, July 10, 1973, pp. 1, 2.

[80] *Khon Suphan*, June 10, 1971, pp. 1, 12.

[81] Budget Bureau, *Ekasarn Ngop-pramarn 2518*, 3,4 (1974): 159, 171; *Khon Suphan*, March 20, 1973, pp. 1, 12; *Khon Suphan*, June 10, 1973, pp. 1, 12.

[82] The Thai government offered to increase the original budget by 35 percent, but Hyundai demanded a 47 percent hike. *Khon Suphan*, August 30, 1974, pp. 1, 8.

[83] *Khon Suphan*, April 10, 1975, p. 1; *Khon Suphan*, May 20, 1975, pp. 1, 8.

[84] *Khon Suphan*, September 10, 1974, p. 3. For similar accounts that show the inefficiency of the state, see *Khon Suphan* January 20, 1971, pp. 1, 12; *Khon Suphan*, July 30, 1971, pp. 1, 12; and *Khon Suphan*, November 20, 1971, p. 1.

avowed to do or boasted of having achieved. Suphanburians, therefore, had only wobbly trust, at best, in the ability, commitment, and sincerity of state officials to undertake local development. Official reports, which complacently praised state-led development works for making "satisfactory" and "steady progress," ignore what was happening at the local level and how ordinary Suphanburians viewed the state machineries and their agents.[85] To be sure, the state-led rural development initiatives were not a total failure. For example, the state built over nine thousand kilometers of provincial highways between 1959 and 1974.[86] On the basis of this kind of aggregate official data, outsiders might consider the developmental state's efforts a success. However, local accounts, which remain completely hidden behind the dry official data, show that many villagers in Suphanburi felt that the state was doing too little. Suphanburi's backwardness, according to these people, was the direct outcome of the state's abysmal failure.

BELITTLING SUPHANBURI: NEGATIVE PROVINCIAL IDENTITY

To the extent that human interaction is essential for the formation of collective identity,[87] Suphanburians living in dispersed villages probably had a relatively weak provincial identity and a correspondingly stronger sense of attachment to their respective villages or districts. To the extent that they had a provincial identity, available evidence suggests that it was negative. The prevailing conditions and perceptions of relative backwardness caused Suphanburians to speak pitifully of their own province, often with a good deal of exaggeration. They had what Tim Oakes calls "a complex of backwardness."[88] In the parlance of social identity theory in psychology, they displayed an "inadequate or negative social identity."[89] In ordinary language, they felt inferior.

Their feelings are well captured in an editorial that the influential local historian Manas once published to recollect and lament Suphanburi's past: "Suphanburi had been dumped [*thort thing*] by the state in a deep jungle, while other provinces from the north to the south prospered [at Suphanburi's expense]."[90] On another occasion, Manas commented: "Suphanburi, for all its proximity to the capital city, had been abandoned by the state. Suphanburi was ... buried in a jungle, despite the fact that it used to be an important place before."[91] A native of Suphanburi, Banharn shares the same memory, recalling that "Suphanburi had been abandoned [by the state] for hundreds of years. Every Suphanburian was complaining about it."[92]

---

[85] NEDB, *The Second National Economic and Social Development Plan 1967–1971*, pp. 181, 190.

[86] NSO, *Statistical Yearbook Thailand 1963* (Bangkok: NSO, 1964), p. 222; NSO, *Statistical Yearbook Thailand 1974–1975* (Bangkok: NSO, 1976), p. 293.

[87] See Emile Durkheim, *The Elementary Forms of the Religious Life*, trans. Joseph Swain (Glencoe, IL: Free Press, 1974); and Emile Durkheim, *The Division of Labor in Society*, trans. W. D. Halls (New York, NY: Free Press, 1984).

[88] Tim Oakes, "China's Provincial Identities: Reviving Regionalism and Reinventing 'Chineseness,'" *Journal of Asian Studies* 59,3 (2000): 683.

[89] Donald Taylor and Fathali Moghaddam, *Theories of Intergroup Relations: International Social Psychological Perspectives* (New York, NY: Praeger, 1994), p. 83.

[90] *Suphanburi Sarn*, December 25, 1987, p. 6.

[91] Manas, *Prawat Luang Phor Tor Wat Jampa*, p. 9.

[92] Khomduean Choetcharatfa, *Cheewa Prawat lae Thasana Banharn Silpa-archa Nayol Ratamontri Khon thi 21 khong Thai* (Bangkok: Soi Thong, 1995), p. 133.

Other examples are equally suggestive of Suphanburians' negative provincial identity. One concerns the failure of the DOH to include Suphanburi in its grandiose, 2,297-million-baht, nationwide highway construction project in 1963. *Khon Suphan* reported this news with a front-page headline that bemoaned Suphanburi's unimportance and marginality: "Building Highways throughout Thailand. Nothing for Suphanburi." Although the DOH used the number of vehicles in each province to justify the selection, *Khon Suphan* flatly dismissed it as an invalid criterion on the grounds that "Suphanburi, with its population reaching almost 500,000, had just as great a need for transportation systems as other provinces."[93] Suphanburi, in short, was denied legitimate access to state resources; it was an apparent loser in a zero-sum inter-provincial competition for development funds, thanks to the unwarranted, blatant favoritism of the state. As a result, Suphanburi was perennially stuck with an extremely poor road network, which the Suphanburians compared to "the bottom of a paper bag" (*kon thung*). The expression meant that Suphanburi was a "dead end" that nobody could pass through; whoever came to Suphanburi from Bangkok had no choice but to turn around and go back because there was no road beyond Suphanburi.[94]

Given such perceptions, when the DOH announced a plan to build a highway from Suphanburi to the neighboring province of Chainat in 1965, *Khon Suphan* predicted with joy that the formerly neglected Suphanburi would "become an important province in the future, with more people and goods passing through."[95] To the Suphanburians' disappointment, however, the construction of the highway came to a complete halt by 1971. This led them to suspect with resentment that "the state has diverted the funds … to some other province that it deems as *more important*."[96] Suphanburians were thus made all the more acutely aware, once again, of their marginal position in the state's national development plan.

From the detached vantage point of the present, outsiders might argue that the state could not have developed all the provinces equally at the same time, or that it was actually doing the best it could to develop rural Thailand as a whole within its budgetary constraints. Outsiders might also ask why the state should have accorded developmental priority to Suphanburi, a province of relatively little economic and strategic importance. Logical explanations, however, fall on deaf ears for those who want something badly. From the subjective viewpoint of Suphanburians, their province needed and deserved roads, schools, and other public goods just as much as did other provinces. The state, however, failed to give Suphanburi the assistance residents thought they deserved, causing Suphanburi to lag behind many other provinces. This kind of disappointment led one newspaper columnist to gripe, with a mixture of pent-up resentment, jealousy, and frustration: "Every [Thai] government has traditionally paid little attention to Suphanburi, leaving it to develop on its own without giving it as much [budgetary] support as it needed." Most dramatically, his

---

[93] *Khon Suphan*, February 10, 1963, p. 1. There is something to this appeal. In 1963, the number of vehicles in Suphanburi (more than 2,400) was the sixteenth highest among the then-sixty-nine provinces in Thailand, excluding Bangkok. Only two provinces in the central region exceeded this number. NSO, *Statistical Yearbook Thailand 1964* (Bangkok: NSO, 1965), pp. 259–61.

[94] *Khon Suphan*, March 23, 1965, pp. 1, 16.

[95] Ibid.

[96] *Khon Suphan*, June 10, 1971, pp. 1, 12; emphasis mine.

editorial referred to Suphanburi as "the child of a mistress [*luuk mia noi*]"—a Thai expression carrying a set of profoundly negative meanings: ignored, inferior, unwanted, disadvantaged, unnoticed, and of secondary importance.[97] Likewise, many elderly people I talked to used the expression *noi jai* (slighted) in recollecting and describing the way Suphanburi was mistreated by the state. Thus, the images of the callous, discriminatory, and negligent state spawned an increasingly bitter awareness of Suphanburi's relative deprivation, which in turn became the perceptual basis for engendering a pitiful, biting, and politicized provincial identity.

While Suphanburians felt inferior, non-Suphanburians felt superior, holding up Suphanburi to ridicule for its backwardness. A local newspaper illustrated this point by retelling a joke with much resentment:

> One day, a Bangkokian went to Suphanburi via Nakhon Pathom Province. On the way back to Bangkok, he stopped over at a coffee shop in Nakhon Pathom. The shop owner looked the man in the face and said, "You've just been to Suphanburi, right?" Amazed, the Bangkokian asked, "How could you tell?" The shop owner answered with laughter, "How could I *not* tell? Dust is all over your face, and that is red dust."[98]

The implication here is that unpaved, gravel roads could be found only Suphanburi, whereas roads in Nakhon Pathom (and elsewhere) were all made of asphalt or concrete. In other words, inferior, dusty roads were regarded as the quintessential symbol of Suphanburi. A car mechanic in Song Phi Nong District (#74) recounted a similar story based on his work experience in the adjacent province of Kanchanaburi in the late 1960s. His repair shop once received a customer whose brand-new car had broken down just a few days after he bought it. A fellow mechanic asked the customer, in jest: "Did you drive to Suphan?" The other mechanics giggled, knowing that roads in Suphanburi were chock-full of potholes. Suphanburi was the butt of these kinds of (lighthearted) jokes, which made the province synonymous with a geographic and social backwater. The absence of roads (and other development projects) did not simply cause inconvenience to Suphanburians in a material sense alone; it also negatively affected Suphanburi's position in the imagined social geography of Thailand.

Given the widely shared image of Suphanburi as a "backward" province, one schoolteacher (#75), who was born in Lopburi Province but now works in Suphanburi, recollected: "In the past, if you were a civil servant and were transferred to Suphanburi, it was considered a demotion. Nobody, except those who were born in Suphanburi, wanted to be assigned here." She continued: "Now, who wants to work in Yala [a southern province plagued by Muslim insurgency] or Yasothon [a northeastern province near the border with Cambodia]? Suphanburi had the same image that these provinces have at present."

Suphanburians themselves share such perceptions. The local historian Manas recalled: "Civil servants who got an official order to be assigned to Suphanburi would run around, beating their chests and pleading not to be transferred." Thus, his editorial, published in 1987, was titled: "50–60 Years Ago, Nobody Wanted to Come

---

[97] *Khon Suphan*, September 10, 1974, p. 3.

[98] *Khon Suphan*, October 25, 1963, p. 5.

to Suphanburi."[99] In particular, the civil servants assigned to U-Thong, a district considered to be one of the least developed in Suphanburi, "felt as if they had been deported [from Thailand]," recalled Dr. Bun-uea, a former Suphanburi MP.[100]

Whether these negative characterizations reflect objective reality is not very important. The point is that they show the subjective sentiments of social shame, inferiority, neglect, and marginalization that many Suphanburians felt in the national (and global) regime of visual and verbal representations, which eulogized modernity and conversely stigmatized backwardness.[101] As a confirmation of Michael Hechter's theory,[102] the social interactions between Suphanburians and non-Suphanburians heightened, rather than lessened, such negative social identity. The stigma that Suphanburians attached to their province's backwardness was shaped by the inferior images that non-Suphanburians imposed on Suphanburi.

Precisely because they felt ashamed, Suphanburians tried to assert their positive provincial identity by playing up what few signs of provincial prestige or distinctiveness they could find. Several seemingly trivial newspaper report are indicative of such attempts. One report boasted that the newly constructed Buddha statue (twenty-six meters tall) at Phai Rongwua Temple in Song Phi Nong District was "the world's largest."[103] Another report gave extensive coverage to a French archeologist who found that the present district of U-Thong was the "oldest" and the "biggest" center of the Dvaravati civilization, dating back to the sixth century. The archeologist was favorably quoted as saying that U-Thong "possessed a larger trap for catching elephants than the ones found elsewhere ... The elephant traps in Ayutthaya, Nakhon Sawan, and Surin [provinces] are just ordinary traps."[104] In reporting the discovery of a ten-meter-high waterfall in Suphanburi in 1962, another report boasted: "Our province has a beautiful waterfall just like other provinces, such as Nakon Nayok, Prachuab, Chanthaburi, Kanchanaburi, and Chiang Mai," and that "we can be proud" of our waterfall even though "it can not really match the waterfall in Chiang Mai or Kanchanaburi" in scale and beauty.[105]

A desire for provincial "greatness" was reflected in another newspaper editorial published in 1965, which urged that a bridge be built across the Tha Chin River—a river that runs through the heart of Suphanburi—to connect the Muang municipality to the sparsely populated western part of Suphanburi. The editorial emphasized the need for this bridge by evoking the image of a once-prosperous Suphanburi during the Ayutthaya Kingdom period. The bridge, it was argued, would stimulate the flow

---

[99] Manas, "50–60 Years Ago, Nobody Wanted to Come to Suphanburi," *Suphanburi Sarn,* December 25, 1987, p. 6. Manas similarly remarked in 1995: "70–80 years ago ... civil servants did not want to be transferred to Suphanburi." Manas, *Prawat Luang Phor Tor Wat Jampa,* pp. 27–28.

[100] Association of Suphanburians, *Hoksip Pii Samakhom Chao Suphanburi,* p. 123; CT Party, *Chart Thai Samphan* 13 (May–June 2001), p. 5.

[101] See Michael Rhum, "'Modernity' and 'Tradition' in 'Thailand,'" *Modern Asian Studies* 30,2 (1996): 325–55; Thongchai Winichakul, "The Quest for 'Siwilai': A Geographical Discourse of Civilizational Thinking in the Late Nineteenth and Early Twentieth-Century Siam," *Journal of Asian Studies* 59,3 (2000): 528–49; and Turton, *Civility and Savagery.*

[102] Michael Hechter, *Internal Colonialism: The Celtic Fringe in British National Development, 1536–1966* (Berkeley, CA: University of California Press, 1975).

[103] *Khon Suphan,* February 8, 1966, p. 1.

[104] *Khon Suphan,* September 15, 1964, pp. 1, 16; *Khon Suphan,* November 10, 1964, p. 16.

[105] *Khon Suphan,* October 10, 1962, p. 1.

of people and goods, and the less developed western part of Suphanburi would then enjoy "prosperity as in the ancient times once again."[106] To outsiders, the imagined past glory of Suphanburi that followed King Naresuan's victory over Burma more than four centuries ago would seem like a thing of the far distant past, which has little resonance in the twentieth century. The seemingly insignificant evocation of the image, however, might be seen as the manifestation of Suphanburians' wistful nostalgia for the lost (putative) "grandeur" of their province. Given the backward conditions in which Suphanburi was mired in the twentieth century, the sharply contrasting image of a once-prosperous Suphanburi in the invented mythical past struck a powerful emotional chord with the local population.

Suphanburians' latent or concealed yearning for a higher social status for their province stemmed from their negative provincial identity. This identity was not the product of Suphanburians' inherent psychological traits; it emerged, instead, as we have seen, out of the historical context of tense state–Suphanburi relations—a context in which Suphanburians from different classes and occupational backgrounds became increasingly conscious of the extent to which the putatively "developmental" state had unjustly neglected their province's development while favoring many other provinces.

PRELUDE TO BANHARN'S EMERGENCE

It is against this historical background that Banharn emerged in the 1960s as a benevolent and munificent local developer. His supporters almost invariably talk about and evaluate his emergence by situating it in the historical context of the "state-made" backwardness that they had to come to terms with firsthand in their everyday lives. That even relatively young Suphanburians recount similar stories suggests that the collective politicized memories of the backward past have been handed down from generation to generation.

Suphanburians, outsiders might argue, may be exaggerating or dramatizing the extent of their province's previous backwardness and the state's lack of responsibility. But that is precisely how they appreciate a series of Banharn's subsequent actions. It is necessary, in other words, for Suphanburians to assign a highly negative meaning to the pre-Banharn past in order to appreciate and accentuate the value of Banharn and his positive place in the history of the province. The negative past is the discursive "dough," as it were, from which the positive present constructed by Banharn is molded and savored. Again, whether the Suphanburians' rueful representations and recollections of the past are wholly based on objectively true facts is irrelevant. They are not interested in such a baffling social scientific search for the "authentic past." For them, the past does not exist as an immutable entity waiting to be discovered or reconstructed through professional historians' painstaking and detached archival research. They take the initiative to confer their own meanings or interpretations on Suphanburi's past in their attempts to construct Banharn as a "good" leader. For example, Waruni Osatharom, a Suphanburi-born, professionally trained historian at Bangkok's elite Thammasat University, recently published a detailed book on the history of Suphanburi that draws extensively on archival materials—probably the only academic book available

---

[106] *Khon Suphan*, December 7, 1965, p. 8.

on the subject.[107] Ordinary Suphanburians, however, are not even aware of its existence. Moreover, Waruni's "expert narratives" do not mention the past backwardness of Suphanburi and the state's failure to rectify it. In other words, the authoritative history of Suphanburi that exists in her book is substantially different from ordinary Suphanburians' memories and "renditions" of the past. Without reading Waruni's (or any other historian's) work, ordinary Suphanburians have come to interpret or reconstruct their social history in their own ways.

The state is now set for Banharn's emergence on Suphanburi's social scene.

---

[107] Waruni, *Muang Suphan.*

CHAPTER THREE

THE RISE OF A LOCAL HERO

On the outskirts of Suphanburi's provincial capital stands a beautiful town shrine (*sarn chaopho lak muang*). It was built six hundred to seven hundred years ago to propitiate a powerful local spirit. The spirit was supposedly so powerful that tax-collecting state officials dispatched to Suphanburi felt it necessary to visit the shrine and to pray for the cooperation of the local people. Prince Damrong and King Chulalongkorn also paid homage to the shrine during their visits to Suphanburi in 1892 and 1904, respectively. As Damrong noted during his visit, Suphanburians feared and respected the spirit to an extraordinary degree.[1] The conditions of the shrine deteriorated over the decades, however, and under these circumstances, Banharn undertook its major renovation in the late 1980s by spending eight million baht. The result is the splendid shrine as it exists now.[2] On weekends, well-wishers flock to the shrine. Civil servants also visit the shrine on being assigned to Suphanburi, as they did a hundred years ago. It is one of the spiritual centers in Suphanburi.

For many Suphanburians, however, the relationship between this shrine and Banharn goes much deeper. It dates back to November 1949, when then-seventeen-year-old Banharn paid a legendary visit to the shrine. As one woman selling lottery tickets outside the shrine (#48) described to me:

> It was a day before he migrated to Bangkok as a worker. He didn't really want to go. He loved his birthplace. He didn't want to leave his parents and friends behind. But he had to, to make money. He was poor, just like us ... He was worried. He didn't know what would happen in Bangkok. He wasn't sure if he would succeed. So he came here to ask for good luck. He said to the spirit, "If I ever meet with success in Bangkok, I'll come back to Suphan to make it prosperous with my money. I promise."

This woman, born in 1951, could not have known whether Banharn really visited the shrine, let alone what he prayed, in 1949. Asked about this, she simply said: "I heard the story from my friends." Indeed, during my fieldwork I heard many other Suphanburians recount a similar story. It was not long before I discovered that

---

[1] Manas Ophakul, *Prawat Luang Phor Tor Wat Jampa* (Suphanburi: n.p., 1995), p. 4; Waruni Osatharom, *Muang Suphan bon Sen Thang kan Plian Plaeng Thang Prawatisat: Phuthasatawat thi 8 – Ton Phuthasatawat thi 25* (Bangkok: Thammasat University Press, 2004), pp. 276–78; *Suphanburi Sarn*, July 25, 1988; *Khon Suphan*, July 16, 1988; and *Khon Suphan*, August 1, 1997.

[2] See Yoshinori Nishizaki, "The Weapon of the Strong: Identity, Community, and Domination in Provincial Thailand" (PhD dissertation, University of Washington, Seattle, WA, 2004), Chapter 7, for details.

Banharn himself told such a story in public in 1995,[3] although it is not clear whether this was the origin of the provincial lore.

Yet Suphanburians do not embrace the apocryphal and seemingly propagandistic mythology simply because Banharn spread it. They believe it because it is well matched by what he has done in practice. Banharn did succeed in Bangkok, and he did come back to Suphanburi to make a series of donations to the cause of local development. That was more than a decade before he became an MP in 1976. In brief, Banharn made good on his alleged promise. He thus emerged, and continues to be honored, as a legendary "Robin Hood" hero who, unlike the callous, miserly, and discriminatory central state, was deeply committed to working for Suphanburi and its people. "We were all waiting for a person like Banharn to come along for a long time," one elderly farmer in Muang District (#104) remarked, playing up the dramatic quality of Banharn's appearance onto the stage of Suphanburi's development. In this and other people's narratives, Banharn met Suphanburians' "summons" by stirring up a whirlwind of much-desired change. This marks the beginning of a long period that continues to the present, a period in which the formerly stagnant and backward Suphanburi started changing for the better, according to Banharn supporters.

These views differ markedly from most scholars' facile ahistorical constructions of Banharn as a dirty strongman who cheated his way into parliament. Many Suphanburians regard Banharn's current political authority as having a deeply moral and historical origin that dates back to the decade before 1976. I trace this origin in the sections that follow. The first section sketches Banharn's economic success in Bangkok and some of his most representative charitable donations in Suphanburi. I will then discuss the Suphanburians' positive assessments of Banharn's actions and his landslide victory in the parliamentary election of 1976, the first election he ever contested in his life.

STRIKING IT RICH IN BANGKOK

The Muang municipality, an area of nine square kilometers inhabited by 47,000 people, occupies the center of Muang District, the most populous among the ten districts of Suphanburi. Everyday life in the municipality revolves around a bustling market lined with shops that sell meat, vegetables, drinks, newspapers, clothes, and other items. In the back of this market, there is an old, small shop called Yong Yu Hong (永裕豐). This is where Banharn was born and lived as a child.

Most Suphanburians are familiar with the general life story of the man who has changed the recent history of their province. The story has been spread over the decades by word of mouth. Several short (nonacademic) biographies, published shortly before and after Banharn became prime minister in 1995, have made his life story all the more famous.[4] In addition, Banharn himself played a part in

---

[3] Chaophraya Yommarat Hospital, *Thiraluek Phithi Perd Tuek Khon Khai Phiset Banharn–Jaemsai Silpa-archa 3* (Suphanburi: Chaophraya Yommarat Hospital, 1997), p. 6.

[4] See, for example, Akhraphon and Rut Manthira, *Senthang suu Nayok Ratamontrii khong Tueng Siao Harn Banharn Silpa-archa* (Bangkok: Nam Fon, 1995), p. 18; Khomduean Choetcharatfa, *Cheewa Prawat lae Thasana Banharn Silpa-archa Nayol Ratamontri Khon thi 21 khong Thai* (Bangkok: Soi Thong, 1995), p. 58; *Krungthep Thurakij Sutsabda*, February 29–March 6, 1992, p. 11; Sarthit Winurat, *Ke Roi Nak Kan Muang* (Bangkok: Wisurut, 1996); and *Sarn Khwam Fan*

disseminating his life story by constructing two museums that display various photos from his childhood.

Banharn was born in August 1932 into a middle-class Chinese (Teochiu) merchant family. His father, Be Saeng Kim (馬成根), had migrated to Suphanburi from Shantou of China's Kwangtung Province in 1907, when the number of Chinese immigrants to Thailand reached a peak.[5] The fourth of six children in the family, Banharn was given a Chinese name, Be Tek Siang (馬德祥), which he retained until the 1940s. His parents sold daily consumables at their shop, Yong Yu Hong. A few hundred meters away is another shop, Chuan Limthong, which sold jewelry. This is where Jaemsai Lekwat, the future wife of Banharn, grew up. She came from an upper-class landowning Chinese family, which, in addition to trading in gold, had interests in rice milling. Banharn and Jaemsai often played together when they were small. An elderly pharmacist (#100) who has known Banharn since his childhood said admiringly, "Jaemsai was Banharn's first love. They are still together. He has one heart [a Thai expression meaning faithful], unlike other politicians who have mistresses."

Banharn likes to present himself as the son of a poor family, or as a sort of Thai Abraham Lincoln who overcame great hardships in life to become a national leader by sheer dint of great effort—an image that some Suphanburians, including the lottery-ticket seller cited earlier, eagerly embrace. This is a myth. As elderly residents of the Muang municipality agree, Banharn's family actually enjoyed at least middle-class status. Sometime after Banharn's birth, his father, Saeng Kim, won a public bid to acquire a small, legal opium plant and alcohol distillery in Suphanburi, investments that considerably raised the family's income.[6] The distillery produced whisky called Mae Nam Suphan (Suphan River). Saeng Kim used his wealth to help out local residents in trouble, and to act as a mediator for disputes. In 1947, he founded the Chinese Association of Suphanburi, of which he became the first president.[7] He also opened a small hotel, Sai Au, which Banharn's elder sister, Sai Jai, managed.[8] These may not be signs of copious wealth, but they are not signs of poverty, either.

Banharn's youth was quite uneventful. He graduated from a local secondary school, Pratheep Withayalai (which no longer exists), at the age of fourteen. After helping his parents with their family business for the next two years, he went to

---

Hoksip Pii Phana Than Banharn Silpa-archa (n.p., 1992). This last item, a booklet, was published in 1992, presumably by Banharn's children, to commemorate his sixtieth birthday.

[5] *Bangkok Post*, May 7, 1996; *Bangkok Post*, September 21, 1996; and William Skinner, *Chinese Society in Thailand: An Analytical History* (Ithaca, NY: Cornell University Press, 1957), pp. 61, 63.

[6] Opium production was one of Thailand's largest, officially sanctioned sources of state revenue well into the twentieth century. Taxes on opium sales provided 18 percent of the nation's revenue in 1926. See Benjamin Batson, *The End of the Absolute Monarchy in Siam* (Singapore: Oxford University Press, 1984), pp. 90, 120; James Ingram, *Economic Change in Thailand, 1850–1970* (Stanford, CA: Stanford University Press, 1971), pp. 177–78, 186–87. It was not until Sarit came to power in 1958 that opium production was outlawed. By this time, however, Banharn's father had passed away—he died in 1954—and his opium factory had been closed down.

[7] Saeng Kim's photo is still hung on the wall of the Chinese Association of Suphanburi.

[8] *Khon Suphan*, August 20, 1969, p. 3; *Krungthep Thurakij Sutsabda*, February 29–March 6, 1992, p. 11.

Bangkok to take an entrance exam for a famous preparatory school, which he failed.[9] Disappointed, he returned to Suphanburi and spent the next year or so learning Chinese and basic tailoring.[10] As one retired civil servant (#101) recalled, Banharn was "just an ordinary boy who dabbled at many things in life. Nobody expected him to become 'Banharn Silpa-archa' that we know now."

What changed Banharn's life—and Suphanburi's history—was his decision to migrate to Bangkok in 1949. As Banharn recalls, he left Suphanburi on a boat —the only mode of transport to Bangkok at the time—on November 11, with only five baht in his pocket. His legendary pledge at the town shrine supposedly took place a day before this departure. His daily job in Bangkok was to help his elder brothers, Somboon and Udom, with their small but growing beverage retail business in a shop named Thai Somboon, located on the bustling Larn Luang Road, an area dominated by immigrant Chinese. He would deliver drinks using a bicycle-drawn cart, for which he earned thirty to forty baht a month.[11] This petty job turned out to be the origin of Banharn's phenomenal economic success. By 1953, just four years after migrating to Bangkok, he had established his own construction company, Saha Srichai, at the age of twenty-one.

Exactly how this dramatic metamorphosis took place remains shrouded in mystery. This is the murkiest part of Banharn's life, the details of which few Suphanburians know. Banharn himself is silent on this issue, suggesting that he has something to hide from the public. It is possible, however, to reconstruct what may have happened by piecing together fragments of available written materials and the oral recollections of Larn Luang residents.

First, Thai Somboon's location was crucial for Banharn's economic success. It was located less than two hundred meters from the Department of Public Works (DPW)—a bureaucratic unit widely regarded as one of the most corrupt in Thailand. The DPW civil servants regularly ordered soft drinks from Thai Somboon. As Banharn delivered them every weekday, he became acquainted with top-ranking DPW officials, some of whom were from Suphanburi. A man of deferential manners, he "knew how to please" civil servants and quickly "became their favorite."[12] He was then offered a job at Thai Yong Phanit (永德興), a successful Sino-Thai construction company, located on Larn Luang Road, just a stone's throw from Thai Somboon. Thai Yong Phanit apparently sought to capitalize on Banharn's connections to the DPW.[13] Banharn, for his part, learned the ins and outs of construction business at Thai Yong Phanit, while deepening his personal ties to DPW officials. This experience led him to found the aforementioned Saha Srichai Construction company (also on Larn Luang) in March 1953, along with Thai Yong Phanit's executives, who probably supplied the start-up capital.[14]

---

[9] Akhraphon and Manthira, *Senthang suu Nayok Ratamontrii*, p.17; Khomduean, *Cheewa Prawat lae Thasana Banharn Silpa-archa*, pp. 34–35.

[10] *Sarn Khwam Fan*, pp. 21–22.

[11] Ibid., pp. 23, 26–28, 46.

[12] Khomduean, *Cheewa Prawat lae Thasana Banharn Silpa-archa*, p. 50.

[13] Established in 1946, Thai Yong Phanit (which no longer exists) built the main office of the Bank of Thailand. Department of Business Development, Ministry of Commerce (DBD/MC), Bangkok Company Files no. 362 and no. 2635; and interviews with Larn Luang residents in May 2004.

[14] DBD/MC, Bangkok Company File no. 3893. For more details, see Nishizaki, "The Weapon of the Strong," chapter 4.

Larn Luang's residents who had met Banharn during this period described him to me in various ways (e.g., hardworking, charming, strange, clever, crooked, and so on), but they are unanimous in their view that the DPW and Thai Yong Phanit turned Banharn, an uneducated nonentity from provincial Thailand, into a budding capitalist in the short space of four years. As one elderly Sino-Thai merchant (#93) recalled, "At that time, there were no skyscrapers, no elaborate buildings, in Thailand, so construction was easy. Anybody who had money, connections, good luck, and a little bit of knowledge could enter the business." Banharn got all these essentials from the DPW and Thai Yong Phanit.

Saha Srichai steadily expanded in subsequent years. Some Suphanburians attribute this expansion to Banharn's sheer hard work. For example, a retired medical doctor (#102), who happened to live near Larn Luang Road while studying in Bangkok, recalled: "The light in his company was always on, until late at night. I came back home one day after midnight, after drinking with my friends. I walked past his company. I saw the light on. I peeped inside. I saw Banharn checking account books alone. He worked on Saturday and Sunday, too. He was always working without resting." In the accounts of this and several other Suphanburians, Banharn figures as a self-made, successful capitalist.

The reality, however, was not so rosy. The patronage of friends and state officials was crucial. The Bangkok Metropolitan Bank, founded in 1950 by the Teochiu capitalist Uthen Techaphaiboon, who personally knew Banharn's brother Somboon, provided loans, business contacts, and other favors to Banharn's fledging company.[15] Then a big break came in 1957, when Field Marshal Sarit Thanarat came to power and initiated massive rural development, including the installation of tap-water systems. Sarit put the DPW in charge of this nationwide project. Thanks to two DPW director-generals, Damrong Chonwijarn (1958–59) and Luang Yuktasewee Wiwat (1959–66), Banharn won an extremely lucrative ten-year monopoly to build tap-water pipes throughout Thailand.[16] Damrong, whose patronage was particularly important, as Banharn's wife, Jaemsai, admits,[17] was from Suphanburi. Banharn had another Suphanburi-born patron, Thawil Sunthorasarnthul, who controlled the DPW as permanent secretary of the Interior Ministry (1963–68) and deputy interior minister (1969–73).[18]

Banharn's detractors would see these connections as the breeding ground of corruption. Interestingly, most Suphanburians I talked to did not deny this; they are not naïve. Most admit that Banharn's economic success probably involved shady deals with powerful bureaucratic patrons. Yet these people quickly point out that

---

[15] *Asiaweek*, July 14, 1995; DBD/MC, Bangkok Company File no. 2070; and *Sarn Khwam Fan*, pp. 34–35. Uthen was later to develop one of Thailand's largest conglomerates, the Techaphaiboon Group. When Banharn established another company, Saha Srichai Chemical, in 1980, he invited Techaphaiboon family members to become its major stockholders. The Techaphaiboon family also became the major stockholders of Siam Occidental Electrochemical, which Banharn established in 1990. See DBD/MC, Bangkok Company Files no. 2164/2523 and no. 7508/2533.

[16] Anant Sanokhan, *Thammai Phom Tong Than Banharn* (Bangkok: Klet Thai, 1988), p. 57; Prachachart Thurakij, *Pert Tua 'Khun Khlang' 15 Phak Kan Muang Thai* (Bangkok: n.p., n.d.), p. 6; The profits from the booming business enabled Banharn to found two additional companies, Nathee Thong and BS International, in 1962 and 1970, respectively. DBD/MC, Bangkok Limited Partnership File no. 527/05 and Bangkok Company File no. 330/2513.

[17] Sarthit, *Ke Roi Nak Kan Muang*, p. 76.

[18] *Khon Suphan*, April 10, 1969, pp. 1, 12; *Khon Suphan*, April 20, 1969, p. 1.

there is *nothing* unusual about Banharn's actions in the economic history of Thailand. They know that virtually all prominent Thai capitalists have attained their present status by depending on, and colluding with, the bureaucracy. Banharn was just one of them. An ascetic work ethic—the key to capitalist growth in Protestant Europe, according to Max Weber[19]—is not enough to get one far in Thailand's business world; hard work must be complemented by official connections. Official patronage is especially important in the highly politicized construction industry, where the market is directly mediated by state agencies. In the 1950s, such patronage was vital for the sheer survival of politically vulnerable Chinese businesses, which were the targets of official harassment and discrimination.[20] Knowing this, one elderly Sino-Thai merchant in Suphanburi (#103) defended Banharn in a typical way: "Can you name any one capitalist who has succeeded while being totally clean? That is impossible in Thailand. If I were him, I would have taken advantage of every connection to any civil servant, too. If you have to offer a little money under the table sometimes, that's part of doing business in Thailand."

According to this merchant and many other Suphanburians, what is unique about Banharn is not how he achieved his wealth, but how he *used* it. He used it for the sake of Suphanburi and its people, following through on his legendary pledge at the town shrine in 1949. He was not simply content with getting rich. This is what distinguishes Banharn sharply from other money-grubbing capitalists, according to his supporters.

DONATION AFTER DONATION

In recounting Banharn's actions in Suphanburi before 1976, his supporters never fail to mention two phrases: generous (*jai kwang*) and charitable (*jai bun*). These words are part of the local vocabulary of praise for Banharn. A series of his high-profile donations to local development give powerful and concrete meanings to these phrases. He turned his money into what John Kane would call "moral capital" or "moral reputation"—a nonmaterial virtue or asset that enables politicians to acquire legitimate authority without resorting to seedy means of establishing social control.[21]

Hospital Ward

Banharn's first major donation in Suphanburi dates back to January 1966, when, at the age of thirty-three, he built a patients' ward at Chaophraya Yommarat Hospital.[22] The unresponsiveness of the central state provided a historical context in which his donation was appreciated by local residents. Chaophraya Yommarat Hospital, the only public hospital in Suphanburi at the time, found it difficult to

---

[19] Max Weber, *The Protestant Ethic and the Spirit of Capitalism*, trans. Talcott Parsons (New York, NY: Routledge, 1996).

[20] Kenneth Landon, *The Chinese in Thailand* (New York, NY: Russell & Russell, 1973), pp. 147–48; Lynn Pan, *Sons of the Yellow Emperor: A History of the Chinese Diaspora* (Boston, MA: Little, Brown and Company, 1990), p. 235; and William Skinner, *Leadership and Power in the Chinese Community of Thailand* (Ithaca, NY: Cornell University Press, 1958), p. 190.

[21] John Kane, *The Politics of Moral Capital* (New York, NY: Cambridge University Press, 2001).

[22] This hospital, founded in 1926, is named after its founder, Chaophraya Yommarat (1862–1938), a Suphanburi-born individual who served as minister of the interior in the period of absolute monarchy.

accommodate a rapidly growing number of patients.[23] Phat Bunyaratphan, governor of Suphanburi, therefore requested funds from the Ministry of Public Health to construct a new patients' ward in 1965. The request was rejected, despite the fact that the first National Economic Development Plan (1961–66) emphasized "expanding and improving the existing hospitals" in the countryside.[24] Suphanburi received only 200,000 baht for undertaking four small-scale projects that were totally unrelated to the requested ward. Suphanburi's share in the construction funds allocated by the Ministry of Public Health nationwide was a mere 0.35 percent.[25] In the following year, Chaophraya Yommarat Hospital received 120,000 baht for building a ward with six rooms,[26] but this amount fell far short of meeting the needs of the hospital. At the same time, Suphanburi's neighboring provinces received much more public funding for building larger patients' wards.[27] Frustrated, Phat was compelled to solicit donations from local residents. It was under these circumstances that Banharn, along with his wife, Jaemsai, made a stunning donation of 700,000 baht.[28]

This sum dwarfed the donations made by other local celebrities.[29] The news of Banharn's unmatched munificence, reported in a local newspaper—an important medium of political communication in provincial Thailand—and also spread by word of mouth, was impressed on many Suphanburians. An elderly Sino-Thai merchant (b. 1929) (#103), who has lived near Chaophraya Yommarat Hospital all his life, remembers that Banharn instantly became the talk of the town among hospital staff, merchants, food vendors, and their customers.

Banharn's donation was quite possibly influenced by the fact that his former schoolmate, Winit Sribunma, and Banharn's brother-in-law, Bundit Lekwat (Jaemsai's elder brother), were both doctors at Chaophraya Yommarat Hospital. Critics of Banharn would view his donation to the hospital as just another case of his characteristic nepotism. This hardly mattered to the local residents, however. As the Sino-Thai merchant quoted above (#103) said, "There is nothing wrong with helping his brother-in-law's hospital get bigger, if he did it to develop Suphanburi." What mattered to the local residents was that Suphanburi would have a new ward thanks to Banharn, whose philanthropy contrasted sharply with the callousness of the central state. As Winit recalled, "The hospital had not received state funds for a long time, and Mr. Banharn came along to offer help."[30] Plainly, Banharn did what the state would not do.

---

[23] Suphanburi's population increased by 32 percent from 448,694 in 1957 to 590,196 in 1967. Uraiwan Kanungsukkasem, *Comparative Population and Health Statistics for Thailand: Regional and Provincial Levels* (Bangkok: Mahidol University Institute for Population and Social Research, 1983).

[24] National Economic Development Board, *The National Economic Development Plan, 1961–1966: Second Phase, 1964–1966* (Bangkok: NEDB, 1964), p. 131.

[25] Budget Bureau, *Ekasarn Ngop-pramarn 2508*, 3,3 (1964): 1043–1187.

[26] Budget Bureau, *Ekasarn Ngop-pramarn 2509*, 3,3 (1965): 1235.

[27] For example, Saraburi, Ratchaburi, Kanchanaburi, and Lopburi received 1,003,000 baht, 810,000 baht, 560,000 baht, and 760,000 baht, respectively. Budget Bureau, *Ekasarn Ngop-pramarn 2508*, 3,3 (1964): 1229–1234.

[28] *Khon Suphan*, January 25, 1966, pp. 1, 15; *Khon Suphan*, November 10, 1968, p. 3.

[29] The second largest donation was 100,000 baht. *Khon Suphan*, January 25, 1966, pp. 1, 15; *Khon Suphan*, February 15, 1966, p. 15.

[30] *Sarn Khwam Fan*, p. 63.

The construction of the ward, a modern two-story building made of ferroconcrete and containing twenty air-conditioned rooms, was completed in 1968. In honor of the most generous donator, the ward was named "Banharn–Jaemsai Ward"—the first symbol of Banharn's contribution to local development. In a pattern that was to become increasingly common in the years to come, his personal mark was thus permanently imprinted on what is essentially a public building that benefits the provincial population at large (figure 3.1).

Figure 3.1 The lettering on this newly built ward of Chaophraya Yommarat Hospital says "Banharn–Jaemsai Silpa-archa Ward." Banharn is in center, Jaemsai, on right[31]

The ward was opened with fanfare in a grand ceremony held in January 1969. The newly appointed Governor Sawat Meephian (1966–75) presided over the ceremony. Also present were high-ranking officials from the Muang municipality and the Provincial Office of Public Health; the grandchildren of Chaophraya Yommarat; and Miss Thailand, whose parents were from Suphanburi.[32] It is unknown how many local residents attended the ceremony, but the presence of Miss Thailand wearing a miniskirt presumably attracted a big audience. During the ceremony, Banharn explained the motive behind his donation in ways that evoked the backward image of Suphanburi and touched a deep chord with the audience: "Once we were born in Suphanburi, we want to see Suphanburi prosper *as much as*

---

[31] *Source*: *Khon Suphan*, January 30, 1969.

[32] *Khon Suphan*, January 30, 1969, pp. 1, 3.

other provinces. I try to help in every possible way."[33] The local newspaper, *Khon Suphan*, further publicized Banharn's donation by covering the ceremony with three front-page photos and by praising him as "a young millionaire with a charitable heart." Banharn used the event to announce his intention to build a new school with his money in the future, giving Suphanburians another socially worthwhile project to anticipate.[34] Thus, the ceremony served as an occasion on which an incipient image of Banharn as a generous patron of the disadvantaged Suphanburi was created with the help of public spectacle and rhetoric.

The Banharn–Jaemsai Ward still exists, bearing Banharn's name and serving as a vivid reminder to the Suphanburians of his generous donation more than forty years ago. Since 1976, Banharn has built two additional patients' wards (also named Banharn–Jaemsai Wards) at Chaophraya Yommarat Hospital with his money. Thanks in no small part to these donations, what was a small hospital in the 1960s has now grown into one of the largest hospitals in the central region.[35]

School Building

Banharn made an equally visible impact in the field of education. It started in August 1968, when he gave a relatively modest donation of 50,000 baht to the Provincial Chief of Education, Mian Khrueasin, at a local ceremony. The donation complemented inadequate state funds that Mian had received from the Ministry of Education (MOE) for repairing ten primary schools in Suphanburi.[36] The ceremony was held at Prasathong Primary School, located just a few minutes' walk from Chaophraya Yommarat Hospital, where the aforementioned Banharn–Jaemsai Ward had been built.

In subsequent years, Banharn made a spate of much more spectacular donations (totaling 3.7 million baht) to build new schools. These schools, constructed in four Suphanburi districts between 1970 and 1977, were named "Banharn–Jaemsai Schools" and were numbered consecutively from I to IV. Again, the stinting nature of the central state had established a historical context that served to highlight, through contrast, Banharn's welcome donations. This contrast between the state and the individual benefactor was clearly illustrated during the process of constructing Banharn–Jaemsai School I in Don Chedi District. Before 1970, this district did not have a single secondary school, forcing its students to travel some thirty kilometers on a dusty, bumpy road to the central Muang District for higher education.[37] To remedy this problem, Provincial Education Chief Mian "requested state funds for many years, but to no avail." Therefore, when Banharn made his first donation of 50,000 baht (noted above), Mian asked him if the money could be used to build a secondary school in Don Chedi rather than to renovate existing buildings. Banharn answered that the money should be spent on repairing the ten schools, as he had

---

[33] Ibid., p. 3, emphasis mine.

[34] Ibid. As will be shown below, Banharn fulfilled this promise.

[35] See Nishizaki, "The Weapon of the Strong," chapter 7, for details.

[36] *Khon Suphan*, August 20, 1968, p. 1.

[37] This road (built in 1954) was made of crushed stones before it was asphalted in 1970–72. Department of Highways (DOH), *Rai-ngan Prachampii 2497* (Bangkok: DOH, 1955), pp. 18, 36; DOH, *Rai-ngan Prachampii 2498* (Bangkok: DOH, 1956), pp. 13, 27; Budget Bureau, *Ekasarn Ngop-pramarn 2514*, 3,4 (1970): 387; Budget Bureau, *Ekasarn Ngop-pramarn 2515*, 3,4 (1971): 382.

originally intended, but that he would make a much bigger donation specifically for Don Chedi in the near future.[38] When Banharn announced his plan to build a new school during the opening ceremony for Banharn–Jaemsai Ward, he apparently had this school in mind.

Banharn kept his promise. In 1969, he donated 500,000 baht to build Don Chedi's first secondary school. A year later, he donated an additional 500,000 baht to the same school. Completed in April 1970, the school, named Banharn–Jaemsai School I, was formally transferred to the MOE in a ceremony attended by then-Minister of Education Sukij Nimmanhemin. The first school bearing Banharn's name thus came into being, with seventy-two students and two teachers.[39] It is now among the largest and the most prestigious secondary schools in Suphanburi (see chapter 4 for details).

Banharn made a similar contribution to Laothong Temple Primary School in Muang District. Established in 1936, the school had only one old wooden building, which by the mid-1970s had been "severely damaged." The building even had holes in the roof, making it impossible to conduct classes on a rainy day. The building was also too small to accommodate a growing number of students, which had reached three hundred by 1971. The school was therefore in urgent need of a new building, but state funds were not forthcoming. The Laothong Temple abbot and the villagers scraped together 316,435 baht from their own pockets, but this sum fell far short of the estimated construction cost of 1.3 million baht. Having heard about this problem, Banharn donated 1.4 million baht to Laothong Temple Primary School—a sum that exceeded the projected construction cost. Out of gratitude for this unsolicited donation, the abbot changed the name of the school to Banharn–Jaemsai School IV.[40] (By this time, Banharn had built three other schools, and each bore his name.) The new school building was completed in 1976. This was just another case demonstrating that Suphanburi's educational development had to rely on a rich benefactor like Banharn to compensate for the limited funds allocated by the "developmental" state.

As was the case with Banharn–Jaemsai Ward at Chaophraya Yommarat Hospital, Banharn's generous donations to education were effectively advertised via grand ceremonies. An array of provincial and national-level "big people," such as Suphanburi's governor, minister of education, and even royal family members, were invited to attend these ceremonies (see table 3.1). For example, on April 20, 1973, Banharn held a cornerstone-laying ceremony for Banharn–Jaemsai School III in Dan Chang District—the first upper-secondary school in Dan Chang—which he was going to construct with personal funds totaling one million baht. The Provincial Office of Education invited Governor Sawat and Minister of Education Aphai Jantawimol to attend the ceremony. A local newspaper advertised the date of the event in advance to maximize popular attendance. The paper also aroused local residents' interest in meeting Banharn in person by publicizing his philosophy,

---

[38] *Sarn Khwam Fan*, pp. 50–51.

[39] Ibid., pp. 52, 56; *Khon Suphan*, April 10, 1969; *Khon Suphan*, April 20, 1969, p. 3; *Khon Suphan*, April 10, 1970, pp. 1, 12; *Khon Suphan*, April 30, 1970, pp. 1, 3, 12.

[40] *Khon Suphan*, March 10, 1975, pp. 1, 2; Banharn–Jaemsai School IV, *Ekasarn Naenam Rongrian nai Phithi Morp Thun Kan Sueksa Munnithi Banharn–Jaemsai* (Suphanburi: Banharn-Jaemsai School IV, 1995), p. 9. For a description of a similar episode regarding the construction of Banharn–Jaemsai School II in Bang Pla Ma district, see *Khon Suphan*, May 10, 1970, p. 1.

Table 3.1 Ceremonies for Commemorating Banharn's Donations to Schools, 1969–77[41]

School Name	Location (District)	Banharn's Donation	Type of Ceremony	Date	Main Guests
B-J I	Don Chedi	1,000,000	Cornerstone-laying	4/20/69	Governor
			Opening	4/25/70	Governor Minister of Education DGE Chief
Tha Chang	Derm Bang	200,000	Inspection	3/??/70	District Education Chief
B-J II	Bang Pla Ma	290,000	Cornerstone-laying	8/19/71	Governor
			Opening	4/20/72	Governor
B-J III	Dan Chang	1,000,000	Cornerstone-laying	4/20/73	Governor Minister of Education DGE Chief
			Opening	7/15/75	King and Queen
B-J IV	Muang	1,400,000	Cornerstone-laying	8/20/75	DLA Chief
			Opening	2/11/77	King's mother and Princess

B-J = Banharn–Jaemsai
DGE = Department of General Education
DLA = Department of Local Administration

which at once played up his altruism and appealed to provincialist sentiments: "We were all born in Suphan. When we have enough to live on and eat, we should all help to make our beloved birthplace [*bankert muang norn thirak khong rao*] prosperous [*charoen rung rueang*]. When we die, we can't take the money with us."[42] Thanks to this publicity, five hundred to six hundred people, consisting of civil servants, merchants, and ordinary citizens, attended the cornerstone-laying ceremony.[43] During the celebration, Governor Sawat addressed the audience to recount the

[41] *Sources*: *Khon Suphan* (April 10, 1969; April 20, 1969; March 10, 1970; April 10, 1970; April 30, 1970; August 20, 1971; April 20, 1972; April 30, 1973; July 10, 1975; July 20, 1975; August 20, 1975; August 30, 1975; February 16, 1977).

[42] *Khon Suphan*, April 10, 1973, pp. 1, 12.

[43] Ibid., pp. 3, 12; *Khon Suphan*, April 20, 1973, p. 3.

circumstances that led up to Banharn's donation. The governor then extolled the other development works Banharn had built, such as Banharn–Jaemsai Schools and Banharn–Jaemsai Ward. He praised Banharn for having made all these contributions "with a pure heart [*borisut jai*]." In his speech, Education Minister Aphai showered similar praise on Banharn: "I have never thought that young people like Banharn and Jaemsai would have the charitable spirits to sacrifice their wealth for the benefit of the community."[44]

Once completed, Banharn–Jaemsai School III was officially opened in a spectacular ceremony held on July 15, 1975. King Bhumibol and Queen Sirikit attended the event as the guests of honor, leaving Dan Chang's residents astounded, impressed, excited, and awestruck. This was the first time that Dan Chang—the northernmost and the most inaccessible district of Suphanburi[45]—had ever had the honor of hosting the royal couple. Their attendance attracted a big crowd —an estimated five thousand to six thousand people, including members of minority ethnic groups, Karens and Songs, who comprised almost 50 percent of Dan Chang's sparse population.[46] A ceremony of this scale was unprecedented in Dan Chang.

Banharn used this event to mobilize numerous initiates of the Village Scouts movement—an intensely nationalist mass movement that the king sponsored during the 1970s to defeat growing communist insurgency in the countryside.[47] Bundit Lekwat, Banharn's brother-in-law and the leader of Suphanburi's Village Scouts, played a pivotal role in mobilizing these initiates.[48] As discussed in Chapter 2, the the Communist Party of Thailand had infiltrated Suphanburi by 1969, and Dan Chang, a mountainous district with a large ethnic minority population, was most seriously affected by the communist insurgency. Against this backdrop, Banharn helped bring Dan Chang's otherwise mutinous population under the gaze and control of the benevolent monarchy that embodied the Thai nation. He also took this occasion to donate 100,000 baht to the royal family to help expand the Village Scouts nationwide (figure 3.2).[49] Paul Handley has written about the pattern of upward social mobility in Bangkok during the 1980s: "High-society Thais and ambitious climbers competed ever more to be seen donating funds and participating in royal events" in return for royal merit.[50] The same thing was happening in Suphanburi in the 1970s. Banharn was a prime example of such "ambitious climbers."

---

[44] *Khon Suphan*, April 30, 1973, p. 12.

[45] The construction of a gravel road linking Dan Chang to another district (U-Thong) started in 1969. The project was not completed until 1974. *Khon Suphan*, July 20, 1969, p. 1; *Khon Suphan*, March 30, 1974, p. 1.

[46] *Khon Suphan*, July 20, 1975, p. 1.

[47] See Katherine Bowie, *Rituals of National Loyalty: An Anthropology of the State and the Village Scout Movement in Thailand* (New York, NY: Columbia University Press, 1997), for details on this movement.

[48] *Khon Suphan*, October 16, 1976, p. 1; *Khon Suphan*, April 10, 1968, p. 1; *Khon Suphan*, April 20, 1968, p. 1.

[49] *Khon Suphan*, July 10, 1975, p. 1; *Khon Suphan*, July 20, 1975, p. 1.

[50] Paul Handley, *The King Never Smiles: A Biography of Thailand's Bhumibol Adulyadej* (New Haven, CT: Yale University Press, 2006), p. 287.

Figure 3.2 Banharn and Jaemsai making a donation to the royal couple during an opening ceremony for Banharn–Jaemsai School III[51]

The royal couple, for their part, reciprocated by inaugurating, and conferring a blessing on, Banharn's school. If their primary motive behind attending the ceremony was to promote the Village Scouts movement and to rally popular support behind the throne, it is still beyond doubt that their attendance considerably enhanced the prestige of Banharn's school. More broadly, the royal couple's attendance, sensationally reported in the local press and even broadcast on the national radio,[52] instantly spread and enshrined Banharn's reputation as a pro-monarchy and anti-communist developer of Suphanburi. In his widely cited paper, Duncan McCargo argues that King Bhumibol's monarchical network, the largest patronage network in post-1973 Thailand, has functioned to place "the right people"—"talented" and "capable people of reformist instincts" who possess "personal virtue"—"in the right jobs."[53] Uneducated and allegedly corrupt rural-based politicians, such as Banharn, who do not live up to the king's high moral standards are marginalized politically. To the extent that this is the case, it is a deep irony that the king incubated or groomed Banharn, if inadvertently, as a legitimate local leader who was later to become Suphanburi's MP. Far from marginalizing Banharn politically, the king effectively co-opted him into the growing rightist network that comprised the palace, the military, bureaucrats, and capitalists. There was a mutually complementary relationship between the two: The king relied on a rich and generous benefactor like Banharn to defeat communism in the countryside, while Banharn depended on the king to build his moral stature at the local level. In short, the king and Banharn needed and used each other for their respective political

---

[51] *Source: Khon Suphan*, July 20, 1975.

[52] *Withayu-sarn Prachamwan*, July 17, 1975.

[53] Duncan McCargo, "Network Monarchy and Legitimacy Crises in Thailand," *Pacific Review* 18,4 (2005): 501, 502, 512.

purposes. Banharn's phenomenal rise in pre-1976 Suphanburi owed much to this synergy; the king was directly implicated in it.

Welfare Charities

Banharn made smaller yet important donations to welfare charities to alleviate the hardships of less fortunate Suphanburians. One example was his donation of clothes worth 1,700 baht to the Provincial Red Cross in 1969. The Red Cross handed out these clothes to villagers in Suphanburi's two least developed districts, Dan Chang and Derm Bang Nang Buat, on July 26.[54] Similarly, on June 12, 1973, Banharn, along with his wife, Jaemsai, and Thapthim Lekwat (Jaemsai's mother), handed out 8,210 baht worth of clothes and notebooks to 207 poor schoolchildren in Muang District.[55]

Furthermore, Banharn started awarding scholarships (named "Banharn–Jaemsai Scholarships") to students from poor families. This practice began on March 15, 1971, when he visited Banharn–Jaemsai School I to award an unspecified number of scholarships in person. He did the same in March the following year. For the next two years, he did not award any scholarships for reasons that are not clear, but on November 26, 1975, he resumed the practice by handing out seventeen scholarships worth 5,100 baht.[56] Likewise, he handed out Banharn–Jaemsai Scholarships at five schools other than his own schools.[57]

One particular episode involving an underfunded primary school illustrates that the incapacity of the central state to provide relief funds for the poor allowed Banharn to appear as a compassionate local benefactor. In November 1970, Pratheep, a private primary school in Sam Chuk District, faced a serious budget crunch.[58] By the late 1960s, the school, run by a Japanese Christian missionary, had become a "sanctuary" for the children of an ethnic minority (Mons) in the nearby Phetchabun Province, where the Communist Party of Thailand had gained much ground. The students' parents, deeply concerned about imminent armed clashes between communist guerrillas and government security forces,[59] entrusted their twenty-three children, aged five to six, to the schoolmaster, promising to come back to fetch them in due course. They thought that it would be safer to leave their children with a non-Thai teacher, whose school fell outside the jurisdiction of the state-controlled MOE. The schoolmaster kindly agreed to take in the children and provided them with shelter and food for free, but then the parents did not return for several months, and there was no telling whether they were dead or had deserted their offspring. As two years passed, Pratheep—a small private school running on a shoestring budget—

---

[54] *Khon Suphan*, July 10, 1969, p. 1.

[55] *Khon Suphan*, June 20, 1973, pp. 1, 12.

[56] Banharn–Jaemsai School I, *Phithi Morp Thun Kan Sueksa Munnithi Banharn–Jaemsai Prachampii 2538* (Suphanburi: Banharn–Jaemsai School I, 1995), page number unspecified.

[57] *Khon Suphan*, November 30, 1974, p. 3; *Khon Suphan*, December 30, 1974; *Khon Suphan*, October 10, 1975, p. 10; *Thin Thai*, September 15, 1975, p. 10.

[58] The information here is based on *Khon Suphan*, November 20, 1970, p. 1, and my interview with the schoolmaster of Pratheep, February 10, 2002.

[59] In 1967, the army started an "indiscriminate use of bombs and napalm" to suppress communist insurgency in northern Thailand. In the same year, the fighting spread to Phetchabun. Saiyud Kerdphol, *The Struggle for Thailand: Counter-insurgency, 1965–1985* (Bangkok: S. Research Center, 1986), pp. 116, 180.

found it increasingly difficult to accommodate and feed the "internal refugee children." When the cold season arrived, the school could not provide enough blankets for the children. In early November 1970, the schoolmaster and his Thai wife (Prakhong Suwanpratheep), who is the granddaughter of one of the founders of the Thai air force, visited Minister of Education Sukit Nimmanhemin in Bangkok to plead for help. In principle, since their school was privately run, it was not entitled to receiving help from the state, but the schoolmaster thought that circumstances were so special as to warrant some emergency relief funds.

Figure 3.3 The Mon tribe schoolchildren at Pratheep School;
the tall man on the left is the schoolmaster I interviewed[60]

Sukit would not or could not provide any help, but out of sympathy he wrote a letter to Banharn to ask for assistance. As mentioned earlier, Sukit had presided over an opening ceremony for Banharn–Jaemsai School I in 1970, so he knew Banharn personally. Soon thereafter, on November 14, 1970, Banharn appeared at Pratheep School and handed out 3,000 baht worth of school uniforms and blankets to all the children in need. Thus, he saved the lives of the minority group children who, under other circumstances, could have been deserted or politically persecuted for being related to communist sympathizers. This news, like news of Banharn's other good deeds, hit the headlines in a local newspaper, along with a photo of the schoolchildren who received his help (figure 3.3).

RESTORING SUPHANBURI'S HONOR AND GLORY

Banharn donated his money, not just to meet the developmental needs of Suphanburians and their communities, but also to take two actions that restored,

---

[60] *Source: Khon Suphan,* November 20, 1970.

protected, or enhanced Suphanburi' fame or honor. These actions further elevated his status as a generous and selfless local hero.

Return of Sangkhalok Bowl

Banharn's first action involved a long-standing controversy surrounding the "Sangkhalok Bowl." The controversy started in 1962, when then-Prime Minister Field Marshal Sarit took this bowl, a priceless ceramic work created during the Sukhothai period (13th–14th centuries), from Suwannaphum Temple, one of the most famous temples in Suphanburi.[61] In return for the bowl, Sarit gave a water jar of little value to the temple's abbot. Although the government issued a statement that Sarit and the abbot agreed amicably to exchange the bowl and the jar, most Suphanburians understood that the abbot was "forced under duress" (*jam jai, doi bankhap jai*) to relinquish the bowl and that Sarit snatched it "unjustly" (*doi mai chorp tham*).[62]

Then, in December 1963, Sarit died, and the Corruption Investigating Commission, established by the government to investigate Sarit's frauds, confiscated his major assets, including the bowl. The abbot of Suwannaphum Temple took this chance to request in writing that the bowl be returned to his temple, explaining how it had ended up in Sarit's hands. The commission reacted slowly, however. It was only in November 1965 that the commission invited the abbot and Phat, then-governor of Suphanburi, to come to Bangkok to ascertain the authenticity of the bowl. This was only a cosmetic gesture. Although the abbot confirmed the bowl to be the one Sarit had taken away, and the commission accordingly promised to return it to Suwannaphum Temple, Suphanburians, to their frustration, saw the commission do nothing but drag its feet for the next four years. Expectations of regaining the bowl had risen high, only to be dashed just like "the wave that had struck against the shore" (*khluen krathop fang*).[63]

This controversy was not simply between Suwannaphum Temple and the Corruption Investigating Commission. It also symbolized a fight between Suphanburi and the arbitrary central state. The commission was the institutional representation of the state, to which Sarit, who had wrested the bowl from Suphanburi, belonged. In mounting a barrage of emotional attacks against the state, a local newspaper asserted that the bowl was "the dearest treasure of all Suphanburians ... The temple's asset is Suphanburians' asset," and that "Suphanburians have the legitimate right to get it back."[64] The question of who

---

[61] The circumstances under which this controversy occurred need some elaboration. On February 16, 1962, Sarit visited Suphanburi to attend an opening ceremony for the newly built Provincial Court. During this ceremony, Governor Phat, wishing to impress Sarit, displayed the Sangkhalok bowl on a table. Phat also boasted of the bowl's incalculable historical value to Sarit. Less than a month later, Sarit's military subordinate appeared at Suwannaphum Temple with a water jar and made a request: "The bowl is so beautiful that I want to give it to my superior [in exchange for the jar]." The abbot agreed, fearing the consequences of refusing the request. Phat admitted later that his silly boasting was to blame for the ensuing mess. *Khon Suphan*, February 20, 1962, pp. 1, 8; *Sarn Khwam Fan*, pp. 46, 48.

[62] *Khon Suphan*, September 5, 1962, pp. 1, 8; *Khon Suphan*, September 20, 1962, pp. 1, 8; *Khon Suphan*, September 7, 1965, p. 1; *Khon Suphan*, April 11, 1967, p. 4.

[63] *Khon Suphan*, March 30, 1969, p. 3.

[64] Ibid.; *Khon Suphan*, March 21, 1967, p. 4.

would take eventual possession of the bowl thus generated an intense interest among Suphanburians. The province's honor was at stake.

Then, in early November 1969, the shocking news leaked out: the government, led by Sarit's successor, Thanom, planned to sell the bowl at a public auction in two weeks. Upon hearing this news, former Governor Phat (who had by this time become governor of Ubon Ratchatani) contacted the provincial newspaper staff on November 2. The latter, in turn, immediately contacted incumbent Governor Sawat. Sawat called an urgent meeting of the Buddhist Association of Suphanburi (of which he was president) to discuss how to deal with the "crisis." Sawat contacted Suphanburi's MPs to plead for help, but in vain.[65] The most powerful of these MPs, Thongyod Jitaweera, was actually in a good position to offer help. His son, Udom, was married to the daughter of Sombat Panitcheewa, an influential Suphanburi-born capitalist who ran a successful Thai–Japanese joint venture—Thai-Asahi Caustic Soda—of which Thanom was a major shareholder.[66] Despite this connection, and more importantly, despite the fact that he was a fellow Suphanburian, Thongyod refused to mediate in the controversy, presumably for fear of offending Thanom.

At his wits' end, Governor Sawat called on Banharn, at his Bangkok home, as the last hope. Banharn instantly agreed to help. He attended the auction held at the Treasury Department in Bangkok on November 14, and bought the bowl for 60,000 baht after a fierce bidding contest against numerous collectors of antique goods from across Thailand.[67] His determination to win the bid amazed other bidders so much that they approached him during and after the auction to ask what he was going to do with the bowl. He gave a simple answer that left them bewildered and speechless: "I will return it to my province."[68]

To celebrate the much-awaited return of Suphanburi's treasure and Banharn's heroic act, Governor Sawat planned a grand public parade consisting of students and brass bands on December 5, 1969, the birthday of the revered King Bhumibol. Yet Banharn declined to be cast in the limelight, saying that he had bought the bowl only to preserve "the glory [*saksri*] of Suphanburi." Rather than take part in the high-profile public celebration, he returned the bowl to Suwannaphum Temple in a subdued ceremony held on November 30.[69] This news, reported sensationally in a provincial newspaper along with a front-page photo of Banharn and his wife kneeling down to return the bowl to the temple abbot, made him famous as a totally unselfish and humble hero who restored Suphanburi's honor. The legendary return of the Sangkhalok Bowl thus established him as a symbolic guardian of Suphanburi's prestige.

More than three decades after this incident, the provincial newspaper *Suphan Post* carried a series of editorials to recount how it happened and what Banharn did.[70] Banharn's heroism has thus been reproduced and perpetuated in the local discourse.

---

[65] *Khon Suphan*, November 20, 1969, pp. 1, 12.

[66] *Khon Suphan*, May 20, 1969, p. 3; Arunee Sopitpongstorn, *Kiarti Srifuengfung: The Boy from Suphanburi* (Bangkok: Sri Yarnie Corporation, 1991).

[67] *Khon Suphan*, November 20, 1969, pp. 1, 12.

[68] *Suphan Post*, November 16, 2001.

[69] *Khon Suphan*, November 20, 1969, pp. 1, 12; *Khon Suphan*, November 30, 1969, pp. 1, 12; *Khon Suphan*, December 10, 1969, pp. 1, 3.

[70] *Suphan Post*, October 1, 2001, p. 5; October 16, 2001, p. 5; November 16, 2001, p. 5.

Revival of Blood of Suphan

Banharn whipped up provincial pride by staging public spectacles of Suphanburi's invented historical greatness on TV and in theater. Specifically, in July and August 1975, he and the Association of Suphanburians in Bangkok revived and performed *Blood of Suphan*, Luang Wichit Wathakan's famous nationalist play that features the legendary heroism and bravery of King Naresuan in the 1593 battle against Burma. Originally written in 1936, the play had enjoyed enormous popularity before and during World War II, thanks to Field Marshal Phibun's patronage.[71] After the war, however, the show's popularity waned. In this context, Banharn, with the support of Luang Wichit's widow, directed the revival of the play to arouse provincialist sentiments among Suphanburians.[72]

News of the revival of *Blood of Suphan* caused excitement in Suphanburi. Luang Wichit, a native of Uthai Thani Province, had written the play to incite nationalism among Thais as a whole, but for Suphanburians, the play was just as much about their province as it was about Thailand. The contents of the play had great provincialist appeal. One line extolled Suphanburians' exemplary courage and unity in the face of enemy attacks: "We have fewer people. We have no weapons for combat. But the blood of Suphan has never been afraid of anybody. When it has to fight, it fights ... The blood of Suphan, wherever it is, will come together. The blood of Suphan has never been cowardly ... It comes together. And it dies together."[73] This line was followed by an intensely patriotic song, also titled *Blood of Suphan*, with the same provincialist message. Its lyrics trumpeted:

> The blood of Suphan is brave in war, tough and bold and never will flee. Never will shiver or tremble before the foe, take dagger or sword, come join in the fight. Come on together, come on together, the blood of Suphan, the blood of Suphan, face the enemy, do not worry or fear.[74]

After weeks of rehearsal, the eagerly awaited play was performed at the National Theater on July 31, 1975. It was also broadcast on national TV channels 7 and 9 on August 2, spreading images of Suphanburi's past glory throughout Thailand. The television performance started appealingly with the song *Blood of Suphan*—a song that Suphanburians "had not listened to for thirty to forty long years"—played ably by the military band under the direction of the Navy Commander-in-Chief and Suphanburi-born Admiral Sa-ngat Chalor-yu.[75] The performing cast consisted entirely of Suphanburians, and featured as its chief actor

---

[71] Scot Barme, *Luang Wichit Wathakan and the Creation of a Thai Identity* (Singapore: Institute of Southeast Asian Studies, 1993), p. 122.

[72] *Khon Suphan*, July 10, 1975, p. 1.

[73] Praonrat Buranamart, *Luang Wichit Wathakan kap Bot Lakhon Prawatisart* (Bangkok: Thammasat University Press, 1985), pp. 100–1.

[74] Barme, *Luang Wichit Wathakan and the Creation of a Thai Identity*, p. 123.

[75] *Khon Suphan*, July 30, 1975, pp. 1, 2; *Khon Suphan*, August 10, 1975, pp. 1, 8. Admiral Sa-ngat was later to lead the successful coups of 1976 and 1977. His relationship to Banharn deepened in the post-1976 period. When Banharn set up two new chemical companies, Saha Srichai Chemical and Siam Occidental Electrochemical, in 1980 and 1990, respectively, he invited Sa-ngat to sit on their board of directors. DBD/MC, Bangkok Company File no. 2164/2523 and No. 7508/2533.

Yodchai Sujit, a tall and handsome Sino-Thai provincial capitalist related by marriage to Banharn.[76] Banharn himself performed in the play. The other performers included Suphanburi-born national celebrities, such as Waiphot Phetsuphan (a Thai country pop music singer), Khwanjit Spiprachan (an award-winning theater performer), and Major General Thawal Aphirakyothin. On the day the play was aired on television, the normally bustling Muang market town was reportedly very quiet, with all the shops and food stalls closed earlier than usual.[77] The majority of local residents apparently stayed at home, glued to TV sets to watch *Blood of Suphan*—the play of Suphanburians, for Suphanburians, and by Suphanburians. Banharn thus restored and enhanced the fame that a formerly prosperous Suphanburi had once supposedly enjoyed in a mythical past.

Banharn used the performance of *Blood of Suphan* to raise money for the military, to support its efforts to combat communist insurgency in the rural provinces. While broadcasting the play, the TV station solicited popular donations to the cause of anti-communism. In addition, when the play was performed at the National Theater, the Association of Suphanburians charged an admission fee of ten baht per person. Banharn donated all the proceeds (from both the TV appeals and ticket sales, totaling over one million baht) to the king, who in turn donated them to the military.[78] Just two weeks earlier (July 15), Banharn, as described above, had donated 100,000 baht to the royal couple when they attended the opening ceremony for Banharn–Jaemsai School III. He now followed it up with this new donation, a much larger one, to show his unwavering support for the royal family's anti-communist drive. Thus Banharn insinuated himself all the more successfully into the monarchical network as a legitimate member; his status in Suphanburi was incubated within this network.

TIDE OF POPULAR SUPPORT

As shown above, starting in the mid-1960s, Banharn used his wealth to perform many public deeds that symbolized and enhanced provincial development and prestige.[79] He performed these deeds in various parts of Suphanburi and with amazing frequency (see table 3.2). He was certainly not the only Suphanburian who made huge donations. In 1967, for instance, a Buddhist monk donated one million baht to build a hospital in Song Phi Nong District.[80] The scarcity of state funds afforded ample opportunities for aspiring leaders to establish moral authority as generous sponsors of local development. Banharn's donations, however, were unparalleled both in number and scale. He had far more economic resources than the majority of his "rivals," and those who did have comparable resources were not as willing to spend them for the benefit of Suphanburians as Banharn was. Two examples of such "miserly" millionaires are Kiat Srifuengfung and Phaiboon Phanitcheewa, who had jointly established the Cathay Trust Group, one of the

---

[76] Yodchai's mother, Hansa, is the half-sister of Banharn's wife, Jaemsai. Interviews with Hansa's kin member, March 2002. This informant (#55) is Hansa's niece.

[77] *Khon Suphan*, July 30, 1975, pp. 1, 2; *Khon Suphan*, August 10, 1975, pp. 1, 8.

[78] *Khon Suphan*, July 30, 1975, p. 2; *Khon Suphan*, August 10, 1975, p. 8; *Khon Suphan*, October 16, 1977, p. 1.

[79] Due to space constraints, I have only described the most representative of Banharn's actions. See Nishizaki, "The Weapon of the Strong," chapter 4, for a fuller account.

[80] *Khon Suphan*, October 1, 1967, pp. 1, 8.

largest economic conglomerates in Thailand, by the 1970s. Both of them, related by blood, are Suphanburi-born and Bangkok-based Sino-Thai capitalists,[81] yet neither made any visible donation in Suphanburi. Thus, Banharn came to dominate what might be called the symbolic marketplace for provincial development and prestige in Suphanburi. His wealth and his readiness to use it put him in the vanguard of Suphanburians trying and desiring to change their socially marginalized province.

Table 3.2 Chronology of Banharn's Contributions to Local Development, 1966–77[82]

Year	Month	Nature of Contribution	District
1966	January	donate money to CY Hospital	Muang
1969	January	opening ceremony for B-J Ward, CY Hospital	Muang
	April	cornerstone-laying ceremony, B-J School I	Don Chedi
	April	donate money to Thai New Year Festival	Muang
	July	donate clothes to Provincial Red Cross	Dan Chang
	November	return Sangkhalok Bowl to Suwannaphum Temple	Muang
	December	build Sri Muang Hotel	Muang
1970	February	cornerstone-laying ceremony for Sai Temple	Muang
	March	rebuild Tha Chang School (Dan Chang)	Dan Chang
	April	opening ceremony for B-J School I	Don Chedi
	May	initiate construction of *monthop*, Phraroop Temple	Muang
	November	donate clothes/blankets to Pratheep School	Muang
1971	March	hand out B-J Scholarships, B-J School I (Don Chedi)	Don Chedi
	April	donate relief money to landless peasants	Bang Pla Ma
	May	cornerstone-laying ceremony, U-Thong Temple	Bang Pla Ma
	June	renovate main hall/crematory, Prasathong Temple	Muang
	August	cornerstone-laying ceremony, B-J School II	Bang Pla Ma
	November	donate money to Sai Temple	Muang
	November	renovate main hall/crematory, Suan Taeng Temple	Muang
1972	March	hand out B-J Scholarships, B-J School I	Don Chedi
	April	opening ceremony, B-J School II	Bang Pla Ma
	June	opening ceremony, Prasathong Temple	Muang

[81] Anant, *Thammai Phom Tong Than Banharn*, p. 53; Arunee, *Kiarti Srifuengfung*; Akira Suehiro, *Capital Accumulation in Thailand, 1855–1985* (Tokyo: Center for East Asian Culture Studies, 1989), pp. 160–63, 223, 229, 247, 298–99.

[82] *Sources*: Various issues of the provincial newspapers *Khon Suphan* (1966–77) and *Thin Thai* (1975–77).

Table 3.2 Chronology of Banharn's Contributions to Local Development, con't

1973	February	cornerstone-laying ceremony, Suan Taeng Temple	Muang
	April	cornerstone-laying ceremony, B-J School III	Dan Chang
	June	hand out clothes/notebooks to school kids	Muang
1974	November	hand out scholarships, Prasathong Primary School	Muang
	December	hand out scholarships, Sa-nguan Ying Secondary School	Muang
1975	July	opening ceremony, B-J School III	Dan Chang
	July	perform "Blood of Suphan" in theater	Bangkok
	August	perform "Blood of Suphan" on TV	Bangkok
	August	cornerstone-laying ceremony, B-J School IV	Muang
	August	opening ceremony, community hall/apartment	Muang
	September	hand out scholarships, Wat Pa Lelai School	Muang
	November	hand out B-J Scholarships, B-J School I	Don Chedi
	November	robes presentation ceremony, U-Thong Temple	Bang Pla Ma
1976	March	boundary-setting ceremony, U-Thong Temple	Bang Pla Ma
1977	February	opening ceremony, B-J School IV	Muang

B-J = Banharn–Jaemsai
CY = Chaophraya Yommarat

If local newspapers both reflect and shape local public opinions,[83] a perusal of *Khon Suphan*, the only provincial newspaper in Suphanburi up to the mid-1970s, shows that Suphanburians' reactions to Banharn's deeds were overwhelmingly positive. In reporting on the construction of Banharn–Jaemsai School I, for example, the newspaper lauded Banharn and Jaemsai as "true-blue Suphanburians"—people who were born in Suphanburi with the "pure blood of Suphan"—who "take good care of our province and help it prosper." All Suphanburians "should be proud of Banharn and Jaemsai."[84] Banharn was also referred to as "the wealthiest master of Suphanburi" and an "exemplary figure" who should be congratulated for his generous donations in "healthcare and education."[85] Similarly, he was praised as a man who "has set an example that many other wealthy people [in Suphanburi] should follow."[86] The newspaper also expressed several hyperbolic wishes, such as: "We would like him to be a hundred times richer [so that he can make more donations]" and "We hope that Mr. Banharn will live for another ten thousand years, so that he can continue to help develop Suphanburi further."[87] Widely publicized in the local press and through ceremonies, Banharn's actions produced a cumulative

---

[83] On this point, see Akhil Gupta, "Blurred Boundaries: The Discourse of Corruption, the Culture of Politics, and the Imagined State," *American Ethnologist* 22,2 (1995): 375–402.

[84] *Khon Suphan*, April 30, 1970, p. 3; *Khon Suphan*, April 10, 1973, p. 12; *Khon Suphan*, April 30, 1973, p. 3.

[85] *Khon Suphan*, April 10, 1973, p. 12.

[86] *Khon Suphan*, May 10, 1973, p. 2.

[87] *Khon Suphan*, March 20, 1970, p. 3; *Khon Suphan*, April 30, 1972, p. 3.

image of him as a bighearted, unselfish man committed to doing a lot for the backward and neglected Suphanburi and its people, in contradistinction to, or on behalf of, the state. He became an integral part of the emergent sense of pride in the gradual "progress" of Suphanburi.

Contributing to the growth of this nascent pride was the timing of Banharn's donations. He made his first donation in 1966, a decade before becoming a politician. According to many Suphanburians, this indicates his genuine and disinterested commitment to developing his birthplace. At that time, Thanom's long-standing military regime held a firm grip on power, and there was no telling whether or when there would ever be an election in the future. Nobody could have foreseen that Thanom's regime would crumble suddenly in the student-led uprising of October 1973. In light of these future uncertainties, it would be incorrect to conclude that Banharn was laying the groundwork for his political career by making a series of donations. In fact, he did not seem to harbor any political ambition at first. For example, when Thanom held a parliamentary election in 1969, Banharn did not run for office. Neither did he run in the election of 1975, the first election after Thanom's fall. That Banharn still kept sacrificing his wealth for Suphanburi's development and fame is clear evidence, as many respondents noted, that he lacked ulterior motives.

A more important factor that reinforced Suphanburians' proud characterizations of Banharn was the negative image they had of the central state. To the extent that they perceived the unsympathetic, tightfisted, and ineffectual state as having given short shrift to the development of peripheral Suphanburi (see chapter 2), Banharn was able to emerge as the very opposite of that state: a benevolent, generous, and efficient developer. Precisely because the state had been widely perceived in such negative terms, Banharn was able to project himself in a favorable light by doing exactly what the state had not done. Wherever the state was not doing enough for Suphanburi's development, he was there to fill the social and economic vacuum and to play on local grievances. There was an inverse correlation between the image of the "absentee developmental state" and Banharn's. Katherine Verdery's fascinating research on the former communist states of Eastern Europe identifies two factors that contribute to the rise of nationalism: the presence of a hero ("a remarkable man") and a common sense of victimhood or suffering.[88] In Suphanburi, the history of state neglect, which had forced its people to endure many kinds of hardships (e.g., they had to build a school using their own funds and labor), provided a context for the rise of provincialist pride that centered on Banharn—Suphanburi's "remarkable man." Pride in Banharn grew because he appealed to a smoldering sense of victimhood that Suphanburians had felt in their daily interactions with state officials.

Etched deeply into the shared memories of ordinary Suphanburians, Banharn's generosity continues to figure prominently in the local discourse at present. In particular, the people who are old enough to remember his donations continue to lavish effusive and unanimous praise on his munificence and altruism, *regardless* of whether they have benefited, directly or indirectly, from his donations. Even a younger generation of people admire Banharn on the same account, having heard about his actions from their (grand)parents. An example is a car mechanic (b. 1952) (#49) in Muang District:

---

[88] Katherine Verdery, *The Political Lives of Dead Bodies: Reburial and Postsocialist Change* (New York, NY: Columbia University Press, 1999), pp. 77–78, 108, 110, 114.

People are basically self-centered. Once you get rich, you don't want to share your money with others. But Banharn was different. He came back from Bangkok to share it with the people of his hometown. It is rare to find a person like him. I'm not sure if I would have done the same if I were him.

The lottery seller (#48) cited at the beginning of this chapter put it just as strongly:

Rich people worship money as if it were God (*wai ngern pen phrachao*). They are greedy ... But Banharn was not an ordinary rich man. He was content with just having enough money to live on. He used most of his money to make our hometown prosper. He used his money unsparingly (*mai an*). Who but Banharn would have done it?

Another person who extols Banharn is the son of a farmer, now a bank teller (b. 1967) (#50), in Dan Chang District. Referring to the past conditions of his home district as "desolate" (*thurakandan*), he praised Banharn's construction of Banharn–Jaemsai School III in 1975:

He volunteered [to build the school]. That's really commendable. I raise my thumb up for him. Who would have thought about sacrificing one's personal money in a place like Dan Chang? A person who just wanted to get famous would have built the school in the city, where there are lots of people.

For these and other Suphanburians, Banharn's legendary, perhaps apocryphal, pledge to the local shrine spirit in 1949—"I will come back to Suphan to make it prosperous with my money"—is not empty cant or propaganda designed to mislead and mystify them; it is, instead, the succinct expression of Banharn's inner conviction, which drove all his actions more than three decades ago. In the shared social memories of these people, he remains the admirable agent, champion, or personification of Suphanburi's incipient change for the better. They identified, and still identify, with him as such.

COMING TO POWER

Reflecting his growing local popularity, Banharn won a few political appointments in the early 1970s. First, in December 1972, he was appointed as a member of the Muang Municipality Council in Suphanburi.[89] Banharn had served in this capacity for less than ten months when a momentous event took place in Bangkok: the student-led uprising of October 1973, which ended twenty-six years of military rule. This so-called "revolution" was essentially an event in Bangkok that had little immediate impact on the countryside, including Suphanburi; practically no ordinary Suphanburian took part in it. For Banharn, however, it was a watershed, for it enabled him to acquire a second formal political position, this time in the central state: a seat in the interim legislative assembly.[90] When the assembly disbanded after

---

[89] *Khon Suphan*, December 30, 1972; *Thai Rath*, December 28, 1972, p. 7.

[90] To simplify a bewildering series of events: on December 10, 1973, the king chose 2,436 members of the interim National Convention from the lists of local notables submitted by provincial governors. Banharn's name was on the list submitted by then-Governor Sawat Meephian. The king handpicked Banharn as one of the seventeen Suphanburians to serve in

the 1975 general election, Banharn was appointed to the senate. Thus, the post-1973 democratization catapulted Banharn, a provincial notable with limited education, onto the stage of national politics in Bangkok.

Given his conspicuously displayed wealth, his command of local support, and his growing prominence at the national level, several major political parties courted Banharn to run for office under their respective banners before the parliamentary election of 1975.[91] However, he fended off these overtures because he was too "tied up" with his business.[92] Before the parliamentary election of 1976, however, Bun-uea Prasertsuwan, a veteran MP from Suphanburi, persuaded a reluctant Banharn to join the Chart Thai Party. Reportedly, it was Bun-uea's statement that made Banharn change his mind: "There is a limit to what you can do to develop Suphanburi with your personal wealth, but as an MP, you would be able to do much more for your hometown."[93]

Meeting Outsiders' Challenges

In the months leading up to the 1976 election, however, Banharn had to face two major challenges that one severe critic from outside Suphanburi posed to his local reputation. The challenges came in 1975 and 1976, when a Bangkok-based firebrand, Police Major Anant Senakhant, came to Suphanburi to attack Banharn in public. Anant was the product of the radical social atmosphere that prevailed after Thailand's transition to democracy in 1973. Calling himself a leader in the crusade against pervasive political corruption, he delivered many open-air "Hyde Park" speeches to attack "corrupt" politicians. In February 1975, for example, he censured Prasit Kanchanawat, then house speaker in parliament and a former executive of the Bangkok Bank, for awarding preferential loans to his political allies.[94] Banharn, an ascendant political figure in Suphanburi, became just another target of Anant's virulent verbal attacks. This proved to be a test of popular support for Banharn.

Articles in *Khon Suphan* provide some detailed accounts of what happened. Anant held two massive anti-Banharn rallies in Suphanburi—first on February 18, 1975, and then on March 13, 1976, a month before the 1976 election. The exact contents of Anant's speeches are unknown, but some of my respondents remember that he castigated Banharn for having amassed his wealth by offering kickbacks to senior DPW officials.[95] By exposing Banharn's tainted background, Anant tried to disabuse Suphanburians of their misplaced support for the "local hero."

Political considerations also motivated Anant's attacks. He was a nephew of Manas Rung-rueng, then mayor of Muang municipality in Suphanburi. Manas was being threatened by Banharn's growing influence among his constituents. In the

---

the National Convention. Then, on December 19, the 2,436 members of this convention selected, from among themselves, 299 members who would compose the interim legislative assembly. Banharn was selected as one of Suphanburi's three representatives in the assembly.

[91] *Sarn Khwam Fan*, p. 83.

[92] *Khon Suphan*, October 30, 1974, p. 3.

[93] *Bangkok Post*, July 17, 1995, p. 4.

[94] *Bangkok Post*, February 21, 1975, p. 1. For accounts of Anant's diatribes against other politicians, see *Bangkok Post* (February 11, 1975, p. 3; February 15, 1975, p. 3; February 18, 1975, p. 3; February 19, 1975, p. 5; February 21, 1975, p. 1).

[95] Anant published a booklet to this effect later. Anant, *Thammai Phom Tong Than Banharn*.

municipal election of January 1975, Manas faced stiff competition from a group of candidates, including former schoolteacher Mrs. Jaranai Injai-uea (the daughter of a prominent landowner, Sa-ngiam Charoensil), all of whom were supported by Banharn.[96] Although none of these people, except Jaranai, won a seat in the municipality council, Manas felt alarmed by Banharn's potential to undermine his position. Manas therefore tried to nip this perceived threat in the bud by masterminding his nephew's public attacks, although he flatly denied any involvement.[97] Whatever his real motives, Anant's rallies posed a threat to Banharn's rising status as a provincial hero.

How did Suphanburians react? Were they swayed, as Anant intended, to an anti-Banharn stance? The answer is "no." In fact, the very opposite happened. Suphanburians became all the more pro-Banharn. In his attempt to undermine Banharn's base of support, Anant, ironically, ended up strengthening it.

Suphanburians' reaction to Anant's first rally is revealing. Shortly after this rally, a number of Suphanburians, calling themselves "the Group of Suphan's Blood," emerged in vociferous opposition to Anant's "inappropriate" behavior. These people distributed leaflets throughout Suphanburi that attacked Anant and defended Banharn with a simple yet powerful message: "Banharn builds goodness for Suphanburi, while Anant destroys [it]." Likewise, another group of "furious" Suphanburians criticized Anant for "insulting [*yiap yam*] a person who has done useful things for Suphanburi." In defending their position, the group cited "a hospital ward, three schools, and temple halls, which Banharn has built by donating no less than 6–7 million baht." Furthermore, on March 14, at least one thousand people from Dan Chang, Don Chedi, and other districts of Suphanburi staged a large protest march against Anant in the provincial capital (figure 3.4). As they marched, they sang and played the song *Blood of Suphan* from Luang Wichit's drama, while blowing bugles and beating drums. They also carried some one hundred placards attacking Anant and defending Banharn. One sign delivered a belligerent message to Anant: "If you come back to Suphanburi again, we'll welcome you with our feet wide open [*ar tiin ton rap*]," which is a vulgar way of saying: "We are ready to start a physical fight with you." In addition, the protesters shouted via a microphone: "If Anant returns to Suphanburi to attack Banharn again, the 'popular force of Suphanburians' [*palang prachacon chao Suphan*] may take the law into their own hands," implying that Anant's physical safety would not be guaranteed. On reaching the Provincial Office, the protest leaders explained to Governor Sawat that their action was not intended to cause a public disturbance, but only to "protect the honor of Suphanburians." They also submitted their demand to Sawat that Anant be forever barred from entering Suphanburi.[98]

Anant's second round of rallies did not cause such an angry reaction. Instead, it was greeted with sheer apathy. Some four hundred to five hundred people

---

[96] Banharn had good reason to support these candidates. Jaranai's uncle was the afore-mentioned Winit, Banharn's former classmate and a doctor at Chaophraya Yommarat Hospital. Another candidate, Somchai Sujit, is the elder brother of Yodchai, who performed *Blood of Suphan* with Banharn. Somchai, along with his mother, Hansa, sits on the board of directors for BS International, a chemical company established by Banharn in 1970. DBD/MC, Bangkok Company File no. 330/2513.

[97] *Khon Suphan*, March 10, 1976, p. 3. Indeed, after having served as municipality mayor for ten years, Manas lost the election of 1985 to Jaranai.

[98] *Khon Suphan*, March 20, 1975, pp. 1, 8.

reportedly turned up at the rallies, but nobody would sit near Anant—in striking contrast to his reception in other provinces, where he had usually been surrounded by large, eager audiences. This was partly because Suphanburians were afraid of being caught in violent incidents that could erupt during his talk. It was also because "the speaker is not anybody important" to them, as one resident commented to a local newspaper reporter. Some people were amazed at Anant's bravery and wondered if "that beast values his life at all."[99]

Figure 3.4 A pro-Banharn rally in front of the Provincial Hall, 1975[100]

One Suphanburian summarized the unintended effect of Anant's actions: "That Anant comes to speak like this [to attack Banharn] is actually making people sympathize with Banharn." This Suphanburian then defended Banharn passionately:

> If you do business with brains, efficiently, and with diligence [as Banharn does], it is only natural that you have a chance to become wealthy. When he [Banharn] has indeed become rich, he still thinks about his birthplace every time he breathes [*thuk lom haijai*]. In the last ten years, Mr. Banharn has built schools, a hospital ward, a temple main hall, and many other things and spent altogether ten million baht on them, which is not little.[101]

Recollecting Anant's attack, one retired schoolteacher in Muang District (#94) referred to her and other Suphanburians' support for Banharn as a collective act of moral obligation and provincial solidarity:

---

[99] *Khon Suphan*, March 20, 1976, p. 1.

[100] *Source: Khon Suphan*, March 20, 1975.

[101] *Khon Suphan*, March 20, 1976, p. 2.

It was ridiculous for him [Anant] to come from outside and think that he could change our opinions in one day. We are not ingrates. We are Suphanburians. When our fellow Suphanburian, a good Suphanburian, is criticized, we must show spirit and band together behind him.

Thus, Suphanburians simply rejected Anant's critiques and reacted with spontaneous and emotional protests, which soon lapsed into outright nonchalance. Anant's attack failed to produce the intended effect of proselytizing Suphanburians. On the contrary, it had the ironic effect of solidifying their support for Banharn by making his achievements even better known, by invoking sympathy with him, and by arousing intense provincialist sentiments. In short, Banharn grew more popular *because of*, rather than despite, Anant's attacks.

A Landslide Victory

The consolidated popular support for Banharn was reflected in the staggering result of the parliamentary election held on April 4, 1976. Banharn did not just win the election; he won by a landslide, capturing the largest number of votes (57,530 votes) among all the candidates in the country. He received an estimated 63 percent of the vote—quite a high figure for a "greenhorn" candidate, aged only forty-three.[102] On the day of the election, leaflets attacking Banharn were distributed, presumably by Anant's supporters,[103] but this last-minute campaign did little to shake Suphanburians' support.

Banharn's stunning victory contrasted with the dismal performance of Thongyod Jitaweera (b. 1909), a veteran MP of Suphanburi who had been elected in 1957, 1969, and 1975. In 1975, he even became minister of commerce. In the 1976 election, however, he suffered a humiliating loss, receiving only 25,509 votes—less than half the votes cast for Banharn. Among the Suphanburians who did not vote for Thongyod is the son of a rice farmer in Bang Pla Ma District (#43). This villager explained his choice to me in plain terms: "Thongyod had been Suphanburi's MP for a long time, but he hadn't built anything in Suphanburi." Thongyod's inaction was also exemplified by his refusal to mediate in the afore-mentioned Sangkhalok Bowl controversy. The villager then contrasted Thongyod's lack of energy and interest in local affairs with the well-demonstrated generosity of Banharn, for whom he has "always voted" since 1976. A policeman in U-Thong District (#76) expressed similar opinions: "I support anybody who develops my birthplace. Thongyod didn't, but Banharn did." The policeman then cited Banharn–Jaemsai School III as the reason why he supported Banharn in 1976. It is worth recalling that this school was built in Dan Chang, outside the policeman's native district of U-Thong. In fact, none of the development works supplied by Banharn before 1976 was located in U-Thong. Asked about this, the policeman answered: "It doesn't matter where Banharn built schools. Dan Chang is part of Suphanburi, and Suphanburi is our home." This policeman, like many others, did not base his support on whether or how much he benefited from Banharn's donations. He looked toward a much broader horizon.

Thus, while the overwhelming vote for Banharn may have raised outsiders' eyebrows, it came as little surprise to many Suphanburians. His landslide victory

---

[102] Calculated from *Khon Suphan*, January 30, 1975, p. 2; *Khon Suphan*, April 10, 1976, p. 2.

[103] *Khon Suphan*, April 10, 1976, p. 2.

was the natural outcome of his heroic generosity and compassion, which allowed him to build up a high stock of "moral capital"; it had nothing to do with unsavory means of establishing dominance, such as vote-buying, violence, and coercion, which are presumed in much of the urban-based discourse to be rife in rural Thailand.

In sum, to understand why Banharn commands many Suphanburians' popular support at present, we must first understand the historical underpinnings of his political authority. History matters. Long before urban-based scholars and journalists constructed him as a corrupt politician, Banharn had established himself at the local level as the admired antithesis to the central state that had rendered Suphanburi backward and socially undistinguished. The result was an incipient sense of provincial pride, of which he became an essential component.

CHAPTER FOUR

INFLUX OF
STATE DEVELOPMENT FUNDS

Virtually all Suphanburians who support Banharn agree that his election victory in 1976 marks a turning point or breakthrough in the history of their province's modernization. If Banharn's donations that started in the 1960s contributed to Suphanburi's nascent development, most Suphanburians see his first election to parliament as an important catalyst for the accelerated development of their province. In the plain words of a construction worker (#21), "If Banharn had not become our MP, Suphan wouldn't be the way it is now. The rate of development has been remarkable since he became an MP ... He did a lot for us before becoming an MP, but he has done even more as an MP."

Exactly how has Banharn developed Suphanburi? An overwhelming 98 percent of his supporters whom I interviewed gave the same answer: by channeling state funds. This is the single most important factor that Suphanburians from all walks of life mentioned to explain how their province has overcome its "legendary" backwardness. Although these people talked effusively about Banharn's donations to local development before 1976, those contributions were relatively few in number, minor in scale, and limited in geographical scope, compared to the development projects that he has undertaken with state funds since 1976. To the extent that the paucity of state funds hindered Suphanburi's development in previous decades, Banharn, as an MP, has resolved that serious problem by penetrating and tapping into the coffers of the "callous" and "miserly" central state. While resenting the inequitable distribution of state funds before 1976 (see chapter 2), many Suphanburians may have viewed the situation as unavoidable or unchangeable. Banharn proved such people wrong, much to their delight, by bringing a formerly unthinkable amount of public monies to the province. Thus he has further enhanced his heroic status in the province.

This chapter starts with a brief description of the political or institutional context that has facilitated the massive infusion of state funds by Banharn. The second part details the scale and quality of his state-funded projects, with a focus on roads and schools.[1] In the third section, I will elaborate on how Suphanburians praise, discount, defend, and justify Banharn's role in the process of budget allocation that has systematically and unfairly favored their province over many others.

---

[1] For Banharn's budgetary contributions to other areas of development (e.g., public health), see Yoshinori Nishizaki, "The Weapon of the Strong: Identity, Community, and Domination in Provincial Thailand" (PhD dissertation, University of Washington, Seattle, WA, 2004), chapters 7 and 8.

INSTITUTIONAL SETTING: THE PATRIMONIAL-DEMOCRATIC STATE

Suphanburians use several key phrases to explain Banharn's eminent success in acquiring public funds. Typical of these are: "He has lots of friends and subordinates in the bureaucracy" and "He knows how to use civil servants." A retired civil servant (#95) in Muang District expounded further with an analogy:

> [The government budget in Thailand] is like the delicious food at the table—for example, a big roast duck. Does a master carve it up equally for all the people present? No. There is no such master. The master gives you a big portion if he knows you well and likes you. If he doesn't like you, you get a small portion, or maybe nothing. Banharn knows how to get close to big shots in the civil service. He himself has become a master in many ministries. That is how Suphan has received lots of public funds.

In academic parlance, these comments underscore one and the same institutional feature of Thailand: the patrimonial nature of the state. Thailand achieved a transition to democracy in 1973, but this transition has represented a change mainly at the level of regime; the fundamental nature of the state, or the way state power is used, has not changed. As in the age of authoritarian rule,[2] public office is still regarded as private property that power holders can manipulate to suit their personal needs. The public–private division is just as blurred in the democratic present as it was in the authoritarian past. This means that the distribution of public goods and services, notably state funds, is as politicized as ever. Funds continue to be dispensed on the basis of personal connections, rather than on merit or in accordance with transparent rules. The difference is that whereas only a narrow circle of elites exerted personal influence over funds allocation in the authoritarian past, the advent of democracy has allowed previously excluded non-elites to attain formal positions in the state and to acquire legitimate access to the state coffers that previously had been closed to them.[3] Banharn, as well as his protégés, family members, and friends, has been among such people.

Banharn's privileged access to the central treasury reflects his high status in the Chart Thai (CT) Party, one of the most institutionalized parties in Thailand. While many other parties simply came and went in Thailand, the CT Party survived many coups and crises after its inception in 1974 (until it was dissolved by the Constitutional Court in December 2008). Of the twenty-nine parties that existed in the 1970s, only the CT and Democrat Parties remained in 2008. After joining the CT Party in 1976, Banharn held its top posts as a reward for his copious donations to the party—deputy secretary-general (1976–78), secretary general (1980–94), and leader (1994–2008). Moreover, every time the CT Party was in power as a coalition government partner—it was in power for seventeen years between 1979 and 2004—Banharn and his cronies obtained key cabinet posts.

---

[2] See Norman Jacobs, *Modernization without Development: Thailand as an Asian Case Study* (New York, NY: Praeger, 1971); and Fred Riggs, *Thailand: The Modernization of a Bureaucratic Polity* (Honolulu, HI: East-West Center Press, 1966).

[3] Yoshinori Nishizaki, "Provincializing Thai Politics," *Kyoto Review of Southeast Asia* 1 (2002), available at http://kyotoreview.cseas.kyoto-u.ac.jp/issue/issue0/article_31.html. Accessed on October 17, 2010.

In addition, numerous civil servants known for their exceptional closeness to Banharn have attained top bureaucratic posts. A good example is Bodi Chunnanond, who controlled the Budget Bureau—a powerful institution that draws up annual budget plans—for over two decades as deputy director-general (1974–83) and director-general (1983–92, 1993–95). In 1995, then-Prime Minister Banharn appointed Bodi as his personal advisor on budgetary matters. In 1996, Bodi even became a finance minister in Banharn's cabinet.

Equally important is Banharn's longstanding membership on the Budget Scrutiny Committee (BSC), a parliamentary committee that has the authority to amend annual budget plans. Most committee members change every year, but Banharn stands out as an exception. He served on the committee every year between 1978 and 1995 (except 1991–92, when parliament was not in session due to the coup of 1991). No other MP has served on the BSC for as long as Banharn has. In addition, the other CT Party MPs of Suphanburi—all Banharn's protégés—have served on the BSC for varying periods of time, making Suphanburi by far the most well-represented province on the committee.[4] Furthermore, Bodi, the aforementioned Budget Bureau director-general, sat on the BSC continuously between 1975 and 1983 as the Budget Bureau's representative. In the subsequent eleven years (1984–95), Bodi served as deputy chairman of the BSC.[5]

All these posts (and many others) enabled Banharn to exert considerable personal leverage over the process through which a huge sum of development funds can be requested, approved, and allocated. In particular, as Thailand's vertiginous economic growth bloated the state treasury from the late 1980s onwards, Banharn funneled a truly impressive array of state-funded development projects into Suphanburi (as will be detailed below). As exemplified by the case of Bodi, any bureaucrat who assisted Banharn in such pork-barrel politics has been amply rewarded with promotions—another kind of "goods and services" that are doled out on a personal basis by the patrimonial state.

The budgets for Suphanburi have not simply increased. The manner in which they are channeled has also become extremely smooth, especially since 1988 when Suphanburi emerged as a unique "one-party dominant province." This is another factor that explains the rapid influx of state funds under Banharn's rule. Before 1988, different MPs of Suphanburi belonged to different parties, with the main rivalry being between the CT Party and the Social Action Party (SAP) (table 4.1). In 1983, however, Thongyod Jitaweera—a senior SAP member who had served as minister of commerce (1975–76), minister of public health (1980–81), and deputy prime minister (1981–83)—suffered a humiliating electoral loss and quit politics. Consequently, the only MP remaining from SAP was Jongchai Thiangtham (b. 1943), a Thammasat University-educated lawyer and Thongyod's protégé. Then, in 1988, Jongchai, apparently lured by the prospect of attaining a cabinet post under Banharn's patronage, defected to the CT Party.[6] Since then, all of the Suphanburi MPs have belonged to the CT Party. Between 1988 and 2001, among all of Thailand's seventy-five provinces, only one other province, Phan-nga, was under the control of one

---

[4] Untitled data obtained at the National Parliament in 2000. See Nishizaki, "The Weapon of the Strong," chapter 5, for details.

[5] *Hoksip Pii Bodi Chunnanond* (Bangkok: Bophit, 1995), p. 10.

[6] While a SAP member, Jongchai had not attained any cabinet post. Meanwhile, the CT Party MPs for Suphanburi had obtained several posts.

party, and it is only because Phan-nga, a province with the sixth smallest population in Thailand, has just one MP.

Table 4.1 Party Affiliations of Suphanburi's MPs, 1976–2001

NAME	1975	1976	1979	1983	1986	1988	1992 (I)	1992 (II)	1995	1996	2001
Banharn Silpa-archa		CT		CT	CT	CT	CT	CT	CT	CT	CT
Bun-uea Prasertsuwan	SJ	CT	CT	CT	CT	CT	CT	CT	CT		
Chumpol Silpa-archa			CT	CT	CT	CT	CT	CT	CT	CT	
Praphat Photsuthon	CT	CT	CT	CT	CT	CT	CT	CT	CT	CT	CT
Jongchai Thiangtham				SAP	SAP	CT	CT	CT	CT	CT	CT
Kanchana Silpa-archa									CT	CT	CT
Nathawuth Prasertsuwan										CT	CT
Worawuth Silpa-archa											CT
Thongyod Jitaweera	SJ	SAP	SAP								
Wirat Watanakrai	CT										
Thi Boonak	PF										
Sakol Watcharathai		CT									
Pramuat Suwannakert			SAP								
Paisarn Saenchai-ngam		SAP									

Notes:
  • CT = Chart Thai Party; SAP = Social Action Party; SJ = Social Justice Party;
    PF = People's Force Party
  • Banharn did not run for office in 1979.
  • The number of parliamentary seats in Suphanburi increased to six in 1995.
Source: Author's research

The significance of this phenomenon is that with all Suphanburi's MPs belonging to the CT Party as his protégés, Banharn has acted as the most important pipeline to the coffers of the patrimonial central state. As a result, the process of requesting and allocating public expenditures has become streamlined, making it possible for Banharn to implement swiftly one development project after another, according to his personal goals or wishes. In stark contrast to the MPs from "multi-party" provinces, Banharn has been able to pursue his vision of development efficiently, without being hampered by wasteful "bickering" (*yaeng*) over state funds among competing MPs. No other Thai MP has been able to straddle the center and local politics more smoothly than has Banharn.

Nowhere has Banharn's influence over the allocation of state budgets been more apparent than in the cases of road construction and school construction, as I discuss next.

ROAD CONSTRUCTION

Makha Lom is a subdistrict located in the northern part of Bang Pla Ma District. On a map, it appears to be only a stone's throw from the provincial capital of Suphanburi. Until some four decades ago, however, it was one of many isolated subdistricts. Banharn changed that. In 1976, he embarked on building a forty-kilometer road that would run through the subdistrict. This was the first road-building project he channeled into Suphanburi as an MP. The project is worth describing here at some length as an illustration of how Banharn put his personal and political connections to good use.

The origin of the project dates back to November 1975, five months before Banharn became an MP. At the time, he knew from all the stories previously reported in a provincial newspaper that Makha Lom residents had been grumbling about a bumpy, unsurfaced road that connected their villages to the provincial capital. The residents had built the road in 1971 by using their own money—a story that is consistent with other local initiatives described in chapter 2. Since it was a makeshift road, however, it soon deteriorated, impeding the transport of catfish, Makha Lom's major income-earning product, to the central market town. To alleviate this problem, the government set out in 1973 to surface an eight-kilometer road from Makha Lom to the provincial capital at a budgeted cost of 500,000 baht. The surfacing project was to be completed by August 1974. Like many other government projects, however, it fell behind schedule, and as of November 1975 it had yet to be completed. Under the circumstances, villagers from more than one hundred families in Makha Lom scraped together 10,000 baht to undertake part of the project on their own (a section one kilometer long and six meters wide).[7] Not surprisingly, these villagers complained bitterly about the inefficiency of the state.

Having read about this story, Banharn, a senator at the time, visited Makha Lom in November 1975 to inspect the road conditions firsthand and to discuss the matter with Makha Lom's subdistrict head, Wichai Duangchan. On the basis of his inspection, Banharn drew up a new, grand project for building a 28-kilometer highway that was to connect the provincial capital not only to Makha Lom but also to Suan Taeng subdistrict, which lies some twenty kilometers beyond Makha Lom. The original eight-kilometer surfacing project was subsumed under this new project. Banharn then wrote a letter to then-Minister of Transport and Communications Siri Siriyothin to request approval of the new project. In the letter, Banharn stressed the importance of his initiative, arguing that the catfish trade would bring annual revenues of three-to-four-hundred-million baht to Suphanburi.[8] Banharn, as he admitted at the time, was unsure if he was "overstepping his bounds," since he was not an MP.[9] Yet he presumably knew that he could count on Siri's favorable response. Both had known each other since they were appointed to the interim Legislative Assembly in December 1973. In addition, Siri, the deputy CT Party leader, was personally very close to the party leader, Pramarn Adireksarn, whose company, Thai-Asahi Caustic Soda, had reaped huge profits in the 1960s by becoming the sole supplier of chlorine to the Public Works Department, thanks to Banharn's mediation.[10] Indeed, Siri approved Banharn's request without raising any

---

[7] *Khon Suphan*, July 20, 1974, pp. 1, 2.

[8] *Khon Suphan*, November 30, 1975, pp. 1, 2; Budget Bureau, *Ekasarn Ngop-pramarn 2520*, 3,4 (1976): 156.

[9] *Khon Suphan*, November 20, 1975, p. 3.

[10] Sarthit Winurat, *Ke Roi Nak Kan Muang* (Bangkok: Wisurut, 1996), p. 76; Anant Sanokhan, *Thammai Phom Tong Than Banharn* (Bangkok: Klet Thai, 1988), p. 53.

objection. The Department of Highways (DOH) then provided 634,000 baht to Suphanburi as a supplementary fund (*ngop sorm saem*) in early 1976.[11]

Upon being elected MP in April 1976, Banharn, now deputy minister of industry, wrote a letter to Chaliao Wacharaphuk, then-DOH director-general, and secured an additional two million baht for the project. This fund allowed Banharn to extend the length of the project from twenty-eight to forty kilometers.[12] Technically speaking, Chaliao was accountable only to the minister of transport and communications; he did not have to agree to Banharn's request. However, he probably thought it prudent not to do otherwise, for he had to hedge against the *distinct* possibility that, given the history of frequent cabinet-member changes in Thailand, Banharn or some other prominent CT member might at any time assume control over his ministry as a new minister and punish him for his "recalcitrance"—a concept that Thai politicians could define to suit their political ends.[13]

Thus, thanks to Banharn's behind-the-scenes maneuverings in the central patrimonial state, Makha Lom residents received a massive road-building project—a much bigger project than they had bargained for. An elderly rice farmer (#77), a staunch supporter of Banharn, who has lived in Makha Lom all her life, recalled the construction project, which was launched soon after his electoral victory:

> One day, I saw a bulldozer coming. Trucks followed one after another. They started appearing from nowhere. Where they came from, I don't know. There were many civil servants, too. I was kind of scared at first. I wondered, "What are they going to do to our village? What are they here for?" One civil servant said, "It's the project of the new MP, Banharn. He is going to resurface your dirt road with asphalt. You won't have to slip on a rainy day any more."

Her neighbor (#96), also a farmer, continued:

> It was unbelievable. All the people here helped build the old road together. We spent a long time, many months, building it, bit by bit. Then those machines and civil servants came and built a new road, a better road. And the construction was over in just a few months, just like that. The road had a very smooth surface ... It linked our village to Suan Taeng [the adjacent subdistrict]. Things became more convenient. My son and his friend went to school in Suan Taeng, and my neighbor's son got a job in the market town.

Completed in 1978, the new road was and still is affectionately called "Banharn Road" (*thanon Banharn*)—a moniker that evokes Banharn's ability to overcome the central state's inefficiencies and to achieve awe-inspiring modernization at the grassroots level.

---

[11] *Khon Suphan*, November 10, 1975, pp. 1, 8; *Khon Suphan*, November 30, 1975, pp. 1, 2, 3; *Khon Suphan*, January 10, 1976, pp. 1, 2.

[12] Budget Bureau, *Ekasarn Ngop-pramarn 2520*, 3,4 (1976): 156, 172; *Khon Suphan*, August 10, 1976, pp. 1, 2.

[13] Indeed, Banharn's younger brother, Chumpol, was appointed deputy minister of communications in March 1981.

Figure 4.1 A highway under construction from Suphanburi to Ayutthaya Province[14]

This is only one of the numerous "Banharn roads" that have appeared throughout Suphanburi, including in areas that are *not* part of his electoral district. As shown in chapter 2, one cardinal mark of Suphanburi's past backwardness was its dearth of roads. Having grown up in Suphanburi in the first half of the twentieth century, Banharn was acutely aware of Suphanburi's physical isolation. Every time he traveled between Bangkok and Suphanburi, he had to take an exhausting, two-day boat trip, in the process of which Suphanburi's remoteness was impressed painfully on his body. Therefore, since his election to parliament, Banharn has made road construction his top priority,[15] to such an extent that Suphanburi now boasts many roads of outstanding quality in Thailand.

Government documents reveal the extent of Banharn's immediate budgetary contributions. Starting in fiscal year (FY) 1977, Suphanburi became the recipient of an unprecedented sum of DOH funds (table 4.2). Between FY1977 and FY1980, the funds for Suphanburi jumped by 489 percent, while the funds for the whole country rose by only 33 percent. Equally striking is an increase in the relative share of funds for Suphanburi. During fiscal years 1966–77, Suphanburi accounted for 1.3 percent of the annual funds allocated nationwide by the DOH. In the four years after FY1977, the comparable figure jumped to 5.9 percent. In FY1980, it reached nearly 12 percent. The significance of this data becomes clearer in light of the fact that Suphanburi accounts for only 1.6 percent of Thailand's population. The initiation of massive road construction by Banharn marked a sharp departure from the pre-1976 period, when Suphanburi was the recipient of a disproportionately small sum of state expenditures. With Banharn as an MP, Suphanburi, once a chronic loser in the zero-

---

[14] This is one of the many places where Banharn initiated road construction so that Suphanburi became more accessible to the outside world. *Source*: DOH, *Rai-ngan Prachampii* 2525, p. 26.

[15] CT Party, *Chart Thai Samphan* 13 (May–June 2001): 15.

sum inter-provincial competition for fiscal resources of the state, now emerged as a main victor.

Table 4.2 Highway Construction Projects for Suphanburi, FY 1966–1980[16]

Fiscal Year	No. of Ongoing Projects	Total Length of Ongoing Projects (km)	Funds for Suphanburi (thousand baht) (A)	Funds for the Whole Country (thousand baht) (B)	Suphanburi's Share of Total (A ÷ B)
1966	1	20.0	5,000	987,995	0.5%
1967	1	15.0	7,680	1,613,209	0.5%
1968	3	30.0	26,210	1,638,571	1.6%
1969	3	29.5	11,000	1,754,150	0.6%
1970	4	133.9	35,700	1,964,413	1.8%
1971	4	94.4	10,650	2,136,017	0.5%
1972	2	176.0	28,600	1,804,670	1.6%
1973	3	169.5	35,500	1,773,154	2.0%
1975	3	186.9	51,600	2,368,467	2.2%
1976	4	192.8	52,350	3,159,832	1.7%
1977	8	320.0	83,730	3,130,996	2.7%
1978	6	300.9	243,420	3,566,387	6.8%
1979	6	370.0	269,000	3,315,927	8.1%
1980	7	385.5	493,800	4,166,933	11.9%

Note: Data for FY 1974 is not available

Starting in 1976, Suphanburi also became the major recipient of funds from the Department of Accelerated Rural Development (DARD), the most important road-building agency at the village level. Founded in 1967 to counter communist infiltration into Thai villages, DARD traditionally operated mainly in the northern and northeastern regions near Laos and Cambodia. Suphanburi (and other central region provinces) took a back seat. The situation changed appreciably after 1976, when a DARD Regional Center—the sixth in Thailand—was established in Suphanburi.[17] Between FY1975 and FY1980, DARD funds for Suphanburi jumped by

---

[16] *Sources*: compiled from Budget Bureau, *Ekasarn Ngop-pramarn* 3,3, various years (1965–67, 1977-79); Budget Bureau, *Ekasarn Ngop-pramarn 2512*, 3,6 (1968); Budget Bureau, *Ekasarn Ngop-pramarn 2513*, 3 (1969); Budget Bureau, *Ekasarn Ngop-pramarn* 3,4, various years (1970–72, 1974–76).

[17] Budget Bureau, *Ekasarn Ngop-pramarn 2520*, 3,5 (1976): 467.

1,404 percent, while comparable funds for the country as a whole rose by only 389 percent.[18]

Since the 1980s, too, Suphanburi has continued to be a main beneficiary of road-construction funds. This became especially noticeable from the early 1990s onward, when Thailand enjoyed an economic boom. In the mid-1990s, DOH expenditures for Suphanburi reached an all-time high, thanks to Banharn's wheeling and dealing in the budgetary process as prime minister. Only the economic crisis of 1997— Banharn's preferential budget allocation was no small contributing factor in this crisis—could put a brake on the inflationary trend (figure 4.2). Yet, within the severe constraints imposed by the crisis, Suphanburi remained a primary recipient of state funds.

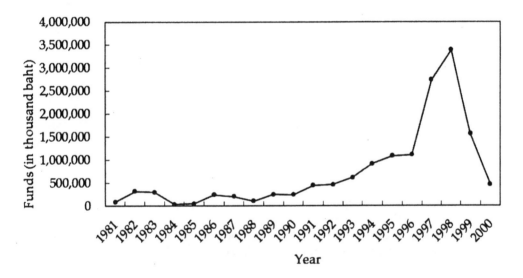

Figure 4.2 Highway Construction Funds for Suphanburi, FY 1981–2000[19]

Comparative analysis demonstrates just how unbalanced the state-funds distribution became in fiscal years 1985–97. Figure 4.3 (below) shows that Suphanburi received far more DOH funds than the other provinces of the central region, except Ayutthaya. The contrast to Chainat and Uthai Thani, the provinces north of Suphanburi, is especially striking. In FY1995, for instance, while Suphanburi received over 1.08 billion baht, these two provinces received 18 million and 22 million baht, respectively.[20] Even Ayutthaya's preeminence does not detract from Suphanburi's uniqueness. The DOH channeled more funds into Ayutthaya primarily

[18] Budget Bureau, *Ekasarn Ngop-pramarn 2518*, 3,5 (1974): 357, 382; Budget Bureau, *Ekasarn Ngop-pramarn 2519*, 3,5 (1975): 407; Budget Bureau, *Ekasarn Ngop-pramarn 2520*, 3,5 (1976): 435, 467; Budget Bureau, *Ekasarn Ngop-pramarn 2521*, 3,4 (1977): 345, 370; Budget Bureau, *Ekasarn Ngop-pramarn 2522*, 3,4 (1978): 308–9, 334; Budget Bureau, *Ekasarn Ngop-pramarn 2523*, 3,4 (1979): 388–89, 417.

[19] *Sources*: Compiled from DOH, *Rai-ngan Prachampii*, various years (1981–84); Budget Bureau, *Ekasarn Ngop-pramarn* 4,3, various years (1984–94); Budget Bureau, *Ekasarn Ngop-pramarn* 4,4, various years (1995–99).

[20] Budget Bureau, *Ekasarn Ngop-pramarn 2538*, 4,3 (1994): 210–13, 260–63, 270–73.

because of the urgency to upgrade the road network between Bangkok and an industrial estate in Ayutthaya that the Thai government set up in the late 1980s to woo foreign capital. In contrast, although Suphanburi has not attracted any foreign capital to date, it still received a disproportionate amount of state monies that it did.

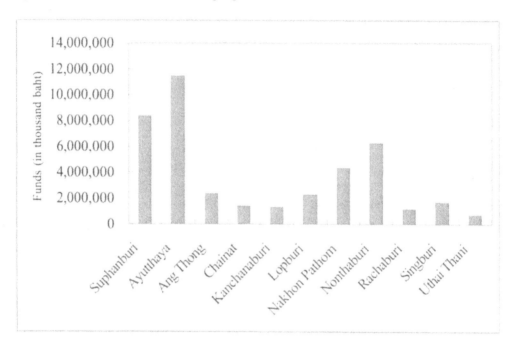

Figure 4.3 A Comparison of Highway Construction Funds for Suphanburi and its Neighboring Provinces, FY 1985–1997[21]

Banharn's direct and indirect control over three major departments in charge of road construction—the DOH, the DARD, and the Department of Public Works (DPW)—was responsible for the massive inflow of development funds. First, he twice served as minister of transport and communications, the post overseeing the DOH (1986–88, 1992). Likewise, he twice became minister of the interior, the post in charge of the DARD and DPW (1990, 1995–96). He controlled all these departments as prime minister, in 1995–96. Moreover, the other CT Party MPs of Suphanburi, all Banharn's clients, have attained cabinet posts in the ministries of interior and communications. Banharn's younger brother Chumpol became deputy minister of transport and communications (1981–83); Praphat Photsuthon, deputy interior minister (1997–2000); and Jongchai Thiangtham, deputy transport and communications minister (2000). The same goes for Banharn's allies in the CT Party, such as Pramarn Adireksarn (interior minister, 1988–90, 1990–91) and Chatichai Choonhavan (prime minister, 1988–91).

No less important, Banharn appointed his bureaucratic cronies to the top posts in relevant departments and ministries. A case in point is Aree Wong-araya, the former governor of Suphanburi (1983–88), who served as deputy permanent secretary and

---

[21] *Sources:* compiled from Budget Bureau, *Ekasarn Ngop-pramarn* 4,3, various years (1984–94); Budget Bureau, *Ekasarn Ngop-pramarn* 4,4, various years (1995–96).

permanent secretary of the Interior Ministry in 1988–95. Two other notable examples are Sathian Wongwichian, DOH director-general (1986–90) and deputy permanent secretary of the Ministry of Transport and Communications (1990–92), and Winit Benjaphong, a Suphanburian-born DOH deputy director-general (1995–2000).[22]

An institutional catalyst for the prodigious infusion of state funds was the establishment of the nation's fourteenth Regional Office of Highways Department (ROHD) in Suphanburi in 1988. Banharn, then minister of transport and communications, appointed the aforementioned Winit as Suphanburi's first ROHD chief. On paper, this office is supposed to undertake highway construction projects in Suphanburi and three surrounding provinces (Uthai Thani, Kanchanaburi, and Chainat). In practice, however, the office has acted as the de facto "front" for Suphanburi's development. It is also worth noting that besides the ROHD, Suphanburi has the Provincial Office of Highways Department (POHD), which was divided into two branches in 1988.[23] That is, Suphanburi, unlike most other provinces (which have only one POHD), has hosted *three* branch offices of the DOH since 1988. These offices have combined to serve as the vital institutional conduits through which a generous stream of state funds constantly flows into Suphanburi, often at the expense of other provinces.

Most of the funds directed by Banharn are "continuous funds" (*ngop phukphan*)—a type of funding that guarantees recipient provinces an uninterrupted flow of funds for several years in a row. For example, once the government decides to allocate a continuous fund of six million baht for a given project over a three-year period, the government is bound to honor this commitment, irrespective of whether there is any unforeseen political change during that time. Given the highly volatile nature of Thai politics (as exemplified by frequent coups and cabinet changes), this type of "guaranteed funding" represents a distinct advantage over the annual funds-allocation process, whereby projects approved by one government might be arbitrarily terminated or scaled down by the next.[24] Banharn made it a policy to secure as many continuous-funds projects as possible whenever he or his allies held any cabinet post. As a result, state funds have poured uninterrupted into Suphanburi despite the rough-and-tumble quality of Thai politics. For example, although the coup of 1976 abruptly ended Banharn's MP status, and parliament did not exist for the next three years, four highway construction projects, for which he had secured continuous funds of more than 331 million baht before the coup, were carried out without a hitch.[25] Similarly, the massive continuous funds that Banharn obtained in the mid-1990s helped cushion the impact of the economic crisis of 1997, sustaining a momentum of development in Suphanburi despite the substantially deflated budget at the national level. A retired college instructor (#97) praised Banharn's prescience, saying, "Banharn is smart. He takes a long-term view [*mong kan klai*]. From the beginning, he has always asked for continuous funds to hedge against future uncertainty."

---

[22] Interviews with DOH officials in May 2002.

[23] DOH, *Kaosip Pii Krom Thang Luang* (Bangkok: DOH, 2002), pp. 159–60.

[24] Interview with a Budget Bureau official, February 5, 2000.

[25] Budget Bureau, *Ekasarn Ngop-pramarn 2520*, 3,4 (1976): 156, 161, 172, 175; Budget Bureau, *Ekasarn Ngop-pramarn 2521*, 3,3 (1977): 112, 121, 128; Budget Bureau, *Ekasarn Ngop-pramarn 2522*, 3,3 (1978): 127, 135; Budget Bureau, *Ekasarn Ngop-pramarn 2523*, 3,3 (1979): 131–32, 138.

A huge sum of public funds has enabled Banharn to build a correspondingly huge number of roads in every nook and cranny of Suphanburi. Suphanburi now stands out from other central-region provinces, both in the absolute and proportional length of highways (table 4.3). The three maps (figures 4.4–4.6) bring into stark relief the phenomenal physical change that Banharn has brought to Suphanburi over time. In 1968, Suphanburi had only five highways, four of which were unsurfaced. Three decades later, fifty-nine paved highways crisscross Suphanburi like a spider's web. The length of highways increased by 1,645 percent, from 111.3 kilometers in 1966 to 1,942.5 kilometers in 2001.[26] Furthermore, the new highways have stimulated the construction of numerous feeder roads (n = 390, as of 2002) that branch out into and interconnect formerly isolated villages. Suphanburi is far ahead of its neighboring provinces in the distances covered by these village-level feeder roads (1,705 kilometers in 2002).[27] One villager (#51), a vendor of soft drinks in Sam Chuk District, described the sense of change he felt by putting Suphanburi in comparative perspective: "I went to visit my relative in Singburi [a province east of Suphanburi]. There was just one unpaved dirt road in his village. I went back there several months later. Nothing had changed. Meanwhile, our village got two asphalt roads. Roads were popping up everywhere, not just in our village. I realized then that Suphan was special. It was developing very fast."

Table 4.3 A Comparison of the Length of Highways in Suphanburi
and its Neighboring Provinces, 2001[28]

Province	Total Length of Highways (km) (A)	Population (B)	Area Size (sq. km.) (C)	No. of People per km (B ÷ A)	Road Density (A ÷ C)
Nakhon Pathom	641.4	671,386	2,168.3	1,047	0.30
Uthai Thani	671.4	318,595	6,730.2	474	0.10
Chainat	672.3	339,329	2,469.7	505	0.27
Kanchanaburi	736.4	724,435	19,483.2	984	0.04
Ratchaburi	753.4	777,105	5,196.1	1,032	0.14
Ayutthaya	825.4	693,230	2,556.6	840	0.32
Saraburi	832.5	546,044	3,576.5	656	0.23
Lopburi	1,126.4	738,370	6,199.7	655	0.18
Suphanburi	1,942.5	825,451	5,358.0	425	0.36

[26] ROHD (Suphanburi branch), *Sarup Phon-ngan Prachampii 2544* (Suphanburi: ROHD, 2002).

[27] Untitled computer data obtained at the DARD and DPW in 2002. The feeder roads are not included in figure 4.6. If included, they would make the map look like a truly dense spider's web.

[28] *Source*: Calculated from computer data obtained at the DOH in 2001

Figure 4.4 Map of Highways in Suphanburi, 1968[29]

Figure 4.5 Map of Highways in Suphanburi, 1975 (inc'l those under construction)[30]

---

[29] Drawn by the Cartography Department, Australian National University. *Sources*: Budget bureau, *Ekasarn Ngop-pramarn 3,3*, various years (1965–67); Budget Bureau, *Ekasarn Ngop-pramarn 2512, 3,6* (1968); Budget Bureau, *Ekasarn Ngop-pramarn 2513, 3* (1969); Budget Bureau, *Ekasarn Ngop-pramarn 2514, 3,4* (1970); DOH, *Rai-ngan Prachampii 2498* (Bangkok: DOH, 1956), p.13; *Khon Suphan* (March 23, 1965; January 18, 1966; October 30, 1970).

[30] Drawn by the Cartography Department, Australian National University. *Sources*: Budget Bureau, *Ekasarn Ngop-pramarn 3,3*, various years (1964–67, 1977–79); Budget Bureau, *Ekasarn Ngop-pramarn 2512, 3,6* (1968); Budget Bureau, *Ekasarn Ngop-pramarn 2513, 3* (1969); Budget

Figure 4.6 Map of Highways in Suphanburi, 2002[31]

The mood of the times that Suphanburians experienced in post-1976 is best captured by the expression, "roads, roads, and still more roads," which Eugen Weber used to describe early twentieth-century France.[32] Before Banharn embarked on massive road construction, space or nature was, as Weber put it, "the master; its distances run wild, overwhelming man." It represented a menace, something intimidating, mysterious, awesome, and daunting. With the advent of roads, however, space has been "conquered, distances [were] tamed, brought to heel, or, rather, increasingly to wheel." If history is "the tale of men struggling against space,"[33] there were signs that Suphanburians were rapidly and finally emerging as victors in this struggle.

The dense network of roads built by Banharn has made possible Suphanburians' unprecedented physical mobility, which has served to shorten the psychological distance among the previously isolated villagers to create a growing sense of extra-

Bureau, *Ekasarn Ngop-pramarn*, 3,4, various years (1970–72, 1974–76); DOH, *Rai-ngan Prachampii 2519* (Bangkok: DOH, 1977), pp. 104, 116; and *Khon Suphan*, March 30, 1974.

[31] Drawn by the Cartography Department, Australian National University. *Source*: A modified version of the map obtained at the ROHD (Suphanburi branch).

[32] Eugen Weber, *Peasants into Frenchmen: The Modernization of Rural France, 1870–1914* (Stanford, CA: Stanford University Press, 1976), p. 195.

[33] Ibid., p. 195.

village provincial awareness. Nothing is more symbolic of this dissolving physical and psychological distance than the completion of a paved highway that links Suphanburi directly to Bangkok. To build this highway, Banharn obtained an astonishing 460 million baht—a five-year continuous fund supplied by the World Bank—from the DOH in 1979.[34] Completed in 1984, the highway, which some Suphanburians proudly call "Banharn Highway," made the distance to Bangkok shorter by sixty kilometers. In terms of time, a road trip to Bangkok was shortened by at least five hours The "Banharn Highway" has thus enabled numerous Suphanburians of all ages and social classes to get to Bangkok for work, education, and entertainment far more easily than had ever been imagined was possible. The highway signifies the opening up of a formerly isolated Suphanburi to the outside world, especially to Bangkok, the center of modernity, civilization, and progress. It is no longer possible to speak of Suphanburians as stuck in a far-flung, "uncivilized" province.

Table 4.4 A Comparison of the Quality of Highways in Suphanburi and its Neighboring Provinces, 2001[35]

Province	Asphalt (km)	Concrete (km)	Laterite (km)	TOTAL (km)
Nakhon Pathom	545.3	96.1		641.4
Uthai Thani	601.0	51.4	19.1	671.5
Chainat	459.9	211.6	0.8	672.3
Kanchanaburi	731.1	5.0	0.3	736.4
Ratchaburi	747.4	6.0		753.4
Ayutthaya	400.9	424.5		825.4
Saraburi	466.4	321.1	45.1	832.6
Lopburi	1,002.5	98.7	25.2	1,126.4
Suphanburi	1,308.9	618.5	15.1	1,942.5
TOTAL	6,263.4	1,832.9	105.6	8,201.9

The huge sum of state funds has not just increased the number of roads in Suphanburi, but has also helped enhance their quality. First, the roads of Suphanburi are exceptionally durable and smooth. Suphanburi has far more concrete and asphalt highways, which are relatively resistant to developing potholes and bumps, than do other central-region provinces (table 4.4, above). The same holds true for village-level feeder roads. Suphanburi ranks third among Thailand's seventy-five provinces in the total length of concrete and asphalt feeder roads (table 4.5, below). None of Suphanburi's neighboring provinces are among the top ten. Suphanburi's

[34] CT Party, *Chart Thai Samphan* 13 (May–June 2001): 15–16; Budget Bureau, *Ekasarn Ngop-pramarn 2523*, 3,3 (1979): 178; Budget Bureau, *Ekasarn Ngop-pramarn 2524*, 3,3 (1980): 84; DOH, *Rai-ngan Prachampii 2523* (Bangkok: DOH, 1981), p. 63; DOH, *Rai-ngan Prachampii 2524* (Bangkok: DOH, 1982), p. 63; DOH, *Rai-ngan Prachampii 2525* (Bangkok: DOH, 1983), page number unspecified; DOH, *Rai-ngan Prachampii 2526* (Bangkok: DOH, 1984), page number unspecified.

[35] *Sources*: ROHD (Suphanburi branch), *Sarup Phon-ngan Prachampii 2544* (Suphanburi: 2002); computer data obtained at the DOH in 2001.

distinctiveness becomes even more pronounced when we consider that, among the top ten provinces, Suphanburi has by far the smallest population and area. Thus, Suphanburi is unmatched in terms of the length of feeder roads per person and per square kilometer.

Table 4.5 The Length of Asphalt/Concrete Feeder Roads: Top Ten Provinces, 2002[36]

Rank	Province	Asphalt (km)	Concrete (km)	Total (km)	Road Density*	No. of People per sq. km.
1	Nakhon Ratchasima	2,275.4	122.8	2,398.1	0.12	1,066
2	Buri Ram	1,641.4	102.7	1,744.1	0.17	856
3	Suphanburi	1,364.3	139.4	1,503.7	0.28	569
4	Ubon Ratchathani	1,232.5	258.1	1,490.6	0.08	1,135
5	Chiang Mai	1,299.8	183.5	1,483.2	0.07	1,011
6	Khon Kaen	1,314.6	133.3	1,447.8	0.13	1,197
7	Udon Thani	1,362.8	48.0	1,410.8	0.09	1,040
8	Nakhon Si Thammarat	1,319.1	86.7	1,405.8	0.14	1,081
9	Songkhla	1,248.4	60.5	1,308.9	0.18	959
10	Phetchabun	1,192.7	114.1	1,306.8	0.10	739

* Measured in terms of kilometers of roads per square kilometer of land

Suphanburi's highways are also exceptionally wide. As of 2001, 359.4 kilometers (18.5 percent) of all the highways in Suphanburi had two or more lanes. Comparable figures for adjacent Kanchanaburi and Uthai Thani Provinces were 27.6 kilometers (3.7 percent) and 42 kilometers (6.2 percent), respectively.[37] The most impressive road in terms of width is the aforementioned Suphanburi–Bangkok highway, which has six lanes for each direction at some points.

Suphanburi's highways, moreover, are well lit. Most of them have a long stretch of modern electric-light poles that give out bright illumination at night. For example, the two-kilometer portion of the Suphanburi–Bangkok highway that passes the central market town of Muang District has eighty-nine towering electric-light poles (about 25 meters in height), each one of which was installed at a cost of 400,000 baht (figure 4.7, below). The 25-kilometer highway between Muang and Don Chedi Districts has 567 slightly shorter electric-light poles that cost 200,000 baht each.[38] In contrast, most highways in Suphanburi's neighboring provinces are dimly lit or have no lights at all. Therefore, they are enveloped in spooky darkness after sunset. To the extent that darkness is a metaphysical mark of backwardness, Suphanburi's brightness vividly represents its escape from that condition.

Thus, thanks to Banharn's injection of state funds, the roads in Suphanburi have now become distinctively long, durable, smooth, wide, and bright. As one indication

---

[36] *Sources:* Calculated from computer data obtained at the DARD and DPW.

[37] ROHD (Suphanburi branch), *Sarup Phon-ngan Prachampii 2544*, p. 7.

[38] Interview with a DOH official, February 1, 2000.

of their exceptional qualities, many roads in Suphanburi have won several regional- and national-level "best highway" contests conducted by the DOH. In 2001, for instance, the 25-kilometer highway between Don Chedi and Muang Districts—the road that had been made of gravel up to the early 1970s[39]—was chosen as "the most beautiful, the most convenient, and the safest highway" in the central region. The DOH announced and disseminated this honor by erecting a big, public signboard along the highway. Another telling indication of the exceptional nature of Suphanburi's roads is in the annual report issued by the DOH in 2000. This report carried twenty-one colorful photos of modern highways the DOH had built nationwide in 1998–99. Of these photos, seven showed the highways in Suphanburi. In addition, the front and back covers of the report featured pictures of Suphanburi's highways.[40] Seeing Suphanburi's highways as the cream of the crop in Thailand, the DOH used them as the symbols of its sophisticated modern road-building technology. Indeed, many roads in Suphanburi look so modern that they would compare favorably with some of the best highways in industrialized nations. The appearance of these high-quality roads concretely embodies a vast improvement over the pre-Banharn era, when Suphanburi was connected to Bangkok by only one unpaved, dusty road.

Figure 4.7. Lamp poles along the Suphanburi–Bangkok Highway

SCHOOL CONSTRUCTION

As in the case of road construction, Banharn's role in educational development became readily apparent immediately after he became an MP. In FY1977, Suphanburi received more than seventeen million baht from the Ministry of Education (MOE)—

---

[39] DOH, *Rai-ngan Prachampii 2497* (Bangkok: DOH, 1955), pp. 18, 36; DOH, *Rai-ngan Prachampii 2498* (Bangkok: DOH, 1956), pp. 13, 27; Budget Bureau, *Ekasarn Ngop-pramarn 2514*, 3,4 (1970): 387; Budget Bureau, *Ekasarn Ngop-pramarn 2515*, 3,4 (1971): 382.

[40] DOH, *Rai-ngan Prachampii 2542* (Bangkok: DOH, 2000).

an unprecedented sum that represents a 534 percent jump from the previous year.[41] Banharn directed this fund to establish two new colleges in Suphanburi. One was the Suphanburi School of Agriculture, one of the ten agricultural schools in Thailand. No other province in the central region had such a school.[42] The other school was the College of Physical Education of Suphanburi (CPES), the eighth physical education college in Thailand.[43] Though it was originally approved in 1972, the proposal to build this college had been shelved for no good reason. Meanwhile, Ratchaburi, Suphanburi's neighboring province, requested a budget for building a similar college. This request, filed by a province that had traditionally obtained a far larger share of state funds than did Suphanburi, raised concerns that the budget earmarked for Suphanburi might be slashed or cancelled. These concerns proved to be premature, for Banharn revived the original proposal soon after he became an MP.[44] Thus, within just one year after he joined parliament, Suphanburi obtained state funds for two brand-new colleges.

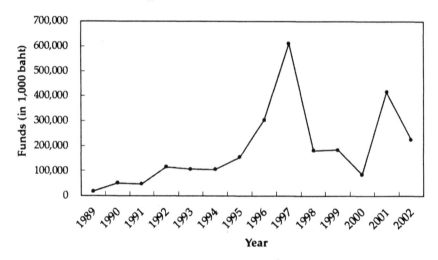

Figure 4.8 School Construction Funds for Suphanburi, 1989-2002[45]

Up to the mid-1980s, MOE funds for Suphanburi stayed at roughly the same level, as Banharn gave priority to road construction. From the late 1980s onward, however, the funds grew exponentially, coinciding with the take-off of Thailand's economy and the emergence of Suphanburi as a "one-party dominant" province (figure 4.8, above). In the mid-1990s, Suphanburi started receiving a sum of state

---

[41] Budget Bureau, *Ekasarn Ngop-pramarn 2519*, 3,6 (1975): 10–363; Budget Bureau, *Ekasarn Ngop-pramarn 2520*, 3,6 (1976): 183–418.

[42] *Khon Suphan*, March 16, 1977, p. 1.

[43] CPES, *Nangsue Anuson Phu Samred Kan Sueksa 2541* (Suphanburi: CPES, 1998); CPES, *Khu Mue Naksueksa Pii Kan Sueksa 2541 Withayalai Phala Sueksa Changwat Suphanburi 2541* (Suphanburi: CPES, 1998), p. 10.

[44] *Khon Suphan*, July 20, 1972, pp. 1, 12; *Khon Suphan*, November 10, 1972, pp. 1, 12; *Khon Suphan*, March 30, 1974, p. 1; *Khon Suphan*, May 1, 1977, p. 8.

[45] *Sources*: compiled from Budget Bureau, *Ekasarn Ngop-pramarn* 4,5, various years (1988–94); Budget Bureau, *Ekasarn Ngop-pramarn* 4,8, various years (1995–99); Budget Bureau, *Ekasarn Ngop-pramarn 2544*, 8,4 (2000).

monies that was utterly disproportionate to the size of its population. As shown in figure 4.9 (below), there is a robust correlation nationally between the provincial population and the funds allocated by the MOE, but Suphanburi represents a conspicuous deviation above the regression line. Even the economic crisis of 1997 did not affect Suphanburi as seriously as it did many other provinces. While the national budget shrank, Suphanburi's share remained relatively large. This is a dramatic reversal of the pattern of funds distribution before 1976.

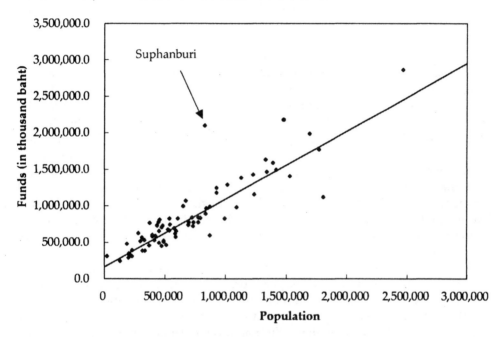

Figure 4.9 Provincial Population and School Construction Funds, FY1995-2001[46]

What accounts for this copious infusion of public spending is the effective stranglehold that Banharn established over the MOE in the late 1990s. First of all, he controlled the MOE as prime minister in 1995–96. While holding this post, he appointed Chaowarin Lathasaksiri, a CT Party MP from Ratchaburi Province, as deputy education minister. Furthermore, in 1995 Banharn appointed his bureaucratic client, Thaweesak Suksawat, to a key post in the Department of Physical Education. Before this appointment, Thaweesak had served as superintendent of the CPES twice (1985–87 and 1993–95).[47] Although the CT Party was in opposition in 1996–97, the party made a quick comeback in 1997. For the next four years, Banharn's family members and CT Party members monopolized the top posts in the MOE. First, in November 1997, his younger brother, Chumpol, became minister of education. When Chumpol resigned in September 1998, Pancha Kesornthong, another CT Party MP from Phetchabun Province, took over. Pancha was replaced in June 1999 by Banharn's well-known protégé Somsak Prisananandhakul, a CT Party MP from Ang

---

[46] *Sources*: compiled from Budget Bureau, *Ekasarn Ngop-pramarn 2538*, 4,5 (1994); Budget Bureau, *Ekasarn Ngop-pramarn* 4,8, various years (1995–99); Budget Bureau, *Ekasarn Ngop-pramarn* 8,4, various years (2000, 2001).

[47] CPES, *Khu Mue Naksueksa Pii Kan Sueksa 2541*, p. 11.

Thong, who had been deputy education minister until then. The post vacated by Somsak's promotion was filled by Banharn's eldest daughter, Kanchana, aged only thirty-four at the time. Both Somsak and Kanchana occupied their respective new posts until January 2001. Although Banharn did not hold any post in the MOE, the appointment of these people turned the ministry into his de facto fiefdom and allowed him to manipulate the budget allotments from behind the scenes as a "shadow" minister. One MOE official was woefully aware of this lopsided, politicized distribution of public funds, but said to me with resignation: "It couldn't be helped. When a person who controls your ministry wants to channel state funds into his province, you have to accommodate his wish, or you will be transferred."[48]

In the period following the economic crisis of 1997, another factor—the so-called "Miyazawa Fund" (*ngop Miyazawa*)—ensured the uninterrupted flow of money into Suphanburi's schools. The Miyazawa Fund, formally called *Khrongkan Ngern Ku Kratun Setakit* (The Loan Project for Stimulating the Economy), is the two-hundred-million-baht loan package that former Japanese Finance Minister Kiichi Miyazawa extended in 1999 to help Thailand weather the economic crisis. The fund aimed primarily to generate (temporary) employment opportunities for rural migrant workers who had lost jobs during the crisis. As the Thai government prepared to distribute the loan to the seventy-six provinces, Banharn successfully claimed a disproportionately large share of it for Suphanburi. According to one official record that an MOE civil servant showed me on the condition of strict anonymity, 14.4 million baht of the Miyazawa Fund was used to renovate eight primary schools in Suphanburi

The massive public spending enabled Banharn to establish many new schools throughout Suphanburi. In 1967, Suphanburi had a total of 414 primary, secondary, and tertiary schools. By 2002, the number increased to 486. The ratio of the number of schools to the provincial population is now comparable, if not superior, to that of other provinces. Thanks to Banharn, Suphanburi has caught up with other provinces. Also, one old building after another at existing schools has been renovated with the funds he channeled, giving these schools a new, modern look.

Banharn's contributions are especially remarkable in the fields of secondary and tertiary school education. Out of the thirty-two secondary and tertiary schools that exist in the province at present, fourteen (43 percent) came into being in the post-1976 period. In addition, Banharn channeled more than 400 million baht from the Ministry of Public Health to establish two new colleges—the Boromarajonani College of Nursing and the Princess Sirinthon College of Public Health—in 1993 and 1995, respectively.[49]

Many of these schools have acquired a dazzling array of impressive, modern facilities that have boosted and spread Suphanburi's fame or prestige nationwide. An outstanding example is the Sports School of Suphanburi (SSS), established in 1991 as the first sports school in Thailand, where highly talented athletes study, live, and eat for free from age five.[50] The origin of the SSS dates back to early 1989, when

---

[48] Interview, March 12, 2000.

[49] Budget Bureau, *Ekasarn Ngop-pramarn 2538*, 4,6 (1994): 280, 303; Budget Bureau, *Ekasarn Ngop-pramarn 2539*, 4,9 (1995): 326; Budget Bureau, *Ekasarn Ngop-pramarn 2540*, 4,9 (1996): 473, 494; Budget Bureau, *Ekasarn Ngop-pramarn 2541*, 4,9 (1997): 193.

[50] *Khon Suphan*, June 1, 1991, p. 9; SSS, *Khu Mue Nakrian lae Phuu Pok Khrong* (Suphanburi: SSS, 1997), p. 5; SSS, *Pratheep haeng Kan Kiilaa* (Suphanburi: SSS, 2000), pp. 22–24, 32.

Banharn proposed that a school devoted exclusively to training international-level athletes be created to put Thailand "on a par with civilized foreign countries."[51] The cabinet, led by then-Prime Minister and CT Party leader Chatichai Choonhavan, approved Banharn's proposal in April 1990. During the next five years, Banharn obtained a four-year MOE fund of 110.8 million baht for the SSS. Thailand's success in wooing the thirteenth Asian Olympic Games (1998) and the government's subsequent decision to hold some of the matches in Suphanburi allowed Banharn to justify this monumental allocation of continuous funds. Between 1995 and 2001, the school, despite the economic crisis of 1997, received an even bigger outlay—nearly 419 million baht—from the MOE.[52] The result is a variety of first-rate, state-of-the-art facilities, such as the 27.5-million-baht Provincial Stadium, with a seating capacity of 12,000 people; Thailand's first running track made of synthetic rubber; and the 99.2-million-baht "Silpa-archa Gymnasium," Thailand's first air-conditioned gymnasium, with a seating capacity of 4,000.[53] These facilities, touted as "the most modern in Thailand," "second to none," and "of international standards,"[54] led one newspaper reporter to write that the SSS is "better equipped than many reputable schools in Bangkok, such as Suan Kularp College or even Triam Udom Suksa."[55] Some facilities even received a royal blessing. For example, a modern swimming pool equipped with underwater cameras, for which Banharn allocated 43.2 million baht,[56] was officially opened by Princess Sirindhorn, the king's second daughter, in a well-attended, spectacular ceremony on May 20, 1994.[57] In a similar grand ceremony held on September 4, 2000, Sirindhorn inaugurated another project at the SSS, a three-story multi-purpose training hall, for which Banharn had secured nearly 95 million baht.[58] These ceremonies, televised throughout the country, considerably enhanced the already high visibility of Banharn's budgetary contributions to the SSS.

---

[51] SSS, *Khu Mue Nakrian lae Phuu Pok Khrong*, p. 5; SSS, *Pratheep haeng Kan Kiilaa*, p. 23.

[52] Budget Bureau, *Ekasarn Ngop-pramarn 2535*, 4,5 (1991): 317; Budget Bureau, *Ekasarn Ngop-pramarn 2536*, 4,5 (1992): 343–44; *Khon Suphan*, October 1, 1992, pp. 1, 2. See Nishizaki, "The Weapon of the Strong," chapter 7, for details.

[53] Budget Bureau, *Ekasarn Ngop-pramarn 2533*, 4,5 (1989): 333; Budget Bureau, *Ekasarn Ngop-pramarn 2535*, 4,5 (1991): 331; Budget Bureau, *Ekasarn Ngop-pramarn 2536*, 4,5 (1992): 362; Budget Bureau, *Ekasarn Ngop-pramarn 2537*, 4,5 (1993): 393; Budget Bureau, *Ekasarn Ngop-pramarn 2541*, 4,13 (1997): 72; *Khon Suphan*, October 1, 1992, pp. 1, 2; *Khon Suphan*, March 16, 1997, pp. 1, 10; *Khon Suphan*, April 1, 1997, pp. 1, 10. Only seven other provinces, such as Chiang Mai, Khon Kaen, and Songkhla, have a stadium with comparable facilities; none of these provinces is in the central region. Similarly, only three other provinces outside the central region—Trang, Yala, and Si Sa Ket—have a gymnasium with a comparable number of seats. Sports Association of Suphanburi (SAS), *Thiraluek Phithi Wang Silarert Arkhan Thi Phak Nakkiilaa Khanat 200 Tiang Changwat Suphanburi* (Suphanburi: SAS, 1998), p. 14; Budget Bureau, *Ekasarn Ngop-pramarn 2538*, 4,7 (1994): 1654; Budget Bureau, *Ekasarn Ngop-pramarn 2539*, 4,13 (1995): 96.

[54] SSS, *Pratheep haeng Kan Kiilaa*, p. 25; *Khon Suphan*, May 2, 1994, pp. 1, 10; SAS, *Thiraluek Phithi Wang Silarert*, pp. 5, 6.

[55] *Bangkok Post*, July 14, 1996, p. 2.

[56] Budget Bureau, *Ekasarn Ngop-pramarn 2535*, 4,5 (1991): 317; Budget Bureau, *Ekasarn Ngop-pramarn 2536*, 4,5 (1992): 343–44; *Khon Suphan*, October 1, 1992, p. 1.

[57] SSS, *Pratheep haeng Kan Kiilaa*, p. 25.

[58] Budget Bureau, *Ekasarn Ngop-pramarn 2539*, 8,7 (1995): 2–305; Budget Bureau, *Ekasarn Ngop-pramarn 2541*, 8,6 (1997): 2–249; SSS, *Pratheep haeng Kan Kiilaa*, pp. 28–30.

The SSS is hardly an exception. Many other secondary and tertiary schools in Suphanburi have developed into large and well-regarded institutions. For instance, Banharn–Jaemsai School I, the first school Banharn established with his own money (see chapter 3), started out with only seventy-two students in 1970, but its enrollment jumped to 1,666 by 1995, thanks to the top-notch facilities that Banharn built with state resources after 1976.[59] During the same period, the physical size of the school also grew, from less than 28,800 square meters to nearly 64,000 square meters. Many of its graduates have gone on to attend some of the most prestigious national universities in Thailand, such as Chulalongkorn, Kasetsat, and Silapakorn.[60] These Suphanburi students, mostly from low-income farming households, have now become doctors, engineers, and civil servants, thus achieving a good deal of upward social mobility. The school has also excelled in sports. In 1994 alone, its twenty-six students won gold and silver medals at provincial-, regional-, and national-level sports competitions. Thailand's women's soccer team, which won the gold medal at the 1995 Southeast Asian Games, held in Chiang Mai City, included eight graduates of Banharn–Jaemsai School I. In due recognition of these achievements, the school received a royal medal three times—in 1981, 1993, and 1997.[61]

It has not always been smooth sailing for Banharn in his efforts to channel state funds into all these schools. He has encountered several obstacles along the way. He has managed to overcome most of them, however, by mobilizing his clients, whose appointments he controls in the central patrimonial state. In 1996, for instance, in the face of repeated and vehement criticism from opposition MPs, the Budget Scrutiny Committee was forced to suspend a sixteen-million-baht project for Kanasoot, Suphanburi's oldest and most prestigious secondary school. This project, involving the construction of a running track, soccer field, and spectator stands with a seating capacity of 2,800, was criticized as too extravagant for a provincial secondary school.[62] To overcome this opposition, Banharn had Wiboon Janchai, Kanasoot's superintendent (1992–97), appear in parliament and stress the "urgent" need for the project on the grounds that Suphanburi could host some of the 1988 Asian Olympics Games, which were to be held in Thailand. Thanks to this justification, the project was revived, although its funds were reduced to less than eleven million baht.[63] Wiboon had good reason to perform this out-of-the-ordinary service for Banharn. Simply, he owed his position to Banharn. Also, before attaining this post, he had served as superintendent of Banharn–Jaemsai School I, in 1988–92. By appearing before parliament, Wiboon tried to repay his personal debt to Banharn for advancing his bureaucratic career.[64]

Another knotty problem Banharn has faced several times concerns the ownership of land on which some of the development projects were to be carried out. For instance, the 16,000 square meters on which a five-story SSS lodging facility

---

[59] For details, see Nishizaki, "The Weapon of the Strong," chapter 7.

[60] In 1995, for instance, seventy-one students entered these universities. Banharn–Jaemsai School I, *Phithi Morp Thun Kan Sueksa Munnithi Banharn–Jaemsai Prachampii 2538* (Suphanburi: 1995), p. 7.

[61] *Khon Suphan*, December 30, 1999, p. 9.

[62] *Bangkok Post*, June 20, 1996.

[63] *Khon Suphan*, August 1, 1996, p. 4.

[64] In 1997, Banharn rewarded Wiboon for this and numerous other services by promoting him to director of the Provincial Office of General Education in Suphanburi.

(the so-called "Athletes' Hotel") was built in 1997–99 originally belonged to the Rice Research Institute of Suphanburi and was under the jurisdiction of the Agricultural Research Department in the Ministry of Agriculture. Likewise, the 80,000 square meters on which the SSS constructed a cycling field, tennis courts, and a soccer field in 2000-01 belonged to the Department of Religions in the MOE.[65] What Banharn did to clear these obstacles is instructive: He simply asked the two departments to make their plots of land available for Suphanburi's development. He did not encounter much resistance. In preparation for the construction of the Athletes' Hotel, for example, Suphanburi's governor Prasert Pliangransi (1995–98), with Banharn's backing, wrote a letter (dated November 23, 1995) to Wichit Benchasil, director-general of the Agricultural Research Department, seeking permission to use its land. A month later, Wichit wrote a formal reply (dated December 22) to say that the request was granted. This fast, positive response is a good indication of the influence Banharn could wield over the Ministry of Agriculture, where he once served as minister (1980–81).[66] Similarly, Banharn had the Department of Religions transfer its land to Suphanburi for the SSS projects by capitalizing on his control over the MOE in the late 1990s.[67]

Donations: Secondary Sources of Development

Although Banharn channeled a huge amount of public monies into Suphanburi, the state has not been the only source of development funds for the province. Banharn continued to donate his personal wealth, as he had done before 1976, to found or renovate various schools in his name.[68] Thus, he has maintained his image as the generous developer of Suphanburi. An example is Banharn–Jaemsai Polytechnic College, which Banharn founded in 1989 by donating five million baht.[69] In the 1990s, Banharn donated 26.7 million baht to found another three schools in his name—Banharn–Jaemsai Schools V to VII located in Song Phi Nong, Sam Chuk, and Derm Bang Nang Buat Districts, respectively.[70]

It is important to note, however, that Banharn's largesse alone was not enough to cover the entire cost of constructing these schools. State funds made up the difference. The shortfalls were due, in part, to Banharn's dwindling personal financial resources. Starting in the late 1980s, the profitability of his four Bangkok-based companies became wildly unpredictable. Saha Srichai Construction, for example, recorded a deficit of nearly twenty-five million baht between 1987 and

---

[65] *Suphan Post*, April 16, 2002, p. 11; *Khon Suphan*, April 16, 2002, p. 9.

[66] This letter (No. 0914/9072) is contained in SAS, *Thiraluek Phithi Wang Silarert*, p. 7.

[67] SSS, *Pratheep haeng Kan Kiilaa*, p. 26.

[68] For Banharn's donations to public health and other fields, see Nishizaki, "The Weapon of the Strong," chapter 8. Banharn has not donated his money to build any road, however.

[69] Banharn–Jaemsai Polytechnic College, *Ekasarn Naenam Withayalai Saraphat Chang Banharn–Jaemsai Changwat Suphanburi* (Suphanburi: n.d.), pp. 1–2; *Khon Suphan*, November 1, 1985, pp. 1, 2; *Khon Suphan*, April 1, 1989, pp. 1, 9; and *Sarn Khwam Fan Hoksip Pii Phana Than Banharn Silpa-archa* (author's name, place of publication, and publisher unspecified, 1992), p. 60. The last booklet was published in 1992, presumably by Banharn's children, to commemorate his sixtieth birthday.

[70] *Thin Thai*, January 16, 1990, pp. 1, 2; *Sarn Khwam Fan*, pp. 58–60; *Khon Suphan*, August 1, 1990, pp. 1, 2; *Khon Suphan*, May 2, 1994, pp. 1, 10; *Khon Suphan*, May 2, 2001, p. 9; *Suphan Post*, May 2, 2001, p. 8.

2002. B. S. International was in the black during the same period, but it reaped a yearly average profit of only 1.2 million baht. Another company, Nathee Thong, went bankrupt in 1990.[71] Before 1973, entry into the construction industry was restricted to a handful of well-connected companies, such as Banharn's. After 1973, however, many companies entered the market by relying on the vastly increased number of political patrons who could now be found at various levels of the state.[72] Banharn's companies lost out in the increasingly crowded and competitive market.[73] This, coupled with the rising prices of land and construction materials during the economic boom, severely constrained his ability to found new schools entirely with his personal wealth. Consequently, he had to turn to the state for supplementary funds. In building Banharn–Jaemsai School VI and Banharn–Jaemsai Polytechnic College, Banharn complemented his donations with a MOE fund of 21.2 million baht and 32.3 million baht, respectively.[74] Cynics might well conclude that he intended to rely on the state from the beginning. As long as he uses some of his own money to found a new school, no matter how small that amount may be, he will be forever honored as its legitimate founder. In any case, the most important fiscal source of provincial development in post-1976 Suphanburi has been the coffers of the patrimonial–democratic state, which Banharn, as Suphanburi's MP, has strategically and frequently tapped and harnessed.

ENDORSING THE PAROCHIAL PROVINCIALIST

As shown above, the post-1976 period saw MP Banharn build a number of high-quality roads and schools in Suphanburi by taking advantage of the patrimonial features of the democratic state. Collectively, these development works, ranging from huge to tiny in scale, visually represent the formerly unimagined transformation of Suphanburi into a modern province. The transformation is monumental for the people who have lived through, or have heard about, Suphanburi's backward past.

Precisely because of such visible, dramatic change, Banharn's ability to procure and allocate funds for his home province has come under a barrage of heavy attacks from opposition parties and Bangkok-based media. In 1987, for example, the opposition parties mounted a widely publicized vote of no-confidence against

---

[71] Department of Business Development, Ministry of Commerce (DBD/MC), Bangkok Company Files no. 3893 and no. 330/2513; DBD/MC, Bangkok Limited Partnership File no. 527/05. See Nishizaki, "The Weapon of the Strong," chapter 6, for details.

[72] Richard Doner and Ansil Ramsay, "Competitive Clientelism and Economic Governance: The Case of Thailand," in *Business and the State in Developing Countries*, ed. Sylvia Maxfield and Ben Ross Schneider (Ithaca, NY: Cornell University Press, 1997), pp. 237–76.

[73] As Banharn himself readily admitted in 2001, "All the factories I have are suffering a loss." CT Party, *Chart Thai Samphan* 13 (May–June 2001): 19. Nonetheless, Banharn has been a major shareholder at other successful companies, including Siam City Cement and Ayutthaya Life Insurance. DBD/MC, Bangkok Company Files no. 243/2512, no. 364/2518, no. 61, and no. 2975.

[74] Budget Bureau, *Ekasarn Ngop-pramarn 2530*, 4,5 (1986): 601; Budget Bureau, *Ekasarn Ngop-pramarn 2531*, 4,5 (1987): 519; Budget Bureau, *Ekasarn Ngop-pramarn 2532*, 4,5 (1988): 564; Budget Bureau, *Ekasarn Ngop-pramarn 2533*, 4,5 (1989): 646–47; Budget Bureau, *Ekasarn Ngop-pramarn 2535*, 4,5 (1991): 527, 600–601; Budget Bureau, *Ekasarn Ngop-pramarn 2536*, 4,5 (1992): 593, 728; Budget Bureau, *Ekasarn Ngop-pramarn 2537*, 4,5 (1993): 565, 786; Budget Bureau, *Ekasarn Ngop-pramarn 2538*, 4,5 (1994): 618, 620, 699; *Khon Suphan*, May 2, 1994, pp. 1, 10.

Banharn, then the minister of transport and communications. They accused him of having his personal appointee, DOH director-general Sathian Wongwichian, channel an unfairly large number of road construction projects into Suphanburi.[75] By the 1990s, Banharn established his unenviable reputation as "the guru of back-room maneuvering to divert government funds to Suphanburi."[76] Accusations of this kind were particularly common while Banharn was prime minister. During a televised parliamentary debate in 1996, an opposition MP accused Banharn of lavishing on Suphanburi the lion's share of the record-breaking 984-billion-baht national budget. The opposition MP referred to all the civil servants who colluded with Banharn as "budget bandits." He then grilled Banharn with the biting question: "How could Suphanburi be more important than Udon Thani, Khon Kaen, or Maha Sarakham [the provinces in the northeast, the poorest region of all in Thailand]?"[77] During another televised session, a group of opposition MPs sarcastically asked Banharn if he had any future plan to move the capital city from Bangkok to Suphanburi.[78] In the words of Alongkorn Palabutr, a prominent Democrat Party MP, "Though he is the country's leader, [Banharn] has the vision of a member of a provincial council who doesn't know how to administer the national budget."[79] Plainly, Banharn has been accused of showing favoritism toward his home turf, and he has been labeled a cunning, narrow-minded, and myopic "virtuoso" of sordid pork-barrel politics that impedes the development of Thailand as a whole.

Ironically, what these kinds of accusations have done in Suphanburi is to make Banharn all the more popular as an heroic MP. Precisely because all the accusations were widely reported in the national media, virtually all Suphanburians have become aware and appreciative of the fact that their province, which received short shrift from the state in the past, is now privileged in the distribution of funds. If not for the extensive media coverage, Banharn's contributions to this historical turnabout would have remained hidden in the stacks of impersonal government documents, to which ordinary Suphanburians have no access. Thus, the media unwittingly helped galvanize many Suphanburians of all ages and social classes into unified support for Banharn as the nation's foremost pork-barrel MP.

This support is reflected in the various ways in which Suphanburians mount an impassioned, partisan endorsement or defense of Banharn's patently parochial funds allocation. One line of defense highlights the "spillover" effects of Suphanburi's development, asserting that the projects built by Banharn benefit non-Suphanburians as much as Suphanburians. The following comments are typical:

> They say that Banharn favors [*ao jai*] Suphanburians alone, but when people in Chainat [Province] go for a vacation in Kanchanaburi [Province], which road do they use?—The road that runs through Suphan. If not for this road, they would

---

[75] Chaisit Phuwaphiromkhwan, *Ekasarn Laktharn Kham Aphiprai Mai Wai Wangjai Ratamontrii Khomanakhom, 21 Tulakhom 2530* (Bangkok: n.p., 1987), pp. 16–29, 61–76, 81–84, 160–161.

[76] *Bangkok Post*, February 27, 1993, p. 3.

[77] *Bangkok Post*, August 17, 1996, p. 3.

[78] *Bangkok Post*, May 25, 1996, p. 3. One of these MPs held up a poster that read: "Suphanburi 2000, Our Capital." See also numerous additional reports in *Bangkok Post* (September 22, 1995, pp. 1, 6; September 23, 1995, p. 3; September 28, 1995, p. 6; November 3, 1995, p. 5; May 20, 1996, p. 3; May 22, 1996, p. 3; May 23, 1996, p. 3; July 14, 1996, p. 2; and August 16, 1996, p. 3).

[79] *Bangkok Post*, May 23, 1996, p. 3.

have to make a long detour. So, it's not fair to say that only Suphan benefits from Banharn's road construction.—Primary school teacher (#79)

Banharn has built many schools in Suphan. Can only students in Suphan attend these schools?—Of course not. Students elsewhere can go. My niece in Ang Thong [Province] does. Can you still say that those schools benefit Suphanburians only? ... So it is not true that Banharn exploits [*ao priap*] other provinces.—Noodle vendor (#47)

The local newspaper *Khon Suphan* put forward a similar defense by claiming that the roads in Suphanburi help alleviate pollution and traffic jams in Bangkok: "People who are not smart criticize our smart MP [Banharn] for building many roads in Suphanburi. But, if not for these roads, which connect the northern and southern regions of Thailand, what would happen to Bangkok, the third dirtiest city in the world?"[80] In other words, these people defend Banharn by playing up the widely accessible or non-excludable nature of public goods.[81]

The majority of Suphanburians offer another defense—perhaps the most potent and vigorous defense. They admit up front that Banharn has unmistakably favored Suphanburi in the allocation of funds, but claim that there is absolutely nothing wrong with that. A low-ranking civil servant (#27) from a farmer's family made a representative comment: "People in other provinces condemn Banharn for developing his home province only. But that is his duty as Suphanburi's MP in the first place ... So why should he be criticized for doing what he is supposed to do? I don't understand. It's nonsense [*mai dai rueang*]." A housemaid (#6) in Muang District put it just as forcefully: "Before criticizing Banharn, those people [outsiders] should criticize *their own* MPs for not doing anything for their provinces. Why should they criticize an MP of another province? They have no right to criticize." These respondents, in other words, defend and support Banharn by turning the criticism of his parochialism on its head. If Banharn is the petty parochial provincialist that the Bangkok-based media and opposition parties say he is, that is exactly what he should be. He is a "good" MP who has manipulated the budget allocation process for Suphanburi's gains.

Many of my respondents raved about Banharn's parochialism in the broad historical context of state–periphery relations, stressing an element of historical justice or retribution that he has brought to Suphanburi. According to these people, the central state used to discriminate against Suphanburi by withholding development funds, but Banharn has now tipped the balance unmistakably in favor of Suphanburi. He has performed a historically important "mission" of redressing and reversing the formerly unequal relationship between the state and Suphanburi. Many Suphanburians may have felt powerless vis-à-vis the discriminatory yet redoubtable central state, but Banharn has given them a real taste of collective empowerment. This is a source of cathartic emotional satisfaction and pride. A farmer (#54) in Sri Prachan District put this well, asserting a strong sense of

---

[80] *Khon Suphan*, December 16, 1992, p. 3.

[81] Banharn himself defended his budget allocations in a similar way. Referring to roads in Suphanburi, he claimed that they "cannot be counted as being for Suphanburi alone because ... everyone has equal access to roads," and that he cannot "prevent people from the South using them to get to the North." *Bangkok Post*, May 22, 1996, p. 3.

entitlement to the state resources that were previously denied to Suphanburi: "Suphanburi used to be disadvantaged [*sia priap*], so Suphanburi is now rightfully advantaged [*dai priap*]. Banharn channels so much money now to make up for all the losses that Suphanburi had incurred before ... Actually, 'channel [*ao*]' is not the right word. Using the word 'pull away' [*dueng*] is better. He pulls the budget that we need away from the government and other provinces."

The Suphanburians who make this kind of comment defend and justify Banharn's favoritism with reference to a cutthroat, zero-sum scramble for state funds among all the provinces. They do not see the allocation of funds by the state as a fair game, whereby all provinces receive an equitable or satisfactory sum—a perception reinforced by their past experiences of having received no or insufficient funds (see chapter 2). To most Suphanburians (as well as the people in other provinces), local development is a sort of social "competition," in which a small number of provinces gain at the expense of many others; "our" loss is "their" gain.[82] Given such a view, Banharn's otherwise condemnable politicized distribution of public spending takes on a quite defensible, legitimate, and even heroic quality. In the words of one college student (#4) in Sam Chuk District, "If Banharn doesn't take all the funds, other MPs will take them, and their provinces will develop more than Suphanburi. That wouldn't be good for us. Better take all we can before others take it." A security guard (#43) in Bang Pla Ma District put it likewise: "If Banharn doesn't bring all the money to us, the taxes we have paid will be used to develop other provinces. I wouldn't like it." Another Suphanburian was quoted in the media as making a similar statement: "Our province always receives a huge share of the national budget [thanks to Banharn]. We know it's not fair to other provinces, but we want roads, schools, and other infrastructure services."[83]

These people do not exactly take pleasure in seeing Suphanburi prosper at the expense of other provinces. Some respondents actually expressed varying degrees of sympathy for other disadvantaged provinces. But even these people ultimately fall back on expressing their endorsement for Banharn's actions. Aware that the central state had historically skimped in its budgetary contributions to Suphanburi, many people have come to value a politician like Banharn, who puts the parochial needs of provincial development above all else. If Suphanburians' interests and preferences are parochial, that is not because they are uneducated, as urban-based scholars would argue. Instead, it is the product of their keen awareness of the historical relations between the central state and Suphanburi. Of course, preference for a Banharn-type politician is not unique to Suphanburi. As Arghiros shows, villagers in Ayutthaya, Suphanburi's adjacent province, similarly define the role or responsibility of politicians as winning a developmental "competition": They "expect that ... politicians at all levels will prioritize the needs of their home area *over those of other areas*."[84] This kind of expectation, however, has been probably stronger in

---

[82] For similar analyses, see Daniel Arghiros, *Democracy, Development, and Decentralization in Provincial Thailand* (Richmond, UK: Curzon, 2001), p. 213; Philip Hirsch, "What is the Thai Village?" in *National Identity and its Defenders, 1939–1989*, ed. Craig Reynolds (Clayton: Monash University Center of Southeast Asian Studies, 1991), p. 332; Ratana Boonmathya, "Contested Concepts of Development in Rural Northeastern Thailand" (PhD dissertation, University of Washington, Seattle, WA, 1997), pp. 131, 145.

[83] *Bangkok Post*, March 21, 2000.

[84] Arghiros, *Democracy, Development, and Decentralization in Provincial Thailand*, p. 213, emphasis mine.

Suphanburi, where peoples' resentful memories of the state-made "backwardness" remain vivid (see chapter 2). Banharn has met—and has exceeded—that expectation.

Interestingly, in objective terms, Banharn's budgetary contributions are not excellent across the board. In many areas of development, such as education and road construction, Banharn has indeed directed a disproportionately huge amount of public funds into Suphanburi. In a few other areas, such as irrigation, however, Suphanburi's share is actually proportionate to its population. I showed several respondents the official statistics that support this "fact." Their reaction was skepticism, outright dismissal, or even hostility. One respondent (#55), a niece of a well-known car-dealing provincial capitalist, snapped: "Where does the data come from? It is not believable. Perhaps, those who gave it to you want to frame [*sai rai*] Banharn." Another respondent, a corn-growing farmer (#56) in Song Phi Nong District, rebutted my data, asserting, "I don't understand math. I am not well educated. But I *know* your data are untrue."

What is notable about these (and other) respondents is that they could have used the official data to counter all the media criticisms concerning Banharn's allegedly blatant favoritism in directing state funds to his home turf. None of them was interested in doing so, however. Far from it, they spurned the official data to reaffirm their stand in support of Banharn's "unfair" funds allocation. In large part, this is because the data contradicted or impaired what they want to believe. To the extent that Banharn's highly conspicuous pork-barrel projects form a solid perceptual basis for articulating the new importance of the previously long-neglected Suphanburi, my respondents were unwilling to have their perceptions undermined by any outsider's unsolicited data. Acknowledging that the data had any merit would have detracted from their pride in what Banharn has done to elevate various Suphanburi villages from their backward conditions. They maintained this pride by snubbing my data.

Cast more broadly, the Suphanburians' accounts reveal the irrelevance of the worldwide ideological debate on high-sounding "Third World democratization." Suphanburians apparently do not interpret or appreciate the value of "democracy" in the same way that most urban-based scholars, policy-makers, and journalists do. To the latter groups, democracy is fundamentally all about a set of lofty yet abstruse political principles, such as freedom, human rights, equality, participation, civilian supremacy, and the like. On this assumption, there has been a normative debate on how to move Thailand's "half-baked" patrimonial democracy in a more transparent, rational-legal direction. In these debates, rural-based politicians such as Banharn are commonly criticized for obstructing the noble move toward better governance.[85] This debate culminated in the passage of the urban-biased "People's Constitution" of 1997, which disadvantaged rural-based politicians and voters. Many ordinary Suphanburians, however, see things differently. To them, the "flawed" democracy, as it has transpired in post-1973 Thailand, is a highly beneficial, if not impeccable, system or mechanism that has allowed Banharn, their "representative" (as an MP is called in Thai), to penetrate the niggardly and discriminatory central state—the formidable Bangkok-centric behemoth—and to "pull away" a formerly unimagined amount of national resources to their home province. To these people, Banharn has been able to do what he has done *precisely* because Thailand's current democracy

---

[85] See, for example, David Murray, "The 1995 National Elections in Thailand: A Step Backward for Democracy," *Asian Survey* 36,4 (1996): 361–75; Philip Robertson, Jr., "The Rise of the Rural Network Politician: Will Thailand's New Elite Endure?" *Asian Survey* 36,9 (1996): 924–41.

remains essentially patrimonial in nature. This feature is not a flaw, but a boon for Suphanburians. If it is a flaw, Banharn has nevertheless turned it ably and clearly to Suphanburi's advantage.

Herein lies the historically grounded, emotion-laden underpinnings or legitimacy of the seemingly defective patrimonial democracy at the local level. Banharn is the *positive* product and personification of this system. Far from representing and perpetuating "bad" democracy, Banharn is regarded as a politician who makes "good" democracy tick at the local level. Ordinary Suphanburians experience and feel the workings and effects of this democracy vividly through the figure of Banharn. Banharn is a window or telescope, as it were, through which Suphanburians can see the broader political processes at work that have handsomely benefited their province. Thus, the politics of his "unjust" or "wasteful" budget allocation, which the Bangkok-based media, opposition parties, and scholars have so heavily criticized, is the very object of admiration and source of provincial pride among many Suphanburians. This helps explain why the urban-based negative image of Banharn as a dirty, pork-barrel MP is commonly brushed aside, disputed, or rejected in Suphanburi.

In a way, my analysis here may appear to corroborate Anek's proposition that the rural electorate values democracy, "not as an ideal, but as a mechanism to draw greater benefits from the political elite to themselves and their communities."[86] I totally agree. However, there is a little more to the case of Suphanburi than what Anek's largely materialist interpretation would lead us to expect. Banharn has not just exchanged tangible infrastructure projects for Suphanburians' support in an instrumental sense; he has also become an integral part of their growing, collective pride in Suphanburi, the various parts of which have been developing rapidly together, thanks to the projects he has sponsored and championed. To the extent that Banharn's well-demonstrated personal generosity before 1976 supplied Suphanburians with a good perceptual basis on which to articulate an emergent sense of provincial pride, he has further solidified that basis since 1976 by bringing home the central state's succulent, high-quality bacon.

---

[86] Anek Laothamatas, "A Tale of Two Democracies: Conflicting Perceptions of Elections and Democracy in Thailand," in *The Politics of Elections in Southeast Asia*, ed. Robert Taylor (New York, NY: Woodrow Wilson Center Press, 1996), p. 221.

CHAPTER FIVE

LOCAL BUREAUCRATS DISCIPLINED

An affable man in his late twenties, Somboon (alias, #5) is from a rice-cultivating tenant farmers' family in U-Thong District. He received eleven years of education. He wanted to go to a technical college, but, like many others in his village, he gave up the idea because he did not want to be a financial burden on his parents, who had to raise three younger children. He now works at a small barber shop in Muang District. Despite not having finished high school, Samboon has a quite valid, if simple, explanation of why some countries develop faster than others—a puzzle that fascinates political economists. In his conversation with me one day, Somboon explained his pet theory at length:

> In every developed country—for example, Japan—civil servants are efficient and hardworking. They have discipline [*winai*]. They live by the principle that they must serve the people. You pay taxes to the government, and civil servants use your money to develop the country. Japan was destroyed by the war. There was nothing then, right? Now Japan is so prosperous ... How has it developed? I think it's because Japanese civil servants work hard for the people. They are honest.

Without raising any objection to his romanticized views of Japanese civil servants, I prodded, "What about Thai civil servants?" Somboon heaved a slight sigh and lashed out at them, though with some humor:

> I don't want to talk about them. No need to talk. They are lazy ... They go to work late ... Once in office, they chat. Before twelve, they leave for lunch. They come back after one, bringing with them cakes and deserts that they have bought outside. They sit down and eat them over coffee. At two, they finally start working. They read this and that document, and sign this and that. At three, they take a break. After 3:30, they do nothing but look at their watches [to wait for office hours to be over].

He continued after a brief interruption:

> But when we, poor people, go to talk to them about our problems, they say, "We are busy now. Come back some other time." They are like this. We must work to get money. I cut your hair, and I get money for it. Otherwise, my family would be starved ... Civil servants are different. They are government employees. If they don't do any work, they still get a salary. It doesn't matter whether they work hard or not. Of course, they don't work. Human beings are basically lazy. ... That's why Thailand is still not developed. We pay taxes, but civil servants do nothing but pocket public money.

Somboon draws a sharp, rather oversimplified contrast between Thai civil servants and their counterparts in the more "developed" countries. Nonetheless, he does touch on a major argument advanced by many noted social scientists: that the institutional capacity of the state to do what it wants to do is ultimately determined by the behavior of local-level state officials.[1] Without using any pompous academic jargon, Somboon described the theory of development in enlivened terms on the basis of his concrete life experiences. His description touches a deep chord with other villagers, who hold just as negative images of civil servants. Somboon probably knows that some civil servants are diligent and scrupulous, but apparently believes that they remain a minority. Or he may have deliberately exaggerated to make his point. In any event, having expressed his frustration, Somboon then made another interesting point, which is the central focus of this chapter:

> But I tell you, Suphan is better off than other provinces. We are lucky, because of our MP. You've heard Banharn's name, right? ... He is very strict. He controls civil servants well, so they must work hard ... They cannot do sloppy work [*ngan chui*]. He is a good administrator [*phu khuap khum thi dii*]. If not for Banharn, there would be lots of corruption, as in other provinces ... Did you see all the big, beautiful roads when you were coming to Suphan? Only Banharn can build such good roads.

Somboon's story—hardly an atypical one—defies the usual image of Banharn as a sleazy, predatory politician. I heard the story shortly after I arrived in Suphanburi. I could not grasp its meaning too well then, but it became clearer as I talked to more people and as I observed Banharn's behavior. His supporters do not believe that Suphanburi has developed rapidly since 1976 simply because he has channeled state funds into the province. Equally important, they praise him for personally monitoring how those funds are actually used by local civil servants (and contractors). He closely oversees every stage of a given project, whether large or small in scale, from implementation to completion. He does not entrust local civil servants to handle development projects competently and efficiently on their own. Most ordinary Suphanburians share this perception on the basis of their past everyday experiences (see chapter 2).

Many local civil servants find Banharn's close supervision officious and annoying, but they all must conform to his directions, given his power over bureaucratic appointments and the allocation of funds in the patrimonial democratic state—a power that has increased considerably since the rise of Suphanburi as a "one-party dominant province" in 1988 (see chapter 4). To the extent that civil servants are reliant on Banharn for jobs and funds, they simply have to do as he says, or they run the risk of being demoted or transferred. As a result, civil servants, as Somboon and many others note with approval, are made to work hard and honestly, as they should, in the interests of local development. In brief, Banharn's leadership has tamed and disciplined the otherwise lazy and exploitative state agents at the local level, according to his supporters.

---

[1] See, for example, Joel Migdal, *Strong Societies and Weak States: State–Society Relations and State Capabilities in the Third World* (Princeton, NJ: Princeton University Press, 1988).

Banharn's leadership style reflects one of his most salient personality traits: meticulousness, or fussiness. He pays inordinately punctilious attention to details. A Chinese word that is often used to describe this character is *longju* (廊主). Derived from the Teochew dialect, *longju* refers to a shop owner or manager generally.[2] The word is also sometimes used to imply a somewhat more specific and traditional, pre-modern type of owner or manager who directly and personally controlled all activities and the employees in his shop.[3] Banharn, the son of a Teochew merchant who grew up in traditional Suphanburi in the 1930s–40s, epitomizes a *longju*. He shows a marked propensity to control every detail and every person concerning Suphanburi—his provincial "shop." For many Suphanburians, especially Sino-Thais, Banharn and *longju* are synonymous; at the mention of the word *longju*, many people think of Banharn. It is indeed Banharn's meticulous leadership that has popularized the word in Suphanburi.[4]

Banharn's leadership style runs counter to the mainstream literature on Thai politics. This literature portrays many rural-based leaders as fitting the image of Janus-faced *nakleng*-type strongmen, who are fearless, violent, and brutal toward their enemies, yet generous and kind toward their supporters.[5] For instance, James Ockey, a noted specialist of Thai politics, pigeonholes Banharn as *nakleng*.[6] In the local setting of Suphanburi, however, Banharn actually displays a hitherto unrecognized non-*nakleng* type of leadership.

SURVEILLANCE OVER DEVELOPMENT PROJECTS

Inspections

Banharn's tendency to exert firm control over the bureaucracy is most vividly manifested in two modes of surveillance that he typically enforces. First is his frequent and meticulous inspection of local development projects. If he has provided state funds for renovating a school, for example, he makes it a rule to visit the school to check up (*truad*) on the progress of the renovation personally and to ensure that the civil servants and contractors in charge are not cutting corners. He is a veritable

---

[2] Shi Jie Hua et al., 世界華僑華人詞典 (Beijing: Beijing University Press, 1993), p. 747; Takejiro Tomita, *Tai-nichi Jiten* [Thai–Japanese Dictionary] (Tenri: Yotokusha, 1990), p. 1917.

[3] Pasuk and Sungsidh translate the word as "an executive manager." This translation might be a bit misleading because it connotes a manager in a modern company. Pasuk Phongpaichit and Sungsidh Piriyarangsan, *Corruption and Democracy in Thailand* (Chiang Mai: Silkworm, 1996), p. 104.

[4] Nikhon Chamnong, *Borihan Ngan Satai Banharn* [Banharn-Style Management] (Bangkok: Mathichon, 2000).

[5] David Johnston, "Bandit, Nakleng, and Peasant in Rural Thai Society," *Contributions to Asian Studies* 15 (1980): 90–101; James Ockey, "Business Leaders, Gangsters, and the Middle Class: Social Groups and Civilian Rule in Thailand" (PhD dissertation, Cornell University, 1992); James Ockey, *Making Democracy: Leadership, Class, Gender, and Political Participation in Thailand* (Honolulu, HI: University of Hawaii Press, 2004), pp. 81–83; Sombat Chantornvong, "Local Godfathers in Thai Politics," in *Money and Power in Provincial Thailand*, ed. Ruth McVey (Honolulu, HI: University of Hawaii Press, 2000), pp. 53–73; Pasuk and Sungsidh, *Corruption and Democracy in Thailand*, pp. 59–60.

[6] James Ockey, "Thai Society and Patterns of Political Leadership," *Asian Survey* 36,4 (1996): 353.

longju, who, according to many respondents, believes in a Thai proverb: "Whenever a cat is away, mice will get happy" (*maew mai yu, nuu raa rerng*).

Banharn's characteristic inspections did not start in the post-1976 period; he had conducted several such inspections before becoming an MP. For example, on February 20, 1970 and May 2, 1971, he inspected the construction of two schools that were being built as a result of his donations in Dan Chang District.[7] His inspections have become even more common since 1976, a pattern that reflects Banharn's appointive and budgetary power in the central patrimonial state. To give a few examples: On January 20, 1990, Banharn inspected the construction of a bridge and a paved riverside walkway in the Muang market town. Once he finished this inspection, he quickly moved on to check road construction projects in two other subdistricts.[8] Likewise, on October 16, 1999, he spent the whole day inspecting the construction of six development works—three roads, one temple, and two schools—in five districts that are separated by a distance of over one hundred kilometers.[9] He regards these development projects, not as impersonal public projects, but as *his* public projects.

Banharn does not inspect construction sites just once; he schedules repeated visits to the same sites over a long period of time until the construction is completed to his satisfaction. A notable example concerns the renovation of Khao Dee Salak Temple, located at the top of a little mountain in U-Thong District. This temple, estimated to be over four hundred years old, is locally known as the place where footprints alleged to be the Buddha's and dating back to the Dvaravati period (in the sixth to tenth century) were found in the 1930s. A group of archeologists was reported to have confirmed the footprints to be "the oldest, the most beautiful, and the most complete Buddha footprints in Thailand."[10] Despite this historic "discovery," however, little had been done since the 1930s to preserve the temple, and its condition steadily deteriorated.[11] Recognizing the significance of the temple, Banharn initiated a major six-year renovation project in 1993 by channeling nearly 34 million baht from the Fine Arts Department of the Ministry of Education.[12] Once this project got under way, he inspected the ongoing renovation fourteen times between 1993 and 1999.[13] Even after the project was completed, he visited the temple six times to inspect how well it was being maintained.[14]

---

[7] *Khon Suphan*, March 10, 1970, pp. 1, 12; *Khon Suphan*, May 10, 1970, p. 1.

[8] *Khon Suphan*, February 1, 1990, p. 2.

[9] *Khon Suphan*, October 16, 1999. See *Thin Thai*, September 1, 1983, pp. 1, 8; *Khon Suphan*, September 1, 1986, p. 3; and *Suphanburi Sarn*, October 25, 1986, pp. 1, 2, for other cases.

[10] *Khon Suphan*, February 1, 2003, p. 4.

[11] *Suphan*, December 2001, p. 7. (*Suphan* is a relatively new monthly newspaper published by the Provincial Office of Suphanburi.)

[12] Budget Bureau, *Ekasarn Ngop-pramarn 2536*, 4,5 (1992): 449; Budget Bureau, *Ekasarn Ngop-pramarn 2537*, 4,5 (1993): 498; Budget Bureau, *Ekasarn Ngop-pramarn 2538*, 4,5 (1994): 562; Budget Bureau, *Ekasarn Ngop-pramarn 2539*, 4,8 (1995): 405; Budget Bureau, *Ekasarn Ngop-pramarn 2540*, 4,8 (1996): 522; Budget Bureau, *Ekasarn Ngop-pramarn 2541*, 4,8 (1997): 157; *Khon Suphan*, May 16, 2000, p. 4; National Archives, *Phithi Yok Phum Khaobin Yord Phra Monthop lae Sompjol Roi Phra Phuthabat thi Wat Khao Dee Salak Changwat Suphanburi*, Jo/2543/3, Files no. 4-5; Provincial Office of Fine Arts, *Kan Buruna Boran Sathan lae Kan Jatsang Monthop Khao Dee Salak* (Suphanburi: Provincial Office of Fine Arts, 1999), pp. 33, 37.

[13] *Khon Suphan* (April 16, 1993, pp. 1, 2; November 1, 1993, p. 1; November 16, 1993, pp. 1, 9; December 30, 1993, pp. 1, 9; July 16, 1996, p. 10; March 16, 1997, p. 4; September 16, 1997, p. 1;

Likewise, while developing a huge wild marsh (named Chawak Marsh) in Derm Bang Nang Buat District into a tourist attraction and a reservoir for the benefit of 340 local farming households, Banharn inspected the project in person twenty-three times between 1998 and 2002.[15] More tellingly, throughout the process of building a new Provincial Hall with public funds of over 374 million baht between 1995 and 1999,[16] Banharn inspected its construction every week.[17]

Another prominent feature of Banharn's inspections is that they often take place outside regular working hours, typically both on Saturday and Sunday and sometimes before 8:00 AM or after 5:00 PM. For example, on December 5, 1995, the birthday of King Bhumibol, then-Prime Minister Banharn traveled to Suphanburi at 10:00 PM (after presiding over a televised grand jubilee in Bangkok) just to check all the electric ornaments that had been put up at various intersections in honor of the king. Once satisfied with their condition, he returned to Bangkok at midnight.[18]

During any inspection, a wide range of government authorities who are dependent on Banharn for promotions and state funds make it a rule to accompany him—a feature that characterizes any routine inspection tour made by King Bhumibol as well.[19] While inspecting any primary school, for instance, Banharn is always accompanied not only by its schoolmaster and teachers, but also by village heads, the chiefs of the Provincial Offices of Education, the relevant district/subdistrict chiefs, and their respective subordinates. Almost invariably, the governor and two deputy governors also accompany Banharn wherever he conducts any kind of inspection in Suphanburi. Sometimes, even high-ranking bureaucrats based in Bangkok take the trouble to tag along with Banharn. Figure 5.1 shows a photograph of one typical inspection, conducted at the aforementioned Khao Dee Salak Temple, during which Barnharn was followed by a long retinue of civil servants representing the U-Thong District Office, the provincial police, and the Provincial Offices of Archeology and Fine Arts. For numerous Suphanburians who have observed this kind of inspection tour with their own eyes, Banharn is at the forefront of state officials pursuing local development, both physically and metaphorically.

June 16, 1998, p. 4; August 16, 1998, p. 1; December 30, 1998, p. 4); and unpublished news stories supplied by an informant at the Provincial Office of Suphanburi.

[14] *Khon Suphan* (June 16, 2000, p. 4; July 1, 2000, pp. 1, 10; August 1, 2000, pp. 1, 10; September 1, 2001, pp. 1, 9; June 1, 2002, p. 1; September 16, 2002, p. 4); *Isara*, June 2002, p. 4.

[15] *Khon Suphan* (March 16, 1998, pp. 1, 10; May 16, 1998, p. 1; June 16, 1998, p. 1; July 1, 1998, p. 1; November 16, 1998, pp. 1, 9; December 1, 1999, pp. 1, 9; May 16, 2000, p. 4; October 1, 2000, p. 1; March 1, 2001, pp. 1, 4; May 2, 2001, p. 1; July 16, 2001, p. 1; October 16, 2001, p. 4; May 16, 2002, p. 4; August 16, 2002, p. 1; November 1, 2002, p. 1; December 1, 2002, p. 3); *Suphan Post* (April 16, 1999, p. 1; October 16, 1999, p. 4; January 1, 2002, p. 8; January 16, 2002, p. 4; October 1, 2002, p. 1); unpublished news stories supplied by an informant at the Provincial Office of Suphanburi.

[16] Budget Bureau, *Ekasarn Ngop-pramarn 2541*, 4,5 (1997): 43-44; Budget Bureau, *Ekasarn Ngop-pramarn 2542*, 4,5 (1998): 34.

[17] *Suphan Post*, August 16, 1999, p. 3; Provincial Office of Suphanburi, *Thiraluek Phithi Perd Phraborom Rachanusawri Phrabat Somdet Phra Junla Jom Klao Chaoyuhua lae Sala Klang Changwat Suphanburi* (Suphanburi: Provincial Office of Suphanburi, 2000), p. 41.

[18] *Khon Suphan*, December 16, 1995, p. 4.

[19] Paul Handley, *The King Never Smiles: A Biography of Thailand's Bhumibol Adulyadej* (New Haven, CT: Yale University Press, 2006), p. 128.

Banharn's behavior during any of his routine inspection tours can best be described as "strict" (*khem nguat, khiaw*), "meticulous" (*la-iad*), and "prudent" (*rorpkorp*)—three words that many respondents often used to describe and rave about his style of review. He checks the quality of any ongoing project thoroughly with civil servants and contractors by his side—a performance that reminds many villagers of King Bhumibol, whose frequent and detailed inspections of rural development projects are widely publicized on TV and in the print media. Consciously or unconsciously, Banharn conducts his routine inspections in the image of the revered king. Evaluating his own character, he stated, "I am very cautious and watchful. I won't allow any loophole [*chongwo*]."[20] If he finds anything unsatisfactory, he scolds the officials in charge, pointing his fingers in their faces—his characteristically domineering gesture, which many civil servants hate (see below).

Figure 5.1 Banharn inspecting the renovation of Khao Dee Salak Temple, December 7, 1998 (courtesy of an informant)

On another occasion, Banharn elaborated on his supervisory role with regard to road construction as follows:

I am the acting control manager for the Department of Highways ... I am very strict. I go and see *everything* on *every* road, whether they are leveling ground, pouring concrete, or laying wooden bases. If my car doesn't shake as it moves on

---

[20] *Khon Suphan*, March 1, 1987, p. 2.

the road, I let [the construction work] pass. If my car shakes, I will have the contractor repair [the bad spot].[21]

Such thorough scrutiny amazed the *Asiaweek* reporters who followed Banharn during one road inspection. They saw him scuffing a road with a deep frown and blasting at an accompanying official from the Department of Highways (DOH): "Not enough cement has been used here. This is why I have to come personally and check all the details. I suggest you get this repaired." The reporters further commented that Banharn's painstaking surveillance was not confined to road construction alone: "Attention to detail is Banharn's forte. Ordering the changing of a lightbulb or chastising contractors over the quality of a varnished floor in a sparkling new basketball stadium is all in a weekend's work for the former premier."[22]

Figure 5.2 Banharn picking up rubbish on the road[23]

Banharn also very carefully checks the aesthetic qualities of various public projects in Suphanburi. Just as some people are finicky about keeping their private homes clean and orderly, Banharn is fastidious about keeping Suphanburi—his provincial "shop" or "home"—clean all the time. In a manner that is reminiscent of

---

[21] Chart Thai (CT) Party, *Chart Thai Samphan* [*Chart Thai Relations*], 13 (May–June 2001), p. 17, emphasis mine.

[22] *Asiaweek*, February 4, 2003, p. 28.

[23] *Source: Suphan Post*, November 16, 2000.

Field Marshal Sarit,[24] Banharn sees beauty, cleanliness, and orderliness as the signs of civilization, and he cannot stand any evidence of dirtiness or disorder. According to one DOH official, as Banharn moves around from one construction site to another in his car, he looks out the window to see if the flowers, trees, and lawns planted in the median strips of major highways are in good condition. He takes note of anything that fails to satisfy him and demands that those civil servants in charge give immediate attention to that problem. It is not uncommon for him to call the chief of the Provincial Office of Highways Department (POHD) from inside his car and say something like, "I'm passing the 100-kilometer point along Highway 321 now. The flowers here are beginning to wilt ... They need more water," or "The lawn on the way to Don Chedi District has not been properly mown. Tell the workers not to be lazy." Also, if he spots any rubbish on the roads or in the median strips, he tells his driver to pull over, gets out of his car, and picks up the rubbish with his bare hands; photographs of such clean-up efforts are sometimes carried in the local press (figure 5.2). He then shows the rubbish to the officials in charge and tells them off for failing to maintain the roads in good condition.[25] Occasionally, he even walks along highways, inspecting the conditions of literally hundreds of trees and flowers.[26]

In addition, on the way to and from any construction site, Banharn sometimes makes a surprise visit to various schools and hospitals to check up on their conditions. As one schoolmaster (#57) in Muang District said, "Mr. Banharn doesn't need any special reason to visit our school or any other school. Suppose he is going from one district to another. He sees a particular school, and if he has enough time and feels like it, he tells the driver, 'Let's stop by at that school for ten minutes.'" The possibility that this kind of unplanned inspection could take place anytime keeps local civil servants constantly on their toes.

Meetings

As another manifestation of his meticulousness, Banharn calls frequent meetings with local civil servants to ensure that all development projects are going smoothly as planned. This is his second means of controlling and monitoring local development.

For example, on April 25, 2002, Banharn held a meeting at Chaophraya Yommarat Hospital, the largest public hospital in Suphanburi, and summoned the directors of all eleven public hospitals in Suphanburi to discuss a budget plan for the following fiscal year. At the meeting, which I observed in person, Banharn had each director report to him how all the budget items they had requested were justified and to what extent the funds allocated in the previous year were used in accordance with the original plans. The directors had to give rational and detailed explanations for every probing question Banharn asked. This was not the formalistic, content-empty ritual that Peter Hinton claims is typical of most bureaucratic meetings in Thailand.[27] There was absolutely no official hoopla or showiness (e.g., the

---

[24] Thak Chaloemtiarana, *Thailand: The Politics of Despotic Paternalism* (Ithaca, NY: Cornell Southeast Asia Program Publications, 2007), pp. 121-23, 148-49.

[25] Interview with a DOH official, February 3, 2000.

[26] See, for example, *Khon Suphan*, September 16, 2000, pp. 1, 10.

[27] Peter Hinton, "Meetings as Rituals: Thai Officials, Western Consultants, and Development Planning in Northern Thailand," in *Patterns and Illusions: Thai History and Thought*, ed. Gehan

presentation of flowers) involved. No attendee was served any food or special drinks beyond a glass of lukewarm water. This was a serious, down-to-earth, no-frills session held in a windowless room with no audience. Banharn appeared genuinely bent on getting satisfactory answers from the hospital directors in this face-to-face setting. Therefore, the atmosphere was very tense. A local newspaper reporter (#80) who had snuck me into the meeting room whispered: "This is like an oral examination at a university, and it's a grueling exam. It's not easy. But if you are a civil servant here, you must pass the exam."

Figure 5.3 Banharn chairing a meeting with civil servants[28]

Another project that spawned a number of meetings involved the renovation of the aforementioned Khao Dee Salak Temple. In initiating this project, Banharn established three committees and appointed himself chairman of all three. A variety of high-ranking civil servants in Suphanburi, ranging from the governor, deputy governors, and district chiefs to directors of the Provincial Offices of Education, Fine Arts, and Archeology, were appointed to these committees.[29] Throughout the renovation project, Banharn called and chaired a meeting with these committee members every two months between April and November 1993, and then every month between November 1993 and 1999 (see figure 5.3). At each of these meetings, Banharn demanded verbal briefings and written reports on the types, prices, and suppliers of construction materials ordered and used for the project, the progress achieved in meeting the targeted schedule for the renovation, the numbers and wages of workers employed, and so forth.[30] Likewise, throughout the process of

Wijeyewardene and E. C. Chapman (Canberra: Richard Davis Fund and Department of Anthropology, Australian National University, 1992), pp. 105–24.

[28] *Source*: *Khon Suphan*, May 2, 2002, p. 4.

[29] *Khon Suphan*, January 16, 2002, p. 8.

[30] Interview with an official from the Fine Arts Department, April 20, 2000.

constructing the Provincial Hall noted above, he called a meeting with the officials in charge every two months.[31] Each meeting of this sort is typically preceded or followed by Banharn's thorough inspection of ongoing construction or renovation in progress. If there is any discrepancy between submitted reports and what he sees firsthand, he demands a satisfactory explanation from the civil servants and contractors in charge.

Banharn makes it a point to call a meeting whenever any matter that concerns Suphanburi comes up. For example, as soon as former Japanese Finance Minister Kiichi Miyazawa announced that Japan would extend a 200-million-baht loan package—the so-called Miyazawa Fund—to Thailand in 1999, Banharn called a meeting with high-ranking civil servants to discuss specifically how the fund was to be used by all the relevant civil service offices in Suphanburi.[32] Sometimes, Banharn calls a meeting to discuss matters that many civil servants regard as trifling. In July 1997, for instance, he summoned as many as one hundred civil servants, including all the district chiefs and municipality mayors in Suphanburi, so that he could preach to them about the need to "maintain the cleanliness, neatness, and beauty of roads all the time."[33] To Banharn, this message was serious enough to justify assembling a large number of bureaucrats.

Omnipresent Normalizing Gaze

Since his election to parliament in 1976, Banharn has mobilized local civil servants to conduct numerous inspections and meetings of the kinds described above. Between 1976 and 2002, he conducted a total of 872 such routine checks in all ten districts of Suphanburi. Even while he was prime minister (1995–96), he managed to find enough time to carry out forty-five inspections and meetings in Suphanburi. The number of inspections and meetings has increased substantially since 1996, reaching a peak, at 102, in 1999—with a monthly average of more than eight.[34] Since he retired as prime minister in 1996, he has not held any cabinet post, which has given him lots of spare time to step up his surveillance efforts in Suphanburi. Banharn's reputation as a strict and nitpicking *longju*-administrator has thus been reinforced and perpetuated.

If we frame Banharn's style of governing in the language of Michel Foucault, his inspections and meetings "discipline and punish" deviant local bureaucrats who fail to live by the standards or norms that he has imposed.[35] These modes of surveillance enable Banharn to "normalize" or regulate the behavior of civil servants. According to Foucault, in an increasingly complex modern society, rulers (are compelled to) rely on a hierarchically organized system of observation, but in Suphanburi, where the social structure is still relatively simple, Banharn can enforce and maintain his

---

[31] Provincial Office of Suphanburi, *Thiraluek Phithi Perd Phraborom Rachanusawri Phrabat Somdet Phra Junla Jom Klao Chaoyuhua lae Sala Klang Changwat Suphanburi*, p. 41.

[32] *Khon Suphan*, April 16, 1999, p. 1.

[33] *Khon Suphan*, July 16, 1997, p. 10.

[34] Author's research based on the provincial newspapers *Khon Suphan*, *Suphan Post*, and *Thin Thai*. The provincial library holdings of these newspapers are incomplete. Therefore, the actual number of inspections and meetings is probably much larger.

[35] Michel Foucault, *Discipline and Punish: The Birth of the Prison*, trans. Alan Sheridan (New York, NY: Vintage Books, 1995).

panoptic control over civil servants directly and effectively, even at the lowest village level. Realistically speaking, given his inherent time constraints, Banharn cannot inspect every project in every village of Suphanburi every week. Neither can he read and digest all the details of literally hundreds of official reports submitted to him. But civil servants *imagine* that they are being watched by Banharn, and that they are the objects of his constant observation and control (see below for further elaboration).

A civil servant (#38) in neighboring Saraburi Province drew an informative contrast between Banharn and Pramarn Adireksarn, a former military general who, until his retirement from politics in 1996, had been continually reelected as Saraburi's MP. On the surface, the two politicians appear similar in several respects. First of all, they are roughly of the same age. Second, both belonged to the Chart Thai Party. Pramarn was its leader between 1975 and 1988, before Banharn took over in 1992. Furthermore, Pramarn has held just as many cabinet posts as Banharn has. Also, both have a business background: Banharn owns Saha Srichai, a Bangkok-based construction company (see chapter 3), while Pramarn ran Thai-Asahi Caustic Soda, a joint venture established in 1964 between Thailand and Japan. The two companies once enjoyed a cozy tripartite relationship with the Department of Public Works (DPW): when Banharn's company monopolized the DPW-funded construction of tap-water pipes in the 1960s, Thai-Asahi became the sole supplier of chlorine for the DPW.[36] For all these similarities, however, the two politicians differ considerably in leadership style. According to my informant, Pramarn was "a modern manager" who believed in the functional specialization of bureaucratic duties. As such, he entrusted civil servants of all levels in Saraburi to perform their respective duties according to their own plans. In sharp contrast, Banharn is a compulsive *longju* or "a total manager" (the informant's own translation), who must stick his nose into everything and personally see to it that civil servants in *his* Suphanburi behave in the way he wants them to. He does not give civil servants leeway to act independently.

Cynics might dismiss Banharn's leadership as a political "show" designed to make him look good in the eyes of Suphanburians. Such an interpretation is not wrong; whatever any politician anywhere does has a thespian quality.[37] However, the sheer frequency of the inspections and meetings Banharn has organized in Suphanburi can be viewed as an indication of his truly thorough nature. Even if one considers his *longju*-style leadership to be the dramaturgical performance of a cunning politician, one also must acknowledge that very few other Thai politicians have put so much energy into keeping up that symbolic act as consistently and for as long as Banharn has. He does not do it just before elections. In this respect, it is worth noting that Banharn resides in Bangkok. This means that to start inspecting a given construction site at 7:00 in the morning (which is quite normal for him), he has to wake up before 6:00, given that it takes at least one hour to travel from his Bangkok home to Suphanburi. After a day of inspections and meetings, he returns to Bangkok in the evening or at night, and, the following morning, he shows up in Suphanburi again. He would not have maintained this exhausting schedule for more than three decades unless meticulousness were part of his nature.

---

[36] Anant Sanokhan, *Thammai Phom Tong Than Banharn* (Bangkok: Klet Thai, 1988), p. 53; Sarthit Winurat, *Ke Roi Nak Kan Muang* (Bangkok: Wisurut, 1996), p. 76.

[37] Murray Edelman, *Constructing the Political Spectacle* (Chicago, IL: University of Chicago Press, 1988); and Erving Goffman, *The Presentation of Self in Everyday Life* (New York, NY: Anchor Books, 1959).

THE HABITUAL COMPLIANCE OF CIVIL SERVANTS

Many local civil servants deeply resent Banharn's nitpicking, officious *longju-*style administration. These people form the nucleus of a group of anti-Banharn Suphanburians. Presumably, the minority of Suphanburians who did not vote for Banharn in the past elections consists mainly of these people (see chapter 8 for more details). As I have observed, only a small number of high-ranking bureaucrats who owe their current positions to Banharn and are likely to be granted further promotions in the near future eagerly and slavishly follow his fussy leadership. Many other bureaucrats are quite resentful and critical.[38]

There are a few mundane reasons for their resentment. First, it is extremely tiring and burdensome to follow Banharn, both literally and figuratively. Since he conducts many inspections and meetings from morning until evening and often on weekends, civil servants who are obligated to accompany him hardly have any time to relax at home with their families. In addition, since they accompany Banharn "voluntarily" outside their regular working hours as part of their self-imposed official duties, they are not paid for their "excessive overtime work." As one civil servant (#58) groused, "Of all the civil servants in Thailand, I bet that those in Suphanburi are the most tired. You work here for one year, and you will look ten years older!" Another civil servant (#81) said with reference to former Governor Wiphat Khongmalai (1998–2003): "Wherever Banharn goes in Suphanburi, Wiphat has to go there … In other provinces, the governor sits back behind the desk and gives orders. In Suphanburi, the governor's job is to be outside, following Banharn and taking his orders." Still another civil servant (#59) grumbled: "They say Japanese workers are workaholics. But Suphanburi's civil servants work just as hard. The difference is that it is in the nature of the Japanese to work hard, but we are forced to be hardworking." The usual image of well-connected civil servants in late developing countries is that they are lazy. In Suphanburi, however, the need to remain in Banharn's favor pushes bureaucrats to be diligent; they cannot afford to slack off.

Second, many civil servants find Banharn's leadership style insulting, for they must put up with a relentless barrage of overbearing actions (e.g., finger-pointing) and harsh words in public. In a society like Thailand's, which puts a premium on saving face, such behavior is particularly unbearable. One senior civil servant (#82) ranted: "Pointing your finger at someone is not part of Thai manners, but Banharn does it all the time without thinking about the feelings of others." I myself have seen him crudely point his finger at his bureaucratic subordinates many times (figure 5.4).

---

[38] Banharn's meticulousness has caused serious friction with other CT Party MPs, too. One is his own brother Chumpol, who resigned as minister of education in 1998 because of Banharn's "constant interference." According to one civil servant in Suphanburi, Chumpol, who holds a master's degree in public administration from Syracuse University, has "a modern head" and could not accept Banharn's "traditional type of administration." Another estranged CT Party MP is Pongpol Adireksarn, the son of the aforementioned Pramarn. Pongpol resigned as minister of agriculture in 2000, because Banharn made him repeatedly submit reports describing how the loan from the Asian Development Bank was being used. When Pongpol failed to supply the precise details that Banharn demanded, Banharn lost his temper and complained to the press: "I have made it a policy that I must be informed of *whatever* is going on at the ministry. I'm tired of asking about *every* development." Pongpol, for his part, was fed up with Banharn's interference and retorted: "I'm not a child. I am nearly fifty-eight." *Bangkok Post*, January 26, 2000, p. 6, emphasis mine.

Figure 5.4 Banharn giving an order to a civil servant in Song Phi Nong District
(June 3, 2002)

A few civil servants recounted one episode that indicates how mortifying it is to have to bear the brunt of Banharn's characteristic fastidiousness and his outbursts of anger. During his routine inspection of the newly constructed Provincial Hall in 1999, Banharn walked into one of the toilets and saw that its wall had been painted in a color different from the one he had requested—his favorite blue. He then lashed out at the accompanying contractor and ordered him to replace the wall with a brand-new one entirely at the company's expense. After Banharn left the scene, the contractor, a man aged over fifty, wept in public, while the civil servants present sympathized with him in silence. To these people, Banharn's reaction was unreasonable; the color of the wall in a toilet was deemed too trivial a matter to justify such harsh scolding and punishment.

Put in the broader historical context of Thai politics, Banharn's fussy *longju*-style of control symbolizes a dramatic reversal of the relative power relationship between civil servants and politicians. In the heyday of the so-called "bureaucratic polity," civil servants enjoyed a relatively higher social status than did the politicians.[39] Politicians had to curry favor with civil servants to obtain favors from the state. Now, the very opposite has transpired in Suphanburi. Civil servants have been completely subordinated to Banharn. Since Banharn is a short man (barely 4' 11"), civil servants must physically stoop down to talk to him—a gesture that accentuates

---

[39] Fred Riggs, *Thailand: The Modernization of a Bureaucratic Polity* (Honolulu, HI: East-West Center Press, 1966).

their humiliating subservience. In the minds of these civil servants, Banharn has exploited democratic institutions at the national level to create an authoritarian bureaucratic culture at the provincial level, a culture in which obsequious compliance is expected, demanded, and rewarded, and any kind of open dissent is dealt with severely.

Banharn is aware that a number of bureaucrats in Suphanburi hate his extreme meticulousness,[40] but, ultimately, he does not seem to care about what they think of him. Their "hidden transcripts," to use James Scott's terminology,[41] are not his concern. What he cares about is their *public* or *outward* behavior. As long as they do what he wants them to do—tag along with him during inspection tours, attend weekly meetings, and submit detailed reports on time—he is not interested in whether they do so eagerly or grudgingly. And they end up doing exactly those chores to fulfill his expectations. Failing to do so could cost them their current posts or state funds. They have no other choice, given the enormous influence that Banharn wields, or is imagined to wield, over bureaucratic appointments and the allocation of funds in the patrimonial–democratic state. One might say that Banharn conducts all the inspections and meetings to test the (outward) loyalty of his bureaucratic clients.

What contributes to civil servants' eager or reluctant obeisance is seeing that their predecessors achieved unusually rapid promotions thanks to their unwavering (public) loyalty to Banharn. These predecessors have set powerful examples for successive civil servants to follow. One such example is Winit Benjaphong, Suphanburi-born former director of the Regional Office of Highways Department (ROHD) (1988–95), who methodically carried out various road construction projects in accordance with Banharn's wishes. In 1995, then-Prime Minister Banharn rewarded Winit by appointing him deputy director-general of the DOH. Another outstanding Banharn protégé is Aree Wong-araya, the former governor of Suphanburi (1984–88), who served as deputy permanent secretary and permanent secretary of the powerful Interior Ministry between 1988 and 1996. While he was Suphanburi's governor, Aree cultivated intimate ties with Banharn by accompanying him on virtually every occasion possible. As one civil servant (#81) jokingly recalled, "Wherever Banharn was, Aree was there. Aree's secretary didn't have to have his daily schedule to know where he was; all she had to know was Banharn's schedule. The two were *paa thongko* [a fried twin dough stick—meaning they were inseparable]."[42]

Whether these (and numerous other) civil servants were genuinely loyal to Banharn we are unable to determine. What is certain, however, is that when they were in Banharn's presence, they followed his lead without showing any signs of resentment, and that they were amply rewarded for their fawning and slavish public behavior. The high ranks achieved by these civil servants serve as reminders to their successors that personal connections with Banharn are more important than administrative competence when it comes to bureaucratic promotions.

---

[40] CT Party, *Chart Thai Samphan*, 13 (May–June 2001), pp. 17, 18.

[41] James Scott, *Domination and the Arts of Resistance: Hidden Transcripts* (New Haven, CT: Yale University Press, 1990).

[42] They even played badminton—Banharn's favorite sport—together several times. See *Khon Suphan* (January 25, 1986, p. 11; August 1, 1989, p. 9; September 1, 1989, p. 9; February 1, 1990, p. 9; April 16, 1990, p. 9).

Consequently, civil servants who desire to advance or protect their current careers have a powerful incentive to tolerate Banharn's fussy leadership and even to pretend that they enjoy following it. In order to maximize their individual career interests, they force themselves to do what they would otherwise regard as too demeaning for socially respected "servants of the king" (as bureaucrats are called in Thai).

Thus, many civil servants in Suphanburi end up helping Banharn enforce the demanding and intrusive style of leadership that they resent so much. What is significant about this ironic, yet highly pragmatic, behavior is that when repeated day after day, week after week, month after month, and then year after year, sycophantic obedience to Banharn becomes a plain habit or routine for civil servants. To draw on Foucault again, in the ritualistic act of forcing themselves to do what they do not want to do again and again, civil servants are constantly and acutely made to realize, and instill in their bodies (as opposed to their minds), Banharn's close surveillance, sustained by his enormous appointive and budget-controlling powers in the central state. They are made to internalize and magnify "thousands of [Banharn's] eyes," as it were, which maintain "permanent, exhaustive, omnipresent surveillance" over their behavior and every stage of every development project in every part of Suphanburi.[43] This actual or imagined surveillance, in turn, serves, paradoxically enough, to drive civil servants to keep performing acts of public or bodily dissimulation—"a politics of 'as if.'"[44] A self-perpetuating process is at work here. One senior civil servant (#83) made a seemingly simple yet revealing remark in this connection: "I wish I didn't have to go to all the inspection tours and meetings. I'm too tired. But I still have to go. Banharn would know if I don't show up, and I would be transferred to Yasothon [a far-flung poor province near Cambodia]. I have a family to support." This statement captures how Banharn' (imagined) surveillance has "disciplined" or "habituated" the bodies of local civil servants to do what he wants them to do.

Contrary to what the literature on rural Thai politics leads us to expect, Banharn's bureaucratic clients in Suphanburi do not function as his vote canvassers at election time. Instead, they serve as willing or unwilling participants in his numerous routine inspections and meetings, both of which reflect his meticulous personality.

SUPPORT FOR THE FUSSY MANAGER

While many civil servants detest Banharn's fussy, intrusive leadership as a deep affront to their high social status, ordinary Suphanburians endorse it enthusiastically, for it has brought a variety of benefits that they had considered unimaginable in the "backward" past. First of all, thanks to Banharn's close supervision, local civil servants have come to implement a variety of development projects very "efficiently."[45] Many Suphanburians, especially Sino-Thais, call Banharn "Thailand's Deng Xiao Ping," and not without good reason. Banharn bears

---

[43] Foucault, *Discipline and Punish*, p. 214.

[44] Lisa Wedeen, *Ambiguities of Domination: Politics, Rhetoric, and Symbols in Contemporary Syria* (Chicago, IL: University of Chicago Press, 1999).

[45] My respondents used several different Thai words to describe this feature, such as *khlong khlaew, yang mii prasitiphap, krachap krachaeng,* and *wong wai.*

an uncannily striking resemblance to Deng, not just in physical appearance but also in the efficiency with which he has carried out various development projects.

Banharn's efficiency was clearly demonstrated during the construction of a school in one remote village (named Ta Pherm Khi) of Dan Chang District in 1998. Located in a mountainous area near the border with Uthai Thani Province and some 190 kilometers away from the provincial capital, this village, inhabited by about two hundred minority tribe people (Karens) from forty-one families, had long been the poorest village of all in Suphanburi. The level of education attained by its residents was also the lowest in Suphanburi, since the village did not have even a primary school.[46] In November 1998, Banharn visited this village to inspect its conditions firsthand. His subsequent action was extraordinarily swift. He called Dilok Phatwichaichoot, then chief of the Provincial Office of Primary School Education, and ordered him to build a new primary school with four classrooms in this village within seventy-two hours. Since this order came out of the blue, Dilok did not have enough construction funds to carry it out. To overcome this problem, Banharn told Dilok to get the construction materials by dismantling a building that was no longer being used at Wat Makham Tao School in the neighboring Derm Bang Nang Buat District. As a provincial *longju*, Banharn knew exactly which school buildings were no longer used and where they were located. Then he ordered the Provincial Administration Organization and the Provincial Offices of Highways and Accelerated Rural Development to provide manpower and trucks in transporting the dismantled materials to Ta Pherm Khi village over a distance of some sixty kilometers. As road construction agencies, the latter two civil service offices have nothing to do with school construction, but Banharn's power over bureaucratic appointments and budget allocations allowed him to mobilize their human and material resources smoothly without being fettered by bureaucratic red tape. At Banharn's behest, Dilok hired fifty-three workers to undertake the construction of the new school on three shifts, twenty-four hours a day.

Thanks to this around-the-clock work schedule, which entailed the mobilization of numerous civil servants and laborers, the construction of the first school in Ta Pherm Khi was completed in just fifty-nine hours.[47] Banharn's leadership made it possible to achieve what many people regarded as utterly impossible. He did not have to inspect the construction often. Nor did he have to call any meeting to supervise the project. Having followed Banharn's leadership for a long time, the civil servants had by this time been "habituated" to complete a development project within the strict time limit he imposed, even though he was not physically present to supervise their behavior. His actual physical presence was unnecessary to maximize bureaucratic efficiency. To modify the aforementioned Thai proverb, "even when the cat is away, the mice have learned *not* to get happy."

Ta Pherm Khi residents were naturally "extremely happy" about the new school. The news of its construction, sensationally reported in the local media and also spread by word of mouth, impressed many people elsewhere in Suphanburi. A reporter for the provincial newspaper *Khon Suphan* expressed amazement and admiration: "Many people must be speechless. How could they build a school in three days when it takes at least four to five days just to build a tiny house?"[48] An

---

[46] *Khon Suphan*, June 16, 1998, pp. 1, 10; *Ban Muang*, October 19, 1998, p. 15.

[47] *Khon Suphan*, December 16, 1998, pp. 1, 9. See chapter 6 for more details on Dilok.

[48] *Khon Suphan*, January 16, 1999, p. 4.

elderly Sino-Thai merchant (#103) in Muang District, who read about this project in a provincial newspaper, was full of praise, too: "You see how much civil servants can actually do. They are capable of doing this kind of thing if they put their minds to it or if someone who has power makes them put their minds to it." Similarly, a security guard (#43) from Bang Pla Ma District praised Banharn's leadership with an analogy:

> Civil servants are similar to spoiled and undisciplined kids. If you just give homework to that type of kid, he won't do it. He will play hooky [*dort rom*]. He will make up all sorts of excuses for not doing it. So you must make the kid sit in front of you and do the homework. You tell him, "If you don't do the work within one hour, you won't get dinner. If you don't want to starve, you do what I tell you. Don't whine. I'm only making you do what you are supposed to do.

These accounts suggest that ordinary Suphanburians view Banharn's *longju* leadership as a means by which they have gained a vicarious sense of collective empowerment relative to the inertia of the state, which had previously caused them to feel a sense of despair.

A civil servant (#60) in Don Chedi District—one of the few pro-Banharn bureaucrats in Suphanburi—recounted another episode in illustrating Banharn's efficiency. In 1999, the sewage system in the Don Chedi municipality broke down without warning. The residents filed an urgent request for help with the municipality mayor, but the municipal government did not have enough funds on hand to carry out the repair. Stumped, the mayor submitted a written request for emergency funds to Banharn. Within just one week, Banharn sent his personal reply to the mayor, informing him that he had arranged for the POHD to channel the highway construction funds left over from the previous year to the Don Chedi municipal government. As a provincial *longju*, he knew which bureaucratic unit in Suphanburi had a reserve of unused funds and the amount of that reserve. The POHD, in principle, is not supposed to use its funds for purposes other than highway construction, but Banharn's order effectively cut through the labyrinth of bureaucratic rules and regulations. The POHD chief, who is firmly under Banharn's control, followed Banharn's order immediately. Thus, within a week, a serious local problem was solved.

The civil servant who shared this story and even showed Banharn's letter to me expressed this opinion: "It is really no surprise to me that Banharn is well liked by villagers. He has been solving small problems like this for Suphanburians for many consecutive years." This civil servant, a local secondary-school graduate, then delivered an invective against the Bangkok-based journalists and scholars who portray Banharn as an incompetent, rural-based politician:

> They don't understand local politics at all. I want to ask them, "Have you ever lived in any village of Suphanburi? Have you ever talked to any villager here?" Villagers in Suphan are not stupid. They vote for a politician who does good things for them. Nothing is simpler. Do you need a college diploma to tell good MPs from bad MPs? No need! Only Bangkokians who make a fetish of diplomas [*baa parinya*] say a thing like that [so that they can] look down on people in the countryside. That's ideology [the civil servant's own word]. A diploma is only a piece of paper. You can buy it in Thailand if you really want it.

This comment took on a particularly poignant meaning at the time of our interview in 1999—just two years after the urban-based intellectuals promulgated the so-called "People's Constitution," which contained a highly illiberal clause decreeing that every MP must have a bachelor's degree. After making the above comment, the civil servant railed against the unwarranted and condescending assumption that justified the "BA clause" in what was widely touted as the most "democratic" constitution in the history of Thailand—that is, the assumption that uneducated rural-based candidates slip into the corridors of power by buying the votes of uneducated rural voters.

A few weeks later, I talked to several people in the area who had been affected by the sewage problem. One of them, a petty merchant (#24), made a characteristic remark that confirmed the civil servant's story:

> Fortunately, Banharn is our MP. If we were in some other province, we would be still having that problem. In other provinces, the problems of poor people like us are continually neglected. But Suphan is different because Banharn can take necessary action decisively [*ded khat*] ... Without him, we would have had to fix the problem on our own.

Andrew Walker's research in Chiang Mai Province supports the view expressed by this merchant. The villagers he interviewed criticized their municipal mayor "for not mobilizing assistance quickly enough" to cope with flash flooding. Furthermore, when these villagers requested state monies for an irrigation project, the mayor told them to "submit a formal written proposal to the local government," thereby taking an impersonal and time-consuming legalistic approach to their request. Thus, the mayor did not fit the villagers' image of an ideal politician—a "quick-acting benevolent patron."[49] In contrast, these villagers expressed their support for former Prime Minister Thaksin because he implemented various projects "very quickly and in a manner that largely bypassed [inefficient] local bureaucracy."[50] Residents in Suphanburi support Banharn for the same reasons.

A few media reports further bring Banharn's leadership into sharp relief. The daily TV program "Villagers in Deep Trouble" (*chaoban dueat rorn*), once featured a group of villagers in the southern province of Trang, who complained about an unsurfaced road in their community: "Our MPs have disappeared as soon as they got elected. We've never seen their faces since the election [of 1996]."[51] This kind of comment is rarely, if ever, heard in Suphanburi, where people have a chance to see Banharn mobilizing civil servants to undertake local development here and there virtually every week. On another day, the same TV program reported that in the provincial council election of February 2000, only nine out of five hundred eligible voters in one village of Trang cast their votes. The rest boycotted the election in silent protest against the incumbent provincial councilors and MPs who, despite the villagers' repeated and desperate pleas over the last two decades, had not kept their

---

[49] Andrew Walker, "The Rural Constitution and the Everyday Politics of Elections in Northern Thailand," *Journal of Contemporary Asia* 38,1 (2008): 92–93.

[50] Ibid., p. 98.

[51] "Villagers in Deep Trouble," ITV, November 19, 1999.

promise to bring electricity to the village.[52] Again, reports of this kind of long-standing neglect of local grievances are seldom heard in Suphanburi.

A second benefit of Banharn's meticulous leadership that many ordinary Suphanburians praise is the (image of) reduced bureaucratic corruption. Since Banharn keeps a close eye on all local development projects, the civil servants who might otherwise be tempted into dishonesty cannot expect to get away with cutting corners. As one DOH official said, "Banharn owns a construction company himself, so he can tell immediately if any substandard materials are being used. He knows all the tricks in the trade. You can't fool him. Nobody would dare."[53] Banharn himself illustrated the value of his approach by drawing a contrast between Suphanburi and the northern provinces of Nakhon Sawan and Tak: "Go and look at the road from Nakhon Sawan to Tak. It's very bad. It has completely crumbled. They have to build it all over again at a cost of 1,000 million baht. It is a waste of money."[54] The implication here is that the MPs of Nakhon Sawan and Tak generally fail to monitor local development projects, allowing predatory civil servants and contractors to siphon off huge profits by doing shoddy jobs. In Suphanburi, by contrast, Banharn demands that all projects meet the high standards he has set. Consequently, state funds reach the village level in full without being devoured by civil servants and their allies along the way—a striking departure from the pre-Banharn past, during which villagers chronically suffered from a lack of state funds (see chapter 2).

To the people who share this view, it is no surprise that a variety of projects of outstanding quality have come to distinguish Suphanburi. Roads and schools are among the most prominent examples, as discussed in chapter 4. In rebutting the widely held perception among Bangkokians that Banharn is a dishonest MP, one student (#4) at the gigantic Sports School of Suphanburi asked a rhetorical question: "Do you think that a corrupt politician could have built it? The school used a construction fund of at least several hundred million baht. If Banharn were corrupt, he could have built a much smaller school. ... His work performance [*phon-ngan*] shows that he is not corrupt."[55]

To be sure, the most important reason for the appearance of all the high-quality development projects is Banharn's ability to infuse massive amounts of state funds into the province. Nonetheless, his direct supervision is also quite important. A handful of other provinces ruled by influential veteran MPs, such as the aforementioned Pramarn Adireksarn of Saraburi and Newin Chidchob of Buriram, have received just as much public funding as Suphanburi has, yet fewer development projects have been initiated in these provinces, and those that have been completed rarely match those of Suphanburi in quality. This variation can be explained by Banharn's uniquely meticulous administration. Many empirical cases in late-developing countries have shown that access to public money alone is not sufficient to guarantee the completion of high-quality public projects. Competent and strict leadership must ensure that public money is not squandered at the receiving end—a fact of which many ordinary Suphanburians are acutely aware, based on

---

[52] "Villagers in Deep Trouble," ITV, February 6, 2000.

[53] Interview, February 3, 2000, Muang District, Suphanburi.

[54] CT Party, *Chart Thai Samphan*, 13 (May–June 2001), p. 17. Banharn's remark is not hollow political rhetoric. During my travel along the Nakhon Sawan–Tak highway in August 2008, I came across many bumpy potholes that had been patched with asphalt.

[55] See chapter 8 for more details on how Banharn's alleged corruption is spurned.

their past experiences. Banharn has filled that role admirably. As Banharn himself said in public, "Suphanburi has the same budget as every other province, but I personally ensure that it is properly used. I make certain that municipal officials do their duty, and I personally inspect different sites in the city on a weekly basis."[56] This is not empty political rhetoric.

Thus, many (though certainly not all) Suphanburians view Banharn, a man who is typically dismissed in the urban-based discourse as a parasite on juicy public projects, as doing his best to stem the corruption that might otherwise run rampant in Suphanburi. This is why Somboon—the barber introduced at the beginning of this chapter—made the remark: "If not for Banharn, there would be lots of corruption, as in other provinces." Whether corruption in Suphanburi *really is* less pervasive than elsewhere is open to question, but that is certainly the cumulative *image* conjured up by Banharn's *longju*-style leadership, displayed so frequently on what Clifford Geertz might call the "provincial theater" of Suphanburi, with numerous civil servants mobilized as the (grudging) supporting cast. Banharn's appointive and budgetary powers in the central state severely constrain the public behavior and speech of a great many civil servants in ways that allow him to project this favorable image in public.

The widely held view of Banharn as an honest developer explains why many villagers go over the heads of local-level civil servants and approach him directly to ask for particular development projects. For example, when he visited Phonsawan, a small outlying village of Song Phi Nong District, on June 3, 2002, one middle-aged female farmer walked up to him deferentially with a handwritten letter. Banharn stopped to ask her, "What is this?" She answered, "I would like you to build a road in our village. It is very inconvenient for us now." Banharn inquired, "How many households are there in your neighborhood?" "About twenty," the villager said. After exchanging a few more words with this petitioner, Banharn put the letter in his pocket. I do not know whether or how he has responded to her plea, but this incident indicates the extent to which ordinary Suphanburians regard local civil servants as untrustworthy and have accordingly come to rely on Banharn to mobilize resources for the efficient delivery of desired development works. In a social context that lacks intermediary political institutions capable of addressing villagers' grievances—no political party in Thailand has any branch below the provincial level—Banharn provides and personifies an informal yet vital form of efficient local governance.

Banharn's strictness or fussiness also compels civil servants to maintain public works in good condition all the time. This is still another benefit of his leadership that many Suphanburians emphasize and appreciate. The thought or fear that no sign of untidiness will escape his careful attention brings enormous pressure to bear on civil servants responsible for the "beautification" of Suphanburi—a far cry from the pre-Banharn past.

Typical examples are the median strips of most highways in Suphanburi, which are embellished with neatly trimmed bonsai-style trees and flowers. To satisfy Banharn's obsessive concern with beauty, cleanliness, and tidiness, DOH workers assiduously sweep roads, collect garbage, trim trees, and mow the lawn on three shifts, six days a week. Suphanburi employs far more of these workers than do other provinces. In 2001, for example, Suphanburi had 1,145 highway maintenance workers, while Kanchanaburi, Chainat, and Uthai Thani had only 372, 284, and 388,

---

[56] *The Nation*, January 28, 2003, p. 2A.

respectively.[57] The ROHD also dispatches trucks equipped with water tanks twice a day to sprinkle water on the median strips throughout Suphanburi. As a result, the roads in Suphanburi have won acclaim as "the best-looking and best-managed" in the country.[58] They even evoke "a touch of Singapore," according to one newspaper reporter.[59] To the extent that rural Thais believe that one aim of development is to "make ... roads and streets clean and to make [their] community tidy and neat,"[60] Suphanburi qualifies as a well-developed province. Banharn has landscaped the median strips to create and project a favorable collective image of Suphanburi to outsiders. Many provinces recently have added attractive landscaping along their own highways to emulate Suphanburi's, and Banharn has been invited to meetings with politicians and civil servants from across the country to share his tips on how to replicate the "Suphanburi model" elsewhere in Thailand.[61] One such politician was former Prime Minister Thaksin, who in 2003 invited Banharn to visit his home constituency, Chiang Mai City, every month and to help restore its beauty to a level that would match Suphanburi's.[62]

Schools have become as neat as the roads. Many teachers take great care to keep their schools free of rubbish. For example, in preparing for Banharn's visit in June 2002, several teachers in the aforementioned Phonsawan village scurried around the playground of their school, checking for any kind of trash. Spotting a cigarette butt on the path on which Banharn was going to walk, one teacher picked it up with his bare hand and put it in a plastic bag. As I looked at him in sheer amazement (and amusement), he said to me and the villagers standing nearby, "Mr. Banharn wouldn't be happy if he saw this."

Moreover, in their efforts to impress Banharn, many schoolmasters have put themselves out to beautify their respective schools with trees and flowers. If they can win Banharn's admiration, they can expect to enhance their chances of promotion. If their schools appear "mediocre" or "untidy" to Banharn, they stand to lose his favor. Some schoolmasters even buy flowers and trees with their own money, seeing it as a necessary "investment" in their future careers. Thus, in the words of one retired schoolteacher (#94) in Muang District, the schoolmasters in Suphanburi are forced to "compete in the de facto province-wide beauty school contest organized by Banharn." This is no laughing matter for some schoolmasters, who must run in this "contest" on a shoestring budget, both personally and institutionally. In one extreme example, recounted by a few informants on the condition of strict anonymity, a schoolmaster, who had been agonizing over how to "do up" his small school, died in office. The doctor could not determine the exact cause of his death, but the teachers

---

[57] ROHD (Suphanburi branch), *Sarup Phon-ngan Prachampii 2544* (Suphanburi: ROHD, 2002), p. 6.

[58] *The Nation*, January 28, 2003, p. 2A.

[59] *Bangkok Post*, September 25, 1995, p. 6.

[60] Ratana Boonmathya, "Contested Concepts of Development in Rural Northeastern Thailand" (PhD dissertation, University of Washington, 1997), p. 130. See also Philip Hirsch, "What is *the* Thai Village?" in *National Identity and its Defenders, 1939–1989*, ed. Craig Reynolds (Clayton: Monash University Center of Southeast Asian Studies, 1991), pp. 331–33.

[61] CT Party, *Chart Thai Samphan*, 13 (2001): 18.

[62] Banharn, however, was not optimistic about the prospects, since "it took him twenty years to make Suphanburi, a much smaller city than Chiang Mai, what it is today." *The Nation*, January 28, 2003, p. 2A.

at the school all believed that it was due to the severe stress and depression that stemmed from his ceaseless attempts to meet Banharn's high expectations.[63]

Last but not least, Banharn's tight control of civil servants is a source of personal emotional gratification for many villagers. The accounts of bureaucrats treating villagers, especially farmers, with contempt are well known. It is not uncommon in Thailand for civil servants to despise, humiliate, or ignore farmers, simply because they are poorly dressed and do not speak the standard Thai vernacular.[64] The villagers in Suphanburi have no shortage of such experiences, as attested by Somboon's story at the beginning of this chapter. Against this social and historical backdrop, the sight of Banharn, a short and poorly educated native of Suphanburi, lording it over much taller and better educated civil servants appointed by the Bangkok-based state, could not be prettier. A middle-aged petty merchant (#25) in Muang District, whose grandparents are farmers, offered a representative comment :

> I get emotionally vindictive satisfaction [*sa-jai*] when I see Banharn scold civil servants who normally act haughtily toward us. They can't say anything in his presence. All they can say is "yes, yes, yes." We need a man like him to put them in their place. Otherwise, they wouldn't do their duty.[65]

In short, Banharn has humbled supercilious and unresponsive civil servants. This is exactly what pleases many villagers in Suphanburi.

Thus, by exercising his meticulous control over local civil servants, Banharn has brought a variety of previously unimaginable benefits to ordinary Suphanburians and has established himself as the antithesis of unscrupulous state officials. This represents heady progress from the past. Some 78 percent of my respondents who commented on Banharn's qualities as a politician cited his "strict," "meticulous," and "efficient" management of local civil servants as the reason for the rapid development of Suphanburi in the post-1976 period. These respondents are all familiar with his *longju*-type leadership, having personally seen, read about, or heard about it in one way or another in the last three decades or so. Out of this constant and frequent exposure to public displays of his actions, they have come to form a very favorable image of him as an energetic and uncompromising provincial manager who pushes otherwise indolent, arrogant, irresponsible, and inefficient local-level agents of the state to perform their duties scrupulously in the interests of the public. Most civil servants in Suphanburi, as elsewhere in Thailand, are from outside the province and are rotated every few years. Therefore, they lack a strong interest in local development. Banharn, however, has set their priorities straight. His actions resonate strongly with the people who remember the hardships of the pre-Banharn past, during which they had to undertake onerous rural development works on their own, without assistance from the state.

The popular endorsement of Banharn's leadership is reflected in the hope expressed by quite a few Suphanburians that he will *never* be prime minister again.

---

[63] Interviews, January 19, 2000, and January 30, 2002, Muang District, Suphanburi..

[64] Ruth McVey, ed., *Money and Power in Provincial Thailand*, p. 4.

[65] A word with rich connotations, *sa-jai* is difficult to translate into English. It refers to the cathartic sensation that one feels when, for example, a person one hates gets into serious trouble or makes a fool of himself.

The reason behind this seemingly odd comment was explained by a car mechanic (#49) in Muang District:

> When he was prime minister, we saw less of him and saw fewer developmental projects [initiated] in Suphanburi because he was busy worrying about how to develop other provinces. As prime minister, he had to take interest in national development. But he was still heavily criticized for being corrupt. It's a great pity. So, why bother with national development? I just want him to be Suphanburi's MP and to continue to develop our birthplace as he has always done. Everybody around here talks like that.

A local newspaper echoed such sentiments when it commented on a spate of Banharn's inspection tours in March 1997, just four months after he was forced to resign as prime minister: "If he were still prime minister, he wouldn't be able to come back to work [for Suphanburians] like this."[66] The newspaper then expressed relief that Banharn was no longer prime minister.[67]

Thus, while scholars and journalists in general write off Banharn as a corrupt politician who is too incompetent to run Thailand, most ordinary Suphanburians see an entirely different politician in him. For these people, he is a quite respectable MP who has developed the once-backward Suphanburi, not only by channeling hefty funds from the Bangkok-focused central state, but also by establishing an efficient provincial administration that makes optimal use of those funds. He may have run Thailand dismally and disastrously, but he has governed his native Suphanburi quite competently. A local journalist spoke for many people in Suphanburi when he said: "I had an opportunity to accompany Banharn [during one of his inspection tours]. Having seen him work, I am not surprised that Suphanburi has prospered the way it has. It's all because he takes his duties seriously."[68] Another columnist put it just as succinctly: "Everything is developing in a good direction" because Banharn is a *"longju."*[69] Thus, Banharn's accomplishments as a thorough and stern manager have become another essential part of Suphanburians' growing pride in the accelerated development of their province since 1976.

---

[66] *Khon Suphan*, March 16, 1997, p. 4.

[67] *Khon Suphan*, October 16, 1997, p. 4.

[68] *Suphan Post*, August 16, 1999, p. 4.

[69] *Khon Suphan*, April 1, 1996, p. 4. See also *Khon Suphan*, January 16, 1999, p. 4; and *Khon Suphan*, December 1, 2000, p. 4, for other positive accounts of Banharn's *longju*-style administration.

CHAPTER SIX

IMAGINING BANHARN-BURI AT THE GRASSROOTS LEVEL

The preceding chapters have shown that Banharn has spearheaded a myriad of public development projects since the 1960s by using a combination of his own money, state funds, and a strict *longju* leadership. Public space in Suphanburi is now filled with such projects, and many ordinary Suphanburians take pride in them as symbols of Banharn's generosity, efficiency, and responsibility as the developer of Suphanburi. Taking an anthropological approach, this chapter examines more closely how such pride in Banharn and his accomplishments in developing Suphanburi are nurtured at the village level, the smallest administrative unit in Thailand.

My argument is that it is not because of Banharn's tangible developmental initiatives alone that Suphanburians have come to take pride in him the way they have. Their pride is also the product of the way those initiatives have been systematically advertised or broadcast to villagers via two symbolic mediums: signboards and ceremonies. Imagine a simple, hypothetical scenario: Banharn channels a state fund to renovate a road in Village A, and he inspects the construction several times until it is completed to his satisfaction. If that were all he does, however, the finished road, no matter how good it may be, would seem to villagers to be just an impersonal construction project, and Banharn would appear as little more than a businesslike politician who supervised the project. At worst, the road might be "anonymous," without being attributed unmistakably to Banharn.[1] Some residents of Village A, and especially outsiders, might never know that the project is Banharn's. Therefore, his developmental projects at the village level need to be actively "marketed" to the public. Otherwise, the pride in Banharn and his accomplishments would not emerge or would take a weaker form.

This is where signboards and ceremonies come into the picture. Once Banharn completes a particular project in a particular place, his local clients—civil servants and contractors—put up a signboard or organize a ceremony to commemorate the finished work and to impress it permanently in villagers' memories as a populist symbol of Banharn's *personal* benevolence, efficiency, and competent leadership. Some of these clients may not be eager to participate in institutionalizing such symbolism, but to the extent that they care about protecting and enhancing their careers and about securing state funds, they do not have much choice, given Banharn's enormous powers, which are rooted in the patrimonial–democratic state. This is especially the case in the post-1988 period, in which Suphanburi's unique

---

[1] To be sure, provincial newspapers, such as *Khon Suphan*, carry stories about Banharn's projects, but not about every single project. Moreover, the provincial newspapers are sold mainly to the middle class in provincial towns; people in small, far-flung villages have limited access to those newspapers.

position as a "one-party dominant province" has given Banharn unchallenged power to allocate state funds for any local contractor and to promote (and demote) any local civil servant in accordance with his personal wishes (see chapters 4 and 5). In this institutional context, Banharn can count on his clients to carry out the methodical advertisement and personalization of public development projects in his name via signboards and ceremonies.

It should be noted at the outset that, unlike their symbolic equivalents in many totalitarian states, these signboards and ceremonies are not aimed at cultivating a hollow and outlandish iconography or personality cult around Banharn. Instead, they convey a specific, believable, and down-to-earth message to whoever reads the signboards or attends the ceremonies: Suphanburi's numerous villages have developed because of Banharn's personal donations and his ability to channel state funds. Many villagers find this message emotionally gratifying, because it appeals to their shared point of concern: rural development.

The signboards and ceremonies, however, do not just commemorate Banharn's specific projects in particular villages of Suphanburi. More importantly for my argument, they make up the semiotic means through which villagers dispersed over geographical distance are incorporated into "Banharn-buri"—a common provincial community spearheaded by the compassionate and efficient developmentalist Banharn. Taken in isolation, signboards and ceremonies represent little more than local ritualistic practices. But as their number has multiplied over the decades, collectively they have come to perform an important integrative function: They induce villagers in one small locality to imagine that Banharn has carried out similar development projects in other locations within the province. This is how villagers' provincial identity, which centers on the imagined concept of Banharn-buri, is generated from the bottom up. Their identity has this firm symbolic foundation at the grassroots level; the identity is not anything artificially imposed on the villages from above.

It may not be the intention of Banharn's clients to foster this collective identity or pride. In all likelihood, they are simply interested in currying favor with Banharn by erecting signboards and organizing ceremonies. But the sum of their actions nevertheless has a significant, unintended effect on ordinary Suphanburians' perceptions of Banharn. Thus, contrary to what much of the literature on rural Thai politics would have us believe, Banharn's clients do not make up a vote-harvesting machine at election time. Instead, they serve as unwitting yet vital agents of symbolic production between elections. They are Banharn's public relations officials or "political entrepreneurs," who assiduously produce numerous signboards and ceremonies, through which ordinary villagers come to embrace and identify with the image of Banharn-buri. As such, Banharn's clients play a pivotal part in the symbolic construction of Suphanburians' provincial identity at the micro-level.

SIGNBOARDS

A typical signboard can be found in Khok Jet Luuk, a small, idyllic village with fewer than 120 rice-cultivating households, located on the fringe of Song Phi Nong, the southernmost district of Suphanburi.[2] In 2000, parallel to a narrow, muddy stream that runs through the village, Banharn built an impeccably smooth asphalt

---

[2] See figure 6.4 for Khok Jet Luuk's location.

road, 1.9 kilometers long and six meters wide, by funneling 4.55 million baht through the Public Works Department—probably the largest amount of state funds that the village had ever received. When this road was completed, a small signboard was erected at its end to advertise the amount of the construction fund, the fiscal year in which the fund was made available, and other details of the construction project. Next to this signboard is another slightly bigger signboard, about three square meters, which carries the message: "The Subdistrict Administration Council of Bang Tathen [under which Khok Jet Luuk falls] and Khok Jet Luuk villagers would like to thank His Excellency Banharn Silpa-archa for helping channel the construction fund" (figure 6.1).

Figure 6.1 A signboard thanking Banharn for channeling a road-construction fund

Two of Banharn's clients—the Bang Tathen Subdistrict Administration Organization (SAO) and the local contractor Thawon Suphanburi Limited Partnership—were responsible for erecting these signboards. Both were directly involved in the construction of the road and had good reason to be thankful to Banharn. The Bang Tathen SAO, for one, is dependent on Banharn for supplementing its small financial base with state funds. As a result of the decentralization policies implemented after 1997, every SAO sets and maintains an independent budget derived from local taxes, and has leeway to undertake village-level development projects on its own. This reform was conducted to bypass and weaken "powerful politicians," such as Banharn, who had dominated local politics by serving as conduits for state monies.[3] However, in the case of projects that require a large sum of funds (normally more than one million baht), SAO still has to rely on

---

[3] Daniel Arghiros, "Political Reform and Civil Society at the Local Level: Thailand's Local Government Reforms," in *Reforming Thai Politics*, ed. Duncan McCargo (Copenhagen: Nordic Institute of Asian Studies, 2002), pp. 223–46.

such politicians—a clear indication of the limits of the widely touted decentralization policy. Thawon Suphanburi, for its part, is well-connected to Banharn. Its owner, Thawon Jampa-ngern (b. 1947), served as vice president (1995–96) and president (1997–2001) of the Association of Suphanburians, of which Banharn is chairman. Thawon also belongs to the Sports Association of Suphanburi and the Suphanburi Chamber of Commerce, both of which are led by Banharn. Furthermore, Thawon is a part-time instructor at Banharn–Jaemsai School IV, located in his home subdistrict of Sanam Chai. Perhaps thanks in part to these connections, Thawon Suphanburi won a total of 324 road construction projects worth more than 350 million baht between 1997 and 2002.[4] Given their dependence on Banharn for state funds, the Bang Tathen SAO and Thawon Suphanburi sought to express their gratitude by erecting the signboard in the expectation of obtaining more funds in the future.

Contrary to what cynics might think, the "Thank you, Banharn" message on the signboard does not put words in the villagers' mouths. The villagers I talked to were extremely grateful for the new road; it is not one of the "highly visible ... infrastructure projects" in rural Thailand that Daniel Arghiros says are "of no particular benefit to the poor."[5] Before Banharn undertook the project, the road—the only road connecting this village to the outside world—was a bumpy, unpaved path. "Do you know what it was like to live in a village like this?" asked one farmer (#52). As an illustration, she recounted how her neighbor's baby nearly died of a high fever before reaching a district hospital situated about twenty kilometers away: "It rained heavily the day before, and the road condition was bad. So it took the parents some two hours to get to the hospital on a motorcycle." Given this condition, the villagers requested that the district office pave the road—their veritable lifeline—with asphalt. The district chief, however, was indifferent and took a dim view of spending public money on a tiny village like Khok Jet Luuk. The situation changed after 1997, when the government created SAOs throughout Thailand. In 1998, the Bang Tathen SAO took the initiative to contact Banharn on the villagers' behalf. The villagers were not too hopeful that he could deliver, given the government's budgetary crunch following the economic crisis of 1997. To their pleasant surprise, Banharn met the request. One villager (#22), therefore, was full of admiration: "Banharn doesn't desert poor people in a small village like ours. Under the circumstances, we would have understood if he had rejected our request. But he sympathized with us and had it approved by parliament."

The new road reminds these villagers of the hardships they had suffered at the hands of indifferent state officials in the past, while at the same time signifying Banharn's role in ameliorating those hardships. In other words, the road is the emotionally evocative site where the villagers are reminded of what their community was like before and how it has changed for the better, thanks to Banharn. Placed in this context, the signboard expresses and reinforces the villagers' collective sentiments of gratitude to Banharn as a benevolent populist. They are not grateful to him simply because local elites say they should be grateful; they are not passive consumers or blind followers of any meaning created by others. They are more than capable of interpreting what they see in their community on the basis of their past experiences.

---

[4] Department of Business Development, Ministry of Commerce (DBD/MC), Suphanburi Limited Partnership File no. 198.

[5] Arghiros, "Political Reform and Civil Society at the Local Level," pp. 233, 234.

Signboards of the same kind can be found at many schools throughout Suphanburi. In the late 1990s, Banharn channeled over 131 million baht from government sources—the Ministry of Education (MOE) and the "Miyazawa Fund," an emergency loan extended to Thailand by the Japanese government after the 1997 economic crisis—into forty-five primary schools in Muang, U-Thong, Song Phi Nong, and Bang Pla Ma Districts. These schools all put up signboards to acknowledge and tout Banharn's role in securing the funding. In addition, many of these schools named their newly constructed buildings "Silpa-archa Building" (*arkharn Silpa-archa*) after Banharn's family name, and have subsequently erected signboards bearing that designation. Before 1976, only those schools built with Banharn's personal fortune were named after him. In the post-1976 period, even those that were built with state funds and Japanese money have been dedicated to him. Thus, what are essentially *public* works that benefit Suphanburi's populace have been advertised, personalized, and immortalized as Banharn's *personal* contributions.

A typical example is Wat Phiharn Daeng Primary School in Muang District,[6] which in 1997 obtained Ministry of Education (MOE) funding of 1,834,000 baht for constructing a ferroconcrete building with four classrooms. Once completed, the building was dedicated and credited to Banharn as "Silpa-archa Building" (figure 6.2, below). Dilok Phatanawichaichoot, chief of the Provincial Office of Primary School Education (POPSE), was responsible for this naming. He was appointed to that post in 1996 by then-Prime Minister Banharn after having served as POPSE chief in Chainat and Chachoengsao provinces. In his eagerness to reciprocate for these appointments and to ingratiate himself with Banharn, Dilok made a behind-the-scenes suggestion to Wat Phiharn Daeng School (as well as the other recipients of MOE and Miyazawa funds) that their new building be named "Silpa-archa Building" to acknowledge and broadcast Banharn's budgetary contribution. The schoolmaster acted on Dilok's suggestion in his own attempt to curry Banharn's favor and possibly to win more projects in the future.[7]

Not to be outdone, the local contractor, Sin Somboon Kan Yotha, installed a marble plaque on the school wall, which thanks Banharn for the construction fund (figure 6.3, below). Founded in 1997, Sin Somboon Kan Yotha is a relative newcomer to the local construction industry, but after erecting the plaque, the company won bids for forty-three projects worth more than 36.8 million baht between 1997 and 2001, including construction projects at two Banharn–Jaemsai Schools.[8] Its owner, Anek Sulisathir, is Banharn's "favorite" (*thuuk jai*), according to one high-ranking civil servant who was directly involved in those projects.[9] Moreover, Sri Somboon Suwattana, another limited partnership founded by Anek in 1989, undertook a total of 143 projects worth more than 301 million baht between 1997 and 2000. They include a dazzling array of mega projects, such as the facilities at the Sports School of

---

[6] See figure 6.4 for the school's location.

[7] Confidential interviews with three MOE civil servants and two schoolteachers who know Dilok personally, March 22 and April 20, 2000. Dilok was handsomely rewarded for his service in 2000, when Banharn, by using his influence over his protégé and then-Minister of Education Somsak Prisananandhakul, appointed Dilok deputy director-general of the Bangkok-based National Office of Primary School Education.

[8] DBD/MC, Suphanburi Limited Partnership File no. 1027.

[9] Confidential interview, April 1, 2002, Muang District, Suphanburi.

Suphanburi (see chapter 4).[10] Anek was thus amply rewarded for having installed the marble plaque at Wat Phiharn Daeng Primary School.

Figure 6.2　Wat Phiharn Daeng Primary School;
the signboard in the center says "Silpa-archa Building"

Figure 6.3　A signboard at Wat Phiharn Daeng Primary School

---

[10] DBD/MC, Suphanburi Limited Partnership File no. 443. See chapter 4 for details on the sports school.

While Banharn's critics condemn these signboards as unfair and illegitimate symbolic appropriations of public projects, many villagers take a more positive view. Typical is a rice farmer-cum-street cleaner (#53), who lives near Phiharn Daeng Temple School, from which she and her daughter graduated. Having described how doors and floors in the old wooden building squeaked, she defended the new "Silpa-archa Building":

> Of course, he [Banharn] deserves it [having his name put on the building]. He is the one who brought the fund to our school. Could Jongchai [another Chart Thai (CT) Party MP of Suphanburi] have brought just as much money? Could Praphat [still another CT Party MP of Suphanburi] have done it? No, only Banharn could do it. The other MPs are good, but their powers [*baramii*] don't equal Banharn's. It is quite understandable. Politicians want to show off their accomplishments. That's the same everywhere. I would do the same thing if I were an MP.

Table 6.1 The Number and Density of "Banharn Signboards," by District, 2004[11]

District	No. of Signboards (A)*	Area size (sq. km) (B)**	Population (C)**	B ÷ A	C ÷ A
Muang	164	540.9	161,056	3	982
U-Thong	40	630.3	122,511	16	3,063
Song Phi Nong	38	750.4	131,067	20	3,449
Bang Pla Ma	39	481.3	85,888	12	2,202
Nong Ya Sai	22	420.2	48,999	19	2,227
Sri Prachan	19	181.0	65,000	10	3,421
Sam Chuk	26	355.9	57,924	14	2,228
Dan Chang	31	1193.6	62,151	39	2,005
Derm Bang Nang Buat	28	552.3	77,456	20	2,766
Don Chedi	25	252.0	46,149	10	1,846

For the villagers who share this kind of view, the "Silpa-archa Buildings" are totally legitimate symbols of Banharn's unmatched ability to draw state funds into formerly neglected small villages. By itself, the "Silpa-archa Building" does not have any intrinsic political meaning or value. What meaning or value it acquires is dependent on the viewers' perspectives. For many villagers in Suphanburi, it acquires a positive meaning, given their politically charged memories of the state's neglect in the past.

Signboards of the sorts I have described above suffuse all the districts of Suphanburi, including those that are *not* Banharn's electoral constituencies (table 6.1; figure 6.4, below). Signboards can be found even at the geographical margins of

---

[11] *Sources*: *Author's Fieldwork. ** Ministry of Interior, *Bantheuk Nak Nokkhrong 2544* (Bangkok: Ministry of Interior, 2002), p. 292.

Suphanburi, such as the sparsely populated upland districts of Dan Chang and Derm Bang Nang Buat. These symbols are particularly well-concentrated in the most populous district of Muang, especially in Muang municipality (figure 6.5, below).[12] The significance of the signboards' concentration becomes clearer when we realize that most of the land in these districts is farmland. In other words, the village communities that lie amid Suphanburi's expansive tracts of farmland teem with signboards that advertise Banharn's tangible contributions to local development. Many Suphanburians have been exposed daily to such signboards since childhood.

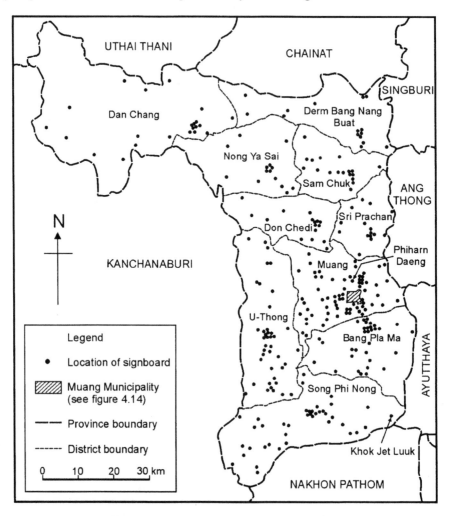

Figure 6.4 Geographical Distribution of "Banharn Signboards" in the Ten Districts of Suphanburi, 2004[13]

---

[12] I do not have comparable data on the other provinces, but my observations, as well as my interviews with non-Suphanburians, indicate that the density of signboards attributed to any particular MP is much less than what is evident in Suphanburi.

[13] Drawn by the Cartography Department, National University of Singapore. *Source*: Author's fieldwork.

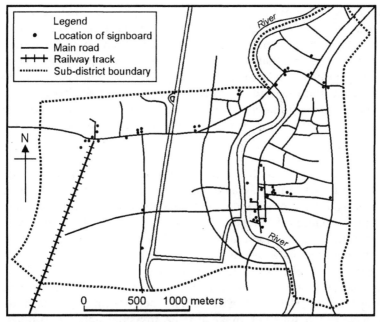

Figure 6.5 Geographical Distribution of "Banharn Signboards" in Muang Municipality[14]

The signboards perform an important social function other than simply extolling and enshrining Banharn's budgetary contributions in spatially limited small villages: They serve as concrete grassroots-level mediums through which people residing in a particular location come to imagine themselves as being part of a larger "Banharn-buri"—a provincial entity that consists of numerous villages developed by Banharn. This is suggested by a casual comment from the Khok Jet Luuk farmer (#52) cited earlier. As I was reading the roadside signboard near her home, she said: "If you are interested in this kind of thing, there are some more around here. One is in the next village, along the main road [located some three kilometers west of Khok Jet Luuk]. Go and see. Banharn built a bridge there. The villagers there had suffered without a bridge before, *just as we had suffered* without a road, but now they don't have to." A petty merchant (#22) who joined our conversation added: "There is still another signboard in Kritsana [a subdistrict located five kilometers to the north]. Banharn built a road there, *just like the one in our village*. And there are a lot more signboards in Muang District. He channels a development fund into every village in Suphan."[15] Neither respondent remembered the specific information given on the signboards (e.g., the sum of funds channeled by Banharn or the year in which the funds were made available), but both respondents knew exactly where Banharn had carried out development projects.

What these seemingly insignificant accounts suggest is that, through their simple yet important everyday acts of moving around in Suphanburi, people come to see "Banharn signboards" erected "here and there" in numerous places that lie beyond

---

[14] Drawn by the Cartography Department, National University of Singapore. *Source*: Author's fieldwork.

[15] These villagers were right. Later on, I did find the signboards they were talking about.

their own village communities. Through this process, they come to see the *comparableness* of many villages firsthand. They become aware that Banharn's contributions to development are not confined to their small localities alone, but extend to many others that were once also neglected by the state. Thus, a development project in one particular village begins to appear as a geographical extension of what the next village with similar social experiences has. To rephrase Benedict Anderson's expression, people come to think of their home village as *"one among many of the same kind* as itself." They come to "think about themselves, and relate themselves to others, in profoundly new ways."[16]

They do not have to visit all the constituent communities of Suphanburi to develop this extra-village identity. Once they realize that a handful of other villages have developed in the same way as their own, they come to assume or imagine that there *must* be countless other villages "somewhere out there" that have similarly benefited from Banharn's actions. Through such realization and expansive imagination, hundreds of thousands of people all over Suphanburi come to nurture a sense of sameness or oneness—identity—a notion that they belong to one and the same unitary trans-local entity. The geographic scope of their parochial village-level identity is gradually stretched, concentrically, to include their own subdistrict, the surrounding subdistricts, the entire district, the neighboring districts, and then all the other districts, which together make up the invisible and amorphous "Banharn-buri." Numerous localities that have, or are imagined to have, "Banharn signboards" are linked up to form this one large coherent provincial whole. Nobody knows (or has to know) all the constituent parts of Suphanburi. Technically, Suphanburi comprises 997 villages, and the names and locations of most of these are unknown to any one local resident. This anonymity, however, is the foundation on which a distinctive provincial identity is continually fashioned and reproduced at the ground level. If such anonymity is "the embryo of the national imagined community,"[17] the same can be said of an imagined provincial community, too. A particular villager may not have "the slightest notion" of any other villages that compose Suphanburi, but she is aware of, and has "complete confidence" in, their existence.[18] Thus, the notion of "Banharn-buri" comes to take on an eerie, ontological quality.

Signboards erected in various parts of Suphanburi, therefore, are not isolated or localized tools of simple signification, let alone shabby, unabashed propaganda, which cynics might make them out to be. They serve as the vital means of political communication and symbolic provincial integration.

CEREMONIES

Development ceremonies similarly serve as a vital means of political communication and symbolic integration in Suphanburi. Typically, such ceremonies are held to commemorate the laying of cornerstones for development projects and to celebrate the official opening of those projects. Banharn is invariably invited as the guest of honor for these ceremonies. Just as signboards enable him to set his seal on projects, his presence at ceremonies allows him to personalize public works and to

---

[16] Benedict Anderson, *Imagined Communities: Reflections on the Origin and the Spread of Nationalism* (London: Verso, 1991), pp. 36, 85, emphasis as in the original.

[17] Ibid., p. 44.

[18] Ibid., pp. 26, 35, 36.

send an unmistakable message to the attendees: "I am the one who made this project possible for you."

Ceremonies held in Banharn's honor are not new. Several such ceremonies were held before 1976 to trumpet Banharn's contributions to local development (see chapter 3). The ceremonies held since 1976, however, differ from those that came before in three important respects. First is the frequency of ceremonies. In the ten-year period before 1976, Banharn held 2.9 ceremonies on average per year. During the next twenty-seven years, the number jumped to twenty-seven per year (table 6.2, below). The increase is especially conspicuous in the post-1996 period. Since resigning as prime minister in 1996, Banharn has not held any cabinet post, which means that he has had lots of "free" time to attend local ceremonies. In a way, he has perhaps been locked in a self-perpetuating process: The more ceremonies held in his honor, the more he has realized how useful they are to him politically, which has driven him to arrange and attend even more such events.

In terms of the precision with which these ceremonies are organized and the visual spectacles of power they create, they increasingly resemble the widely publicized ceremonies attended by King Bhumibol and other royal family members each year. From his firsthand experience of having hosted royal ceremonies,[19] Banharn must have realized how effective "the plodding regime of royal ritual and social ceremony" was for establishing and sanctifying the king's authority.[20] This has perhaps motivated Banharn to emulate the fine example set by the benevolent king and to step up his own ceremonial presence in Suphanburi. Banharn, it might be said, is to Suphanburi what the king is to Thailand in this respect.

A second difference concerns the "geography of ceremonies." Before 1976, Banharn's ceremonies were held in a relatively small number of places. Over the last three decades, however, the geographical scope of host sites has expanded to cover almost all 110 subdistricts of Suphanburi (figures 6.6–6.8, below). Banharn has used even the remotest villages as a "public theater" on which to perform local development ceremonies. He is the indefatigable, omnipresent "maestro" of ceremonies. When he was sick or busy with his duties in Bangkok, his wife (Jaemsai), his eldest daughter (Kanchana), and/or his son (Worawuth) have attended ceremonies in his place to evoke his presence.

What has allowed Banharn to increase his ceremonial presence over great geographical distances is the expanding and excellent network of roads that he himself has built. The roads do not simply signify the physical transformation of the formerly inaccessible Suphanburi, as discussed in chapter 4; they also serve as "the infrastructure of ceremonial production," which has enabled Banharn to attain a very high level of physical mobility in performing development ceremonies in various places of Suphanburi, including its far-flung corners.

---

[19] As shown in chapters 3 and 4, Banharn invited royal family members to preside over opening ceremonies for several local development projects (e.g., schools) in the 1970s.

[20] Paul Handley, *The King Never Smiles: A Biography of Thailand's Bhumibol Adulyadej* (New Haven, CT: Yale University Press, 2006), p. 365.

Table 6.2 The Number of Development Ceremonies Held by Banharn, 1966–2002[21]

	Jan	Feb	Mar	Apr	May	Jun	Jul	Aug	Sep	Oct	Nov	Dec	Total
1966	1												1
1967													0
1968								1					1
1969	1			2			1				1		5
1970	1	1	1	1							1		5
1971					2			1					3
1972				1									1
1973	1	1		1		1							4
1974											1	1	2
1975		1					3	1	1		1		7
1976				1	2			3	1	1	2		10
1977	2	1	2	2		1		1	2	1	1	2	15
1978	2		3						2	2	1		10
1979	1		1		1	2			1	3	4	2	15
1980	1		1	5	1	1	1	7		1	4	2	24
1981	2	1	2	1		2		3	1	3		1	16
1982	1						2	3	1	5		3	15
1983	2		3			1		1	2		2	2	13
1984	1		3	1		1		1	1	3			11
1985	2	1	2				2	1	5		3	2	18
1986	3		4	4	2		1	1		7	3		25
1987	2	2	2	5	3		5		5	3	2		29
1988	2	2	2	5			1		6	1	6		25
1989	2	2			1	2	7	1		1	5		21
1990	8	2	2	2	2	2	3	6	1	2	4	1	35
1991	2	1	1					2	1			1	8
1992	2						2		2		1	1	8
1993	1	1		2	1		2			2	3	1	13
1994	2	1			2		5	1				2	13

[21] *Sources*: Various copies of the provincial newspapers *Khon Suphan, Suphan Post, Thin Thai,* and *Suphanburi Sarn*; personal observations.

Table 6.2 The Number of Development Ceremonies held by Banharn,
1966–2002, con't

	Jan	Feb	Mar	Apr	May	Jun	Jul	Aug	Sep	Oct	Nov	Dec	Total
1995	1	1					1	2	1	4	1	2	13
1996	6	6	1	1	2	1	4	*	*	*	*	2	23
1997	4	3	9	5	2	1	7	2	2	3	4	6	48
1998	3	4	4	4	3	5		3	1	3	1	11	42
1999	4	3	6	6	3	6	10	7	15	7	9	9	85
2000	11	11	6	4	2	4	3	9	5	2	1	1	59
2001	3	4	4	4	2	2	4	6	4	4	8	8	53
2002	11	2	3	12	9	4	5	9	12	2	9	6	84
Total	85	50	63	69	40	36	69	72	72	60	78	66	760

* There is no data for August–November 1996

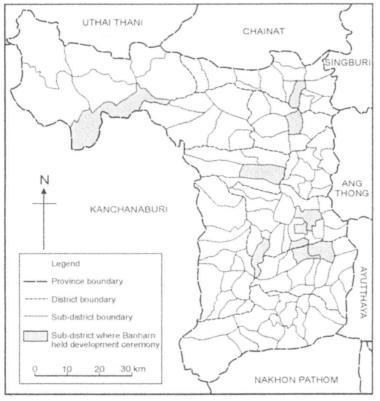

Figure 6.6 Subdistricts where Banharn Held Development Ceremonies before 1976[22]

---

[22] *Sources*: Various copies of the provincial newspapers *Khon Suphan, Suphan Post, Thin Thai,* and *Suphanburi Sarn.*

Figure 6.7 Subdistricts where Banharn Held Development Ceremonies by 1988[23]

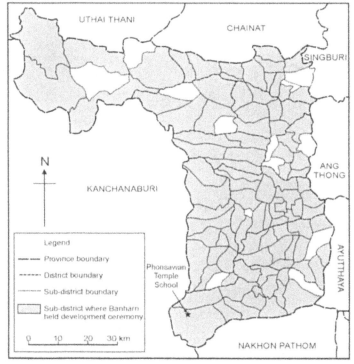

Figure 6.8 Subdistricts where Banharn Held Development Ceremonies by 2003[24]

---

[23] *Sources*: ibid.

A third difference concerns the power relationships between Banharn and local civil servants. Before 1976, Banharn organized his own dedication ceremonies by inviting high-ranking local bureaucrats as guests of honor. Now it is the other way around. All Banharn has to do now is to physically appear at ceremonies, which are meticulously planned and executed by numerous civil servants. These clients constitute what might be called "an institutionalized ceremonial network"— "impresarios, directors ... the supporting cast, stage crew, and audience,"[25] which Banharn can easily activate and mobilize whenever and wherever he wants to hold a development ceremony in Suphanburi. Some clients may not wish to organize or attend Banharn's dedication celebrations, but, as noted earlier, given his enormous powers over bureaucratic promotions and funds allocations in the patrimonial-democratic state, they have little choice but to assist him in the ceremonial construction of his authority. In other cases, local civil servants may view it as an important source of their own legitimacy to be seen and photographed with Banharn in the presence of ordinary villagers. In either case, Banharn may be testing these civil servants' personal loyalty to him by having them organize and attend ceremonies in his honor.

An illustrative example of Banharn's development ceremonies was held on June 3, 2002, at Phonsawan Temple Primary School, located in an outlying village of Song Phi Nong District, near the border with Kanchanaburi Province.[26] The village is connected to the outside world by a narrow asphalt road, which Banharn had built in 1988–90 by channeling 51.2 million baht from the Department of Highways.[27] The Phonsawan Temple School, with more than two hundred students, used to be in serious disrepair until 2000, when Banharn channeled 1.72 million baht to replace its old wooden structure with a new ferroconcrete building with four classrooms. The allocation of this fund, as in the case of the aforementioned road-pavement project, was a pleasant surprise to many villagers because Thailand was, at the time, still reeling from the devastating effects of the 1997 economic crisis. "Without having too much hope," one villager (#78) explained, "the schoolmaster contacted a member of the Provincial Administration Organization who is Banharn's relative. Just a year later, the school received the requested budget for a new building." The completion of this building was celebrated via a ceremony, the contents of which I briefly describe here as an illustration of how Banharn's reputation as a compassionate and efficient developer is created and trumpeted at the village level.[28]

The ceremony was organized by one of Banharn's well-known protégés: Kit Kiantisomkit, POPSE chief. Kit first contacted Banharn to set a date for the ceremony. Then, in consultation with relevant district-level officials, Kit drew up a detailed program for the event (figure 6.9, below), which Phonsawan Temple School distributed to all village households, encouraging (but never forcing) residents to attend. At Kit's behest, the school also erected a large and colorful signboard in front of its gate, announcing the date and time of the ceremony (figure 6.10, below). A son

---

[24] *Sources:* ibid., and author's research.

[25] Clifford Geertz, *Negara: The Theater State in Nineteenth-Century Bali* (Princeton, NJ: Princeton University Press, 1980), p. 13.

[26] See figure 6.8 for this school's location.

[27] Budget Bureau, *Ekasarn Ngop-pramarn 2533* 4,3 (1989): 218–19.

[28] Unless otherwise noted, the following account is based on my firsthand observation of the ceremony.

(#23) of a corn-growing farmer spoke for many Phonsawan villagers when, two weeks before the dedication, he said to me: "It's unbelievable that the former prime minister is taking the trouble to come to our small village."

PROGRAM
Opening the Signboard and Commemorating the Completion of a Building
Phonsawan Temple Primary School
Village 6, Nong Bo Subdistrict, Song Phi Nong District, Suphanburi
by
His Excellency Banharn Silpa-archa
21st Prime Minister

June 3, 2002

09:00 - Civil servants, merchants, people, school administrators, and guests of honor gather at the ceremony venue

09:30 - Sangha ceremony
   - Chief of Elementary School Education Commission lights candles to pay respect to three gems [*ratana trai*]
   - Master of ceremony requests that precepts be read
   - Monks chant Buddhist incantation
   - High-ranking civil servants and guests of honor make offerings
   - Monks give blessings

10:30 - H. E. Banharn Silpa-archa, 21st prime minister and the main guest of honor, arrives at the ceremony venue. Guests of honor, the Group of Housewives, teachers, and students present wreaths and flowers.
   - Chief of Provincial Office of Primary School Education gives an address.
   - Main guest of honor [Banharn] hands out medals to the people who have donated money to the school
   - Main guest of honor [Banharn] declares the building open and removes he cloth covering the signboard of Phonsawan Temple School
   - Monks read a *pali* verse to ask for good luck. Brass band plays good omen song [*phlaeng maharerk*].
   - Main guest of honor [Banharn] inspects the building and the exhibition by students

11:30 - Conduct *thord pha pa* ceremony
12:00 - People and guests of honor have meal together

Dress Code
   - Civil servants, subdistrict heads, village heads, and local government officials must be dressed in khaki clothes
   - Teachers and members of citizens' groups must be dressed according to the orders of their superiors
   - People in general must be dressed appropriately

Figure 6.9 A Program for an Opening Ceremony at
Phonsawan Temple Primary School[29]

---

[29] *Source*: Translation of a leaflet obtained from a villager.

Thanks to all this publicity, the ceremony, held on a muggy Sunday, attracted a crowd of some 250 people, men and women, young and old. By 8:00 AM, nearly three hours before Banharn's scheduled arrival, more than fifty villagers, almost all farmers wearing their everyday clothes and sandals, had arrived at the school. They were sitting and talking in a relaxed mood under a big, makeshift tent (figure 6.11, below). At the same time, several teachers from Phonsawan Temple School moved around the venue, ensuring that the sound equipment and other devices were in the right places and in good condition. As time passed, the number of villagers swelled. Dozens of high-ranking local civil servants (e.g., district chief, SAO members, and village heads) also arrived from all over the district, although many of them would probably have liked to stay at home on a Sunday. Also present at the ceremony was a brass band of twenty-seven students dispatched by Thap Kradan, another primary school in Song Phi Nong District.[30] The master of ceremonies (MC) was Phajon Burunarot, superintendent of Don Makluea Temple School in the adjacent U-Thong District, who is locally well known for his oratorical skills.[31] Thus, POPSE Chief Kit successfully mobilized quite a few people from both within and outside the Phonsawan village as "the supporting cast, stage crew, and audience."

The MC Phajon started addressing the audience through a microphone at around 8:20. Among the matters he talked about in rapid succession was how the schools in Suphanburi as a whole, including his own and Phonsawan's, had changed for the better in the last three decades, thanks to Banharn's funds allocations and donations. Phajon thus reminded the Phonsawan villagers that their school was not the only recipient of state monies channeled by Banharn. In other words, the MC included Phonsawan Temple School in a broader, extra-village frame of reference, within which Banharn's development projects were to be situated and appreciated. The fact that Phajon himself was from outside Phonsawan made the frame of reference all the more salient.

Phajon continued to play up Banharn's achievements by drawing an (exaggerated) binary contrast between Suphanburi and other provinces:

> People in other provinces ask, "Why do people in Suphanburi like Banharn so much?" For example, they wonder why we welcome him with flowers wherever he goes in Suphanburi. This is what they wonder about us. I often have a chance to meet teachers from other provinces, so I know. But they don't understand. Banharn takes a deep interest in Suphanburi. Suphanburi is different from other provinces, thanks to Banharn. Take as an example many signs of Suphanburi's current prosperity [*khwam charoen*], such as roads, schools, hospitals, and many others, which other provinces can't match [*suu mai dai*] … Why is Suphanburi prosperous like this now? Who is responsible for it? It's all because we have a

---

[30] In 1999, Banharn channeled more than 1.834 million baht for constructing a building with four classrooms at Wat Thap Kradan School. He then held an opening ceremony for the building in January 2002, five months before the ceremony in Phonsawan. *Suphan Post*, January 16, 2002, p. 4.

[31] By serving as master of ceremonies at Phonsawan, Phajon sought to express his gratitude to Banharn for the patronage his school had received. In 1998, Banharn allocated more than five million baht to Don Makluea Temple School to construct a four-story building with fifteen classrooms. This was followed by an opening ceremony for the building in January 1999. Author's research at Don Makluea; *Khon Suphan*, February 1, 1999, p. 4.

good MP who takes a deep interest in Suphanburi ... I once asked Banharn, "You've been developing Suphan like this for a long time. Don't you feel tired?" He said, "No." But, he is a normal human being just like us, so I believe he is actually tired, but he never says that in public ... Of all the prime ministers in Thai history, he is one of the most hardworking.

Figure 6.10 A signboard announcing Banharn's upcoming visit

Figure 6.11 A newly constructed building at Phonsawan Temple School; to its right is the covered ceremony venue

Propagandistic as they may sound to outsiders, those words seemed to delight the Phonsawan villagers. Nobody showed any sign of stifled or open cynicism, much less opposition. On the contrary, many listened attentively to Phajon with a satisfied grin, as the MC's speech, delivered with smooth-as-silk eloquence and passion, contained an emotionally appealing and exhilarating message for the villagers: Suphanburi, of which Phonsawan is a part, has acquired a variety of high-quality development projects, and has become the object of outsiders' curiosity, thanks to the compassionate and industrious leader that they were about to meet. To draw on Eric Hobsbawm's analysis of the symbolic construction of political authority, Phajon succeeded in "broadcasting [Banharn's goodness] on a wavelength to which the public was ready to tune in."[32]

The audience's enthusiasm and excitement rose shortly after 10:00, when Phajon, keeping in close touch with Banharn's driver over a mobile phone (a tool essential for the precise organization of a ceremony), announced: "Mr. Banharn is arriving in about twenty minutes, at 10:30, as scheduled ... So, please line up to welcome him." All the people then stood up, moved towards the school gate, and formed two beautiful straight lines, about 150 meters long, with small flowers in their hands. As Banharn's minivan arrived and he got out,[33] the brass band played a salute, and a horde of civil servants greeted him with a submissive and fawning *wai*—a Thai manner of putting hands together to greet seniors. Banharn walked between the lines, receiving flowers from the villagers, many of whom looked awestruck by the appearance of a former prime minister (figures 6.12–6.13, below).

Figure 6.12 Villagers form long lines to welcome Banharn

---

[32] Eric Hobsbawm, "Mass-Producing Traditions: Europe, 1870–1914," in *The Invention of Tradition*, ed. Eric Hobsbawm and Terence Ranger (New York, NY: Cambridge University Press, 1992), p. 263.

[33] Unlike many other MPs, Banharn never takes a ride in a flashy European car, at least while he is in Suphanburi.

Figure 6.13 Banharn receives flowers from villagers

Once everyone was seated, with Banharn in front (a seating arrangement which represented the power hierarchy of the attendees), Kit addressed the audience. He started by thanking Banharn for "developing all the villages of Suphanburi, including Phonsawan, for decades." In particular, he thanked Banharn for responding favorably and swiftly to the fund request filed by a small village school like Phonsawan. Kit did not mention exactly how Banharn obtained the fund. Interestingly, however, he used the word *don bandarn* (the spirit or magic to make the impossible possible) to describe Banharn's budgetary influence in faraway Bangkok—the geographical embodiment of the central Goliath state. The state, to most villagers, is little more than a distant and huge "black box" in Bangkok, the precise workings of which remain completely mysterious to them. Kit's speech evoked the image of Banharn somehow cracking open this esoteric black box, penetrating deep into it, and using his "supernatural power" to obtain much-needed funds from it.

The ceremony's climax came when Banharn and an entourage of high-ranking bureaucrats, including Kit, gathered in front of the newly constructed building. As Banharn pushed a button set up on a podium, a cloth that had been covering the building wall was pulled back to unveil a nicely decorated "Thank you, H. E. Banharn" signboard, which had been erected by a local contractor (figures 6.14–6.15, below).[34] Simultaneously, a series of firecrackers was lit and exploded with a roar, and the brass band played music with drums and trumpets to underscore the auspicious moment. Then, nine local Buddhist monks—nine (*kao*), which also means "progress" in Thai (although spelled differently), is considered an auspicious number—chanted a pali verse (*chaiya monkhol khatha*), to which the villagers listened and prayed solemnly by putting their hands together (figures 6.16–6.17, below). As

---

[34] Between 1997 and 2000, this contractor, Suphan U-Thong Phanit, undertook 316 projects worth over 252 million baht in Suphanburi. DBD/MC, Suphanburi Limited Partnership File no. 120/2505.

the monks finished chanting, Banharn stepped off the podium, talked to the brass band members for a while, and proceeded to inspect the new building. The ceremony, which lasted for more than two hours, thus came to an end.

Figure 6.14 Banharn officially opens a new building
accompanied by a brass band in the background

Figure 6.15 An unveiled signboard, which says: "We thank H. E. Banharn
Silpa-archa, 21st Prime Minister, for helping allocate a fund of 1,710,000 baht to
construct a building with four rooms at Phonsawan Temple School"

Figure 6.16 Monks chant a *pali* verse

Figure 6.17 Villagers listen and pray as monks chant

The Phonsawan ceremony, the successful and smooth organization of which required the coordination of numerous local civil servants, celebrated, dramatized, and sanctified Banharn's budgetary contribution to the physical metamorphosis of a small, dilapidated school building in Suphanburi's periphery. The ceremony juxtaposed the old building from the pre-Banharn past against a brand-new structure that presented itself right before the villagers' eyes. Making adroit use of vivid spectacles, music, and words, the ceremony served as an effective instrument for broadcasting and constructing Banharn as a caring and powerful populist "missionary" of development who made this change possible in an agrarian village located far from the provincial capital. To the extent that the paramount task of a politician is to display and broadcast favorable images of his authority over long geographical distances,[35] Banharn did just that through this ceremony.

The image of Banharn's authority was all the more strongly impressed on the villagers as they came into face-to-face contact with him; he did not appear snobbish and standoffish, as do many other MPs. For these villagers, "politics" (*kan muang*) was not an impersonal, distant affair reported in the Bangkok-based mass media. Neither was "local administration" (*kan bokkhrong thong thin*) an abstract concept that exists only in dry, annual bureaucratic reports. The Phonsawan villagers saw and felt both in front of them: Banharn *was* politics and local administration. While this physical closeness signified and engendered emotional bonds between Banharn and the villagers, however, the solemnity of the atmosphere, created by the presence of many high-ranking bureaucrats, the making of formal speeches, the playing of auspicious music, and the chanting of Buddhist monks, simultaneously created a measure of distance between the two. In short, Banharn was neither too distant from the villagers nor too close to them. This felicitous combination of closeness and distance imbued Banharn's village-level authority with affection, awe, and respect at once. The making of political authority, as several scholars analyze it, is a public show that politicians perform to create, reinforce, and perpetuate images, impressions, or meanings that are favorable to their rule.[36] The ceremony I have described here was important to Banharn in this respect.

This ceremony was not unique. Similar ceremonies attended by Banharn have been held virtually everywhere in Suphanburi with amazing frequency over the last four decades, cumulatively involving vast numbers of Suphanburians as the audience. Over 90 percent of the Suphanburians I talked to in different parts of the province said that they had attended or heard about Banharn's ceremonies during the last four decades. In this historical and social context, all these ceremonies have contributed to fostering and entrenching Banharn's positive image as a perennially tireless and benevolent local developer.

This point is best exemplified by the case of a middle-aged farmer (#78) in Phonsawan, who attended the ceremony described above. In the early 1970s, this farmer had attended another ceremony that Banharn held to commemorate the construction of a small primary school in her home district of Bang Pla Ma, situated some fifty kilometers from Phonsawan. According to a local newspaper, Banharn

---

[35] Jeffrey Herbst, *States and Power in Africa: Comparative Lessons in Authority and Control* (Princeton, NJ: Princeton University Press, 2000).

[36] See Murray Edelman, *Constructing the Political Spectacle* (Chicago, IL: University of Chicago Press, 1988); and Erving Goffman, *The Presentation of Self in Everyday Life* (New York, NY: Anchor Books, 1959).

donated 290,000 baht to build this school, which was subsequently named after him and his wife.[37] The farmer does not know this detail, but Banharn's generosity has left an indelible mark on her memory. She compared what she witnessed in Phonsawan with what she had seen in her native village more than thirty years ago:

> Banharn was young back then. He has now aged. His hair has grown gray, and he has wrinkles. He is more than 70 now. He's not a young man any more. But at his age, he is still doing what he was doing years ago. He is still going around Suphan to build various things for villagers like us and to celebrate their completion with the villagers. That has not changed at all after all these years. He is still the same. Is there anybody who is more sincere and hardworking than him?

For this kind of villager, the ceremony in Phonsawan did more than just reinforce Banharn's commendable role in developing one remote area of Suphanburi. It also served to (re)confirm the similarity of Phonsawan to other villages. All the villages and their residents for whom Banharn had *ever* held a development ceremony were connected together in time and space; the temporal and spatial distances that separate the past ceremonies and the one in Phonsawan were erased, as it were, to conjure up the image of sameness. To draw on Anderson's expression again, the Phonsawan villagers came to think of their village community as "*one among many of the same kind* as itself."[38]

Once the ceremony ended, the Phonsawan villagers probably imagined Banharn as a leader constantly on the go, attending similar events in countless other locations throughout Suphanburi that they had never visited or even heard of before. The announcements by POPSE Chief Kit and MC Phajon that Banharn "has been developing *all* the villages of Suphanburi" served to magnify the villagers' imagination by discounting Phonsawan's uniqueness. While seeing Banharn leave after the ceremony, the farmer's son cited earlier (#23) made a comment that is simple yet richly suggestive of this imagination: "Where will he go next week? Maybe U-Thong or Bang Pla Ma [District] ... Where was he last week?" When exposed to Banharn's development ceremonies "here and there" over a long period of time, the villagers come to get what Anderson might call "a hypnotic confirmation of the solidity of a single community" that is "moving steadily down (or up) history."[39] Their parochial village-level identity is thus broadened or scaled up to the higher level of subdistrict, district, and province.

Given this kind of imagination, the Phonsawan ceremony—a seemingly trivial ceremony held for a small, purely local audience—takes on considerable importance as the means of provincial integration. The ceremony signified that Phonsawan was no longer the isolated, neglected village that it once had been. Although physically linked to the outside world by only one road, Phonsawan now symbolically joined many other villages "out there," where Banharn had undertaken, or was going to undertake, some kind of state-funded or personal development project. The Phonsawan villagers are sure of the existence of those villages, even if they do not know what they are called and where they are located. This odd anonymity, which

---

[37] *Khon Suphan*, August 20, 1971, p. 1.

[38] Anderson, *Imagined Communities*, p. 85, emphasis as in the original.

[39] Ibid., pp. 26, 27.

Anderson calls "visible invisibility,"[40] is the essential ingredient of which villagers' pride in Banharn's real or imagined accomplishments is made. Insofar as villagers living in a particular locality develop a provincial identity through the everyday process of seeing "Banharn signboards," the ceremonial participation serves to reaffirm and reinforce that identity. In this sense, the ceremonies held in Phonsawan and other villages are not dispensable "icings on the cake" that cynical outsiders might portray them to be; they provide and mark enormously important occasions, through which hundreds of formerly dispersed small villages are symbolically and incrementally spun into an invisible collectivity—the broad imagined provincial entity of Banharn-buri—which Banharn has developed over the decades.

THE IMAGE OF BANHARN-BURI

Influenced by the way Banharn's numerous real or imagined development initiatives have been broadcast at the grassroots level, many villagers I talked to expressed a sense of strong and positive identification with the concept of Banharn-buri. An example is a farmer (#52) in the aforementioned Khok Jet Luuk, where Banharn built a 4.5-million-baht asphalt road in 2000. In admiring this road, the farmer said: "I went to Ang Thong [Province] last month to visit my niece. Her village doesn't have this kind of road. You can find it only in Suphan. Banharn goes around Suphan, carrying out projects like this everywhere. Why else do we call Suphanburi 'Banharn-buri'?" About ninety kilometers north of Khok Jet Luuk, a middle-aged farmer (#86) in Derm Bang Nang Buat, the northernmost district of Suphanburi, made a similar comment in praising a secondary school near his home, which Banharn built in 1999 by donating fifteen million baht: "He has done so much for us for many years in a row. There is no other MP like him anywhere. The official name of our province is Suphanburi, but actually it might as well be called Banharn-buri. After all, it is Banharn who has developed Suphan to be the way it is now ... We don't call our home Banharn-buri simply because Banharn is our MP."

Another farmer (#87) in Dan Chang District, located thirty kilometers west of Derm Bang Nang Buat, put it even more strongly by contrasting Suphanburi to Saraburi Province, where his relatives live:

> Saraburi had a nationally famous MP, Pramarn Adireksarn [a former CT Party leader before Banharn took over]. But do the people there call Saraburi "Pramarn-buri"? No, because he didn't do much there. Has he ever built any school with his own money? No. Did he channel public money to build roads in small villages like ours? No, not much. If he channeled any project, did he continually check up on its progress? No. If you go to Saraburi, ask people around, and you'll see. Only Banharn does those things. That's why we call Suphanburi "Banharn-buri." Other than Suphanburi, there is no province in Thailand that is nicknamed after its MP ... People in other provinces have never seen the faces of their MPs. Some people don't even know the names of their MPs. In Suphan, who doesn't know that Banharn is an MP?

These villagers are just three of the many Suphanburians who call their province "Banharn-buri." To echo Anderson, these people have never met, and will never

---

[40] Ibid., p. 44.

meet, each other.[41] They often have not visited or heard of each other's village, either. Yet they are all bound by one common perception that they belong to Banharn-buri—a provincial community that has escaped previous conditions of backwardness, thanks to a combination of Banharn's generous donations, his allocation of state funds, and his close supervision of local civil servants. Banharn has incorporated people living in different parts of Suphanburi into a single, imagined provincial community, of which he is the unmistakable architect.

Banharn has not simply achieved symbolic provincial integration, however. He has also given Suphanburians a strong sense of pride that derives from his unparalleled contributions to developing various villages in formerly "backward" Suphanburi. The designation "Banharn-buri" is the concise, condensed manifestation of this symbolically constructed provincial pride. It reveals the Suphanburians' keen understanding or imagination of what their province used to be and what it has become under Banharn's rule. The expression "Banharn-buri" is also used to differentiate the rapidly developing Suphanburi from the "stagnant" provinces that are bereft of an MP of Banharn's stature. It reflects Suphanburians' "we–they" mentality that serves to heighten or crystallize their positive provincial identity.

The social process through which this identity has emerged has less to do with the key elements of collective identity formation that are identified in the literature: newspapers, maps, novels, education, social interaction, culture, museums, and so on.[42] Of crucial importance to Suphanburians' provincial identity are a range of Banharn's development works, the meanings of which are disseminated and enshrined at the grassroots level through signboards and ceremonies. Several scholars have paid due attention to ceremonies as sources or instruments of collective identity formation.[43] Yet these scholars put their analytical emphasis on just one or two ceremonies held in a particular place at a particular point in time, without paying adequate attention to the spatial and temporal density of ceremonies. Banharn's success suggests the importance of adopting more longitudinal and wider geographical perspectives when examining the role of ceremonies in village-level collective identity formation.

---

[41] Ibid., p. 6.

[42] See, for example, Anderson, *Imagined Communities*; Michael Hechter, *Internal Colonialism: The Celtic Fringe in British National Development, 1536–1966* (Berkeley, CA: University of California Press, 1975); Charles F. Keyes, *Isan: Regionalism in Northeastern Thailand* (Ithaca, NY: Cornell Southeast Asia Program, 1967); and Thongchai Winichakul, *Siam Mapped: A History of the Geo-Body of Siam* (Honolulu, HI: University of Hawaii Press, 1994).

[43] See, for example, Emile Durkheim, *The Elementary Forms of the Religious Life*, trans. Joseph Swain (Glencoe, IL: Free Press, 1974); and Douglas Haynes, "Imperial Ritual in a Local Setting: The Ceremonial Order in Surat, 1890–1939," *Modern Asian Studies* 24,3 (1990): 493–527.

CHAPTER SEVEN

PRIDE IN IMAGINED BANHARN-BURI

In January 2000, a middle-aged merchant (#26) in U-Thong District returned from Chainat Province, where she had visited her elder sister. The merchant said to me half-jokingly:

> Every time I go there, I realize how important MPs can be. Fifty years ago, Suphanburi was at the same level of development as Chainat, but now the two are very different. Suphan has become so prosperous [*charoen*] thanks to Banharn, but Chainat has hardly changed. It is still what it was before.

She then made a lighthearted, bold prediction: "In fifty years from now, Chainat will probably be still the way it is now." This merchant is among the many Suphanburians who, with exaggeration and humor, poke fun at, put down, and even despise the (putative) "underdevelopment" or "stagnation" of other provinces and, at the same time, hold up Suphanburi as "modern" (*tan samai*), "developed" (*phattana*), or "progressive" (*charoen kao naa*). According to these characterizations, the other provinces remain mired in backwardness (*laa lang*), while Suphanburi has surged ahead and will continue to do so.

Such narratives (which are not uncommon) reveal one extremely important effect of Banharn's actions on Suphanburians' explicit or latent social consciousness—an enhanced sense of collective superiority. As we have seen, the Suphanburians who remember the backward conditions of the past are effusive about the *temporal* progress or development of their province that Banharn has brought about over time. However, that is not the only way in which Suphanburians assess and appreciate his actions. They also heap praise on his achievements for having developed Suphanburi *in relation to* other provinces. Suphanburians do not live in a social vacuum; they live in an inter-provincial social environment, where they continually read and hear about the seventy-four other rural provinces of Thailand, and interact with numerous people from these provinces. Thus, when they evaluate Suphanburi's historical development over the last four decades, they naturally do so by comparing Suphanburi to other provinces, and especially to neighboring provinces such as Chainat. In so doing, they are prone to uphold the superiority of Suphanburi's development, often with a good deal of exaggeration—a tendency exemplified by the merchant's comment quoted above. Narratives of this kind illustrate the most interesting and the strongest forms of Suphanburians' collective pride in Banharn as the developer of their province.

This chapter will first shed light on outsiders' admiration or envy of Banharn's achievements as a component of Suphanburians' positive provincial identity. Plainly, Suphanburians are proud of their province because many non-Suphanburians are envious of it. I will then discuss the Suphanburians' comments that reflect this provincial pride.

NON-SUPHANBURIANS' ADMIRATION AND ENVY

The high-quality development works, both large and small in scale, that Banharn has built in various parts of Suphanburi have had an impact on the popular discourse in other parts of rural Thailand. As a result of their increasingly frequent inter-provincial travels, migration, and marriages, coupled with the wider distribution of communications technology (e.g., televisions, radios, newspapers, mobile phones), many Thais living outside Suphanburi have seen, read about, and heard about the wide range of public works in Suphanburi that their provinces do not have or cannot match in number or quality. Consequently, they have become increasingly aware of Suphanburi's distinctiveness and consequently have come to express a mixture of admiration, envy, and sour resentment towards Suphanburi.

Examples abound. One Bangkok-based newspaper lauded Suphanburi for having "wider roads, bigger and glossier public buildings, more schools, more hospitals, more public facilities of all kinds."[1] Another newspaper published this observation: "Clean and well-built roads, modern infrastructure, and efficient public utilities make Suphanburi stand out from other provinces in the country. Once an impoverished farming province, now locals [*sic*] feel privileged to be born there because Suphanburi has set standards other provinces will find hard to keep up with."[2] Roads, in particular, are the objects of non-Suphanburians' admiration. During their excursion to Suphanburi, a group of college students from Bangkok rated Suphanburi's roads as better and more beautiful than those in the capital city.[3] Indeed, many roads in Suphanburi, as discussed in chapter 5, are so well maintained and decorated that they are admired for evoking "a touch of Singapore."[4] Likewise, *Thai Rath*, a widely circulated Thai-language national newspaper, admired Suphanburi for having "roads as wide as [the airport's] runways" and "super-good [*jaew*] public works," which "put other provinces to shame." The newspaper also published a letter sent by one resident in the northern province of Nakhon Sawan, who grumbled bitterly: "I was born in Nakhon Sawan and have lived here all my life. All this while, I haven't seen Nakhon Sawan develop in the same way as other provinces." Foremost among those "other provinces" was Suphanburi. The letter asked why Suphanburi has many excellent public works when "our hometown, the Muang municipality of Nakhon Sawan, can't have anything good."[5]

My conversations with non-Suphanburian respondents ($n = 171$) in twenty-seven provinces lent support to these media reports. In response to my question, "At the mention of Suphanburi, what comes to your mind?" some 80 percent of the respondents, including those who had *never* been to Suphanburi, answered "roads," which they praised in various ways. For instance, a hotel receptionist (#16) from the northeastern province of Mukdaharn recalled being "impressed" with Suphanburi's four-lane roads during her first visit in 1997, for in Mukdaharn "even the biggest highway has only one lane." Her parents were just as amazed by the towering electric-light poles that line Suphanburi's highways. A factory worker (#39) in Saraburi Province commended the "beauty" and "orderliness" of Suphanburi's

---

[1] *The Nation*, April 18, 2000, A5.

[2] *Bangkok Post*, April 17, 2003, p. 8.

[3] *Khon Suphan*, February 16, 1994, p. 3.

[4] *Bangkok Post*, September 25, 1995, p. 6.

[5] *Thai Rath*, July 24, 1998, p. 6.

roads, which she contrasted to Saraburi's "noisy, crowded, polluted, and chaotic" roads. A civil servant (#92) in the northern province of Phayao commented in jest while admiring Suphanburi's well-lit highways at night: "They are so bright that you can even see ants moving!" The sentiments of these people were well summarized by the exaggerated statement of one college student (#18) in Kanchanaburi Province: "When I am in Suphanburi, I don't feel I am in the Thai countryside."

Schools in Suphanburi have also won the admiration of nonresidents. The aforementioned hotel receptionist from Mukdaharn said: "In Suphanburi, even the schools in small villages are made of concrete. They don't have to worry about the roof leaking when it rains. Not like in Mukdaharn." One girl from Phayao Province (#19), who studied at the Suphanburi College of Dramatic Arts, one of the tertiary schools that Banharn established by channeling state funds of more than 481 million baht in 1991–99,[6] recalled:

> I had to travel seven hundred kilometers from my home to get a higher education because there is no college of this sort in Phayao. Phayao has just a few colleges, so the educational opportunities are limited. That is why many young girls from poor families in Phayao must turn to prostitution [for which Phayao has become infamous]. The girls in Suphanburi are lucky.

Another student in Phayao (#2) was full of praise for the "modern facilities" at the Sports School of Suphanburi (SSS), which he saw on TV in 2006 when Suphanburi hosted the annual National Sports Competition, a well-attended interprovincial competition. He then belittled Phayao in contrast: "Look at our stadium. It's so small. Phayao can never [*mai mee wan*] host a national-level sports competition, as Suphanburi does so often." There is much to this student's statement. The SSS's superb facilities, for which Banharn has channeled a phenomenal sum of state monies since the early 1990s (see chapter 4), have allowed Suphanburi to host many high-profile sports competitions, to a point where the province is recognized as "a golden town of sports."[7] Between 1990 and 2003, Suphanburi played host to a total of thirty-nine games at the national and international levels, most of which were televised live throughout Thailand.[8] In marked contrast, many other provinces, including Phayao, have not hosted a single national-level, let alone international, competition, simply because they do not have the necessary facilities.

Many nonresidents attribute the apparent disparity between their provinces and Suphanburi to the "Banharn factor." In so doing, they express admiration for

---

[6] Budget Bureau, *Ekasarn Ngop-pramarn 2535*, 4,5 (1991): 430–31; Budget Bureau, *Ekasarn Ngop-pramarn 2536*, 4,5 (1992): 469–71; Budget Bureau, *Ekasarn Ngop-pramarn 2537*, 4,5 (1993): 524–27; Budget Bureau, *Ekasarn Ngop-pramarn 2538*, 4,5 (1994): 589; Budget Bureau, *Ekasarn Ngop-pramarn 2539*, 4,8 (1995): 432; Budget Bureau, *Ekasarn Ngop-pramarn 2540*, 4,8 (1996): 601–2, 607, 611; Budget Bureau, *Ekasarn Ngop-pramarn 2541*, 4,8 (1997): 204–05; Budget Bureau, *Ekasarn Ngop-pramarn 2542*, 4,8 (1998): 161–62; Suphanburi College of Dramatic Arts, *Withayalai Nathasin Suphanburi* (Suphanburi: n.d.), pp. 75–77.

[7] Sports Association of Suphanburi (SAS), *Thirteenth Asian Games Suphanburi* (Suphanburi: SAS, 1998), p. 9.

[8] SAS, *Chomrom Basketball Changwat Suphanburi* (Suphanburi: SAS, 1994); SAS, *Khrop Rorp Haa Pii Samakhom Kiilaa Changwat Suphanburi* (Suphanburi: SAS, 1997), pp. 36–38; SAS, *Thirteenth Asian Games Suphanburi*; SSS, *Kan Khaeng Khan Kiilaa Rawang Rongrian Kiilaa Thua Prathet Khrang Thi Song* (Suphanburi: SSS, 1998); various issues of *Khon Suphan* and *Suphan Post*. See Nishizaki, "The Weapon of the Strong," chapter 9, for more details.

Banharn as the architect of the "modern" Suphanburi—admiration that often verges on frustration or anger at their own MPs. For example, a man (#70) from the southern province of Petchaburi, who now works as a civil servant's chauffeur in Suphanburi, lambasted Piya Angkinan, Petchaburi's nationally well-known godfather, for being "better at killing people" than building roads and schools. "When I first came to Suphanburi [in the early 1990s]," the chauffeur recalled, "I couldn't help wonder, 'What has our MP been doing? What has he done to match what Banharn has done?'" Another respondent, a janitor (#40) in Saraburi said that her province's MPs "are not bad, but they don't love Saraburi the way Banharn loves Suphan. Banharn loves his birthplace and his people very much, so he has done so much for them." Still another respondent, a merchant (#41) in Phayao Province, deplored the fact that Ladawan Wongsriwong, a nationally prominent female MP from Phayao, was "too weak to emulate Banharn. It takes a male MP to channel funds from the state." On the basis of his extensive fieldwork in Ayutthaya, Suphanburi's neighboring province to the east, Daniel Arghiros noted similar views. He reports that when comparing Montri Pongpanich, Ayutthaya's long-standing MP, to Banharn, many villagers "admired the fact that ... Banharn ... had transformed ... Suphanburi with highways, hospitals, and schools ..."[9]

Those nonresidents who admire Banharn naturally wish that their MPs had more of his attributes, or even that Banharn were their MP. For instance, one civil servant (#71) in Kanchanaburi, Suphanburi's adjacent province, said: "If only we had an MP like Banharn, Kanchanaburi could develop like Suphan. And if only Banharn becomes prime minister again, the whole countryside will reach the same level of development as Suphan." Similarly, a young bookstore clerk (#17) from Nakhon Pathom, a neighboring province of Suphanburi, illustrated her view by recounting a humorous episode. She once had a (mild) argument with her mother, a petty merchant, who "constantly grumbles about the difference between Suphanburi and Nakhon Pathom and asks, 'Why is our province [underdeveloped] like this?'" Bored with this question, my respondent snapped at her mother: "Who elected the MPs we have in the first place? We have only ourselves to blame for not electing a person like Banharn. So, stop complaining." The mother retorted: "Who can we vote for? Is there anyone like Banharn here? We don't have much choice." My respondent then concluded with laughter: "We wouldn't have to have a silly argument like this again if Banharn ran for office in Nakhon Pathom in the next election!" In a report that lent credence to these views, a columnist for one major national newspaper wrote that his office often receives letters from non-Suphanburians, criticizing their MPs for not developing their provinces the way Banharn has developed Suphanburi.[10] Thus, although many MPs have attacked Banharn for being too partial to his province (see chapter 4), there is much reason to believe that their voters actually want them to emulate his actions.

Such sentiments are particularly strong in provinces adjacent to Suphanburi, where Banharn's achievements are extremely well known thanks to frequent inter-provincial travels (made possible by all the roads he has built) and the circulation of Suphanburi's provincial newspaper, *Khon Suphan*.[11] A down-to-earth politician,

---

[9] Daniel Arghiros, *Democracy, Development, and Decentralization in Provincial Thailand* (Richmond, UK: Curzon, 2001), p. 213.

[10] *Thai Rath*, July 24, 1998, p. 6.

[11] About one thousand copies of *Khon Suphan* are sold in both Ang Thong and Chainat.

Banharn is aware of the wishes of the people in these provinces.[12] He has therefore repeatedly tried to rally electoral support for his Chart Thai (CT) Party by evoking the image of a "developed" Suphanburi. For example, before the 2001 parliamentary election, he had a large signboard erected at a busy intersection in Chainat Province that exhorted: "If you want Chainat to develop like Suphanburi, vote for the CT Party."[13] Similarly, during a campaign rally in Singburi Province in 1995, he pledged to build four-lane provincial highways and asphalt roads in every village within four years, just like in Suphanburi.[14] At another rally, he played up his party's electoral appeal by referring to the adjacent Ang Thong, Kanchanaburi, Singburi, and Nakhon Pathom provinces as Suphanburi's "satellites" and by announcing, "Prosperity is only meters away from Suphanburi."[15]

Campaign tactics of this kind paid off, at least until Thaksin's mighty Thai Rak Thai Party emerged to dominate the electoral system in 2001. My research indicates that in eight elections held between 1983 and 2001, the CT Party won 27.5 percent of the seats in the eleven neighboring provinces of Suphanburi, despite the fact that more than ten parties contested each of these elections. Many non-Suphanburians were apparently convinced by Banharn's rhetoric—so much so that a Solidarity Party candidate in Nakhon Pathom warned the electorate before the 1995 election: "[F]ree yourselves of Suphanburi. Don't turn Nakhon Pathom into a colony of Suphanburi."[16] Suphanburi has become something of a centripetal icon of rural development, behind which popular support in these provinces can be successfully mobilized. The extant literature generally contends that ideology is irrelevant in Thai politics, but there are signs that what one former farmer (#43) in Suphanburi called "developmentalism" (*phathana-niyom*) has emerged as an incipient, yet immensely appealing, ideology for the electorate in the provinces that are labeled "backward" (as Suphanburi once was).

Few other MPs, however, have been able to ride the "rural developmentalism" bandwagon. For example, in the most recent parliamentary election of December 2007, a Puea Phaendin Party leader, Suvit Khunkitti, ran for office, promising to turn his home province of Khon Kaen into "Suvit Buri." As he said during the election campaign, "If Mr. Banharn could develop Suphan Buri ... impressing people so much that they couldn't help calling the province Banharn Buri, why can't I convert Khon Kaen into Suvit Buri?"[17] He lost the election, however, because the voters were not convinced that he had the potential to deliver on the promise. He had served as Khon Kaen's MP between 1986 and 2005, yet during this time he had done little to further development in the province in the way Banharn has in Suphanburi. Despite the apparent failures of their own representatives, however, many rural voters

---

Interview with *Khon Suphan*'s staff, November 15, 1999. Moreover, newspapers in these provinces (e.g., *Phalang Thai* in Ang Thong, *Chart Pracha* in Kanchanaburi, and *Chart Pracha* in Lopburi) regularly carry stories about the projects undertaken by Banharn in Suphanburi.

[12] *Khon Suphan*, August 1, 1993, p. 3.

[13] Personal observation in Chainat, January 2001.

[14] *Bangkok Post*, June 18, 1995, p. 4. See also *Bangkok Post*, June 11, 1995, p. 1; and *Bangkok Post*, June 27, 1995, p. 9, for similar campaign slogans employed in Ang Thong and Kanchanaburi.

[15] *Bangkok Post*, June 25, 1995, p. 4.

[16] *Bangkok Post*, June 10, 1995, p. 6.

[17] *Bangkok Post*, November 20, 2007, p. 3.

outside Suphanburi continue to view Banharn-buri as one (if not the only) attractive model of provincial development that their MPs should try to emulate.

PRAISING SUPHANBURI'S (PUTATIVE) SUPERIORITY

Over the years, the sentiments of Thais residing outside Suphanburi have been transmitted to Suphanburians in person and/or through the grapevine and the media. As a result, virtually all Suphanburians have become cognizant of the development works in their own province that are superior in quality and number to their counterparts in other places. Increased inter-provincial travels, marriages, and communications have allowed not only non-Suphanburians but also Suphanburians to see, hear about, and read about such projects. Plainly Suphanburians have come to realize: "We are special. We have what other provinces don't have." The perceived uniqueness of Suphanburi has become the semiotic basis on which Suphanburians have acquired an intense form of provincial identity.

This identity finds expression in a variety of social narratives—everyday stories, jokes, (unfounded) gossip, and myths—which Suphanburians recount among themselves and to outsiders about Banharn's achievements in making Suphanburi *more* developed than other provinces. In particular, because of their geographical proximity, Suphanburi's neighboring provinces—most notably, Ang Thong, Chainat, Uthai Thani, and Singburi—most often figure as objects of comparison. These provinces, where the envy of Suphanburi's development is most strongly expressed, are invoked in Suphanburians' narratives as convenient tropes for backwardness. In other words, these provinces serve as discursive foils for Suphanburi's (imagined) superior development.

To illustrate, my respondents ($n = 229$), who represent all ages, social classes, and the ten districts of Suphanburi, pointed to a wide variety of public works as the "indubitable" evidence of Suphanburi's superior development. The most frequently cited projects (cited by 211) were roads. Just as outsiders regard roads as the quintessential symbols of Suphanburi's development, so do Suphanburians. In this connection, many respondents cracked essentially the same joke to me by singling out Ang Thong Province: "If you are traveling on a bus or in a car from Ang Thong to Suphanburi, how can you tell, without looking at road signs, whether you are still in Ang Thong or have reached Suphan? Very easy! Just hold a drink in your hand. If it shakes and spills onto your hand, you are in Ang Thong. If it doesn't, you are in Suphan!" Banharn himself told a similar joke: "When you enter Suphanburi [in a car], you fall asleep. When you enter other places, you wake up."[18] The meaning is obvious: All the roads in Suphanburi are smooth, whereas Ang Thong's roads are bumpy. Thus, one janitor (#3) asked a rhetorical question with a chuckle: "Why do they bother to put up those signboards saying, 'Welcome to Suphanburi'? There is no need for them." According to another Suphanburian, a vendor of drinks (#84) in Don Tarl subdistrict (which borders Ang Thong), even the revered King Bhumibol told the "drinks-never-shake-in-Suphanburi" story to his entourage. Another common joke goes: "If you are driving at night, you can turn off your headlights as soon as you reach Suphanburi. That saves you energy." This joke extols all the modern electric-light poles erected along roadways in Suphanburi, conjuring up another binary contrast, a contrast between "bright Suphanburi" and "the dark other

---

[18] CT Party, *Chart Thai Samphan*, 13 (May–June 2001), p. 17.

provinces." Before the 1970s, there were jokes that ridiculed Suphanburi for its bumpy and dusty roads (see chapter 2). Now the tables have turned.

Pride in the superiority of Suphanburi's roads is embedded and reflected in numerous other accounts that set up an imaginary, simplified "us versus them" dichotomy between Suphanburi and other provinces. Again, Suphanburi's neighboring provinces are the targets of easy and frivolous caricature in many of these accounts. Here are some representative examples:

A drinks vendor (#84) in Muang District: "I often get lost while traveling on Suphan's highways because they are so intricate. Our road system is too developed for me [laughter]. But I never have that problem while in Ang Thong!"

A farmer (#61) in Song Phi Nong District, referring to her sister in Chainat Province: "The road in her village is so bad that I have to slow down my motorcycle to ten kilometers per hour. Otherwise, it would be dangerous. But in Suphan, I can speed at sixty kilometers [per hour]."

A civil servant (#28) whose husband is from Kampheng Phet Province: "Even the roads in central Kampheng Phet can't match the roads in outlying areas of Suphan. The roads in Suphan are 'kirei' [a Japanese word for beautiful] and the roads in Kampheng Phet are 'kiree' [a Thai word for ugly]."

A rice farmer (#104) in Muang District: "Suphan's roads are excellent [*sutyord*]. You might call Suphan the second capital of Thailand. It should actually be the capital. Bangkok is too crowded, so they should move the capital here."

A noodle vendor (#29) in Nong Ya Sai District: "I heard a story that royal family members like to visit Suphanburi because our roads are so good and pleasant to the eyes. The trip is safe and enjoyable. But they don't like visiting other provinces so much because of the narrow and bad roads there."

A security guard (#62) in Sri Prachan District: "The tall electric poles are in Suphan only. You can't find anything of this sort anywhere else in Thailand. ... Look at all those beautiful trees and flowers. Some other provinces have trees and flowers, but they are less beautiful because they are not well maintained."

A student intern (#9) speaking sarcastically beside his supervisor from the southern province of Trang: "All the roads in Suphan have been surfaced with asphalt and concrete. But I'm not sure about other provinces. I wonder if there is any asphalt road in Trang."

My respondents expressed similarly strong pride in Suphanburi's schools. To give some typical examples:

A motorcyclist (#30) in Dan Chang District: "Good students in Uthai Thai [Province] must come to Suphan to pursue higher education because no schools are up to standard there. They have only lousy [*yae*] schools."

A retired civil servant (#97) in Muang District: "I have visited most of the provinces in Thailand as part of my job. I can tell from this experience that our schools' facilities are among the best in the country. Banharn is turning Suphan into the educational center of Thailand."

A schoolteacher (#31), whose wife is from Buriram Province in the northeast: "Old school buildings in Suphanburi, even those in far corners, have been renovated. If there is any old building left, I bet it will be renovated within a few years ... Compare Suphan to Buriram. Many schools there keep on using old, rotting buildings that were built many decades ago. Not modern."

A policeman (#32) in Sam Chuk District: "The SSS is the largest sports school in Thailand. Most players on the national soccer team were trained there. Without the SSS, Thailand might be creamed even by Burma. If there were more schools like the SSS in Thailand, we could beat Japan, too."[19]

Because collective memories of Suphanburi's backwardness in the not-so-distant past are still strong and have been orally transmitted from generation to generation, all the roads and schools built by Banharn constitute emotionally resonant visible symbols of Suphanburi's current development. As such, the roads and schools have become the crucial sources of Suphanburians' provincial pride.

Yet one might ask at this point: Even if Suphanburians may be justified in looking down on their adjacent provinces as "backward," how do they maintain Suphanburi's superiority against a handful of other provinces, such as Chiang Mai and Nakhon Ratchasima, which Thais in general consider to be the most developed after Bangkok? The quality of many roads and schools (as well as other public works) in these provinces can match those in Suphanburi. Many of my respondents admitted this, if rather reluctantly at times. At the same time, however, they defended and played up Suphanburi's uniqueness. Their responses can be grouped into three types.

First, some respondents contended that other "advanced" provinces were blessed with "inherent advantages." As one food stall owner (#63) explained, "Chiang Mai and Nakhon Ratchasima are much bigger in area and have many more people than Suphan does, so the government naturally must pay much attention to their development. Of course, they are well developed. It is no surprise." The respondents who made this kind of comment attributed the development of some other provinces to geographic and demographic factors, which were beyond Suphanburi's control. Compared to those "naturally favored" provinces, Suphanburi does not have any inherent advantage, yet it is still quite well developed. Thus, even a concession that Suphanburi does not enjoy a monopoly over superior development works would not detract from its distinctiveness.

A second way to defend Suphanburi's uniqueness was to restrict the scope of comparison or to highlight the fields in which Suphanburi had established a clear

---

[19] This statement is not groundless. Between 1992 and 2003, thirty-six male students of the SSS made it to Thailand's national soccer team. During the same period, a total of 293 SSS students, both men and women, represented Thailand in over ten categories of sports at various international competitions, such as the Asian Olympics. Thus, the school has produced many of the best athletes in Thailand. SSS, *Pratheep haeng Kan Kiilaa* (Suphanburi: SSS, 2000), pp. 21, 26–27; written information obtained at the SSS in May 2005.

"competitive edge" over other provinces. As a photocopying clerk (#7) remarked: "Roads in Nakhon Ratchasima may be just as wide as those in Suphan. But in terms of cleanliness and smoothness, their roads are no match for ours." Similarly, a restaurant waiter (#8) said: "I've been to Chiang Mai. Yes, it has big roads with median strips, but the trees and flowers planted there were almost wilting, not like those in Suphan, which are more fresh and beautiful."

Third, some respondents emphasized the *speed* (as opposed to the level) of Suphanburi's development. A drinks vendor (#73) in Sri Prachan District offered a representative remark: "If you are talking about the modernity of schools, Suphan and Chiang Mai are at the same level. But if you look at the last ten years or so, Suphan has developed much faster than Chiang Mai." She concluded: "At the current rate, it is [only] a matter of time before Suphan will overtake the provinces that are ahead of it now." This kind of response concedes that Suphanburi still lags behind some provinces in the *level* of its development, but argues that Suphanburi has enjoyed an unrivaled *rate* of development. Therefore, according to this view, Suphanburi is "comparable" (*thaokan*) or "not inferior" (*mai noinaa*) to some other supposedly "more developed" provinces.

All this is not to say, of course, that every Suphanburian interprets Banharn's development projects in the same positive way. Different works hold different meanings or values for different people. For example, to Banharn's detractors (mostly bureaucrats), to this day all the gargantuan roads signify nothing but his nefarious corruption. Some respondents also associated rapid road construction with impersonal capitalist development that has eroded their closely knit villages.[20] Yet the vast majority of my respondents, including even those who hated Banharn, played up ways in which the improved roads had made their daily travels to schools, the market, and so on more convenient and had promoted a more vigorous exchange of commercial goods. Some of these respondents, especially women, also noted that it had become much safer to go out at night because the roads were well lit and facilitated more effective police surveillance. Likewise, many respondents praised Banharn's construction of schools for having made education more accessible to the provincial population at large. Thus, Suphanburians conferred multiple and sometimes conflicting meanings on Banharn's developmental projects; the symbolic universe of Suphanburi is not uniform (see also chapter 8).

Nonetheless, in a context where residents of rural Thailand have been socialized into believing that development is a "competition,"[21] many Suphanburians endorsed Banharn's projects as emotionally gratifying symbols that represented their province's triumph in this competition. If these initiatives were ostentatious and

---

[20] For a similar view, see James C. Scott, *Seeing like a State: How Certain Schemes to Improve the Human Condition Have Failed* (New Haven, CT: Yale University Press, 1998), pp. 103–46. For other studies of the effects and implications of road construction in late-developing countries, see Jeffrey Herbst, *States and Power in Africa: Comparative Lessons in Authority and Control* (Princeton, NJ: Princeton University Press, 2000); Hermann Kreutzmann, "The Karakoram Highway: The Impact of Road Construction on Mountain Societies," *Modern Asian Studies* 25,4 (1991): 711–36; and Thak Chaloemtiarana, *Thailand: The Politics of Despotic Paternalism* (Bangkok: Social Science Association of Thailand, 1979), pp. 228–29, 264–67.

[21] Arghiros, *Democracy, Development, and Decentralization in Provincial Thailand*, p. 213; Philip Hirsch, "What is the Thai Village?" in *National Identity and its Defenders, 1939–1989*, ed. Craig Reynolds (Clayton, Australia: Monash University Center of Southeast Asian Studies, 1991), p. 332; Ratana Boonmathya, "Contested Concepts of Development in Rural Northeastern Thailand" (PhD dissertation, University of Washington, 1997), pp. 131, 145.

extravagant pork-barrel projects (as anti-Banharn scholars and journalists would characterize them), that is exactly what pleases most Suphanburians. In the language of Ronald Inglehart, Suphanburians have not yet reached a "postmodernist" or "post-materialist" stage, where they would take a dim view of glitzy modernization projects.[22] Just as middle-class Thais in general enjoy displaying their large, expensive cars as status symbols, many Suphanburians take delight in flaunting or bragging to outsiders about their big and beautiful development works, citing these projects as indisputable proof of Suphanburi's higher social status at present. Banharn's development projects, in other words, have taken on the semiotic character of "prestige goods" on display.[23]

Comparing Banharn to "Bad" MPs

Many residents of Suphanburi highlighted several qualities of Banharn to explain what they proudly viewed as the marked difference in development between their province and others. Among those qualities (cited by more than 80 percent of my respondents) were his generosity, his inimitable ability to channel funds from the state, and his hardworking and meticulous nature, manifested by his constant surveillance over local civil servants. According to my respondents, these qualities set Banharn sharply and positively apart from MPs in other provinces. Other MPs simply did not measure up to Banharn. This difference in the quality of MPs was often cited to explain why Suphanburi had been able to surpass many other provinces in the level and/or speed of development in just a few decades. Plainly, Suphanburi had developed rapidly because it had Banharn, whereas other provinces lagged behind because they did not have an MP of Banharn's caliber.

Many respondents illustrated this point by drawing a sharp contrast between Banharn and some other "unconcerned" or "incapable" MPs. For example, a vendor of drinks (#64), whose wife comes from the northern province of Kampheng Phet, spoke approvingly about Banharn's many generous donations:

> A man like him is hard to come by. Even though he has become a national-level politician, he has never forgotten about his birthplace. He loves his birthplace and Suphan's people very much, so he is glad to spend lots of his money for us. Other MPs would keep all the money to themselves. If MPs in Kampheng Phet were a little more like Banharn, there would be better roads, hospitals, and schools up there.

His wife chipped in by citing a Thai proverb: "They [MPs in Kampheng Phet] are like 'toads on a festival float' [*khangkok khuen wor*]."[24] A security guard (#43) from Bang Pla Ma District made a similar point by criticizing Sanan Kachonprasert, a veteran MP from the northern province of Phichit and former secretary-general of the Democrat Party:

---

[22] Ronald Inglehart, *Modernization and Postmodernization: Cultural, Economic, and Political Change in 43 Societies* (Princeton, NJ: Princeton University Press, 1997).

[23] For similar views, see Qin Shao, *Culturing Modernity: The Nantong Model, 1890–1930* (Stanford, CA: Stanford University Press, 2004).

[24] This proverb is used to deride persons who come from lowly backgrounds, yet start acting arrogant as soon as they attain a higher social status.

Sanan has so much political power, so you would expect Phichit to be well developed, but it is actually underveloped. If you go there, you'll see. There are no good public works there, such as the ones we have in Suphan. Why? Because Sanan does nothing but drink expensive foreign wine [for which he is widely reported to have a weakness]. He spends more than 200,000 baht on importing just one bottle of foreign wine. Banharn would spend that kind of money building a school in Suphanburi.

Another respondent, a schoolteacher (#85) in Muang District, hailed Banharn's successes as a pork-barrel politician by using Montri Phongpanich, a nationally famous MP from the adjacent industrial province of Ayutthaya, as a contrasting case:

Look at all the things Banharn has built here—temples, schools, roads, hospitals, and many others. Compare all these to what Ayutthaya has. Ayutthaya is closer to Bangkok, but it has nothing but factories. Other than that, it's not developed. Even Montri couldn't match Banharn … Montri couldn't bring as much money to Ayutthaya as Banharn does to Suphan. You see how much difference MPs can make.

Interestingly, among the "bad" MPs, the one most commonly cited by my respondents was Chuan Leekpai, former leader of the Democrat Party, who is widely regarded as one of the most honest politicians in Thailand. Banharn and Chuan once vied fiercely for the premiership in 1995, and after Banharn became prime minister, Chuan mounted vehement attacks against him as the opposition leader. Chuan also served as prime minister in 1999–2001, when I conducted most of my fieldwork. For these reasons, many respondents cited Chuan in assessing Banharn's value or performance as an MP. For example, a college student (#9) asked a rhetorical question to highlight Banharn's munificence: "Can you name any one thing that Chuan has built in Trang [a southern province where Chuan is from] with his own money? Nothing! He is stingy and greedy. He never thinks about using his own money for his birthplace, not like Banharn." In praising Banharn's meticulous supervision of construction projects, another respondent, a car mechanic (#49), started his analysis with a casual observation: "Chuan is a lawyer. So, he is not close to the people." The mechanic then elaborated:

Once Banharn implements a project in Suphan, he makes it a point to come back to Suphan to follow up [*tit tam*] on its progress every week, until the day it is completed to his satisfaction. He takes a direct interest in every project. He never abandons it. What does Chuan do? He just sits in an air-conditioned office … He lets irresponsible and corrupt local officials take full charge. He seldom goes back to Trang to inspect local projects. Of course, the level of Suphan's development is superior [*nuea*] to Trang's.

This respondent and several others even went so far as to claim or insinuate, albeit without any evidence, that Chuan pocketed the state funds that he was supposed to channel into his home province. These Suphanburians regarded Chuan, the quintessence of morally correct *phudi*-type politicians for many urban-based voters,[25] as a dishonest and inactive politician. In other words, Chuan was used as a foil for Banharn, a definitively good MP for Suphanburians.

Enjoying Others' Imagined Envy

Suphanburians' proud and exaggerated accounts of their province's progress are reinforced by their conviction or imagination that fellow Thais living outside the province recognize, admire, envy, and resent Banharn's high-profile accomplishments as a provincial developer. While it is true that many outsiders are envious of Suphanburi's advancement, however, others actually express cynical nonchalance or flatly deny that Suphanburi is more developed than other provinces. For example, one civil servant (#42) in Ayutthaya Province denigrated Suphanburi, saying: "Suphanburi ... has only good roads. Other than that, Suphanburi is still quite backward." Similarly, a merchant (#72) in Lopburi Province said: "Actually, the roads in Lopburi are just as good as Suphan's. People in Suphan just don't know." Suphanburians are well aware that such skeptics exist, but they have convenient ways to resolve, explain away, or rationalize such "anomalous cases."

One illustrative response was offered by a hotel employee (#10):

OK, suppose I have a brand-new European car, and you don't. I ask you, 'Are you jealous of me?' What would you say? You would never say 'yes' to my face, right? You would say, 'I am happy with what I have now,' although deep down in your heart, you are very jealous. Nobody wants to admit being jealous. That is human nature.

In other words, nonresidents who fall short in their admiration of Suphanburi are dismissed as dissimulating their indifference or as crying sour grapes.

For many Suphanburians, the fact that Banharn has been so heavily criticized for lavishing state funds on his home province (see chapter 4) is further irrefutable evidence of outsiders' jealousy. According to one elderly rice farmer (#104), Bangkokians attacked Banharn because they were "envious" and "fearful" that they might "lose the honor of living in the national capital to Suphanburi." He elaborated: "They used to look down on us as backward. Now they see we have better roads. They know that, at this rate, Banharn will succeed in moving the capital to Suphan. So they try to stop him by criticizing him." Another respondent (#11), an unemployed young man with a bachelor's degree from a university in Bangkok, explained philosophically: "If you and I are competing for the same job and I get it, you would be jealous, right? You would get so angry that you would say all sorts of nasty things about me." These respondents viewed all the criticisms concerning Banharn's preferential allocation of funds as stemming from outsiders' anger, which is a manifestation of their jealousy. This imagined jealousy pleased Suphanburians because it confirmed their already strong conviction that Suphanburi has attained a position of superiority in the developmental hierarchy of Thailand.

Thus, often the criticisms hurled at Banharn backfire among Suphanburians. The more outsiders criticize him for showing favoritism toward Suphanburi, the more

---

[25] See James Ockey, "Thai Society and Patterns of Political Leadership," *Asian Survey* 36,4 (1996): 345–60.

praise Suphanburians heap on him for making their province special. The more envious non-Suphanburians are or are imagined to be, the more emotional satisfaction Suphanburians derive from Banharn's actions. There is a positive correlation between the two.[26]

DEVELOPMENT IS IN THE EYE OF THE BEHOLDER

Viewed from the detached perspective of outsiders, many of the Suphanburians' accounts are clearly exaggerated, oversimplified, and caricatured. Some are patently spurious. For example, not all the roads in Suphanburi are as smooth and bright as my respondents made them out to be; Suphanburi has its share of bumpy and dimly lit roads. It is one thing to boast that many development projects in Suphanburi are high-quality (which *is* true), but it is quite another to make sweeping, value-ridden generalizations about the excellent quality of *all* projects in the province. For those who wish to attain and maintain a positive social identity, however, this line is very easy and tempting to cross. In the process of crossing the line, they consciously or unconsciously accentuate the conspicuous marks of Suphanburi's development and ignore or discount any remaining signs of its backwardness.

In other words, Suphanburians do not engage in an impartial comparative assessment of development. Rather, what they *want* to believe—that Suphanburi's development is superior to that of other provinces—guides, influences, or clouds their appraisal. In their eagerness to retain this belief, they arbitrarily and conveniently play up selected pieces of available information that appear to validate it, and turn deaf ears and blind eyes to other pieces of information that do not. The result is a range of highly subjective and prejudiced narratives—"rudimentary classifications," using Edward Said's language[27]—that relegate other provinces to the status of vastly inferior, backward "others." These narratives are simply *necessary* for Suphanburians to uphold the superiority of their province. Drawing further on Said's insightful analysis, we might say that the "others" do not have to accept or agree with the schematic distinction drawn by producers of the discourse—in this case, Suphanburians. "It is enough" for Suphanburians to "set up" the distinction in their minds and tell narratives that help them visualize that distinction.[28] Through the mundane act of recounting and hearing such narratives based on "a very unrigorous idea" of the "backward" provinces that lie somewhere "out there,"[29] beyond the familiar territory of Banharn-buri, Suphanburians obtain, reaffirm, and magnify their provincial pride. Their provincial identity is dependent on the construction and maintenance of those subjective accounts.

It is important to note, however, that Suphanburians' pride is not an absurd illusion or figment of their imaginations, detached from objective reality. The pride has a firm, tangible basis in the form of numerous development works, which Banharn has supplied over the decades by using a combination of his personal wealth and his institutional power rooted in the central patrimonial state. These

---

[26] For a theory regarding the enjoyment derived from other people's envy of oneself and one's group, see Jon Elster, *Alchemies of the Mind: Rationality and the Emotions* (New York, NY: Cambridge University Press, 1999), pp. 142–43.

[27] Edward Said, *Orientalism* (New York, NY: Vintage Books, 1979), p. 53.

[28] Ibid., p. 54.

[29] Ibid.

development works, as well as ubiquitous signboards and frequent ceremonies advertising those accomplishments to the public—all of which collectively make up what might be called Banharn's "symbolic capital"— constitute the solid semiotic ground, on the base of which Suphanburians feel justified in generating various overdrawn categorizations that cast their province in a relatively favorable light. In a historical context where rural Thailand (*ban nork*) has traditionally been relegated to the inferior "backward" category, its people desire to seek and accentuate any visible signifier or even trapping of "development" in an attempt to move up the social status hierarchy and to escape the stigma associated with backwardness.[30] For many people of Suphanburi, all the development projects carried out by Banharn constitute one type of such signifiers. As such, Banharn's projects have become the material objects around which a sense of highly subjective provincial pride is mobilized, forged, and reinforced; they constitute the sites of Suphanburians' provincial identity production and reproduction.

In their attempts to prove that Suphanburians have been misled or fooled by Banharn, political scientists might try to examine the extent to which their narratives are objectively true. Such an exercise would be pointless, however. Suphanburians' narratives have overlapping elements of reality, imagination, misrepresentation, exaggeration, and (unintentional) distortion mixed into them. Like beauty, Suphanburi's development is in the eye of the beholder. Trying to determine the objectivity of their accounts would therefore produce inconclusive results at best. Suphanburians would not be interested in such a detached empirical test anyway. They believe what they want to believe. Their narratives, just like any other subjective narratives that reflect one's deeply cherished beliefs, are impervious to scientific or logical refutation.

The significance of Suphanburians' (exaggerated) narratives lies in the plain fact that they are told *at all* and that they reflect a very strong and positive provincial identity—"provincialism" (*changwat-niyom*), as one farmer's son (#43) called it— which a great many people living in the ten districts, 110 subdistricts, and more than nine hundred villages of Suphanburi have come to embrace. As noted in chapter 2, Suphanburi used to be regarded and ridiculed as a backward province, and its residents would speak of their own province with a sense of shame, as exemplified by such self-belittling expressions as "the bottom of a paper bag" and "the child of a mistress." But now, Suphanburi boasts many nationally renowned symbols of development, which other Thais admire, envy, and resent. These symbols are the vivid and concrete signifiers of the otherwise abstract and shapeless "geo-body" of Banharn-buri.[31] A whole range of Suphanburi's citizens—farmers, civil servants, capitalists, workers, students, merchants, and others—have been integrated into, and have come to identify strongly and positively with, that imagined provincial community that transcends the otherwise divisive differences of class, gender, age, occupation, and educational attainment. Following Benedict Anderson, we may note

---

[30] See also Yoshinori Nishizaki, "The Gargantuan Project and Modernity in Provincial Thailand," *Asia Pacific Journal of Anthropology* 8,3 (2007): 217–33. For a fascinating account of how the same desire led Siamese kings to imitate things Western, see Maurizio Peleggi, *Lords of Things: The Fashioning of the Siamese Monarchy's Modern Image* (Honolulu, HI: University of Hawaii Press, 2002).

[31] The concept of "geo-body" here draws on Thongchai Winichakul, *Siam Mapped: A History of the Geo-Body of Siam* (Honolulu, HI: University of Hawaii Press, 1994).

that most of these people have never met, and will never meet, each other,[32] yet they are all bound by the common perception that they are part of Banharn-buri, a uniquely progressive provincial entity that Banharn has developed over the last four decades. Before Banharn's emergence as a leader, these people may have identified with "Suphanburi" as an impersonal unit of territorial administration, but many had lacked strong emotional bonds with that unit. Banharn's achievement has been to turn these subjects of bureaucratic governance into proud Suphanburians by creating a deeply personal social community with which they can identify positively.

The manifestations of this positive collective identity are all the stereotyped generalizations and simplifications that discursively construct or uphold Suphanburi as a cut above other (putatively) "still backward" provinces. Suphanburians now find themselves in a position to tell such narratives and to draw a new version of an "imagined social geography of Thailand," in which the formerly inferior Suphanburi now enjoys the high social status that it lacked before. The relative social position of Suphanburi has been completely reversed. Nothing is more symbolic of this reversal than the jokes that Suphanburians now tell, mocking the roads in other provinces. This represents a striking departure from the pre-Banharn past, when jokes were more likely to mock Suphanburi's roads. In brief, the way in which Suphanburians collectively represent their province to outsiders has fundamentally changed. Banharn has made Suphanburians proud to be Suphanburians. He has brought about this dramatic transformation of their social identity in the short space of four decades, a transformation that would have been dismissed as utterly unbelievable before.

Suphanburians' strong provincial identity translates into their effusive and staunch support for Banharn as the engineer of the "new Suphanburi." One daughter (#7) from a sugarcane-growing family in Song Phi Nong District chided: "If there is anybody who doesn't like Banharn, that person should move out of Suphanburi immediately. The person doesn't deserve to be here." Other respondents expressed their support or loyalty in equally intense terms, referring to Banharn as their "pride" (*pen thi phum jai*), the "darling of Suphanburi" (*khwan muang*), "the most beloved" (*sut thi rak*) individual, and so on. Given all the negative news stories concerning his alleged corruption, very few of these people worshipped Banharn as "a spotless saint" or "a living god" in the same way that Thais in general idolize King Bhumibol. Still, they constructed highly favorable portrayals of Banharn as a respectable and adored politician. Simply, Banharn is what they make of him.

According to these people, Banharn has not just orchestrated the emergence of the "new Suphanburi" that makes them proud. He has also come to personify that provincial community. As such, he has become the vital component or source of Suphanburians' positive provincial identity. The designation "Banharn-buri" is the crystallized expression of this collective identity. Banharn is Suphanburi, and Suphanburi is Banharn. The two are synonymous. The rise of Suphanburians' provincial pride, as reflected in the remarkable conflation of these two concepts, forms the solid social–psychological foundation on which Banharn's unchallenged domination is based.

Scholars of Thai politics who fix their attention on the sordid aspects of Banharn's rule alone—I do not deny that there are such aspects—overlook this

---

[32] Benedict Anderson, *Imagined Communities: Reflections on the Origin and the Spread of Nationalism* (London: Verso, 1991), p. 6.

nonmaterial social–pyschological basis of his authority. To echo the anthropologist Katherine Verdery's trenchant critique of political science,[33] such scholars' "narrow and flat" analytical focus "desiccates" or "impoverishes" Suphanburians' "enchanting" perceptions of how their provincial society has evolved over the decades, thanks to Banharn. The sources of his political authority over the province are more complex than casual outside observers can appreciate. Banharn's actions, as represented by his munificent donations, his monumental successes in initiating pork-barrel projects, and his strict supervision of local civil servants, have set in motion a new phase of provincial development that continues to this day—a phase in which Suphanburi has caught up with, and has overtaken, many other formerly advanced provinces. Banharn has enhanced the prestige, reputation, image, and status of a province that was previously on the social margins of Thailand. Their perceptions or imaginations regarding this change have enabled Suphanburians to overcome a sense of social inferiority and to feel a strong provincial pride that they did not feel before. Paying due attention to this social–psychological change helps us better understand why Banharn, whom urban-based intellectuals consider a depraved politician, continues to attract the strong support of Suphanburians.

---

[33] Katherine Verdery, *The Political Lives of Dead Bodies: Reburial and Postsocialist Change* (New York, NY: Columbia University Press, 1999), pp. 26, 127.

CHAPTER EIGHT

DEFENDING THE "BAD" POLITICIAN

Banharn is a Janus-faced politician. On one hand, from the perspective of many Suphanburians, he is a compassionate, efficient, and strict leader who has developed their province since the 1960s in contradiction to, or on behalf of, the central state. On the other hand, many scholars and journalists have constructed his image very differently, portraying him as a despicable, rural-based MP by leveling various kinds of criticisms or allegations concerning his malfeasance and ineptitude. Given the firm control that these critics have held over the means of discourse production (e.g., newspapers, TV programs, and scholarly works) in Thailand and abroad, this negative image of Banharn has become dominant. The image has taken such deep hold that well-educated residents of Bangkok typically cite and denounce Banharn as the archetype of Thailand's "bad" MPs, politicians who hamper the substantive growth of democracy in Thailand.

How do Banharn's supporters in Suphanburi counter such negative characterizations? This chapter will show the various ways in which they defend, rationalize, justify, and even praise what outsiders view as Barnharn's less-than-admirable qualities as a politician. Precisely because the outsiders' severe criticisms and allegations threaten, challenge, or damage his local reputation as the heroic provincial developer, many Suphanburians are driven to react against them in all sorts of partisan and even opinionated and contrived ways in their efforts to bolster their pride in him. Chapter 4 and, to a lesser extent, chapter 7, discussed this sort of reaction with regard to Banharn's favoritism in state funds allocation. This chapter will take up two other common charges made against Banharn: (1) that he is corrupt, and (2) that he has failed to industrialize Suphanburi and reduce poverty. I will also discuss the signs of covert resistance to his dominance initiated by a small number of his detractors in Suphanburi and the reasons why the resistance has been largely unsuccessful. I conclude by speculating briefly on the prospects for change in post-Banharn Suphanburi.

IS BANHARN CORRUPT?

A criticism commonly leveled against Banharn concerns his alleged misuse of office. As mentioned in chapter 1, his long-standing political career, spanning more than thirty years, abounds with well-publicized, if unsubstantiated, accusations about his office-based corruption and nepotism. Some accusations involve relatively minor issues.[1] More seriously, he has been accused, on numerous occasions, of siphoning off public funds and accepting kickbacks from business interests for

---

[1] For example, in the early 1980s, Banharn was accused of having altered his birth certificate and educational qualifications in order to qualify as an electoral candidate. In the mid-1990s, he was suspected of having obtained a MA degree in law from Ramkhamhaeng University by submitting a plagiarized thesis.

granting contracts. In 1988, for example, a number of opposition MPs charged then-Minister of Transport and Communications Banharn with awarding road-building projects to a handful of companies that were closely connected to him.[2] The military coup of February 1991, instigated (ostensibly) to eliminate rampant corruption in the elected civilian government, targeted Banharn, among many other MPs.

These accusations are not groundless. Indeed, the huge number of development projects that Banharn has injected into Suphanburi has enriched several of his "crony" contractors. One beneficiary has been Sri Saeng Public Works, a Bangkok-based company run by Banharn's close friend, Siroj Wongsirojkul. In 1993–98, the company undertook 1,678 million baht worth of highway construction projects in Suphanburi.[3] Siroj is a major shareholder in Saha Srichai, a chemical company established by Banharn in 1980. Saha Srichai, in turn, is a major shareholder in Sri Saeng Public Works.[4] Another major beneficiary of Banharn's pork-barrel projects is Sai Samphan, owned by kin of Sriphol Limthong, the nephew of Banharn's wife. Between 1997 and 2000, Sai Samphan won more than 601 million baht worth of road construction projects (n = 191) in Suphanburi.[5] One man (#65), whose fledging construction company went bankrupt in 2002 because he "lacked good ties to the powerful MP [in Suphanburi]," confided in me: "Personal ties are all that matter here. If you don't have them, you lose out." The presence of these (and other) well-connected contractors reinforces the widely held suspicion that Banharn has feathered his own nest by selectively awarding pork-barrel projects and accepting payments for such favors.

In the course of their conversations with me, a number of pro-Banharn respondents (n = 151) addressed the issue of his alleged corruption. They *all* had read or heard about the issue in the media; they were quite well-informed, not ignorant. Their responses fall into two broad categories: (1) a flat or reserved rejection of the accusation that Banharn is corrupt, and (2) an open or reluctant admission that he is or may be corrupt, accompanied by a counterargument that he has strong redeeming qualities that compensate for his dishonest dealings.

Typical of the first kind of response was the blunt dismissal—"nonsense" (*rai sara*)—uttered by a retired medical doctor (#102) who has known Banharn since he was a coffee-delivery boy in Bangkok in the 1950s. This man offered a passionate defense of Banharn: "I have never believed any of those stories about his corruption. He used to be poor, and he has pulled himself up on his own [*duay lamkaeng tua eng*]. I remember how hard he used to work. He is not the type of person who takes money under the table." Another respondent, a construction worker (#21) in Muang District, defended Banharn by making a distinction between the past and the present: "I think this problem [Banharn's corruption] is a thing of the past. He was perhaps corrupt before entering politics. Doing business in Thailand must involve corruption … But now, he is not like that. Everybody makes mistakes in life. If you keep making the same mistake, you should be criticized, but if you repent and

[2] Chaisit Phuwaphiromkhwan, *Ekasarn Laktharn Kham Aphiprai Mai Wai Wangjai Ratamontrii Khomanakhom, 21 Tulakhom 2530* (Bangkok: n.p., 1987).

[3] Untitled computer data obtained at the Department of Highways in 2002; *Bangkok Post*, November 3, 1995, p. 5.

[4] Department of Business Development, Ministry of Commerce (DBD/MC), Bangkok Company Files no. 2164/2523 and no. 1319/2510.

[5] DBD/MC, Suphanburi Limited Partnership File no. 60.

amend yourself [*klap tua*], we should be forgiving." Some other respondents took sides with Banharn by distinguishing between Bangkok and Suphanburi. As a waitress (#13) in Sri Prachan District put it, "I don't know what he does in Bangkok, but at least in Suphan, he doesn't 'eat' [a Thai euphemism for pocketing public funds]."

Most people who offered the first kind of defense made the extremely interesting claim that Banharn was actually in the vanguard of the province-wide crusade against corruption. Given his constant and meticulous surveillance of public construction projects as a *longju*-type leader, civil servants and contractors would not dare misuse public funds for fear of being caught and punished through demotion or transfer (see chapter 5). In the words of a farmer (#87) whose sister lives in Uthai Thani Province:

> Contractors in her district are deceitful. They build substandard roads on purpose, knowing that the roads will develop potholes soon. The district chief then requests more funds for repair from MPs. These people are in cahoots [*som ruu ruam khit*]. This is how they all get rich—by building bad roads. But Banharn doesn't let it happen in Suphan. The road in our village was built more than five years ago, but it has never had to be repaired. It's as good as ever.

A primary school teacher (#88) expressed a similar opinion:

> Civil servants in Suphan find it very hard to pocket state funds because Banharn is always keeping an eye on them. He has worked at a construction company before, and he owns a construction company in Bangkok, so he can tell substandard materials from good materials immediately … And he knows the prices of construction materials. So, nobody would dare try to fool him. Public money is therefore used more effectively here.

According to the people who share these kinds of views, it is simply preposterous to accuse Banharn of skimming profits off development projects.

Another common defense of Banharn asserted that receiving kickbacks from businesses does not constitute corruption in Thailand's social or cultural context. One rice farmer (#54) in Sri Prachan District offered this analysis:

> Suppose you are a contractor. You have won a project channeled by Banharn. Then you must give something back to him to show your appreciation. It may be a little money, whisky, dinner, or whatever. Giving nothing back and continuing to receive benefits is ugly and inappropriate. It is against Thai culture. Do you call gift-giving corruption? I call it a Thai custom.

This sort of defense rejects what one might call the "universalist" definition of corruption. Plainly, this kind of response sends a message to outsiders: "What is corruption to you is not corruption to us." If outsiders try to judge and construct Banharn as a corrupt MP by using their yardsticks, Suphanburians are ready to pass the opposite judgment on him by using *their own* yardstick. According to the latter, what Banharn has done is within totally legitimate bounds; his behavior conforms perfectly to Thai cultural norms.

Some other respondents based their vindication of Banharn's innocence less on emotion-ridden impressions than on logical reasoning. For example, an Internet café manager (#33), holder of a bachelor's degree, claimed: "If he were really guilty, he would be in jail now. But he is not. That means he is innocent." Several other respondents reasoned that Banharn had grown so wealthy before becoming a politician that "he doesn't have any need to 'eat' [misappropriate public funds]." Outsiders would find these defenses naïve and unpersuasive. They would argue, for instance, that the richer one gets, the more insatiable one's appetite for money becomes. Also, given the notoriously weak division between public and private in Thailand, powerful politicians, such as Banharn, can easily get around the law by buying off the police and judges, so the fact that he has not been convicted of any crime means little. My respondents were oblivious to, or refused to recognize, these obvious holes in the logic of their "airtight" defenses.

How, then, did these pro-Banharn Suphanburians explain the fact that so many reports of his corruption had appeared? How did they counter the perception of most outsiders that "there is no smoke without fire"? Most often, they placed the blame for these allegations on Banharn's political rivals. As one lottery seller (#48) put it, "Thais are jealous by nature. If you get rich and powerful, others will try to find every fault with you … Sometimes they make up a story [*ku rueang*]. That's the character [*nisai*] of Thais." Making a play on words, this respondent referred to the "politicians" (*nak kan muang*) who accuse Banharn of corruption as "national troublemakers" (*nak kuan muang*). Some other respondents expressed doubts about the ethical standards of the Thai media. A civil-service clerk (#34) commented: "What the newspapers in Bangkok say about Banharn isn't true. They report anything to frame [*sai rai*] anybody in power. That's not good. They should report the truth." The worker's son, a secondary-school student (#1), added a terse comment: "They think we are gullible. We are not."

A second category of defenses—more numerous than the first type—conceded that Banharn might be or is actually corrupt, but played down or even justified his corruption. For example, several respondents pardoned his corruption by comparing him to the other MPs, whom they claim are much worse. A primary-school teacher (#66) in Sam Chuk District made an obvious reference to Kamnan Po and Piya Angkinan, the nationally well-known *jao pho* (godfathers): "At least, he [Banharn] doesn't kill people, unlike politicians in Chonburi and Petchaburi. Corruption is better than killing." A security guard (#43) from Bang Pla Ma District defended Banharn, saying that, unlike Sanan Kachonprasert, a famous MP from Phichit Province, who "spends more than 200,000 baht on importing just one bottle of foreign wine," "Banharn always eats simple twenty-baht duck rice" at an open-air food stall in the provincial capital. According to this respondent, Banharn may "eat" (public funds), but not to the extent that would enable him to spend 200,000 baht on one bottle of foreign wine—an ostentatious luxury that many rural Thais associate with egregious corruption in high places. Still another respondent, a female teacher (#67), minimized the seriousness of Banharn's corruption by contrasting him with the former president of the United States, Bill Clinton: "Didn't Clinton use his power to sleep with women? To me, that is worse than taking a little bribe." To these respondents, Banharn's corruption, even though it should be condemned, still stays within innocuous or permissible limits.

Another type of response, given by over half of my respondents, asserted that Banharn's corruption was not exceptional among Thai politicians. A remark by one gatekeeper (#35) is typical: "Banharn is not the only corrupt politician in Thailand. So why pick on him alone? It's not fair." A civil-service clerk (#81) offered a similar judgment: "Every politician everywhere is corrupt ... Banharn is just one of them. So, why make a big issue of his case?" The respondents who gave this kind of answer sympathized with Banharn for being singled out by his critics, when many other equally guilty Thai politicians should also have been targeted.

A number of Suphanburians ventured beyond mere expressions of sympathy for Banharn and offered more active, spirited, and interesting justifications for his alleged corruption. By far the most common defense in this regard was to argue that Banharn channels part of the public money he embezzles into Suphanburi in the form of tangible development projects. A security guard (#36), a former farmer, stated philosophically:

> All Thai politicians must eat [pocket public funds] ... But we shouldn't criticize them just because they eat. The important thing is how much they eat and what they do with what they eat. Do they eat a lot, but keep it all to themselves, or do they use part of it for their hometowns? ... Banharn eats, but he gives a lot to us. Look at all the things he has built.

This security guard's colleague (#12) elaborated from a comparative perspective: "Some people in Suphan might be unhappy about Banharn's corruption, but once they go to other provinces and see what kind of conditions they are in, even they come to appreciate his achievements and say to themselves, 'Taking a little money is OK' [*kin nitdio ko mai pen rai*]." A senior civil servant (#68) in U-Thong District illustrated this point by giving arbitrary figures off the top of his head: "In Chainat, an MP eats 40 percent of the funds channeled, a contractor eats 20 percent, and only 40 percent is used to build roads. What kind of roads do they get? Very poor quality ... In Suphan, Banharn eats 10 percent and a contractor 5 percent. He spends the rest building high-quality, durable roads, which make Suphan famous." This respondent concluded with a challenge: "So, let me ask you, 'Which MP is better, Chainat's MP or Banharn?'"

These respondents were well aware of Banharn's "crony" contractors (some of them rattled off the names of these contractors to me), but they brushed off or discounted the gravity of his alleged corruption by arguing that there had been a sort of "give-and-take" between Suphanburians and Banharn. According to these respondents, what ordinary Suphanburians have received from Banharn in the form of highly visible public projects far outweighs what they may have lost as a result of his invisible corruption. While admitting upfront that Banharn may be or is corrupt, these Suphanburians quickly assert that he is not rotten to the core. He has a redeeming quality that cancels out his weakness. As a civil servant (#27) summarized, "Human beings all have strengths and weaknesses. There is nobody in the world who doesn't have any fault ... Banharn has notable weaknesses such as being corrupt, but he has more strengths. We must then accept him as good. We must judge his worth in terms of those strengths."

Put another way, these people do not consider Banharn's corruption to have breached their conceptions of what is moral or what is a legitimate use of public power. Andrew Walker's research in Chiang Mai Province is directly relevant to Banharn's case. The villagers he interviewed accepted it as "quite normal" that politicians would "derive some private benefit from public office." They condoned the politicians' misappropriation of public funds, so long as this behavior did not adversely affect the collective interests of their community.[6] Such values, norms, or expectations at the grassroots level, which make up what Walker calls "the rural constitution," help explain the Suphanburians' defense of Banharn's alleged malfeasance.

Some other respondents took an equally pragmatic and partisan view of Banharn's corruption, arguing that it was a *necessary* condition for developing Suphanburi, given the institutional context of Thailand, in which clientelism, rather than merit or need, determines the distribution of state funds. One merchant in U-Thong (#26) spelled out the "logic" behind this argument:

> Suphan was backward and disadvantaged before. Banharn wanted to develop it, so he had to bring state funds into Suphan. But he couldn't do it all alone. He had to rely on his bureaucratic clients. To return favors for their support, he had to give them a little money under the table occasionally. But he did that to develop Suphan. So, this is corruption for the sake of Suphan. That's OK.

In the same vein, another respondent, an elderly merchant (#98) in Muang District, likened Banharn's corruption to a social "lubricant" (*namman lor luen*) for the otherwise squeaky and immobile Thai bureaucracy:

> Just by offering a little money under the table to a few senior bureaucrats, Banharn can get their whole department or ministry to serve the needs of Suphan. If he doesn't pay them, he may still be able to get funds for us, but not much. But he knows that if he pays them a little money, he can get ten times more funds. That is what he has been doing to develop Suphan.

A security guard (#43) from Bang Pla Ma District offered a similar defense by questioning the advantage of having impeccably honest MPs. To make his point, he contrasted Suphanburi to the southern province of Trang, where former Prime Minister Chuan Leekpai, reputedly one of the most honest Thai politicians, has been an MP since 1975: "In Thailand, an honest politician can't do much to develop his province. Have you ever been to Trang? It is the home of the current prime minister, Chuan [in 1999], but it is still so backward … You know why? Because Chuan is too honest, to the point of being stupid [*sue jon ser*]. He does everything according to the law." Likewise, a senior civil servant (#89) in charge of education in Muang District said matter-of-factly:

---

[6] Andrew Walker, "The Rural Constitution and the Everyday Politics of Elections in Northern Thailand," *Journal of Contemporary Asia* 38,1 (2008): 95. Tolerance of corruption is not confined to provincial Thailand. One study found that Filipino villagers are willing to "wink when officials pocket some public funds as long as this is not excessive." As one farmer put it, "If there are ten glasses, an official may get two for himself, but not all ten." Fernando Zialcita, "Perspectives on Legitimacy in Ilocos Norte," in *From Marcos to Aquino: Local Perspectives on Political Transition in the Philippines*, ed. Benedict Kerkvliet and Resil Mojares (Manila: Ateneo de Manila University Press, 1991), p. 271. For a similar example in Burma, see Ardeth Maung Thawnghmung, *Behind the Teak Curtain: Authoritarianism, Agricultural Policies, and Political Legitimacy in Rural Burma* (London: Kegan and Paul, 2003), p. 7.

A politician with unclean hands who does much to develop our hometown is better than a politician with clean hands who does little to develop. It's a matter of which you see as more important: development or honesty. Of course, if there were an honest developer, I would vote for him, but realistically, can you find any MP like that in Thailand?

I asked this civil servant and several others a hypothetical question: "If Chuan would run for office in Suphanburi in the next election, would you vote for him or Banharn?" They all answered "Banharn" without hesitation, averring that Chuan's impractical, "goody-goody" honesty would hamper Suphanburi's continual progress.

These respondents are keenly aware of the attribute that an MP must possess to channel development funds from the state in the institutional milieu of Thailand: a willingness to use public office in a particularistic fashion. Banharn has amply demonstrated that he has this attribute. It has enabled him to cut through the otherwise cumbersome bureaucratic red tape and to get things done "efficiently" and "swiftly," according to many Suphanburians who admire the way he works. By contrast, they describe Chuan as too slow *because* he is too honest and cautious. Thai politics is so full of intrigue that ordinary citizens need a "dirty" politician to obtain what they want from the state. Suphanburi has been able to acquire all the high-quality projects the way it has precisely because Banharn knows when and how to bend the law and is willing to dirty his hands. This is "corruption for the sake of Suphanburi," as described by the respondent cited above. The end justifies the means; all is fair, not just in love and war, but also in developing Suphanburi.

Thus, many (if not all) Suphanburians see Banharn's corruption not as a liability, but as an *asset* that has allowed the formerly disadvantaged Suphanburi to rectify the historical injustice that had been perpetrated by the negligent central state. His corruption, which outsiders so often criticize (with good reason), assumes a quite positive meaning in Suphanburi. A construction worker (#21) expressed the value of Banharn's "heroic" corruption in a way that illustrated many Suphanburians' strong sense of comradeship with him: "Banharn may be corrupt, but he is *our* corrupt MP." For this kind of resident, even Banharn's corruption is a source of provincial pride.

HAS BANHARN FAILED TO INDUSTRIALIZE SUPHANBURI AND ADDRESS POVERTY?

Another common criticism of Banharn is that he has merely modernized the outward appearance of Suphanburi without substantially improving the lives of its individual citizens.[7] As shown in chapter 1, Suphanburi's economy is still characterized by a low level of industrialization and a correspondingly heavy reliance on agriculture. This stands in contrast to Suphanburi's neighboring provinces, such as Ayutthaya, which have achieved major structural changes to their former agrarian economies by wooing (mainly foreign) industrial capital. Consequently, people in these provinces enjoy better employment opportunities and higher per capita income. This does not mean that Suphanburians are mired in wretched poverty. Far from it—most have actually experienced an appreciable rise in their living standards under Banharn's rule. As a result, almost all Suphanburians, including farmers and workers, live fairly decent lives; nobody is homeless and is

---

[7] See *Bangkok Post*, September 25, 1995, p. 6, and December 24, 1995, p. 3.

starving to death.[8] Most Suphanburians, however, are *relatively* poorer than their counterparts in other industrialized Thai provinces.

One such person—and one of my closest informants—is Somsak (#43), an unassuming middle-aged man from a tenant rice-growing family in Phai Kong Din of Bang Pla Ma District. He lives in a small dusty wooden house that is only accessible by boat across a narrow stream. The house has no chairs and tables; it has only a small black-and-white TV set, a refrigerator, an electric fan with no cover, and a portable radio—all amenities that Somsak bought secondhand in the two decades before 1999. The house is serviced by electricity and tap water, but to save on utility costs, Somsak normally bathes in the muddy stream that flows in front of his house—a practice he blames for his receding hairline. Somsak, with just seven years of education, had worked as a waiter, bartender, and a construction worker in Bangkok until he was fired during the 1997 economic crisis and returned to Suphanburi to live with his aging parents. Thanks to the help of a former classmate, he landed his current job as a security guard in Muang District. He works six days a week for a monthly wage of 2,600 baht (approximately US$70). Since he cannot afford a motorcycle, let alone a car, he spends nearly an hour commuting from his home in Bang Pla Ma to his workplace by non-air-conditioned bus. When he is on an evening shift, he sleeps overnight at a roofed construction site near his workplace, since there is no bus service between Muang and Bang Pla Ma after 6 PM. While Somsak has lived on his meager income, his relative in Ayutthaya Province, whose son works at a Japanese electronics company (OKI), has purchased a new motorcycle and has had his old house renovated.

Somsak would be considered "poor" by the standards of urban-based scholars, and indeed Somsak calls himself "poor, just like many others in Suphanburi." How, then, do citizens like Somsak address Banharn's failure to industrialize Suphanburi, which is obviously one major cause of their relative poverty? Scholars who regard individual-level economic interests as of paramount importance would expect these people to be unhappy with Banharn, but that is not the case.

A small number of my respondents (some 15 percent) denied that most provinces, except a few such as Chiang Mai and Chonburi, have a higher per capita average income than Suphanburi. They conceded that other provinces may have more factories than Suphanburi, but thought that the impact of this difference on the level of income was minimal. The rest of my respondents, including Somsak, were "good sports," in the sense that they readily admitted that Suphanburi lags behind many provinces in its levels of industrialization and workers' income. At the same time, these people rationalized, defended, or even praised the path of development that Banharn had pursued. They agreed that lack of industrialization was one major cause of their relative poverty, but claimed that pursuing industrialization was not a desirable solution to the problem.

The most common line of defense they offered questioned and even disparaged the developmental trajectory that other industrialized provinces had followed. These provinces had succeeded in raising their per capita income by pursuing industrialization, but they had paid very high prices for it that substantially offset the economic gains. Among the adverse effects of industrialization are air and water pollution. A college student (#4) from a rice-cultivating family in Sam Chuk District

---

[8] This may be the socioeconomic precondition for the type of political dominance that Banharn has constructed. I thank Ben Kerkvliet for pushing me to reflect on this point.

gave a typical reply: "People in Ayutthaya get higher income, but they have to jeopardize their health because the air is dirty. But in Suphan, the air is still fresh. Suphan has developed while preserving clean air. Ayutthaya has developed by destroying the environment. Suphan is much more livable." Her friend, also a college student (#14), concurred: "Health is more important than having several hundred baht more each month." These respondents defended Suphanburi's slower economic growth by constructing a binary contrast between "clean Suphanburi" and "polluted other provinces." Since they knew that Suphanburi was inferior in terms of industrialization, they played up another dimension of comparison in which it was (presumed to be) superior.

Secondly, my respondents viewed the people in industrialized provinces as growing increasingly materialistic, greedy, selfish, and impersonal. According to Somsak, many people in Ayutthaya, including his relative with the motorcycle, now "value money as the most important thing in life. They were not like that twenty years ago." He provided an illustration: "If I'm short on money to buy a meal, I can stop by my neighbor's house and get a free meal. In Suphan, poor people help each other. In Ayutthaya, you'll be chased away from the neighbor's house. They only think about themselves without caring for others [*hen kae tua, tua khrai tua man*]." Somsak's mother agreed, saying, "People in Ayutthaya are becoming like Bangkokians." According to these views, the erosion of time-honored village norms prescribing mutual assistance indicates the deplorable erosion of traditional Buddhist values that has accompanied the pattern of growth in Bangkok and other industrialized regions. In Suphanburi, by contrast, people still behave as good Thais: pious, temperate, and kindhearted.

Whether such perceptions reflect the reality is highly debatable; I have met a number of materialistic and self-centered Suphanburians. But the important point is that many citizens of Suphanburi believe their subjective observation to be true, and that holding on to this belief is indispensable for upholding Suphanburi's moral (as opposed to economic) superiority to other industrialized provinces. This does not mean that Suphanburians' negative view of industrialization is somehow inherent in their culture. Instead, their beliefs should be interpreted as the ideational effect of the particular type of development that Banharn has pursued. Suphanburians have been led to accentuate some areas of development as more important than others because this allows them to maintain their pride in their province.

Equating industrialization with the loss of Thai morals has become all the more pronounced in Suphanburi since the economic crisis of 1997. King Bhumibol's public admonition against greed reinforced this tendency. According to the king, the economic boom of the early 1990s, fueled by fast-track, mindless industrialization, enriched many ordinary Thais, but along the way they developed an insatiable appetite for ostentatious living, until they learned a painful lesson the hard way in 1997. In the wake of the crisis, the king called for a soul-searching reappraisal of the previous approach to development and preached to the Thai population about the virtue of "having just enough to live on"—the didactic, abstract principle of the so-called "self-sufficient economy (*setakit phophiang*)."[9] Many of my respondents used this teaching to justify the lack of industrialization in Suphanburi. For example, a senior schoolteacher (#67) claimed that Suphanburi was "not severely hit by the

---

[9] Kevin Hewison, "Resisting Globalization: A Study of Localism in Thailand," *Pacific Review* 13,2 (2000): 279–96.

crisis because we had always practiced what the king preached. But that was not the case with the people in Ayutthaya." If the crisis hit Ayutthaya, she concluded, "they had it coming [*kam tam sanong*]." Another respondent, a gas-station attendant (#15) in Bang Pla Ma District, made a similar point: "Suphanburians may have lower incomes, but it is not that we have no money at all. We have enough to live on, a place to live, and clothes to wear. What more should we need? That's how the king tells us to live." Somsak (#43) also echoed this view.

These comments do not suggest that Suphanburians are content with being relatively poor indefinitely. Rather, what they suggest is that the virtue of frugality, as preached by the king, has allowed many Suphanburians to extol the merit of living in a non-industrialized agrarian province. The king's teaching has supplied them with another powerful and seemingly valid way to categorize industrialized provinces as decadent and to rationalize Suphanburi's apparent relative inferiority.

Given these kinds of views, the majority of my respondents praised Banharn for being "wise" and "longsighted" (*mong kan klai*) enough to steer Suphanburi clear of environmentally harmful and morally decadent industrialization. Their perception was sustained by one pervasive local myth, which a civil servant (#69) in Nong Ya Sai District described in 1999 as follows:

> About a decade ago, at the peak of the economic boom, several Japanese firms wanted to build industrial factories in Suphanburi, seeing great potential for growth in our excellent road network. But Banharn didn't like industrial firms. He knew that the effects of industrialization were not all positive. He wanted Suphanburi to be an educational center instead, so he said "no" to the Japanese firms. Since then, Banharn has made it a public policy not to attract any foreign capital to Suphanburi. As a result, foreign investors have stayed away from Suphanburi. Suphanburi has therefore been spared what happened to other industrialized provinces.

The authenticity of this story is questionable. In fact, one official (#37) at the Provincial Office of Commerce dismissed it as totally unfounded. As a capitalist who holds vital stakes in the construction industry, Banharn actually tried to *promote* Suphanburi's industrialization in the late 1980s, as exemplified by his establishment of the Western Regional Office of Industrial Promotion in Muang District.[10] He even held a cornerstone-laying ceremony for this office.[11] Back then, he made no bones about his intention to "turn Suphanburi into an industrial province,"[12] arguing that "more factories must be built in Suphanburi for sure."[13] Most Suphanburians who laud Banharn for refusing to promote industrialization do not know about his past policy, have forgotten about it, purposely ignore it, or simply say that he has changed his mind (which is the case with Somsak). In any case, these Suphanburians now embrace the belief that Banharn has never been seriously interested in industrialization, and they hail him as a man of inimitable foresight. The sheer number of schools that Banharn has recently built and the fact that he initiated a

---

[10] *Khon Suphan*, June 16, 1989, pp. 1, 2.

[11] *Khon Suphan*, November 16, 1990, pp. 1, 9.

[12] *Khon Suphan*, November 16, 1988, p. 1.

[13] *Khon Suphan*, September 16, 1988, p. 2.

local project called "Clean and Pollution-free Suphanburi" in 1997 reinforce their belief.[14]

Thus, many lower-class Suphanburians avoid drawing a causal connection between their poverty and Banharn's failure to industrialize the province. Instead, these people, especially farmers, blame their poverty on the factors that have little to do with Banharn, such as: (1) vagaries of the weather or natural disasters (e.g., flood, drought, and crop diseases); (2) their limited educational attainments, which restrict job opportunities; (3) price fluctuations in the agrarian market, or the government's inability to shore up rice prices; (4) expensive farming inputs (e.g., fertilizers), or lack of state subsidies for those inputs; and (5) the practices of greedy rice millers/middlemen (who cheat in weighing crops) and their collusion with corrupt local government officials. Many farmers feel particularly bitter about the last three factors, as they represent conditions resulting from the government's historical neglect of their problems. A former rice-cultivating farmer (#90) from Song Phi Nong District lamented: "It has been like this everywhere in Thailand. The government is no good. They don't help farmers. They are not interested." This man, named Phongsak, blamed the government's incompetence or insincerity for his mounting debts in the past, which forced him to quit farming in 1993 and to start a new life as a vendor of fried noodles.

What is interesting to note about this kind of account is that although Banharn is technically a part of the state that has historically squeezed the farming sector (he was once at the pinnacle of the state), few farmers in Suphanburi, including Phongsak, see him as being implicated in their economic problems. On the contrary, they see him as doing the best he can to alleviate their poverty in his own ways. They cite two of his major accomplishments to support their claims.

One is his impressive record of sponsoring the construction and improvement of the province's infrastructure. For instance, Somsak (#43) said of the Suphanburi–Bangkok highway that he uses daily in commuting to his work—the so-called "Banharn Highway" built in the early 1980s with a fund of 460 million baht (see chapter 4): "If Banharn had not built the road, I would be jobless and far poorer than I am now … Imagine how many people like me are dependent on that single road alone for jobs." Somsak also hailed Banharn's effort to improve the educational system, saying:

> If only there were a man like him when I was a student, I might have been able to study a little longer, and I might have a better job now … But now, there are fewer people like me. He emphasizes the virtue of education, builds schools, and gives scholarships to students who want to study at a higher level. I hope my daughter [who lives with his ex-wife] will go to a Banharn–Jaemsai School.

Similarly, Phongsak (#90), the aforementioned vendor of fried noodles, proudly talked of his twenty-year-old daughter, who attends the Boromarajonani College of Nursing, for which Banharn provided almost 123 million baht in state funds in 1993–99.[15] He is hopeful that, after graduation, his daughter will work at Chaophraya

---

[14] *Khon Suphan*, July 16, 1997, p. 1; *Khon Suphan*, December 16, 1997, p. 4.

[15] Budget Bureau, *Ekasarn Ngop-pramarn 2538*, 4,6 (1994): 280, 303; Budget Bureau, *Ekasarn Ngop-pramarn 2539*, 4,9 (1995): 326; Budget Bureau, *Ekasarn Ngop-pramarn 2540*, 4,9 (1996): 473, 494. See also chapter 4.

Yommarat Hospital, the largest public hospital in Suphanburi. "She will then help our family earn a more steady income. If not for the college, she might be a farmer now," Phongsak said.

In addition to noting Banharn's construction projects, many respondents cited the pro-farmer policies that he had adopted or supported in the past.[16] Unfortunately, according to my respondents, these well-intentioned policies have never materialized, or have never been sustained over an extended period of time, because they were blocked or rescinded by faceless, "bad" MPs who have vested interests in suppressing farmers economically. As Phongsak (#90) said, "Just one or two politicians cannot solve farmers' problems. Everybody has to cooperate. Banharn tries to enforce policies to help us, but he is obstructed by other MPs who have connections to the rice millers. Some MPs are rice millers themselves." Consequently, farmers' poverty persists as a deeply embedded structural problem of Thai society, a problem that "even an MP of Banharn's caliber cannot solve" (*so so khanat Banharn ko kae khai mai dai*). Phongsak, as well as many others, seemed to view the problem as one caused by all sorts of wicked policies and practices that emanate from the invisible, yet powerful, central state that has been "out there" in Bangkok "all along." He perceived Banharn as making valiant efforts to confront and tame this Goliath to the benefit of the poor in Suphanburi. Thus, far from being seen as a leader who has contributed to, much less caused, the continuing (relative) poverty of low-income Suphanburians, Banharn is perceived as playing a part, however small, in addressing the farmers' intractable economic problem.

In sum, Suphanburians mount all sorts of subjective and even dogmatic defenses that spurn, minimize, gloss over, or rationalize the outsiders' criticisms of Banharn as a politician. Many of these responses clearly conflict with each other. Some defenses, for example, admit that he is corrupt, while others categorically deny it. Also, some defenses are convincing, whereas others sound strained. Yet these arguments that vindicate Banharn have one thing in common, despite all the contradictions they contain and the varying degrees of their persuasiveness: They all ultimately serve the same function of preserving and bolstering the coherent, hegemonic image of Banharn as the heroic creator of the present-day "developed" Suphanburi. This image lies at the core of, and unifies, a system of disparate and even contradictory narratives that Suphanburians recount to justify and reaffirm their support for their leader and thereby to reinforce their positive provincial identity. Keeping this deeply cherished image intact requires that Suphanburians come up with a variety of partisan and ad hoc defenses of Banharn. The significance of these defenses lies not in their coherence or persuasiveness, but in the overall social function they serve. Suphanburians' support for Banharn is therefore immune to outsiders' critiques of his misconduct and incompetence, no matter how formidable or legitimate these critiques may be.

This support allows Banharn to fend off or trivialize outsiders' critiques. He once commented on a media report that his administration suffered from a "public faith deficit" among the voters in Bangkok. "You can't possibly base your judgment only

---

[16] For example, after being elected MP in 1976, Banharn persuaded the minister of agriculture to provide 275 tons of subsidized fertilizers to farmers in Suphanburi. *Khon Suphan*, September 10, 1976, pp. 1, 8. For similar stories, see *Khon Suphan*, April 16, 1980; *Khon Suphan*, August 16, 1980; and *Khon Suphan*, September 1, 1980. For an account of his attempt to guarantee minimum rice prices, see *Khon Suphan*, February 16, 1992, pp. 1, 9.

on Bangkokians. Bangkok does not represent the whole country."[17] He knows all too well where his base of support is.

FEEBLE POLITICAL OPPOSITION

Banharn's political authority in Suphanburi is not totally uncontested. He has his share of severe critics. These detractors, mostly rank-and-file civil servants, comprised some 11 percent of the people I interviewed. There were several reasons for their opposition to his rule. First, they believed he was corrupt, as reported in the media. Second, they hated being mobilized to attend frequent inspection tours, meetings, and ceremonies held in his honor. Third, they resented his constant, fastidious interference in civil service affairs (see chapter 5). These people do not simply sit still, letting Banharn's authority go unchallenged; they have taken several actions, both covert and overt, to chip away at the political base that sustains his authority. Banharn's domination, just like any other politician's, is not total (and will never be).

A few examples are illustrative. One is the daring action that a group of disgruntled primary school teachers took in early 2002 to vent their frustration. They sent two letters to then-Prime Minister Thaksin, exposing the collusive relationship that had developed between Banharn and two chiefs of the Provincial Office of Primary School Education—Dilok Phatanawichaichoot (1996–2000) and Kit Kiantisomkit (2000–2006). In particular, the letters, which my informant allowed me secretly to photocopy, revealed how Dilok milked profits from various school construction projects and called him a "corrupt and dishonest" civil servant and a "vampire [*phi krasue*] who sucks the blood of the Ministry of Education." The letters asserted further that Dilok worked as a vote canvasser for the Chart Thai (CT) Party instead of maintaining political neutrality as a civil servant, and that he was responsible for having various state-funded school-building projects named inappropriately in Banharn's honor. The letters also complained: "Civil servants in Suphanburi … are forced [*khom khuean*] to welcome the prominent politician of Suphanburi [Banharn] many times every year."[18] Although Thaksin did not take any action in response to these complaints, presumably because Banharn's CT Party was a member of his coalition government, this episode is indicative of the festering resentment harbored by some local civil servants.

Other civil servants have mounted their offensive in more subtle ways. A case in point concerns a billboard erected by the Provincial Office of Accelerated Rural Development (POARD) in 1999 to publicize the technical specifications of a newly constructed asphalt road in Nong Krathu village, Song Phi Nong District. At the bottom, the signboard notes, in small letters, that the construction fund for the road "came from the taxpayers' money." What makes this signboard interesting is that it has been erected right next to a large sign mounted by Nong Krathu subdistrict officials and a local contractor, which thanks Banharn for the road construction fund. The POARD's billboard effectively challenges this sign and sends an implicit message to Nong Krathu residents that, since they pay taxes to benefit from public

---

[17] *Bangkok Post*, August 15, 1996, p. 1.

[18] See Yoshinori Nishizaki, "The Weapon of the Strong: Identity, Community, and Domination in Provincial Thailand" (PhD dissertation, University of Washington, 2004), chapter 10, for details.

works, they do not need to say special thanks to Banharn for supplying them. A Suphanburi-born TV anchorman and former senator, Somkiat Onwimon, represented the views of these civil servants in public when he said:

> [Suphanburians] have long been misled into thinking Mr. Banharn is solely responsible for public projects in the province, even to the point where they believe he paid for the projects out of his own pocket. Little [do] they know the money spent on dozens of public utilities and ... infrastructure, ranging from roads to public schools ... which invariably bear the name of Banharn–Jaemsai, actually come from the pockets of taxpayers nationwide.[19]

Thus, while the majority of Suphanburians support Banharn's rule, one can nonetheless detect some evidence of a counterhegemonic discourse. Banharn's opponents try to contest and subvert his authority in various places and through various means.

There are residents of Suphanburi who are not civil servants, yet who have opposed Banharn for valid reasons. A representative case concerns twenty-two farming families in Pho Khiew of Muang District, where Banharn built a government complex in 1996. As the Provincial Office tried to clear the land (348 *rai* in size), these families, who claimed to have inherited the land from their ancestors in 1915 and had land titles to support their claims, refused to vacate, even though they were assured official compensation payments that amounted to sixteen million baht.[20] They put up a surprisingly tenacious resistance by lying flat on the ground to block the passage of bulldozers and trucks.[21] In the end, the provincial authorities, apparently with Banharn's tacit consent, evicted these farmers from the construction site, claiming that it was "public" land. In the process, violence broke out, and several villagers were arrested. The farmers were indignant. One of them was quoted as saying, "Development has brought nothing but grief ... It's good to bring civilization here, but don't let that hurt the people."[22] Consequently, Banharn's image was stained. The leader of the protest declared, "We had loved Than Banharn very much, that's why we voted for him. We are extremely saddened that he could be so oppressive against Suphanburi citizens. If he continues with the project, we will vote for him no more."[23] A civil servant who comes into regular contact with Pho Khiew residents confirmed that Banharn's popularity has been on the wane in that area since the forced eviction.[24] In his rush to undertake the megaproject, Banharn employed heavy-handed unilateral tactics that directly hurt the interests of a group of economically precarious low-income Suphanburians, generating profound resentment in its wake.

All these dissenting voices, however, have failed to coalesce into a major province-wide public movement against Banharn. There are three reasons for this.

---

[19] *Bangkok Post*, January 4, 2009, p. 5.

[20] *Bangkok Post*, April 13, 1996. Sixty-five other families agreed to vacate by accepting the compensation. *Bangkok Post*, April 20, 1996.

[21] *Bangkok Post*, January 9, 1996, p. 3; *Bangkok Post*, February 23, 1996, p. 1; *Bangkok Post*, February 26, 1996, p. 19.

[22] *Bangkok Post*, September 25, 1995, p. 6.

[23] *Bangkok Post*, February 29, 1996, p. 8.

[24] Confidential interview, April 22, 1999.

First, anti-Banharn Suphanburians are in the minority. They are limited, by and large, to rank-and-file civil servants, whose number in the provincial population is minuscule. Even at the peak of the economic boom in 1995, civil servants (n = 7,272) constituted a mere 5.4 percent of all gainfully employed Suphanburians,[25] and not every civil servant hates Banharn. Many are actually his stalwart supporters. Furthermore, the kind of incident described above, in which Banharn's development projects impinged on his constituents' economic interests, seems to be an exception rather than the rule.

Second, there is no rival politician who can galvanize the anti-Banharn elements and rally their support. Wirat Watanakrai, a former village head in U-Thong District, was a potential rival, but his challenge eventually fizzled. A long-standing, redoubtable critic of Banharn since the late 1970s, Wirat contested the parliamentary elections of 1988, 1992, 1995, and 1996, adopting a campaign slogan that made his opposition to Banharn explicit.[26] Although he performed dismally in each of these elections (his influence was confined to just a few subdistricts in U-Thong), he remained a champion of the anti-Banharn cause. But Wirat was co-opted by the CT Party in 1999, when his son, Phatthaphong, was elected to the U-Thong Municipality Council thanks to Banharn's support.[27] Seeing Wirat as an irritating thorn in the side, Banharn removed it by applying a little ointment.

Third, anti-Banharn civil servants refrain from publicizing their opposition for fear that Banharn's supporters might expose or misquote them and that they might be punished with a transfer or demotion as a result. So long as Banharn controls bureaucratic appointments in the patrimonial central state, his potential opponents must confine their critical discourse within the circles of their trusted friends and colleagues, and they cannot risk forming a public political alliance with other anti-Banharn elements outside the bureaucracy, such as the aforementioned farmers in Pho Kiew.

Thus, opposition to Banharn remains small and disorganized, and is too weak to challenge his control over the symbolic universe of Suphanburi. As a result, what most ordinary Suphanburians see, hear, and read on a daily basis—a system of social meanings in which they live their daily lives—continues to be dominated by the geographically and temporally accumulated stock of Banharn's symbolic capital: the development projects, both large and small in scale, which he has supplied in various parts of Suphanburi over the last four decades, coupled with the numerous signboards and ceremonies that broadcast news of those projects. To live in Suphanburi is to live in this symbolic universe, which reproduces the positive image of the rapidly developing provincial community created by Banharn. Nobody has been able to mount a successful symbolic offensive to threaten or challenge this robust spatiotemporally nurtured image. Disgruntled anti-Banharn civil servants would view his symbolic capital as ideological propaganda aimed at brainwashing or indoctrinating the pliant populace in Suphanburi. In their public behavior,

---

[25] Provincial Statistical Office of Suphanburi, *Samut Rai-ngan Sathiti Changwat: Suphanburi 2539* (Suphanburi: Provincial Statistical Office of Suphanburi, 1997), pp. 14, 41, 55.

[26] Wirat was elected as a CT Party MP from Suphanburi in 1975. In 1976, he ran for office again under the CT Party banner, along with Banharn, who had just joined the party. Wirat suffered a mortifying loss, however, while Banharn, a political novice at the time, scored a landslide victory (see chapter 3). Wirat garnered only 21,779 votes, less than half the votes for Banharn (57,530). This probably soured Wirat's relationship with Banharn.

[27] Confidential interview with a high-ranking civil servant in U-Thong, January 29, 2000.

however, most of these civil servants still choose, albeit grudgingly, to help create such symbolic capital in their eagerness to maximize their chances for promotions and access to state funds (see chapters 5 and 6). In other words, these civil servants are complicit in reproducing, advertising, and enshrining the regime of the very politician they resent. Thus, the hegemonic system of beliefs that underpin Banharn's reputation as Suphanburi's legendary developer remains firmly in place.

It is not too surprising, then, that Banharn consistently won a large share of his constituency's votes in every election he contested, although this share decreased noticeably after 1996 as a result of growing opposition to his rule (table 8.1). Along the way, he came under severe attacks from his opponents, yet none of these attacks came close to undermining his base of support. If anything, some of them strengthened the voters' support for him. The campaign mounted by Banharn's barbed-tongued, longtime rival, Police Major Anant Senakhant, in 1988 had this reverse effect. As described in chapter 3, Anant held massive anti-Banharn rallies in 1975 and 1976. For reasons that are not clear, Anant then kept a low profile for the next twelve years, but, before the 1988 election, he delivered another public tirade against Banharn. Unlike the previous rallies in which he attacked Banharn independently, the 1988 rally was financially supported by a political party, the Seri Niyom. Anant was also backed by the aforementioned Wirat Watanakrai, the village head of U-Thong District, who ran for office under the Seri Niyom Party banner in the 1988 election. Buoyed by all this institutional and personal support, Anant "lashed out fiercely" (*du dueat phet rorn*) at Banharn,[28] held him responsible for spreading an epidemic of sordid money politics in Thailand, and called him "a poison and danger [*pen phit pen phai*] for democracy" and "the representative of evils." Anant further asserted that Banharn might "outwardly look like a wonderful angel [*thewada prod*]," but he was actually "a Dracula [*phi porp*] that sucks Suphanburians' blood."[29] Anant also resorted to scare tactics by arranging to have a dummy corpse set up in front of the house of one CT Party vote canvasser.[30]

Anant's vehement attacks only made Suphanburians "furious and vengeful" (*pen dueat pen khaen*). Organizing "the Group of Suphan's Blood" protest (as in 1976), these Suphanburians, aroused by hatred of the outsider who insulted their hero, demonstrated stronger support for Banharn. A provincial newspaper aptly described the ironic effect of Anant's action when it reported (by using a rhyme), "Ying da, ying dang" (The more [Anant] denounced, the more famous [Banharn] became).[31]

Anant and his allies were not the only individuals who dared to challenge Banharn. Before the election of September 1992, the candidates fielded by the Liberal Justice Party attacked Banharn, calling his supporters "stupid" for believing in his deceptive appearance of generosity.[32] This attack was mounted when the reputation of Banharn and the CT Party was at its nadir nationally. Following the coup of 1991, the military froze the assets of several "unusually rich" (i.e., corrupt) politicians, including Banharn. He was eventually cleared of the corruption charge, but he was widely suspected of having bought his way out of trouble. In addition, in the violent clash between the military and civilian demonstrators in May 1992, the CT Party

---

[28] *Khon Suphan*, August 1, 1988, p. 1.

[29] Anant Sanokhan, *Thammai Phom Tong Than Banharn* (Bangkok: Klet Thai, 1988), pp. 21, 23.

[30] *Khon Suphan*, August 1, 1988, p. 1.

[31] Ibid.

[32] *Khon Suphan*, September 16, 1992, p. 2.

sided with the military, leading the national media to label it "a devil's party."[33] Thus, the already negative images of Banharn and the CT Party were severely tarnished before the 1992 election. The Liberal Justice Party candidates saw this as a golden opportunity to unseat Banharn from power in Suphanburi.

Table 8.1 Votes for Banharn, 1976–2007[34]

Year	Number of Votes for Banharn (A)	Total Number of Votes Cast (B)	A ÷ B
1976	* 57,530	91,731	62.7%
1983	99,104	145,821	68.0%
1986	151,095	?	?
1988	120,149	171,285	70.1%
(I) 1992	* 165,614	189,466	87.4%
(II) 1992	181,572	194,137	93.5%
1995	* 218,376	244,455	89.3%
1996	223,724	236,909	94.4%
2001	49,816	57,972	85.9%
2005	58,610	74,905	78.2%
2007	209,989	267,559	78.4%

* indicates the largest number of votes in Thailand.
The elections of 2001 and 2005 were held under a new electoral law, as a result of which Banharn's previous constituency was divided into four districts.

Their attacks backfired. Far from undermining the base of support for Banharn, they ended up expanding it. For example, one opposition candidate, Photchara Yuwangprasit, held an anti-Banharn rally in Kho Khok Tao, Muang District. Despite the fact that Photchara was born in this subdistrict, local residents refused to support him, and they expressed profound dissatisfaction with him for attacking Banharn, who had done so much to develop their province. One villager questioned whether Photchara "can do anything for us [other than to attack other people]?"[35] Consequently, Photchara received only 5,921 votes, in contrast to the 181,572 votes for Banharn. More than 90 percent of all the votes cast in Kho Khok Tao went to Banharn.[36] The Liberal Justice Party had severely underestimated the resilient strength of local support for Banharn.

---

[33] David Murray, *Angels and Devils: Thai Politics from February 1991 to September 1992: A Struggle for Democracy?* (Bangkok: White Orchid Press, 1996).

[34] *Sources*: Data obtained at the Division of Elections, Ministry of Interior; Election Commission, *Khomun Sathiti lae Phon Kan Lueak Tang Sammachik Sapha Phu Thaen Ratsadon*, various years (2001, 2005, 2007).

[35] *Khon Suphan*, September 16, 1992, p. 2.

[36] Ministry of Interior, *Phon Kan Lueak Tang Sammachik Sapha Phu Thaen Ratsadon 2535* (Bangkok: Ministry of Interior, 1992), p. 152.

Popular support for Banharn was even more firmly consolidated in the parliamentary election of 1995. As widely reported in the national media, this election was essentially a contest between Banharn's CT Party and the Democrat Party led by Chuan Leekpai, a Thammasat-educated and morally upright politician who enjoyed the support of most voters in Bangkok. Banharn was bent on winning this election, so he did not hesitate to recruit nationally well-known criminals, godfathers, and thugs into the CT Party, so long as they had proven their ability to deliver votes. Among those recruited were Kamnan Po (a murderous gangster in Chonburi Province), Narong Wongwan (a suspected drug trafficker in northern Thailand), and Vatthana Asavaheme (another alleged drug dealer from Samut Prakan Province, south of Bangkok). The latter two had been denied entry into the United States on account of their suspected involvement in the narcotics trade. The response to this electoral strategy from middle-class residents of Bangkok was overwhelmingly negative—a poignant reminder to Banharn of how little political capital he had accumulated in Thailand's capital. Foreign investors, too, showed deep concern about the prospect of Banharn's ascendance to power. Most Suphanburians, however, saw the 1995 election as a golden opportunity to have Banharn become Thailand's first Suphanburi-born prime minister. Because he was so viciously criticized in the media, these people stood firmly behind him. One farmer (#61) in Song Phi Nong District recalled: "We said to each other, 'We must stick together to help Banharn.' If he becomes prime minister, he will do even more to develop Suphan. If we miss this chance, we may have to wait for another hundred years ... If Chuan becomes prime minister, only the south will develop." Nodding in agreement, this farmer's neighbor (#91) said: "All Suphanburians voted for him. We had to, to say thanks to him for all the things he had done for Suphanburi ... If anybody didn't vote for him, that person was not a true Suphanburian."

Thus, despite the fact that the Democrat Party characterized the 1995 election as a contest that offered Thai voters a simple choice between a "good" man (Chuan) and a "bad" man (Banharn), the overwhelming majority of Suphanburians chose the latter. Banharn's clients did much to build a groundswell of zealous, partisan support for him on this occasion. When Banharn visited Suphanburi a month before the election, several secondary schools that had benefited from his budget allocations mobilized hundreds of their students and musical bands to organize and lead a splendid procession through the provincial capital, carrying banners that appealed to the already strong provincialist sentiments of the crowd: "Vote Banharn for premier for the prestige of Suphanburi's People" and "This is the first time in history that Suphanburi will have a prime minister."[37] In an outcome that surprised few people in his own province, Banharn won the election by garnering more votes than any other candidate in the country. With his subsequent assumption of power as prime minister, Suphanburians' pride in Banharn reached an all-time high. By voting for Banharn and having him elected as prime minister, these people reaffirmed and consolidated their positive social identity as members of "Banharn-buri."[38]

---

[37] *Bangkok Post*, June 6, 1995, p. 6.

[38] One might say that every parliamentary election has performed the social function of unifying Suphanburians behind Banharn, just as in southern Thailand, where people consolidate their regional identity by voting for the Democrat Party. See Marc Askew, *Performing Political Identity: The Democrat Party in Southern Thailand* (Chiang Mai: Silkworm, 2008).

The extent to which Banharn enjoys Suphanburians' support is reflected in the growing *quietness* of electoral campaigns in the province. Over the years, the familiar ingredients of Thai elections, such as smear campaigns and loud rallies, have become more and more conspicuous by their absence in Suphanburi. Opposition parties have fielded candidates, but only to meet the legal quota regarding the number of candidates that must be fielded nationwide. These "dummy candidates" were therefore not serious about winning; opposition parties were well aware of the futility of conducting expensive election campaigns in the province. In the election of 2005, for instance, the Thai Rak Thai (TRT) Party announced its intention to grab at least two of the six seats in Suphanburi, but the party leader, Thaksin Shinawatra, did not even bother to attend an election rally in support of the TRT candidates who were running there.[39] On election day, the majority of Suphanburi's voters remained steadfastly loyal to Banharn, although they had benefited a great deal from Thaksin's pro-poor social policies over the previous four years.

One voter summed up the sentiments of his fellow constituents when he said: "As long as Banharn doesn't wash his hands of politics, who could beat him? Nobody—because his achievements [in having developed Suphanburi] are so conspicuous. It is difficult for [Suphanburi's] people to forget [what he has done]."[40] Likewise, a retired civil servant (#101) in the Muang market town looked back on Suphanburi's recent history and commented:

> Those people who accuse Banharn of vote-buying and other bad things just don't know how much he has done for Suphanburi ... Anyone who remembers what Suphanburi was like forty, fifty years ago would agree. Those who badmouth him don't know our history. They shouldn't talk [about Banharn]. They have no right to talk.

This kind of view forms the heart of Suphanburians' accounts, which reflect and generate their collective pride in Banharn and his construction of "Banharn-buri."

THE FUTURE OF BANHARN-BURI: WITHERING AWAY?

Let me end these empirical chapters on a speculative note. Banharn-buri is essentially a *personal*, not a family, dynasty. It is founded on Suphanburian's positive identification with him and his personal contributions to provincial development. As such, Banharn-buri is potentially vulnerable to disintegration when Banharn, now aged seventy-eight (as of 2010), passes away.

To avert this possibility and ensure the smooth transfer of political power to his Silpa-archa clan, Banharn started grooming his eldest daughter, Kanchana (b. 1961), and his only son, Worawuth (b. 1973), in the mid-1990s to become Suphanburi's MPs. Thanks to his characteristic behind-the-scenes maneuverings, both attained ministerial posts, but only once, and for a short duration.[41] To the extent that Banharn-buri has been routinized or institutionalized, its strength is based on Banharn's personal appointive and budgetary powers in the central patrimonial

---

[39] *Bangkok Post*, January 11, 2005, p. 6.

[40] *Khon Suphan*, September 16, 1992, p. 2.

[41] Kanchana was deputy minister of education in 1999–2001, while Worawuth served as deputy minister of transport and communications in 2008.

democratic state, which neither Kanchana nor Worawuth has been able to match. Both are simply too young and too weak politically to emulate what Banharn has done. In addition, since Banharn does not have any economic interests in Suphanburi—his companies are all based in Bangkok (see chapter 3)—neither Kanchana nor Worawuth has a firm, local economic base from which to exert his or her political control over the province. Therefore, Banharn-buri may be far less enduring than the many land-based family dynasties in the Philippines, which have been successfully bequeathed from father to child over many generations.[42] The latter have been able to survive the deaths of their founders. Banharn-buri may not. Banharn's eventual death might well expose its inherent fragility.

One politician who could fill Banharn's shoes in the future is Pridi Charoensil, a retired colonel in the Provincial Police of Suphanburi. Pridi is the younger brother of Muang Municipality's mayor, Jaranai Injai-uea (1985–), who owed her first successful election in 1985 to Banharn's support. This marked the beginning of a cozy relationship between Pridi and Banharn. Thanks to Banharn's help, Pridi was transferred from the southern Muslim province of Yala and achieved promotion to the rank of colonel.[43] In return, Pridi served as a vote canvasser for Banharn. A fissure opened between the two in 2000, however, when Thailand had its first senatorial election. Pridi expressed a keen interest in running for office and expected to receive Banharn's endorsement, but Banharn refused to support him. Local rumor had it that Banharn, who essentially mistrusts anyone other than his family members, was deeply concerned about a potential scenario that might develop after his death—the possibility that Pridi, once elected, would use his office to expand his already strong influence at the expense of Kanchana and Worawuth. That would frustrate Banharn's ambition to see "Banharn-buri" pass into the hands of his daughter or son in the form of "Kanchana-buri" or "Worawuth-buri." Banharn therefore endorsed politically lackluster and pliant Manas Rung-rueang, former Muang Municipality mayor (Jaranai's predecessor), whose loyalty to Banharn was actually quite suspect.[44] Incensed, Pridi split with Banharn and ran for office by receiving covert support from Thaksin's TRT Party. Although he lost to Manas,[45] he challenged Banharn again in the parliamentary election of 2005 by running against his son, Worawuth, under the TRT Party banner. Pridi lost again (despite Thaksin's help), but many Suphanburians believe that he has not given up his political ambition. He is believed to be biding his time before he makes his presence felt following Banharn's death.

---

[42] Alfred McCoy, ed., *An Anarchy of Families: State and Family in the Philippines* (Madison, WI: University of Wisconsin Press, 1993).

[43] *Bangkok Post*, March 15, 2000.

[44] Once an influential politician in Suphanburi, Manas was alarmed by Banharn's growing popularity in the 1960s. Therefore, when Banharn ran for office in the parliamentary election of 1976, Manas tried to sabotage his election (see chapter 3).

[45] Pridi initially won the election, which deeply humiliated Banharn. Subsequently, Banharn took heavy-handed, no-holds-barred action to block Pridi's assumption of office. He ordered then-Governor Wiphat Khongmalai to file an official complaint with the Election Commission, claiming that Pridi engaged in vote-buying. The Election Commission declared the election results void and called for a reelection in May. Manas won the reelection, but this time Pridi leveled the same vote-buying accusation at Manas, which led the Electoral Commission to call for another reelection in July. Manas won this third election and assumed office as a new senator. *Bangkok Post*, March 12, 2000.

On coming to power, Pridi (or anybody else with similar political ambitions) might try to revisit or even undo the recent history of Suphanburi that Banharn has composed, as it were. The future generations of Suphanburians who do not know Banharn might be susceptible to such reinterpretations of the past. Or they might simply feel blasé about his achievements. That might be the fate of any regime whose dominance is based mainly on social memories[46]—in the case of Banharn-buri, these are the collective memories of the province's "backward" past. As the memories gradually and inevitably fade away or become fragmented, so will Banharn's authority.

Furthermore, if a powerful MP of Banharn's type appears in any of Suphanburi's neighboring provinces after his death, the relative social position of Suphanburi could decline correspondingly. Conditions are propitious for the rise of "a second Banharn" in the provinces that are currently branded "backward." Suphanburi had suffered such a label before, and it was under that historical condition that Banharn attained his current position. Therefore, as Sallie Yea analyzes in her fascinating study on regional rivalry in South Korea, "imaginary (social) maps are never finally drawn." They are like "a palimpsest, where earlier inscriptions are erased and others drawn over them."[47] The social geography of power is not immutable. It is subject to contestation and reconstitution. The future of politics and development in post-Banharn Suphanburi is therefore not certain and secure. Neither is Banharn's posthumous place in the history of Suphanburi.

Banharn is probably well aware of these disturbing possibilities. His sponsorship of the modern and extravagant Banharn Silpa-archa Museum, in Muang District, can be interpreted as evidence of his insecurity. This museum, completed in 2004 at a cost of over 300 million baht,[48] presents and honors a condensed and accessible history of Suphanburi's recent development of Suphanburi under Banharn's rule. Despite the fact that admission is free, the museum is usually empty; few ordinary Suphanburians, to my knowledge, have visited it. They have little reason to do so, since the museum presents what they already know so well. The target audience is not the Suphanburians who are alive now. Banharn has built the museum, I believe, for the hundreds of thousands of Suphanburians who will be born in the decades to come, long after his death. The future generations will need to be taught and reminded of what he had accomplished before they were born. The construction of the museum is the manifestation of Banharn's desire to enshrine himself at the top of the "Who's Who" list in Suphanburi and to pass the positive legacies of his rule to the future in the service of his children.

This project has acquired all the more importance since December 2008, when the Constitutional Court disbanded the CT Party, the second oldest existing party in Thailand, which Banharn had led since 1994, on account of the electoral fraud committed by one of its executives. In addition, the court stripped Banharn, as well as Kanchana and Worawuth, of political power for a period of five years—a decision

---

[46] Hue-Tam Ho Tai, ed., *The Country of Memory: Remaking the Past in Late Socialist Vietnam* (Berkeley, CA: University of California Press, 2001).

[47] Sallie Yea, "Maps of Resistance and Geographies of Dissent in the Cholla Region of South Korea," *Korean Studies* 24 (2000): 90.

[48] The museum was built in part with Banharn's personal funds and in part with donations from local elites.

that has left many Suphanburians appalled.[49] Thus, Banharn has been deprived of his firm, institutionalized footing in the patrimonial democratic state that had "incubated" his political career since the 1970s. This is a terrible blow for a politician whose local-level legitimacy had rested on his ability to manipulate formal institutions of the center to the benefit of his local constituencies. The same fate befell three other CT Party MPs of Suphanburi, who are all Banharn's protégés— Nathawuth Prasertsuwan, Yutthana Photsuthon, and Samerkan Thiangtham. These three MPs come from the families that have received various benefits in return for supporting Banharn over the decades. Nathawuth is the son of a former MP for Suphanburi, Bun-uea Prasertsuwan (b. 1919), who attained a series of political posts thanks to Banharn's machinations: deputy agriculture minister, minister attached to the prime minister's office, deputy prime minister, and House Speaker. Yutthana is the cousin of another former MP of Suphanburi and deputy CT Party leader, Praphat Photsuthon (b. 1949), who had served as deputy finance minister, deputy interior minister, and minister of agriculture. In addition, Praphat's two family-based construction companies—Ruam Mitr Muang Rae and Prasong Phon—have reaped handsome profits from the infrastructure projects directed by Banharn.[50] Samerkan, the third CT Party member stripped of his position, is the eldest son of another former MP of Suphanburi, Jongchai Thiangtham (b. 1943), who had served as deputy minister of labor and welfare and deputy minister of transport and communications despite his shady reputation as a gambler and his close association with Chat Tao-poon, Bangkok's notorious gangster.[51] As a result of the Constitutional Court ruling, these families, which had underpinned Banharn's patronage network, lost their political bases in Suphnaburi. The ruling also frustrated the ambitions of these families to secure intra-family transfers of power by relying on Banharn. It was speculated in some circles that these developments might spell the end of Banharn's long-standing hold on politics in Suphanburi.

Yet Banharn has quickly adapted to these changes and minimized their adverse impact by establishing a new party, Chart Thai Phattana (Thai National Development) Party. He then invited his younger brother Chumpol to become its leader. The two had not been on speaking terms since 1998, when Chompol, then-minister of education, quit the post and left the CT Party in protest against Banharn's constant *longju*-style meddling in the affairs of his ministry (see chapter 5). But to cope with the exigencies that transpired as the result of the 2008 court ruling, Banharn, a politician always known for his Machiavellian flexibility, buried the hatchet with Chumpol.[52]

Subsequently, in the by-election of January 2009, Banharn had his local clients run for office successfully under the banner of Chumpol's new party. This means that the five new MPs of Suphanburi are all under Banharn's control. One is Nitiwat Chansawang (b. 1978). He is Banharn's (distant) cousin, related by marriage to the younger sister of Somchai Sujit, a prominent Sino-Thai capitalist in Suphanburi, whose mother is the half-sister of Banharn's wife, Jaemsai. Another new MP is Nopphadol Matrasri (b. 1969), former president of the Provincial Administration Organization of Suphanburi. He and his younger brother Adisak (a village head in

---

[49] See also *Bangkok Post*, January 4, 2009.

[50] DBD/MC, Suphanburi Company Files no. 685/2514 and no. 3195/2530.

[51] *Bangkok Post*, April 8, 1996, p. 4; *Bangkok Post*, May 21, 1994, p. 1.

[52] *Bangkok Post*, August 1, 2009.

U-Thong District) run Matrasri Jakrakon, a major contracting enterprise that undertook more than 1,247-million-baht worth of (mostly road-building) projects channeled by Banharn between 1996 and 2002.[53] In addition, their father, Khiang, a former village head, was Banharn's vote canvasser. The other three MPs—Charnchai Prasertsuwan, Patcharee Pothasuthon, and Jaraja Thiengtham—are all family members of former MPs: Charnchai is Nathawuth's brother, Patcharee is Praphat's niece, and Jaraja is Jongchai's younger brother. The election of these clients allows Banharn to continue to exert his influence, if indirectly and less strongly than before, over budget allocations and bureaucratic appointments in the central state. In other words, although he has been deprived of his official political power, the institutional "shell" of patrimonial democracy within which he has thrived as a politician remains intact, and he has found enough room for maneuver within this shell to prevent his historically constructed personal provincial dynasty from crumbling, at least for the time being. He has once again proven his remarkable resilience as a politician.

Whether Kanchana or Worawuth will eventually succeed in converting their father's dynasty into some form of family dynasty remains to be seen. For my immediate purpose, however, whatever might happen in the foreseeable or distant future will not change the fact that the majority of Suphanburians place Banharn's accomplishments at the core of their historical narratives concerning their province's development. For these people, Banharn is a legendary hero who has single-handedly attended to developing the formerly backward Suphanburi on behalf of the central state and has enhanced the social status, image, and reputation of the province. As such, he continues to occupy a central and honored place in the Suphanburians' oral and written representations of their recent history.

---

[53] DBD/MC, Suphanburi Limited Partnership File no. 414.

CHAPTER NINE

BANHARN IN THEORETICAL AND COMPARATIVE PERSPECTIVES

Banharn has come a long way. An anonymous migrant worker who once delivered coffee in Bangkok in the 1950s is now the invincible leader of Suphanburi. I have unraveled the long historical process through which he has attained his present status, despite (or even because of) his alleged corruption. A key element of this process is the rise of Suphanburians' provincial pride, which is based on their subjective assessment of Banharn's contributions to local development. To speak of Banharn's current dominance is, in no small measure, to speak of this provincial pride. This concluding chapter explores the broad implications of my empirical argument by casting it in theoretical and comparative perspectives.

TAKING COLLECTIVE PRIDE SERIOUSLY

The essence of politics is domination and obedience. Across time and space, all rulers have tried to make legitimate or illegitimate use of their power to win their subjects' ready or grudging obedience. The rulers may sometimes resort to compromise and persuasion, but that is part of the tactics they employ to pursue their paramount political goal—to make their subjects comply with their rule. Some rulers, however, have been more successful than others in achieving this goal. Put another way, people obey some rulers but not others. Why? This is a fundamental question in the voluminous literature on state-society relations.

Scholars have advanced a variety of answers to this fascinating yet baffling question. One answer is the use of coercion, violence, or fear.[1] Another is political culture—individuals' values, norms, and beliefs that form the basis of political authority.[2] Max Weber identified three ideal types of authority: rational–legal, charismatic, and traditional.[3] Proponents of rational choice theory highlight an instrumental nature of compliance based on tangible material benefits.[4] Other answers include class/state structures, ideology, patron–client ties, road density, and habitual compliance.[5] This list, while not an exhaustive one, shows the variety of

---

[1] Among others, see John Sidel, *Capital, Coercion, and Crime: Bossism in the Philippines* (Stanford, CA: Stanford University Press, 1999).

[2] The most famous work would be: Robert Putnam, *Making Democracy Work: Civic Traditions in Modern Italy* (Princeton, NJ: Princeton University Press, 1993).

[3] Max Weber, *The Theory of Social and Economic Organization*, trans. A. M. Henderson and Talcott Parsons (New York, NY: Free Press, 1964), pp. 324–86.

[4] See, for example, William Brustein, *The Logic of Evil: The Social Origins of the Nazi Party, 1925–33* (New Haven, CT: Yale University Press, 1996).

[5] For representative works that offer these respective answers, see Theda Skocpol, *States and Social Revolutions: A Comparative Analysis of France, Russia, and China* (Cambridge, NY:

answers offered in the existing literature to explain the causes or mechanisms of domination and compliance.

My study, a single case study of Banharn's political domination, does not debunk these (and other) explanations. It does draw our attention, however, to one social–psychological element of legitimate political authority that the extant literature has overlooked or underestimated: positive social identity or collective pride. Many residents of Suphanburi gain and buttress this pride by constructing and recounting a variety of subjective accounts that exalt the transformation of the previously "undeveloped" Suphanburi into a "well-developed" province, and by crediting Banharn's leadership for this change.

Two kinds of literature—one on collective social narratives, and the other on social identity in psychology—inform this argument in mutually compatible ways.

Collective Social Narratives

Suphanburians' accounts of Banharn's accomplishments take on the character of what Jeffrey Paige calls "collective social narratives." Drawing on George Steinmetz,[6] Paige uses the concept of "social narratives" to refer to the stories that a particular individual "tells about a social group of which he or she is a member." When the majority of persons in the same social group tell similar kinds of stories, it produces "a collective portrait of a group or 'collective narrative.'" Paige calls the assortment of such accounts "collective social narratives."[7]

Collective social narratives are akin to the narratives that we tell about ourselves at the individual level—stories about where we come from and how we have become the way we are. Such narratives typically feature benchmark events in our lives and a cast of personalities who have profoundly influenced our lives (e.g., "I was born in a small town in Kentucky … What changed my life forever was my encounter with a primary school teacher … While in college, I met another teacher who has shaped my intellectual outlook"). We tell such narratives in ways that give a particular order, structure, or meaning to our otherwise bewilderingly complex and messy life experiences. Put another way, these narratives have an overarching theme or motif, according to which we reconstruct our life stories. Events and personalities that fit and reinforce the leitmotif are played up, while those that do not are played down, glossed over, or simply excluded. The narratives are therefore basically subjective in nature. Whether or not they are objectively "true" is irrelevant. What is important is that, by telling subjective stories about ourselves, we affirm and reaffirm who we are and how we have become the way we are. The stories, in other words, reflect and shape our personal identity.

Cambridge University Press, 1979); Antonio Gramsci, *Selections from the Prison Notebooks*, trans. and ed. Quintin Hoare and Geoffrey Smith (New York, NY: International Publishers, 1971); James C. Scott, *The Moral Economy of the Peasant* (New Haven, CT: Yale University Press, 1976); Jeffrey Herbst, *States and Power in Africa: Comparative Lessons in Authority and Control* (Princeton, NJ: Princeton University Press, 2000); and Lisa Wedeen, *Ambiguities of Domination: Politics, Rhetoric, and Symbols in Contemporary Syria* (Chicago, IL: University of Chicago Press, 1999).

[6] George Steinmetz, "Reflections on the Role of Social Narratives in Working Class Formation: Narrative Theory in the Social Sciences," *Social Science History* 16,3 (1992): 489–516.

[7] Jeffery Paige, *Coffee and Power: Revolution and the Rise of Democracy in Central America* (Cambridge, MA: Harvard University Press, 1997), p. 341.

Collective social narratives extend personal-level narratives to the level of society. As Paige explains, they have "a beginning, middle, and an end," which are all linked together seamlessly by a sequence of events, a cast of personages, and a set of their actions. What influences the selection and evaluation of these events, characters, and actions is "the organizing principle"—a central theme that gives "meaning, coherence, and moral purpose" to the otherwise disorganized hodgepodge of stories.[8] This unifying theme gives us a clear sense of collective identity: what our community was in the past, what it is now, why or how it has reached the present, and how it differs from other communities. Put another way, a group's collective identity is dependent on the organizing theme that group adopts and the kinds of social narratives its members construct, embrace, and recount on the basis of that theme. As in the case of individual-level narratives, some social narratives may be gloomy,[9] but the point is that social narratives form the discursive basis on which all human beings obtain or construct their social identity. To ask if those narratives are correct representations of undeniable truth or reality is as pointless as asking whether our collective identity as members of a particular village, city, nation, and so forth is true or real.

Suphanburians' accounts of the recent history of their province are consistent with the pattern discussed above. The narratives start with negative (and often exaggerated) recollections and representations of Suphanburi's past backwardness, a condition that had been created by the discriminatory Bangkok-centered central state. In these narratives, Suphanburi's history then enters a new phase with the emergence of Banharn as a benevolent and efficient hero, a champion of development, who is juxtaposed against the callous and inept central state and its officials. First, he started developing Suphanburi by using his personal wealth in the mid-1960s—an action that fulfilled his legendary pledge to the local shrine spirit. Second, after becoming an MP in 1976, he began contributing even more to Suphanburi's development by supplementing his personal donations with state funds. By taking advantage of his new political position in the central state, he was able to pour an unprecedented amount of development funds into Suphanburi, often at the expense of other provinces. He also tightly monitored how local civil servants used the state funds he channeled to the province. As a result, a large number of public development projects were secured and admirably completed in Suphanburi, many of which are admired and envied by other Thais. Thus, the formerly "backward" Suphanburi won a reputation as a "developed" province in the new social geography of Thailand. This is the (temporary) "happy ending" of Suphanburi's provincial development.

Suphanburians' social narratives revolve around this unfolding historical development "drama," in which Banharn has consistently occupied center stage, first as a philanthropic individual (1966–76), and then as a powerful "pork-barrel" MP and a strict, watchful manager of lazy local civil servants (1976–present). If every collective social narrative starts with an account of a social "problem" that a cast of

---

[8] Paige, *Coffee and Power*, p. 341. See also William Sewell, "Introduction: Narratives and Social Identities," *Social Science History* 16,3 (1992): 483; Margaret Somers, "Narrativity, Narrative Identity, and Social Action: Rethinking English Working-Class Formation," *Social Science History* 16,3 (1992): 603.

[9] See James C. Scott, *Weapons of the Weak: Everyday Forms of Peasant Resistance* (New Haven, CT: Yale University Press, 1985), for a prime example.

characters and a sequence of their actions have resolved,[10] the stigmatized backwardness of Suphanburi is that problem for the predominant social narratives in Suphanburi, and Banharn is the main character who has provided the solution. This is the central theme or organizing principle of Suphanburians' social narratives.

In these narratives, the negative media reports concerning Banharn's graft and incompetence as a politician are subjectively rejected, discounted, or rationalized (e.g., "Every Thai politician is corrupt, so it's not fair to target Banharn") because they impair the coherence of the central organizing principle. The same holds true for the remaining evidence of Suphanburi's relative backwardness, evidence that Suphanburi ought to have achieved more economic or industrial progress than it has under Banharn's rule. In their eagerness to preserve Banharn as the heroic developer of Suphanburi, many people consciously or unconsciously minimize or justify his apparent failures to substantially raise their standards of living (e.g., "Suphanburi still has unpolluted air because it is not industrialized").

It would be a mistake to see these Suphanburians as passive and helpless consumers of Banharn's unabashed ideological project. They do not hold the beliefs they do because they have been ideologically "brainwashed" or "duped" by Banharn or his agents. It is true that Banharn, like any other politician, has propagated ideas or images that are favorable to his rule, and ordinary Suphanburians have embraced some of those ideas or images. But that is not because they are uncritical and uneducated (as urban-based scholars often make them out to be), but because they have critically assessed his actions on their own and have concluded that he has consistently stood up for Suphanburi's interests in ways that match his words. Moreover, many Suphanburians defend Banharn's ineptitude as a politician in various ways, despite the fact that he has never told them how to do so. These people are more than capable of coming up with social narratives of their own without having them supplied from above by well-educated elites. In many respects, these people are "historians" in their own right; they are active and autonomous agents engaged in interpreting how their province has evolved over time and what kind of place Banharn occupies in this history. In so doing, they have "emplotted" their provincial history in ways that often differ from, contradict, or even challenge well-educated scholars' authoritative interpretations—or what Paige calls "expert narratives."[11]

I do not mean to deny the validity of scholars' narratives in favor of the "lay narratives" created by these Suphanburians. Both may be valid. Banharn is at once a "good" and "bad" politician, depending on the interpreter's interests and preferences. As far as Suphanburi's residents are concerned, the former image applies. Of course, not all Suphanburians tell positive narratives about Banharn; his domination, just like any other politician's, is not a seamless web. As shown in chapters 5 and 8, some people embrace a counterhegemonic discourse that constructs him as a "bad" politician. Such views, however, remain a minority. Banharn stays firmly in the saddle of local power as long as the majority of the provincial population continues to hold him up as a legendary "Robin Hood," who has transformed the history and social position of Suphanburi by challenging, penetrating, and taming the irresponsible central state.

---

[10] Paige, *Coffee and Power*, p. 341.

[11] Ibid., p. 342.

Social Identity Theory

Social identity theory (SIT) allows us to recast the same argument in terms of social psychology. Developed in Europe to challenge the hegemony of individual-centered American social psychology, SIT makes a simple yet powerful argument on the basis of numerous experiments. This theory contends that human beings seek to enhance the status, image, prestige, and reputation of a social group of which they are members. According to SIT, this is the natural and inevitable product of social interaction. Just as individuals are driven to seek a sense of positive self-identity or self-esteem (*amour-propre*) in the process of coming into contact with each other,[12] constant human interaction causes social group members to develop a fundamental desire or need to "belong to groups that compare favorably with, and are distinct from, other groups." Belonging to such a group gives human beings "positive evaluations for themselves" or positive social identities, which they all desire or need.[13] Contrary to the assumptions of rational-choice theory, human beings are not always or primarily interested in maximizing their material interests at the individual level. They are just as much members of various social groups as they are "freely-floating individual particles."[14] As such, their interests are shaped or constrained by the society in which they live. One of those interests is to seek a positive social identity or, in other words, to take pride in any social group they belong to. This quest or penchant for collective pride is "the psychological 'motor' behind the individual's actions in the intergroup context."[15] To draw on David Laitin's phrase, this is "a point of concern" for all human beings.[16]

This does not mean that all human beings possess a positive social identity. As a result of social interaction and comparisons, they may end up feeling inferior. In the parlance of SIT, they may display an "inadequate" or "negative social identity"—"a social identity that is not as positive as one with which the individual is satisfied."[17] Residents of Suphanburi suffered from this condition during those years when they considered their home province to be relatively backward compared to others. According to SIT, people with an inadequate or negative social identity try to shed or overcome it by supporting "social competition" or "social action," which "would lead to desirable changes in the situation [in which their group is inferior and disadvantaged]." They do not resign themselves to the inferior social status imposed on them by dominant higher-status groups. They perceive the existing status hierarchy as unjust and illegitimate, and believe that another hierarchical system, in which their group enjoys higher social status, can and should be created through

---

[12] Jean-Jacques Rousseau, "Discourse on the Origin and Foundations of Inequality among Men," in *Modern Political Thought: Readings from Machiavelli and Nietzsche*, ed. David Wootton (Indianapolis, IN: Hacket Publishing, 1996).

[13] Donald Taylor and Fathali Moghaddam, *Theories of Intergroup Relations: International Social Psychological Perspectives* (New York, NY: Praeger, 1994), p. 83.

[14] Henri Tajfel, "Individuals and Groups in Social Psychology," *British Journal of Social and Clinical Psychology* 18 (1979): 187–88. See also Henri Tajfel, *Social Identity and Intergroup Relations* (New York, NY: Cambridge University Press, 1982).

[15] Taylor and Moghaddam, *Theories of Intergroup Relations*, p. 79.

[16] David Laitin, *Hegemony and Culture: Politics and Religious Change among the Yoruba* (Chicago, IL: University of Chicago Press, 1986), p. 29.

[17] Taylor and Moghaddam, *Theories of Intergroup Relations*, p. 83.

conscious human efforts.[18] They make or support active attempts to catch up with and overtake superior social groups. Relative group status is not an immutable given. Purposive human actions can rearrange an existing social hierarchy. In the case of Suphanburi, those human actions are represented by a series of deeds that Banharn has performed since the 1960s in the name of provincial development and in a way that has contrasted with the image of the negligent central state.[19]

In interpreting these "social actions" by Banharn, Suphanburians produce and reproduce a variety of "collective social narratives" that categorize their province, if humorously and flippantly, as a cut above all or many other Thai provinces. Such accounts reflect a new social geography of Thailand that people of Suphanburi visualize in their minds. This imagined—but not totally illusionary—social geography is the source of their provincial pride or positive social identity, signs of confidence they did not have before.

As noted earlier, however, the Suphanburians' interpretations involve a good deal of subjectivity; they are not based on an objective, impartial, or detached assessment of Banharn's actions and the level of their province's overall development. This is consistent with the second major finding of SIT: Human beings, in their eagerness to acquire a positive social identity, knowingly or unknowingly process and (mis)interpret available information in ways that accentuate the uniqueness of their social group. A drive for a positive social identity turns human beings into partial and arbitrary judges of available information. One noted proponent of SIT calls this human propensity "the perceptual accentuation effects" of social interaction.[20] At the same time, human beings tend to make light of or dismiss any data or information that detracts from their group's distinctiveness. A desire or need to attain a positive social identity drives human beings to assess what they see and hear in ways that serve to confirm and bolster that social identity.

Put differently, human beings are only pseudo-scientists or "intuitive scientists."[21] They may claim to be "objective," but that is a self-deceiving illusion. An objective assessment of reality is not their concern; they are more interested in

---

[18] Ibid., p. 84; Henri Tajfel, "Social Categorization, Social Identity and Social Comparison," in *Differentiation between Social Groups: Studies in the Social Psychology of Intergroup Relations*, ed. Henri Tajfel (New York, NY: Academic Press, 1978), p. 64.

[19] SIT enables us to make better sense of some other seemingly unintelligible phenomena. An example is many Malaysians' support for former Prime Minister Mahathir's grandiose and economically unviable development projects—the soaring Petronas Towers, the Proton Saga (the first automobile to be made in the "Third World"), and the Penang Bridge (the third longest bridge in the world, "six times the length of the Marcos Bridge" in the Philippines). These Malaysians supported Mahathir's ultimate collective goal: to show that Malaysia can "compete successfully against other rivals ... and to 'stand as tall as others'" and to create a society that is "psychologically subservient to none and respected by the peoples of other nations." See *Asiaweek* (July 19, 1985; September 27, 1985; and November 15, 1985); Gordon Means, *Malaysian Politics: The Second Generation* (Singapore: Oxford University Press, 1991), p. 96; R. S. Milne and Diane Mauzy, *Malaysian Politics under Mahathir* (London: Routledge, 1999), p. 64; Khoo Boo Teik, *Paradoxes of Mahathirism: An Intellectual Biography of Mahathir Mohamad* (Kuala Lumpur: Oxford University Press, 1995), pp. 66, 183, 329.

[20] Penelope Oakes, "The Categorization Process: Cognition and the Group in the Social Psychology of Stereotyping," in *Social Groups and Identities: Developing the Legacy of Henri Tajfel*, ed. Peter Robinson (Oxford: Butterworth-Heinemann, 1996), p. 97.

[21] Charles Lord, Lee Ross, and Mark Lepper, "Biased Assimilation and Attitude Polarization: The Effects of Prior Theories on Subsequently Considered Evidence," *Journal of Personality and Social Psychology* 37,11 (1979): 2099, 2108.

imputing "favorable rather than accurate evaluations" to their own groups.[22] Since they want to believe that the social group to which they belong is as good as any other or is better than others, they will play up every piece of positive information that appears to corroborate that belief, while questioning or brushing off the validity, reliability, relevance, and representativeness of any negative data that would contradict, undermine, or invalidate it.[23] Suphanburians' social narratives can be understood in this light. Precisely because they desire to belong to a province that is no longer considered a laggard in development, they are prone to extol Banharn's outstanding contributions to provincial development, while (deliberately) ignoring or playing down his lack of achievements.

This is best manifested by a gamut of Suphanburians' biased or crude overstatements that have little or no factual basis (e.g., "Chainat is twenty years behind Suphanburi," "All the roads in Ang Thong are bumpy."). These are nothing less than what SIT calls "social stereotypes"—the value-laden, over-generalizing, and contrasting images meant to distinguish in-groups from out-groups—that inevitably emerge from the subjective and repeated process of seeking a positive collective identity.[24] As posited by SIT, if social stereotypes represent a gross distortion of reality, they are the deplorable yet *logical* product of our all-too-human drive for positive group distinction. Cognitive psychologists view stereotypes as the result of either "dysfunctions of the personality" or "shortcomings of cognition." Stereotypes, therefore, can be corrected by "more accurate information" and "better education." Proponents of SIT disagree. Stereotypes stem not from our cognitive or perceptual defects, but from our basic, characteristically human psychological need to attain a positive group identity. Social stereotypes are therefore hard to eliminate; they are not something that would simply disappear if well-informed, well-educated outsiders pointed out their speciousness. As Penelope Oakes and her coauthors concluded succinctly, "As long as there are social groups ... there will be stereotypes."[25] From such a standpoint, we might view the variety of Suphanburians' tendentious misrepresentations of reality as the building blocks and expressions of their heightened collective pride in Banharn and his contributions to provincial development. A desire or need to maintain this pride pushes them to construct

---

[22] Taylor and Moghaddam, *Theories of Intergroup Relations*, p. 79.

[23] Drawing on social psychology, one political scientist similarly notes that human beings "process information given to them in such a way as to fit their preconceived ideas, desired images, or what they want to believe." Murray Edelman, *The Symbolic Uses of Politics* (Urbana, IL: University of Illinois Press, 1976), pp. 12–13. The same human proclivity is corroborated by another social–psychology theory, "confirmatory attribution" theory. James Kulik, "Confirmatory Attribution and the Perpetuation of Social Beliefs," *Journal of Personality and Social Psychology* 44,6 (1983): 1171–81; James Kulik, Paul Sledge, and Heike Mahler, "Self-Confirmatory Attribution and the Perpetuation of Self-Beliefs," *Journal of Personality and Social Psychology* 50,3 (1986): 587–94.

[24] See John Jost and Mahzarin Banaji, "The Role of Stereotyping in System-Justification and the Production of False-consciousness," *British Journal of Social Psychology* 33 (1994): 1–27; Oakes, "The Categorization Process," p. 99; M. Snyder, E. D. Tanke, and E. Berscheid, "Social Perception and Interpersonal Behavior: On the Self-fulfilling Nature of Social Stereotypes," *Journal of Personality and Social Psychology* 35 (1977): 656–66.

[25] Penelope Oakes, Katherine Reynolds, Alexander Haslam, and John Turner, "Part of Life's Rich Tapestry: Stereotyping and the Politics of Intergroup Relations," *Advances in Group Processes* 16 (1999): 154.

favorable interpretations of Banharn's actions in the various partisan and hyperbolic ways they do.

All this is not to say, of course, that Suphanburians care exclusively or primarily about gaining a positive social identity. They are concerned just as much about bread-and-butter issues of economic survival at the individual level. Within the severe constraints imposed on their lives by Thailand's capitalist economy, many people struggle to make both ends meet on a daily basis. But this does not mean, logically and empirically, that they do not care about the prestige, image, social status, or reputation of Suphanburi. On the contrary, they are deeply conscious of such nonmaterial collective issues, and they covet anything that makes Suphanburi look good or superior. They satisfy this desire by playing up Banharn's role in provincial development as the central theme of their social narratives. Some of these people, especially farmers, may be dissatisfied with their individual living conditions, but human beings have collective non-economic interests, which may not always or necessarily coincide with their individual-level economic interests. Plainly, people can be proud of a social group that falls short of meeting their daily economic needs to their full satisfaction. The fact that even the Suphanburians who would be considered "poor" by outsiders construct Banharn as their provincial hero serves as a reminder of this complex duality of human beings, a duality often overlooked in the individual-centered rationalist and Marxist paradigms.

Thus, as long as we simply examine the extent to which Banharn has furthered individual Suphanburians' economic interests, we cannot adequately understand why he continues to command their eager support the way he does. The key to understanding this phenomenon would be to recast Suphanburians in line with the SIT model of individuals and to direct our attention to what Banharn has done to meet their nonmaterial social–psychological needs or interests. That is, we need to highlight the long historical process through which Banharn has symbolically created a uniquely modern and socially distinguished provincial community; has incorporated into that community a vast number of people who were once physically and psychologically isolated from each other; and has given them a strong and positive provincial identity that they lacked before.

This positive social identity is a potent and effective ideational instrument that facilitates Banharn's domination, which makes the use of unscrupulous means of social control (e.g., coercion, vote-buying) superfluous. To use Migdal's analogy,[26] the Suphanburians' positive group identity is one kind of "mortar" that unites a large number of these citizens in an otherwise cacophonous and centrifugal provincial society. It endears Suphanburians to Banharn, creating strong emotional bonds between them. Domination based on, and cemented by, the mortar of positive social identity is also quite durable, if certainly not impervious to challenges from below, because it enjoys a higher level of legitimacy. This is why Banharn, a seemingly despicable politician for urban Thais, continues to win many Suphanburians' voluntary support and compliance with his rule, while many other Thai politicians have been voted out of office.

Political scientists in general have paid relatively little attention to the importance of positive social identity as a social–psychological component of

---

[26] Joel Migdal, "Studying the State," in *Comparative Politics: Rationality, Culture, and Structure,* ed. Mark Lichbach and Alan Zuckerman (New York, NY: Cambridge University Press, 1997), p. 213.

domination and compliance. It is one of those factors that they may take for granted. Its importance is perhaps regarded as an axiom, but despite or precisely because of this, political scientists have not taken social identity as seriously as they should have.[27] Methodologically, social identity is such an elusive concept that it defies easy quantification. Therefore, political scientists have paid the lion's share of attention to more observable or quantifiable variables, such as violence, instrumental exchanges of goods and services, institutional autonomy, class structures, and cultural values. The relative neglect of social identity is a serious oversight. The case of Banharn shows that social identity is one crucial—if not the only or the most important— factor underpinning powerful and legitimate domination. As such, it merits more scholarly attention than it has received to date.

COMPARATIVE CASES

One might ask whether there is any other Thai MP whose dominance rests on provincial pride. I am unable to give a firm answer, since I have not done comparable research on all the Thai MPs in the past and at present (which would be a Herculean task). But my educated guess is that Banharn is unique. Some politicians, such as Suvit Khunkitti, a former MP of Khon Kaen Province, may have wanted to emulate Banharn's construction of provincial pride, but he met with little success (see chapter 7).

A politician who comes somewhat close to Banharn might be (oddly enough) Chuan Leekpai, reputedly one of the most honest politicians in Thailand, who has served as an MP of Trang Province in the south (1975–present) and as prime minister (1992–95, 1997–2000). As Askew's detailed study shows, the voters in the southern region, including Trang, are intensely proud of Chuan because he embodies moral values such as honesty and loyalty, which make up the socially constructed, romanticized notion of "virtuous southern culture." This is why Chuan has met with phenomenal success equal to Banharn's in maintaining his political power in Trang, and the Democrat Party, of which Chuan was the leader until 2003, has maintained its unchallenged stronghold in the south. Chuan, however, differs from Banharn in two respects.[28] First, the collective identity he has constructed is regional, rather than provincial. Second, this identity is based on the moral virtue of honesty, for which Chuan is nationally well known. Given the fact that this virtue is universally upheld, it is no surprise that people in Trang and the south in general take pride in him. Banharn, in contrast, is notorious as a crooked politician, so that one would expect the people of Suphanburi to have little reason to be proud of him. Yet, they are. In fact, many even take pride in his alleged corruption, as illustrated in chapter 8.

---

[27] There are, however, several notable exceptions in the field of international relations. See R. P. Dore, "The Prestige Factor in International Affairs," *International Affairs* 51,2 (1975): 290–307; Daniel Markey, "The Prestige Motive in International Relations" (PhD dissertation, Princeton University, 2000); Jonathan Mercer, "Anarchy and Identity," *International Organization* 49,2 (1995): 229–52; Eric Noerper, "The Tiger's Leap: The Korean Drive for National Prestige and World Approval" (PhD dissertation, Tufts University, 1993); and Scott Sagan, "Why Do States Build Nuclear Weapons? Three Models in Search of a Bomb," *International Security* 21,3 (1996): 68.

[28] Marc Askew, *Performing Political Identity: The Democrat Party in Southern Thailand* (Chiang Mai: Silkworm, 2008).

Two other Thai politicians who seemingly resemble Banharn are Chai Chidchob (b. 1928) and his son Newin Chidchob (b. 1958), MPs from Buriram Province in the northeast. At present, Chai is the speaker of the House of Representatives, while Newin is the "shadow" leader of the Bhumjaithai (Proud Thais) Party, whose defection from the Thaksin camp in December 2008 ushered in the rise to power of the current Democrat Party-led government.[29] Like Banharn, both Chai and Newin are notorious for their alleged misuse of office,[30] yet they have repeatedly won major electoral victories in Buriram since 1983 and 1988, respectively.[31] This, in part, reflects the voters' appreciation of their accomplishments in developing Buriram. Since becoming MPs, Chai and Newin have used their institutional positions in the state— e.g., cabinet portfolios and membership in the parliamentary Budget Scrutiny Committee (BSC)[32]—to pump a large number of state-funded development projects into Buriram, many of which are credited to them via signboards.[33] The most notable of these projects involved the construction of roads. As shown in chapter 4, Buriram is ranked second among the seventy-five provinces of Thailand in terms of the total length of asphalt and concrete roads at the village level. As one Buriram villager said proudly, "Roads in our village are paved with asphalt gravel provided by Mr. Newin ... Laterite roads known for kicking up red dust are nearly all gone."[34] Another report confirms: "Asphalt roads are seen almost everywhere in Buriram."[35] As a result, Buriram has developed rapidly, to a point where it is said to be "as prosperous as Suphanburi."[36] The local dominance of the Chidchob clan had become so solid by 1996 that it could be "equaled in strength by ... Banharn Silpa-archa's grip on his native Suphanburi."[37] As some local people say, Newin "has won the hearts of many villagers." Even his political opponent admits, "If you speak about Mr. Newin in a negative way in Buriram, the people there may hit back at you. People just love him."[38]

These reports, however, need to be taken with a pinch of salt. First of all, Chai and Newin do not take the credit for all the development projects in Buriram in the way Banharn does in Suphanburi, because, unlike Suphanburi, Buriram has never been dominated by a single political party and its representatives. Between 1996 and

---

[29] The Constitutional Court ruling of May 2007 banned Newin from holding a political post for the next five years.

[30] For instance, Newin was once accused of having illegally obtained loans worth millions of baht from the Bangkok Bank of Commerce and of using them to take over firms on the stock market of Thailand. *Bangkok Post*, October 20, 1996, p. 1.

[31] In addition, Newin's wife (Karuna) got elected to parliament in 1996, 2001, and 2005, and his younger brother (Saksayam) won elections to parliament in 2001 and 2005. Saksayam, too, was banned from politics for five years in 2007.

[32] Between 1986 and 2000, Chai served on the BSC for ten years, making him the second longest-serving member after Banharn. Untitled data obtained at the National Parliament in 2000. Newin has served as deputy minister of finance (1995–96), deputy minister of agriculture (1997–2001, 2002, 2005), deputy minister of commerce (2002), and Minister to the Office of the Prime Minister (2005).

[33] *Bangkok Post*, July 8, 1996, p. 7.

[34] *Bangkok Post*, March 14, 1996, p. 9.

[35] *Bangkok Post*, July 22, 1996, p. 4.

[36] *Bangkok Post*, June 12, 1995, p. 6.

[37] *Bangkok Post*, July 22, 1996, p. 4.

[38] *Bangkok Post*, July 8, 1996, p. 6. See also *Bangkok Post*, July 22, 1996, p. 4.

2001, for example, ten MPs of Buriram, including Chai and Newin, belonged to four different political parties. As a result, political power is fragmented there, preventing Chai and Newin from establishing themselves as *the* provincial developers.

More importantly, many reports, as well as my interviews with several Buriram-born voters, indicate that the Chidchob clan has relied more on "dark influence" (*itthiphon muet*)—vote-buying, violence, and coercion—as instruments of domination than on the more attractive "carrot" of development projects. In one well-known case that came to light before the parliamentary election of 1995, the police conducted a raid on the house of Newin's vote canvasser and found eleven-million-baht worth of 100-baht banknotes with Newin's electoral identification numbers attached to them.[39] In December 1999, Newin's elder brother Thaweesak was suspected of hiring professional gunmen to make an assassination attempt on Panawat Liangphongphan, a rival Democrat MP of Buriram.[40] According to another report, "Rumors are rife [in Buriram] about people opposed to Mr. Newin being abducted and taken to Cambodia."[41] The financial bases of the Chidchob family's pervasive "dark influence" are their several local businesses, such as Silachai Buriram, which has monopolized government rock quarry concessions.[42] In addition, Newin's second wife, Karuna (MP of Buriram, 1996–2007), whom he married in 1994, is from a prominent contractor's family in Chiang Mai Province. Her father (Khanaen Supha) owns six companies, most notably Chiang Mai Construction (founded in 1979).[43] By 2008, Chai, along with his wife (La-ong), had accumulated assets of more than 144 million baht,[44] while Newin and Karuna had more than 1,000 million baht, making the Chidchob family one of the wealthiest political clans in Thailand.[45] All this wealth has enabled them to build up province-wide networks of dark influence, which they wield at election time to their advantage. Thus, Chai and Newin are more objects of some voters' moral repulsion than they are the focus of provincial pride in Buriram.[46]

An even more illuminating contrasting case, which I will detail below, concerns Narong Wongwan, an alleged drug tycoon and former MP of Phrae Province, in northern Thailand. Despite his (allegedly) shady background, Narong, like Banharn, never used violence to attain and maintain his power. Yet, in contrast to Banharn,

---

[39] *Bangkok Post*, June 30, 1995, p.1; *The Nation*, June 30, 1995, A1. In the senate election of March 2001, the Election Commission disqualified the electoral victory of Usanee, Newin's elder sister, on account of vote-buying.

[40] *The Nation*, December 29, 1999, and January 4, 2000; *Bangkok Post*, December 18, 2001.

[41] *Bangkok Post*, July 8, 1996, p. 9. See also *The Nation*, January 4, 2000, for a similar report.

[42] Department of Business Development, Ministry of Commerce (DBD/MC), Buriram Company File no. 0315534000071.

[43] DBD/MC, Chiang Mai Company File no. 0505522000347.

[44] National Counter Corruption Committee, Party List MP File no. 431.

[45] National Counter Corruption Committee, Minister File no. 41.

[46] Although systematic research is wanting, my preliminary research suggests that Newin and Chai are characteristic of many other violence-prone rural strongmen who have recently suffered humiliating electoral losses, such as Vatthana Asavaheme of Samut Prakan Province and Piya Angkinan of Phetchaburi Province. Vatthana, a suspected drug dealer, lost the election of 2001, along with his younger brother (Somporn) and son (Phunporn), after having been elected as Samut Prakan's MP continuously since 1975. Similarly, Piya, Phetburi's MP since 1975, lost the elections of 2001, 2005, and 2007. For an analysis of Piya and his family's historical domination in Phetchaburi, see Pasuk Phongpaichit and Sungsidh Piriyarangsan, *Corruption and Democracy in Thailand* (Chiang Mai: Silkworm, 1996), pp. 76–80.

Narong constructed his political authority mainly or exclusively based on personal patronage ties. In the end, he was made painfully aware of the fragility of this type of domination in 1995, when he lost a parliamentary seat. Thus, this case brings into sharp relief the robustness of Banharn's rule based on provincial pride.

I will follow the case of Narong Wongwan with a discussion of three politicians from other countries in Asia—Kakuei Tanaka of Japan, Ferdinand Marcos of the Philippines, and Kim Dae Jung of South Korea. While Banharn may be unique in Thailand, these three non-Thai politicians resemble him to a remarkable degree. Tanaka, Marcos, and Kim are all from areas once considered to be among the most "backward" in their respective countries, and they used their official power to boost the image of their home provinces or regions. Their actions had the cumulative effect of enhancing the collective pride of their constituents. The three politicians thus retained their constituents' support in the face of outsiders' severe criticisms, in much the same manner that Banharn has done in Suphanburi. Taken together, these four comparative cases, drawn from inside and outside Thailand, lend additional empirical support to my argument that a positive social identity is one essential component of political domination.

Narong Wongwan

Narong Wongwan (1925–present) was a long-standing MP (1979–95) of Phrae, a northern Thai province near the border with Laos. He was born into a local elite family, in which his grandfather was *chao muang* (governor) of Phrae in the days of the absolute monarchy. The family initially engaged in logging businesses in Chiang Mai and Chiang Rai provinces. From this economic base, the family ventured into phenomenally lucrative tobacco-curing and tobacco-exporting enterprises during Narong's time.[47] By the 1990s, Narong had become a wealthy tycoon who controlled several multi-million-baht companies in northern Thailand, such as Thepawong, Siam Tobacco Export Corporation, Thai Tobacco Industrial, and General Tobbaco. He is also a major shareholder in Chiang Rai Borikan, a real-estate company founded in 1960. Narong, as well as his three sons (Anuson, Anuwat, Asawin), daughter (Asaniphon), and daughter-in-law (Samonsri), is the major shareholder for these companies.[48] Finally, Narong is a suspected drug trafficker who was once denied entry into the United States.

At first glance, Narong bears a striking resemblance to Banharn in several respects. First, both belong to roughly the same generation of politicians. Their careers as MPs also started at about the same time: Narong was elected to parliament for the first time in 1979, just three years after Banharn. Second, like Banharn, Narong always won a landslide electoral victory in Phrae. In fact, the two often vied with each other for the honor of receiving "the largest number of votes in Thailand." In addition, the two politicians held many key ministerial and party posts.[49] As the

---

[47] Pasuk and Sungsidh, *Corruption and Democracy in Thailand*, p. 80; *Bangkok Post*, March 29, 1992, p. 1.

[48] These companies were founded in 1949, 1965, 1970, and 1974, respectively. They are all located in Chiang Mai Province, except Thapawong, which is in Chiang Rai. DBD/MC, Chiang Rai Company Files no. 0525492000034 and no. 0575503000019; Chiang Mai Company Files no. 0505508000084, no. 0505513000208, and no. 0545517000024.

[49] Narong was the leader of Ruam Thai Party (1986–91) and Samakkhi Tham Party (1991–92). He served as deputy minister of agriculture (1981), minister of agriculture (1983–86, 1990–91),

leader of the once-powerful Therd Thai faction that controlled some thirty MPs, Narong, like Banharn, long remained one of Thailand's most influential political wheeler-dealers. Had the US government not intervened to reveal his suspected involvement in the drug trade, he would have become prime minister after the election of March 1992, in which his military-backed Samakkhi Tham (Moral Unity) Party won the largest number of votes. Finally, like Banharn, Narong was widely believed to be corrupt. The military junta, which staged a successful coup in 1991 on the pretext of eliminating political corruption, listed Narong, along with Banharn, as one of the "unusually rich" (i.e., corrupt) cabinet ministers.

For all these similarities, however, Narong differs from Banharn in one crucial respect: Narong did not use his enormous personal wealth or state-based resources to launch development projects in Phrae in the way Banharn has done in Suphanburi. Between 1985 and 1995, for example, Phrae received a road construction fund of 473.4 million baht from the Department of Highways (DOH). By contrast, Banharn channeled a DOH fund exceeding 3,900 million baht into Suphanburi during the same period.[50] As a consequence, Phrae remained, and still remains, a province with relatively few conspicuous development projects. Moreover, Narong seldom returned to Phrae and showed little interest in local development. As one Phrae resident griped, Narong "stays in Bangkok a lot," and this absence from his home province "upsets many people."[51] Given all the material and human resources at his disposal, Narong could have done what Banharn has done, but he apparently did not have the will to do so. Few people in Phrae, therefore, felt a strong emotional attachment to Narong.

What enabled Narong to attain and stay in power was his vast patronage network—a political machine—which he effectively mobilized at election time to drum up support on his behalf. This network won him a string of easy victories between 1979 and 1992. In this sense, he was a typical rural-based boss, of the kind depicted in the standard literature on Thai politics.[52] The limit of patronage politics, however, became acutely apparent by the time he contested the election of 1995. A patronage network, by definition, can be maintained only as long as a patron is able to dispense concrete material benefits to his clients, and this is how Narong had maintained his electoral machine before 1995. His patronage resources sharply dwindled after 1992, however, when the US started tightening the screws on drug traffickers worldwide. As Narong's economic base shrank, so did his political machine. Shortly before the 1995 election, his most "trusted" vote canvasser in Phrae,

---

and deputy prime minister (1992).

[50] Budget Bureau, *Ekasarn Ngop-pramarn 2528*, 4,3 (1984): 113–266; Budget Bureau, *Ekasarn Ngop-pramarn 2529*, 4,3 (1985): 81–199; Budget Bureau, *Ekasarn Ngop-pramarn 2530*, 4,3 (1986): 81–174; Budget Bureau, *Ekasarn Ngop-pramarn 2531*, 4,3 (1987): 101–227; Budget Bureau, *Ekasarn Ngop-pramarn 2532*, 4,3 (1988): 125–298; Budget Bureau, *Ekasarn Ngop-pramarn 2533*, 4,3 (1989): 111–300; Budget Bureau, *Ekasarn Ngop-pramarn 2534*, 4,3 (1990): 113–298; Budget Bureau, *Ekasarn Ngop-pramarn 2535*, 4,3 (1991): 99–306; Budget Bureau, *Ekasarn Ngop-pramarn 2536*, 4,3 (1992): 119–314; Budget Bureau, *Ekasarn Ngop-pramarn 2537*, 4,3 (1993): 109–330; Budget Bureau, *Ekasarn Ngop-pramarn 2538*, 4,3 (1994): 127–324.

[51] *Bangkok Post*, June, 1995, p. 3.

[52] James Ockey, "Business Leaders, Gangsters, and the Middle Class: Social Groups and Civilian Rule in Thailand" (PhD dissertation, Cornell University, 1992), p. 160; Pasuk and Sungsidh, *Corruption and Democracy in Thailand*, pp. 80–81.

Sanit Supasiri, split with him.[53] When Sanit defected, so did his immediate clients, leaving Narong suddenly deprived of a huge electoral machine. On top of that, Sanit had his thirty-nine-year-old daughter, Siriwan Prasarjarksatru, contest the 1995 election against Narong in a political showdown. Sanit now constructed a new electoral network that worked directly in the service of his own daughter. Another key vote canvasser in this network was Siriwan's husband, Police Colonel Tha-ngai Prasajarksatru, a "very popular" senior policeman in Phrae. Other vote canvassers for Siriwan included her relatives and close friends, who served in the Provincial Administration Organization.[54] Phrae's voters then deserted Narong and switched their support to Siriwan.

These developments produced a stunning result in the 1995 election: Siriwan, a young female political novice who had never run for office before, scored a comfortable victory, while the much more senior and seasoned Narong, aged seventy at the time, suffered a humiliating loss. Of the nine candidates in his constituency, three, including Siriwan, garnered more votes than did Narong.[55] Narong reportedly received financial support from the telecommunications tycoon and future prime minister, Thaksin, whose father, Lert, had been Narong's close associate. However, even this support was not enough to assure Narong's electoral success.[56] Thus, his long-standing "invincible" domination came to an unexpected, abrupt end in 1995. This defeat made him decide to wash his hands of politics altogether. In striking contrast, Banharn won the 1995 election hands down by receiving some 89 percent of the votes in his constituency and subsequently became prime minister.

While Narong's loss shocked outside observers who had taken his dominance for granted, it came as little surprise to many local voters. As one tricycle driver said, Phrae's voters "are no longer stupid," and they wanted to "give him a lesson." They were critical of Narong's "lack of energy" and wanted to elect an MP who could "bring development" to their home province. The driver continued: "Narong has been too complacent about his political support and, to the chagrin of many of his supporters, has shifted his attention away from his hometown during the past few years."[57]

My fieldwork in Phrae in 1999 supported these views. Few people had any favorable account of Narong to relate. They portrayed him as a "washed-up" politician who failed to develop Phrae, or as a disgrace who besmirched the image and reputation of Phrae with his alleged drug trafficking. In her conversation with me in 1999, one female factory worker in Den Chai District recalled, "He was born in Phrae, but he didn't love his birthplace as much as he should have. He monopolized all the wealth for himself, family, and friends." She continued, "Why should we have voted for someone who gave our hometown a bad name?" Similarly, a group of villagers in Song District of Phrae recollected that when a road linking their village to

---

[53] In the previous election of March 1992, Sanit ran for office along with Narong, although he lost.

[54] *The Nation*, June 28, 1988, p. 8; *Bangkok Post*, June 19, 1995, p. 3; *Bangkok Post*, October 26, 1996, p. 2.

[55] Ministry of Interior, *Khomun Sathiti lae Phon Kan Lueak Tang Sammachik Sapha Phu Thaen Ratsadon 2 Karakadakhom 2538* (Bangkok: Ministry of Interior, 1995), p. 95.

[56] See *Bangkok Post* (June 8, 1995, p. 5; June 22, 1995, p. 4; July 17, 1995, p. 7; July 18, 1995, p. 6).

[57] *Bangkok Post*, July 16, 1995, p. 20.

the provincial capital was severely damaged due to floods sometime before 1995, they could not turn to Narong for help because he was living in Chiang Rai. One of the residents complained bitterly: "He was an MP from Phrae. Then how come he didn't live here to take care of us? Why live in another province? It doesn't make sense." In these and other people's accounts, Narong was portrayed as a politician they wished to forget about. Some people simply remembered so little about him that they had nothing to say.

The contrasting results of the 1995 election suggest one important reason why many Thai MPs, including Narong, have simply come and gone, whereas Banharn has for years scored resounding electoral victories. Domination based on a positive social identity is much more resilient than domination based on simple patronage politics. This is not to say that Banharn has not relied on patronage. As shown in previous chapters, he has dispensed numerous favors (e.g., bureaucratic promotions, development funds) to create an extensive network of local clients. In this respect, Banharn is no different from many other MPs. The key difference, however, lies in what he has done with his patronage network. Most MPs, including Narong, have merely turned their respective patronage networks into vote-harvesting machines that can be conveniently mobilized at election time. This is an easy and politically attractive choice in terms of the time and resources required. A candidate who takes this option only has to invest his or her personal time and resources just before each election. As some studies have shown, many villagers do see the benefits dispensed by an electoral machine as legitimate.[58] But a relationship dependent on instrumentalist exchange is relatively shallow. If and when the supply of benefits dwindles, so does reciprocal support. This is the fate that befell Narong in 1995.

Banharn, in contrast, has chosen a much more exhausting and time-consuming strategy. He has used his network of clients to produce and advertise a myriad of visible symbols of provincial development through signboards, ceremonies, inspection tours, and meetings. These symbols have become the base for the local social narratives that enshrine him as a hardworking and sincere provincial developer. Based on the attendant collective pride, Banharn's domination has enjoyed more legitimacy and has proven to be much more resistant to fracture than Narong's. He has been handsomely rewarded for taking the hard option.

Kakuei Tanaka

Kakuei Tanaka (1918–1993), the former Japanese prime minister arrested for accepting kickbacks from big business, represents a case quite similar to that of Banharn. The resemblances between Tanaka and Banharn are striking, indeed. Both received only eight years of education,[59] and had amassed their fortunes in the construction business before venturing into national politics.[60] Furthermore, Tanaka

---

[58] See Daniel Arghiros, *Political Structures and Strategies: A Study of Electoral Politics in Central Rural Thailand*, Occasional Paper No. 31 (Hull: University of Hull, Center for South-East Asian Studies, 1995).

[59] On paper, Banharn has a master's degree from Ramkhamhaeng University, an open-admission university in Bangkok. But he is suspected to have obtained the degree by submitting a plagiarized thesis.

[60] Tanaka's company, founded in 1943, grew rapidly. When the Pacific War ended in 1945, it was undertaking a construction project in Korea. Toru Hayano, *Tanaka Kakuei to 'Sengo' no Seishin* (Tokyo: Asahi Shinbun, 1995), p. 18.

is regarded as the personification of sordid money politics, for which Japan has become notorious in recent years. For these reasons, Banharn is sometimes referred to as Thailand's Kakuei Tanaka. Tanaka is to the Japanese what Banharn is to the Thais.

The most striking common characteristic linking the two, however, is the strength of their local support. Like Banharn, Tanaka, despite all the corruption charges leveled against him, was—and still is—extremely popular in his home prefecture of Niigata. This is because during his long political career, which spanned more than forty years, he poured a huge amount of development funds into Niigata, a prefecture that forms the heart of *Ura-Nihon* (backside Japan)—a pejorative designation for the backward and socially marginalized area that lies across the Sea of Japan from the Korean Peninsula.[61]

There were several reasons for Niigata's perennial backwardness. First, Niigata was (and still is) geographically handicapped. During Niigata's long, harsh winter, the high waves in the Sea of Japan made it hard to engage in fishing, one of the main sources of income for the people in Niigata. In addition, icy winds blowing from the sea caused heavy snowfall, hampering the flow of people and goods—a reason why Niigata, along with its adjacent prefectures, is called "Snow Country." Also, the high mountain ranges in the south and the east constituted natural barriers to effective transportation, shutting off Niigata from Tokyo and other cities on the Pacific coast. Moreover, the Shinano River, the second longest river in Japan, would overflow each year, causing often catastrophic damage to Niigata's already depressed agriculture-based economy. Local farmers lived in constant fear of disaster and famine.[62]

Niigata's backwardness did not stem from its natural conditions alone. More importantly, it was exacerbated by the central state, as was true in the case of Suphanburi. Since the Meiji Restoration, the state had given priority to development in the Pacific Rim areas, including Tokyo and Osaka. As a result, Niigata and other prefectures in the "backside Japan" were neglected. While "frontside Japan" prospered, "backside Japan" stagnated.[63] This imbalance was reflected in the extremely high rate of temporary or permanent out-migration from Niigata. Because of the dearth of jobs during the long icy winters, virtually all male farmers would leave Niigata in late October each year and migrate to more prosperous prefectures in search of seasonal employment. They did not, or could not, come back home until April. They had to spend even the New Year holidays—generally the most festive time for the Japanese—far away from their homes and families.[64] Permanent emigration was equally serious. In 1888, Niigata had the largest population of all the prefectures in Japan,[65] but in subsequent years it became rapidly depopulated, thanks to the massive outflow of emigrants.

---

[61] Tadao Furumaya, *Ura Nippon: Kindai Nippon wo Toinaosu* (Tokyo: Iwanami Shinsho, 1997); Michael Lewis, *Becoming Apart: National Power and Local Politics in Toyama, 1868–1945* (Cambridge, MA: Harvard East Asian Studies, 2000).

[62] Hayano, *Tanaka Kakuei to 'Sengo' no Seishin*, p. 38; Jacob Schlesinger, *Shadow Shoguns: The Rise and Fall of Japan's Postwar Political Machine* (New York, NY: Simon & Schuster, 1997), pp. 36–37.

[63] Schlesinger, *Shadow Shoguns*, pp. 37–38.

[64] Hayano, *Tanaka Kakuei to 'Sengo' no Seishin*, p. 54.

[65] http://www.hrr.mlit.go.jp/library/hokuriku2003/si/1-06/01jinkou/03meiji/03meiji.html, accessed on October 18, 2006.

To ameliorate these conditions, Diet members from Niigata pleaded for government funding on the grounds that "people who live in the unblessed snow country are always neglected by the central government," despite the fact that "snow country people are also Japanese citizens." These repeated and desperate pleas were ignored by the government, which considered Niigata to be of secondary importance—a situation akin to what Suphanburians experienced in the pre-Banharn past (see chapter 2). As in Suphanburi, perceptions of relative deprivation generated a sense of bitter resentment toward the central state among the residents of Niigata. One farmer lamented, "The largest number of migrant workers [from Niigata] have been used in the big cities of *omote Nippon* [frontside Japan]. We built the subways and buildings, bullet trains and highways, but we have never received the benefits."[66] "People over there [in Tokyo] have never seen the snow," Tanaka himself cried out. As Schlesinger puts it aptly, the "snow" in this terse statement "meant not just nature's hardship but the indignities and neglect heaped on top by the national government."[67] Underneath the glamorous and well-studied story of Japan's "economic miracle" in the post-Edo period lie the lesser known stories of underprivileged prefectures such as Niigata.

From the time when he was first elected to the Diet in 1947, Tanaka worked hard on improving the lot of Niigata's citizens. This was his paramount concern from the beginning, especially in 1972–74, when he served as the first Niigata-born prime minister in Japanese history. As a person born into a peasant family in Niigata, he was acutely aware of his prefecture's backwardness, just as Banharn was of Suphanburi's. Bent on rectifying this condition, Tanaka made visible contributions to local development, including the construction and elevation of numerous riverbanks to reduce floods. Many of these reinforced riverbanks now feature monuments of Tanaka that have been erected by Niigata residents as tokens of their gratitude. Equally important are the large number of roads, bridges, railways, and tunnels built by Tanaka, which now interconnect formerly isolated parts of Niigata and also link Niigata to Tokyo. Niigata is also the only prefecture in "backside Japan" to be served by the bullet train—a cardinal mark of modernity in postwar Japan. Thanks to these transportation networks, it now takes less than two hours to reach Tokyo from Niigata. Moreover, the massive infrastructure projects implemented by Tanaka have created jobs and have stimulated more vigorous commerce in the prefecture, thereby reducing the need for permanent or temporary emigration.[68] He achieved all this by channeling more public funds into Niigata than into any of Japan's forty-six other prefectures. "On a per capita basis, the snow country got two and a half times the national average" in public works funds. Not surprisingly, Tanaka came under heavy fire for showering favors on his home prefecture. He was unfazed, however, saying: "This is the last thing I can stop."[69]

Many outside critics view Tanaka's infrastructure projects as the breeding ground for his corruption.[70] His critics typically target the Etsuzankai (The

---

[66] Schlesinger, *Shadow Shoguns*, pp. 38, 39.

[67] Ibid., p. 99.

[68] Ibid., p. 44; Gilbert Rozman, "Backdoor Japan: The Search for a Way out via Regionalism and Decentralization," *Journal of Japanese Studies* 25,1 (1999): 15.

[69] Schlesinger, *Shadow Shoguns*, p. 103.

[70] James Babb, *Tanaka: The Making of Postwar Japan* (Edinburgh: Pearson Education, 2000); Chalmers Johnson, "Tanaka Kakuei, Structural Corruption, and the Advent of Machine

Association for Crossing the Mountains), a group of Tanaka's local supporters established in 1953. The Etsuzankai served as an institutional conduit through which Tanaka pumped one pork-barrel project after another—"big money," in short—into Niigata from the central government. Accordingly, over the years the Etsuzankai mushroomed into a huge corruption-ridden local electoral machine for Tanaka. These critiques, while certainly not wrong, are one-sided, however. They mask the profoundly deep and politicized meaning contained in the symbolic designation, "Crossing the Mountains." The designation meant much more than the simple physical act of crossing the mountain ranges that separated Niigata from Tokyo; it was the condensed expression of Niigata people's collective yearning to overcome the backwardness that had effectively been imposed on them by the discriminatory central state.[71] Tanaka made this dream come true. As Banharn has done in Suphanburi, Tanaka redressed what local people had perceived as the historical injustice that their home prefecture had suffered at the hands of the central government. By pumping developmental resources into Niigata, he gave his constituents their due. Niigata's farmers, in particular, found immense emotional gratification in this change, because Tanaka was a poorly educated man from humble origins just like them, yet he was powerful enough to push much better educated, elite bureaucrats in Tokyo—the embodiment of the callous central state— to secure a disproportionate amount of funds for the formerly disadvantaged prefecture.[72]

As a result of Tanaka's actions, "Niigata's sense of remoteness dissipated, and the country seemed to join the rest of Japan."[73] He put Niigata on a par with, if not ahead of, many other prefectures. Tanaka thus became a veritable Robin Hood developmental hero. According to one survey conducted in Niigata, which asked, "Of all the people that Niigata has produced since the Meiji period, who are you most proud of?" more than 50 percent of the respondents chose Tanaka, and he won more votes than any other individual.[74] Scholars who reduce Tanaka's actions to dirty pork-barrel politics cannot sufficiently explain why Niigata's people took so much pride in him.

The pride in Tanaka translated into emergent pride in Niigata. Residents of the prefecture came to acquire "a sense that they all belonged to the one and the same local community" developed by Tanaka.[75] The rise of this comradeship in the prefecture—a kind of positive social identity—cut across the divisions of age, class, and occupations. Plainly, whoever rallied behind Tanaka's slogan, "Develop Niigata, Our Home," embraced the collective identity centered on pride in his accomplishments.

Politics in Japan," *Journal of Japanese Studies* 12,1 (1986): 1–28; Gavan McCormack, *The Emptiness of Japanese Affluence* (New York, NY: M. E. Sharpe, 2001), pp. 25–77; Schlesinger, *Shadow Shoguns*, pp. 107–45; Brian Woodall, *Japan under Construction: Corruption, Politics, and Public Works* (Berkeley, CA: University of California Press, 1996).

[71] Schlesinger, *Shadow Shoguns*, p. 42.

[72] Ibid., p. 102; Yo Mizuki, *Tanaka Kakuei Sono Kyozen to Kyoaku* (Tokyo: Nihon Keizai Shinbunsha, 1998), pp. 68, 107.

[73] Schlesinger, *Shadow Shoguns*, p. 44.

[74] Mizuki, *Tanaka Kakuei Sono Kyozen to Kyoaku*, p. 289.

[75] Hayano, *Tanaka Kakuei to 'Sengo' no Seishin*, p. 198.

In light of this context, we can better understand why Tanaka repeatedly won landslide victories at the polls, despite all the corruption scandals that plagued his political career. As Schlesinger relates, many voters in Niigata turned deaf ears to the scandals, regarding them as an "inhuman ... frame-up" by the "degree-holding elite because [Tanaka] is not a university graduate" or as "a plot" to "crush the one man who had stood up for the snow country against the Pacific Coast cabal." Others believed that Tanaka was corrupt. But for these people, he was not a criminal in a negative sense; he was "*Niigata's* [heroic] criminal." "If the parent had not robbed," one mayor in Niigata explained, comparing Tanaka to the father of a poor family, "the children would have died."[76] As is the case with Banharn, the more the national media criticized Tanaka, the more passionately Niigata's voters supported and defended him, often in highly partisan ways that uninitiated outsiders found irrational.

This defensive group response was exemplified by the outcome of the general election in 1976, held one year after Tanaka was arrested for his sensationally publicized involvement in the Lockheed bribery scandal.[77] Contrary to popular expectations, Tanaka scored a landslide victory, receiving 168,522 votes—more than three times the votes for the candidate who came in second.[78] His arrest did little to shake the support of his constituents. As one woman explained, "Tanaka *sensei* is a politician who loves his homeland ... We will believe and support Tanaka *sensei* no matter what."[79] More strikingly, in the election of December 1983, held just two months after the Tokyo District Court found Tanaka guilty of accepting bribes, he scored another overwhelming victory, receiving a record-breaking 220,761 votes; the candidate who placed second garnered only 48,324 votes.[80] In his conversation with me, one elderly farmer in Niigata, an ardent supporter of Tanaka over the decades, explained and recollected his decision to vote for Tanaka at the time as follows:

> [Tanaka] *sensei* had helped us when we were in hard times. Now *sensei* was facing hard times. We said to ourselves, "It is time for us to unify to show our loyalty and gratitude to him. It is time for Niigata to show to the rest of Japan how much we appreciate *sensei's* achievements." We couldn't abandon him just because of one or two incidents ... I know why people elsewhere badmouthed *sensei*, and I don't blame them. But for many of us, the people in Niigata, there couldn't have been a better Diet member than *sensei* ... We could never forget what he had done for us. We were in his debt. We are forever in his debt ... We would have been called ingrates [if we had not voted for Tanaka].

To illustrate his point, this man pointed his finger at one inter-prefectural road that Tanaka built through Niigata, saying, "If not for *sensei*, who would have paid

---

[76] Schlesinger, *Shadow Shoguns*, pp. 98, 99, 100, emphasis mine.

[77] This scandal involved the US-based aerospace company Lockheed, which bribed Tanaka (and other individuals in Japan) to buy its airplanes.

[78] Hayano, *Tanaka Kakuei to 'Sengo' no Seishin*, p. 303.

[79] Schlesinger, *Shadow Shoguns*, p. 105. Normally meaning "teacher," the term *sensei* is also used to refer with respect to politicians.

[80] Hayano, *Tanaka Kakuei to 'Sengo' no Seishin*, p. 303.

attention to developing Niigata? Only the Pacific Coast area would have developed. We would be still stuck in heavy snow."[81]

Thus, for many people in Niigata, Tanaka has become an integral component of their emotionally charged, prefectural identity. This does not mean, of course, that everyone in Niigata holds a favorable view of Tanaka, but the majority of the prefecture's residents—especially the elderly who remember the socioeconomic conditions in the pre-Tanaka era—recount narratives that honor him as the creator of the "no-longer-backward" Niigata in the changing social geography of post-Meiji Japan. His achievements are now neatly displayed and enshrined in the Museum for Commemorating Kakuei Tanaka, built in 1998, in his hometown. At the same time, the legacies of his rule linger on in the form of his daughter Makiko, a controversial, sharp-tongued member of the Lower House, representing Niigata since 1993. Caught in a situation reminiscent of her father's career, Makiko was forced to resign from her post in August 2002 amid a well-publicized scandal concerning her malfeasance. Seven months earlier, she had been kicked out of her party, the Liberal Democratic Party (LDP). In the general election held in November 2003, however, she won reelection, despite the fact that she ran as an independent. A sixty-six-year-old resident of Nagaoka, one of the cities in Niigata through which the bullet train now runs, thanks to Tanaka, explained his support for her: "It was all thanks to Kakuei that Nagaoka has grown this much ... It doesn't matter whether Makiko is in the LDP or is an independent. I am voting for the 'Tanaka Party.'"[82]

Ferdinand Marcos

Another politician who resembles Banharn is Ferdinand Marcos (1917–89) of the Philippines. Filipinos (and non-Filipinos) in general regard Marcos as the president who plundered the state.[83] However, in his home region of Ilocos, located in the northernmost part of the Philippines, Marcos is still fondly remembered as "the best leader the Philippines ever had."[84] His pictures are "hung in government offices throughout the Ilocano districts."[85] A survey, conducted a few years after his fall from power in 1986, similarly found that for many Ilocanos, "whether farmers, teachers, or businessmen, Marcos approximated their concept of a true leader."[86]

As was true in the cases of Banharn and Tanaka, these positive images of Marcos emerged because he boosted Ilocanos' collective pride by developing their home region. During the US colonial and early independence periods, Ilocos was regarded

---

[81] Interview in Niigata, January 9, 2007.

[82] *Japan Times*, October 2003.

[83] Belinda Aquino, *Politics of Plunder: The Philippines under Marcos* (Quezon City: University of the Philippines College of Public Administration, 1987); James Boyce, *The Philippines: The Political Economy of Growth and Impoverishment in the Marcos Era* (Honolulu, HI: University of Hawaii Press, 1993); John Bresnan, *Crisis in the Philippines: The Marcos Era and Beyond* (Princeton, NJ: Princeton University Press, 1986); and Paul Hutchcroft, *Booty Capitalism: The Politics of Banking in the Philippines* (Ithaca, NY: Cornell University Press, 1998).

[84] *Asiaweek*, June 2, 1995, p. 80.

[85] Robert Reid and Eileen Guerrero, *Corazon Aquino and the Brushfire Revolution* (Baton Rouge, LA: Louisiana State University, 1995), p. 38.

[86] Fernando Zialcita, "Perspectives on Legitimacy in Ilocos Norte," in *From Marcos to Aquino: Local Perspectives on Political Transition in the Philippines*, ed. Benedict Kerkvliet and Resil Mojares (Manila: Ateneo de Manila University Press, 1991), p. 274.

as "a backwater upcountry,"[87] as were Suphanburi and Niigata at one time. A rugged mountainous region "most vulnerable to typhoons and flooding," Ilocos is "cursed with a harsher environment than other regions." Exposed constantly to the fear of natural disasters, and yet deprived of welfare services from the central government, Ilocanos were forced to develop a large number of community-based self-help associations; Ilocos, in fact, had a higher number of such associations than any other region in the country. Left to their own devices, the Ilocanos had to live "with ... less money, and less comfort than their countrymen in other, lusher regions ... of Luzon."[88] Much of their income came from the production of tobacco and the remittances sent by their family members who had migrated to Hawaii and the American west coast.[89] It was common, therefore, for Filipinos in general to "jeer at their [Ilocanos'] backwardness ...."[90] Objectively speaking, Ilocos may not have been among the most destitute regions in the Philippines, but the popular perceptions of the region, reinforced by its great distance from Manila, suggested otherwise.

Under these circumstances, Marcos became a regional hero for Ilocanos. During his terms as a congressman, senator, and president (1949–86), Ilocos "benefited from a disproportionate share of infrastructure projects and government jobs," whereas other provinces, especially the provinces of Marcos's political rivals, were denied funds. Road construction was Marcos's top priority. Thus, Ilocos became the recipient of "miles of cement pavement and the best roads in the republic." Bridges and schools sprang up "literally by the thousands." In addition, Marcos built an airport and a five-star hotel, which considerably improved the image of Ilocos.[91] He also recruited an unprecedented number of fellow Ilocanos into the bureaucracy, the congress, the military, and the courts. At the same time, he "returned regularly to Ilocos ... to meet with his people," sending a strong symbolic message that "he had not forgotten his origins."[92]

The result of these actions was resilient support for Marcos at the local level. While his massive pork-barrel projects and shameless "Ilocanization" of Filipino politics invited severe criticisms from outsiders, the six million ordinary Ilocanos took pride in their region, which Marcos turned into the object of others' envy and antagonism. Plainly, "Marcos's ascent to power tipped the scales" in favor of Ilocos.[93] Accordingly, many Ilocanos "revered Marcos as one of their own," as the developer of their long-neglected, disadvantaged region.[94] On the day of the national assembly election in 1984, for example, one Ilocano, with "his eyes ablaze with fierce loyalty to

---

[87] Personal communication with Patricio Abinales, November 11, 2008.

[88] Greg Bankoff, "The Dangers of Going It Alone: Social Capital and the Origins of Community Resilience in the Philippines," *Continuity and Change* 22,2 (2007): 341–42, 346; Sandra Burton, *Impossible Dream: The Marcoses, the Aquinos, and the Unfinished Revolution* (New York, NY: Warner Books, 1989), p. 37; and William Rempel, *Delusions of a Dictator: The Mind of Marcos as Revealed in His Secret Diaries* (Boston, MA: Little, Brown and Company, 1993), p. 10.

[89] Personal communication with Ben Kerkvliet in 2007.

[90] Zialcita, "Perspectives on Legitimacy in Ilocos Norte," p. 283.

[91] David Timberman, *A Changeless Land: Continuity and Change in Philippine Politics* (Singapore: Institute of Southeast Asian Studies, 1991), p. 96; Rempel, *Delusions of a Dictator*, p. 19; and David Wurfel, *Filipino Politics: Development and Decay* (Ithaca, NY: Cornell University Press, 1988), p. 272.

[92] Zialcita, "Perspectives on Legitimacy in Ilocos Norte," p. 274.

[93] Ibid., p. 284.

[94] Reid and Guerrero, *Corazon Aquino and the Brushfire Revolution*, p. 38.

the region's favorite son," commented to an outsider that "the vote will be one hundred percent for the KBL [Kilusang Bagong Lipunan, a party led by Marcos] in this town, as it should be all over the Philippines today."[95]

Ilocanos' strong sense of identification with Marcos is reflected, as one study found, in a variety of grassroots-level social narratives that defend his alleged wrongdoings. For example, few Ilocanos believe that Marcos was as corrupt as is widely reported. They do not blame Marcos, either, for the multi-billion dollar debt that the Philippines incurred under his presidency. Instead, they put the blame on his wife, Imelda, an allegedly typical Visayan known to have "extravagant" and "expensive tastes." In contrast, they uphold Marcos as a model of what every good Ilocano man should be: frugal and humble. He "cared little for meat [a sign of opulent living]" in his daily meals and preferred "boiled vegetables flavored with fermented fishpaste"—a symbol of humble living. Even during the fancy wedding ceremony for his daughter, Marcos is believed to have asked for "a simple dish of bittermelons." While in the presidential palace, he "ate with his fingers—just like an ordinary farmer."[96]

Furthermore, although conventional wisdom has it that Marcos was the mastermind behind the assassination of his archrival, Benigno Aquino Jr., in 1983, few Ilocanos share this view. The majority of Ilocanos also embrace the narratives that challenge the widely reported accounts of the People's Power Revolution of 1986. They believe that, far from blocking the smooth assumption of power by Benigno's widow, Cory Aquino, Marcos actually won the presidential election of 1986. They criticize the National Movement for Free Elections, a supposedly neutral body that oversaw the 1986 election, for "being partial to Aquino." Aquino's supporters were "poor sports, so they could not admit that their candidate lost ... they were Manila people who disliked Marcos, an Ilocano." Equally interesting is the local belief that Juan Ponce Enrile and Fidel Ramos, Marcos's trusted subordinates, whose last-minute betrayal clinched his downfall, "turned against Marcos because Cory paid them to do so." Nonetheless, Marcos "willingly stepped down from the presidency" to disperse the huge crowd of protesters, which many Ilocanos interpret as "further proof" of his humility. In their eyes, Aquino was not the heroine who restored democracy to the Philippines, as is commonly believed. Far from it. She instead represented an "undemocratic" government that "forcibly" displaced Marcos, their hero and the legitimate winner of the 1986 election, from power.[97] Unsubstantiated, exaggerated, and unpersuasive as these "articles of faith" may seem to outsiders, the narratives form a "legitimate" discourse at the local level and play an important part in sustaining Ilocanos' pride in Marcos, just as their counterparts in Suphanburi bolster their pride in Banharn.

Of course, not all Ilocanos supported Marcos. Yet many do continue to honor him as the man who developed backward Ilocos. To preserve this image, they have come up with all sorts of imagined stories or pieces of gossip. This is why Ilocos still remains "the Solid North," the "fiercely loyal bastion" of popular support for Marcos,[98] even nearly two decades after his death. His lingering legacy is reflected, in part, in the firm dynastic control that has been bequeathed to his son Ferdinand

---

[95] Burton, *Impossible Dream*, p. 217.

[96] Zialcita, "Perspectives on Legitimacy in Ilocos Norte," pp. 275, 276–77.

[97] Ibid., pp. 276, 278–80.

[98] Rempel, *Delusions of a Dictator*, pp. 15, 127.

Marcos Jr., the governor (1983–86, 1998–2007) and congressman (1992–95, 2007–present) of Ilocos Norte, and his daughter Imee, a congresswoman from Ilocos Norte (1998–2007). To be sure, many factors, such as coercion and control over the local economy, have helped insure this dynastic succession, yet we cannot understand it fully without considering the regional pride that Marcos engendered.

In recent years, Imee has striven to counter the negative images that Filipinos in general have of her late father. This has led her to initiate an ambitious project to rewrite the widely accepted history of Marcos's presidency.[99] This ideological project may well be superfluous for the supporters of Marcos in Ilocos. They do not need such reminders from the elite to enhance their respect for the region's former benefactor; they are capable of developing their own narratives.

Kim Dae Jung

Kim Dae Jung (1925–2009), former president of South Korea, is another politician akin to Banharn. He hails from the predominantly agricultural southwestern region of Cholla, which has been socially marginalized and discriminated against as the most backward region in South Korea. Cholla is also denigrated as a hotbed of violent radicalism, a reputation built on events such as the Tonghak peasant rebellion of 1894 and the Kwangju pro-democracy uprising of 1980, in which an estimated two-hundred civilians were brutally killed by the military.

Social discrimination against Cholla has a deep historical root in Korea. It dates back to the premodern "Three Kingdoms Era" (18 BCE–668 CE), during which three regional dynasties—Koguryo, Paekche (which corresponds roughly to Cholla), and Silla (which covers the southeastern region of present-day Kyongsang)—vied for hegemony. Years of bitter struggles led to the subjugation of Paekche by Silla in 660—a fact that has traditionally given Kyongsang's people a sense of superiority over Cholla. Later, King Wang Kon, the founder of the Koryo Dynasty (918–1392) that unified the Korean Peninsula, issued the notorious "Ten Injunctions," which formally prohibited the hiring of Paekche's people to serve in the government and the military, branding them "treacherous and disharmonious." The injunctions were strictly adhered to for the next four hundred years. The discrimination against Cholla was thus "legitimized." During the Choson period (1392–1910), Cholla's status remained as low as ever. One official document, for instance, labeled Cholla "a bad province, full of thieves, murderers, and pirates."[100]

Leaders of the post-independence state intensified the social stigma associated with Cholla. On coming to power in the military coup of 1961, General Park Chun Hee used his dictatorial authority to bestow an array of benefits on his home region of Kyongsang, Cholla's long-standing regional rival, as a way to consolidate his local base of support. The bulk of industrial factories and infrastructure projects were concentrated in Kyongsang, and Cholla was deliberately left out. Park also actively

---

[99] *The Philippines Star*, October 3, 2006.

[100] Sallie Yea, "Maps of Resistance and Geographies of Dissent in the Cholla Region of South Korea," *Korean Studies* 24 (2000): 72–74; Sallie Yea, "Reinventing the Region: The Cultural Politics of Place in Kwangju City and South Cholla Province," in *Contentious Kwangju: The May 18 Uprising in Korea's Past and Present*, ed. Gi-Wook Shin and Kyung Moon Hwang (Lanham, MD: Rowman & Littlefield, 2003), pp. 112–15; and Eui-Young Yu, "Regionalism in the South Korean Job Market: An Analysis of Regional-Origin Inequality among Migrants in Seoul," *Pacific Affairs* 63,1 (1990): 26.

recruited a large number of people from Kyongsang into the government, the bureaucracy, and the military, whereas Cholla-born workers who moved to Seoul faced open discrimination in finding even ordinary jobs.[101] Contrary to the conventional wisdom among political economists,[102] the developmental authoritarian state under Park was not insulated from society in a way that enabled it to enforce prescient economic policies in the interests of Korea as a whole. Far from it. In fact, petty regional politics drove Park's policy choices.[103] Although Park was assassinated in October 1979, his anti-Cholla policies were perpetuated under the leadership of three of his successors—Chun Doo Hwan, Roh Tae Woo, and Kim Young Sam, who all came from Kyongsang.

Even the advent of vibrant electoral politics in 1987 did little to redress the unequal allocation of resources by the central state. The new democratic system actually aggravated the already politicized pattern of distributing resources.[104] As a result, Cholla, once a wealthy rice-growing region, lagged even farther behind politically, economically, and socially under a functioning democracy than it had under military authoritarian rule. Cholla thus came to occupy a "stigmatized" position in the consciousness of Koreans outside the region. According to one journalist, South Koreans in general "regard people from this [Cholla] region as socially inferior—poor, uncouth, and unruly. Many respectable Korean families would be appalled if their daughter wished to marry a man from Cholla."[105]

Cholla's people were naturally resentful. They felt unjustly disadvantaged and "isolated from the mainstream of development."[106] They came to "share a common 'persecution consciousness'" or "a sense of 'victimization,'"[107] as illustrated in their flourishing anti-state *minjung* (populist) writings and dramas. Such perceptions led Cholla's people to belittle their own region as "backward," as Suphanburians once did regarding their own province. A negative collective identity intensified in

---

[101] Jang Jip Choi, "Political Cleavages in South Korea," in *State and Society in Contemporary Korea*, ed. Hagen Koo (Ithaca, NY: Cornell University Press, 1993), pp. 35–36, fn. 24; Manwoo Lee, *The Odyssey of Korean Democracy: Korean Politics, 1987–1990* (New York, NY: Praeger, 1990), pp. 49–51; Sallie Yea, "Regionalism and Political–Economic Differentiation in Korean Development: Power Maintenance and the State as Hegemonic Power Bloc," *Korea Journal* 34,2 (1994): 20.

[102] Alice Amsden, *Asia's Next Giant: South Korea and Late Industrialization* (New York, NY: Oxford University Press, 1989); and Peter Evans, *Embedded Autonomy: States and Industrial Transformation* (Princeton, NJ: Princeton University Press, 1995).

[103] Hyeok Yong Kwon, "Targeting Public Spending in a New Democracy: Evidence from South Korea," *British Journal of Political Science* 35,2 (2005): 340.

[104] Ibid.

[105] http://news.bbc.co.uk/1/hi/world/asia-pacific/788861.stm, accessed in November 2004. See also Yea, "Maps of Resistance and Geographies of Dissent in the Cholla Region of South Korea," p. 89.

[106] C. I. Eugene Kim, "The Meaning of the 1971 Korean Elections: A Pattern of Political Development," *Asian Survey* 12,3 (1972): 218; C. I. Eugene Kim, Young-Whan Kihl, and Doock-Kyou Chung, "Voter Turnout and the Meaning of Elections in South Korea," *Asian Survey* 13,11 (1973): 1965.

[107] Wang-Bae Kim, "Regionalism: Its Origins and Substance with Competition and Exclusion," *Korea Journal* 43,2 (2003): 18.

opposition to the state-imposed process of blatant political, economic, and social marginalization and exclusion.[108]

Against this historical backdrop, Kim Dae Jung came to be recognized as a heroic figure in Cholla. Elected to the National Assembly in 1961, Kim openly stood up to Park Chung Hee. In the presidential election of 1971, he almost defeated Park. Kim's main political platform was actually democratization, but since Park and other military leaders were all from Kyongsang, the platform became tantamount, for Cholla's people, to a noble campaign against Kyongsang's regional hegemony. Kim rose as the "challenger to the regional discrimination in political opportunity and material concessions ... and hence as the major campaigner for the southwest."[109] In short, Kim bolstered his popularity by capitalizing on the sense of smoldering discontent in Cholla and by projecting himself as a politician who best represented the interests of Cholla. That was the most effective way to establish a local base of support. Kim thus became the champion of both democracy and pan-Cholla regionalism. For Cholla's people, democratization meant giving their region the "fair deal" that it deserved, yet had long been denied.

Viewing Kim as a serious threat to its power, the military, led by Park, tried to kill him in 1971 and 1973. When these attempts failed, the regime arrested him in 1976. After the Kwangju uprising of 1980, he was arrested again and was sentenced to death (although he was allowed to flee to the United States, instead). The result of all this repression was ironic for the military, for "the more Park persecuted Kim, the more Kim's popularity grew ... in Cholla."[110] Precisely because of this persecution, Kim "was increasingly identified with the Cholla region" as its "favorite son" and "became the rallying point of the Cholla people."[111]

Presidential election results give a clear indication of the growing popular support for Kim in Cholla. In the elections of 1971, 1987, 1992, and 1997, he received 62.3 percent, 88.4 percent, 91 percent, and 92.9 percent of the votes in Cholla, respectively. His supporters "transcended age, sex, class, generation, and occupation." As a vivid manifestation of the "regionalization of voting," Kim's opponents fared dismally in Cholla each time. In the presidential election of 1992, for instance, Kim Young Sam from Kyongsang received only 4.8 percent of the votes in Cholla. Although in Kyongsang, 60.4 percent of the votes went to Kim Young Sam and only 10.3 percent to Kim Dae Jung, the difference was not as stark as in Cholla, where Kim Dae Jung commanded an extremely high level of partisan support.[112] This overwhelming support for Kim made the Kyongsang-dominated government even less inclined to allocate more public expenditure for Cholla,[113] which in turn made

---

[108] Sallie Yea, "The Culture and Politics of Resistance in South Korea," *Futures* 31 (1999): 221–34; Yea, "Reinventing the Region," p. 120; Yea, "Regionalism and Political–Economic Differentiation in Korean Development," p. 22.

[109] Yea, "Regionalism and Political–Economic Differentiation in Korean Development," pp. 20-21.

[110] http://www.cnn.com/SPECIALS/200/korea/story/leader/kim.dae.jung, accessed on November 1, 2004.

[111] Kim, "The Meaning of the 1971 Korean Elections," pp. 216, 218–19.

[112] Hochul Sonn, "Regional Cleavage in Korean Politics and Elections," *Korea Journal* 43, 2 (2003): 41, 43, 47, 49; Yea, "Regionalism and Political–Economic Differentiation in Korean Development," pp. 21, 22; Lee, *The Odyssey of Korean Democracy*, p. 82; Kwon, "Targeting Public Spending in a New Democracy," pp. 328–29.

[113] Kwon, "Targeting Public Spending in a New Democracy," p. 338.

Kim all the more popular there. He lost the elections of 1971, 1987, and 1992 because of his failure to garner enough support outside Cholla, but in the 1997 election, held amid the devastating economic crisis, he finally grasped victory, thanks to his strategic partnership with another regionally based politician. In February 1998, Kim thus became the first South Korean president from Cholla.

Kim's rise to the presidency signified and heralded the much-awaited ascendancy of Cholla. Contrary to his repeated pre- and post-election promises to eliminate parochial regionalism from Korean society,[114] Kim (allegedly) implemented policies that reinforced it. He used his presidential power to "disproportionately allocate important bureaucratic and governmental positions to persons from his native Cholla region, as well as … considerable development funds to the region."[115] This led the opposition Grand National Party to accuse him of adopting "a double standard on regionalism" and to comment: "It is ironic that President Kim, a clear beneficiary of political regionalism, touts efforts to overcome it."[116] This may have been the political propaganda used by the opposition to discredit Kim; one recent study shows that Kim (as well as other presidents in democratic South Korea) actually pursued policies that benefited all regions equally.[117] In any case, all the accusations only gratified Cholla's residents. During his first visit to the region as president in August 1998, Kim received "a hero's welcome."[118]

Cholla's people were not effusive simply because of the material benefits that Kim (supposedly) bestowed on them. More importantly, his presidency in general, coupled with his winning the Nobel Peace Prize in 2000, symbolized the first rewriting of the country's highly skewed social geography, in which Cholla had been relegated to an inferior, humiliating position. The fact that Kim was the first Cholla-born president was more important in enhancing the collective pride of Cholla's people than the specific benefits he channeled to the region.[119] Given "centuries of discrimination and marginalization behind them," the region's social identity could not be transformed overnight, but, as one keen observer noted, after Kim's rise to presidency, "the indications that a new manifestation of regionalism has set in are becoming more evident by the day." She detected "a shift in outlook in which the previous sense of powerlessness, deprivation, and marginalization has become muted, if not reversed."[120]

A major, concerted effort by the state to reappraise the meaning of the Kwangju uprising of 1980 in South Korean history has strengthened regional pride even further. Instead of writing off this event as an anti-state subversive rebellion (as the military regime had done), the civilian government has situated it as one of the most

---

[114] *Korea Times*, August 25, 1998; *Korea Herald* (February 2, 1999; April 23, 1999; May 17, 1999; November 3, 2000).

[115] Yea, "Maps of Resistance and Geographies of Dissent in the Cholla Region of South Korea," pp. 89–90. For specific examples, see *Korea Times* (August 25, 1998; September 28, 2000; March 2, 2000; April 2, 2003).

[116] *Korea Times*, March 2, 2000.

[117] Yusaku Horiuchi and Seungjoo Lee, "The Presidency, Regionalism, and Distributive Politics in South Korea," *Comparative Political Studies* 41,6 (2008): 861–82.

[118] *Korea Herald*, August 26, 1998.

[119] I thank Erik Mobrand for calling my attention to this point.

[120] Yea, "Maps of Resistance and Geographies of Dissent in the Cholla Region of South Korea," pp. 89–90.

important catalysts for democratization in South Korea. Thus, the image of Kwangju City and, by extension, the Cholla region that encompasses Kwangju, has been redefined; it is no longer considered a radical, dangerous, and defiant region, but is now more widely recognized as the place where South Korea's valiant struggle for democracy originated. This project actually got under way while Kim Young Sam, the first elected civilian president in postwar Korea, was in power (1993–97), but Kim Dae Jung, with his vital interests in the reinvention of Kwangju's image, actively promoted and sponsored the project.[121]

Kim Dae Jung's presidency (1998–2003) thus figures as a landmark event in the long "dark" history of Cholla. It is in this context that we can better understand why he commanded resilient support in the region, despite all the bribery charges made against his family members during his administration.

Cursory as they may be, these four comparative cases drawn from four different countries lend additional empirical support to my argument based on Banharn's case. They underscore the importance of a positive social identity as a vital social–psychological component of (locally bounded) legitimate political authority. The seemingly unchallenged domination of Narong was actually based on a flimsy foundation, whereas that of Tanaka, Marcos, and Kim each had a much more solid base. What distinguishes the second set of politicians from Narong is the presence of collective pride felt by their respective constituents. These comparative cases, therefore, suggest the applicability of my argument beyond Suphanburi and Banharn.

CONCLUDING THOUGHTS: "IGNORANT RURAL THAIS" REVISITED

Let me wrap up by returning to Banharn's case and considering its broad implications in light of recent developments in Thai politics. In the dominant urban-based public discourse in Thailand, it has been a common and largely uncontested practice to depict the rural masses as having little education and as holding fast to traditional cultural values that hinder the substantive democratization of Thailand. Commercial advertisements, TV dramas, movies, and songs reinforce this image, portraying rural folks as uncouth and unenlightened country bumpkins. The image has shaped, and has been shaped by, the prevailing views among scholars, intellectuals, and journalists that rural voters, especially farmers, are easy prey to vote-buying, violence, coercion, and other instruments of domination that are commonly employed by *chao pho* (godfathers) and other dishonest rural-based politicians, such as Banharn. For example, on the basis of his mechanical survey in Bangkok and four northern provinces, one political scientist makes the simple and unedifying point that Bangkokians "had more democratic attitudes" than rural voters. The latter "lack knowledge about legal, procedural, and institutional aspects of democracy," and simply expect their MPs to provide material benefits. The scholar concludes, echoing modernization theorists: "This combination of little political knowledge along with an expectation of the fulfillment of particularistic material needs forms part of a larger attitudinal complex that enables local figures, often

---

[121] Sallie Yea, "Rewriting Rebellion and Mapping Memory in South Korea: The (Re)presentation of the 1980 Kwangju Uprising through Mangwol-dong Cemetery," *Urban Studies* 39,9 (2002): 1551–72; *Korea Times*, August 26, 1998.

involved in illegal business activities, to win elections and engage in corruptions of all kinds so long as they continue to deliver the goods to their constituencies."[122]

This kind of stereotyped view of rural voters provided a powerful rationale for the passage of the "People's Constitution" of 1997, hailed as the most "democratic" constitution in the history of Thailand. Some of its clauses, which established the independent Electoral Commission and required that all MPs have a bachelor's degree, were institutional hedges against the election of uneducated and "immoral" rural-based MPs, who were assumed to attain political office by deceiving, buying off, or intimidating uneducated, pliant voters.[123]

The rule of Prime Minister Thaksin (2001–06), who enjoyed enormous popularity in the countryside for his "money-dumping populist" policies (e.g., universal health care made available to each Thai citizen for 30 baht per hospital visit, the one-million-baht village fund scheme), added considerably to this urban-based bias against the rural masses.[124] After the Constitutional Court nullified the victory of Thaksin's Thai Rak Thai (TRT) Party in the snap election of April 2006 and called for another election, an elderly man in Bangkok expressed the profound concern or pessimism shared among many "well-educated" Bangkokians. No party, according to this man, would ever be able to defeat the TRT in any future election. This was because:

> The farmers will decide Thailand's future. Thaksin is very clever—he has their votes, *the votes of the uneducated*. These people cannot possibly know about his activities. They are too busy earning their bread. Any gifts or financial gain that come their way just add to his fame.[125]

The media mogul Sondhi Limthongkul whipped up popular support for his anti-Thaksin and (putatively) royalist "yellow-shirt" movement—the People's Alliance for Democracy—by exploiting this kind of widespread snobbery among the middle class in Bangkok concerning "the tyranny of the rural majority."[126]

Against this backdrop, the military manipulated the growing populist–royalist rhetoric to justify the coup of September 2006 that drove Thaksin from power.[127] According to the coup leader, General Sondhi Boonyaratglin, this unconstitutional usurpation of power was necessary because "many Thais still lack[ed] a proper

---

[122] Jim LoGerfo, "Attitudes toward Democracy among Bangkok and Rural Northern Thais: The Great Divide," *Asian Survey* 36,9 (1996): 908, 918.

[123] William Callahan, "The Discourse of Vote Buying and Political Reform in Thailand," *Pacific Affairs* 78,1 (2005): 95–113; Kasian Techapira, "Toppling Thaksin," *New Left Review* 39 (2006): 14–15; Erik Kuhonta, "The Paradox of Thailand's 1997 'People's Constitution': Be Careful What You Wish For," *Asian Survey* 48,3 (2008): 375, 378–79; and Duncan McCargo, ed., *Reforming Thai Politics* (Copenhagen: Nordic Institute of Asian Studies Press, 2002).

[124] Kasian, "Toppling Thaksin," pp. 27–29; Pasuk Phongpaichit and Chris Baker, "Thaksin's Populism," *Journal of Contemporary Asia* 38,1 (2008): 62–83.

[125] BBC News, http://news.bbc.co.uk/1/hi/world/asia-pacific/4751407.stm, accessed on October 16, 2006, emphasis mine.

[126] Kasian, "Toppling Thaksin," p. 15.

[127] Ukrist Pathmanand, "A Different *Coup d'Etat?*" *Journal of Contemporary Asia* 38,1 (2008): 124–42.

understanding of democracy,"[128] and those uninformed Thais fervently supported Thaksin, a "dictatorial" politician who lacked respect for the revered monarchy. The palace-sanctioned coup was followed by a series of other heavy-handed, top-down actions aimed at eliminating Thaksin's influence in Thai politics—the Constitutional Court ruling of May 2007, which dissolved the TRT Party and barred its 111 top-ranking members from politics for five years; the replacement of the 1997 People's Constitution, which had inadvertently favored the TRT Party, with a new "anti-Thaksin" charter; another Constitutional Court ruling of September 2008, which unseated Prime Minister Samak Sundaravej, leader of the TRT-reincarnated People's Power Party (PPP); and still another Constitutional Court ruling of December 2008, which dissolved the PPP (and Banharn's Chart Thai Party, as discussed in chapter 8) and forced the resignation of Prime Minister Somchai Wongsawat, Thaksin's brother-in-law. The last ruling paved the way for the rise of Abhisit Vejjajiva, leader of the royalist Democrat Party, as the new prime minister.

Yet these actions taken or supported by the military, the Privy Council, the judiciary, and reform-minded urban intellectuals—the institutions and individuals that comprise the "network monarchy"[129]—have done nothing but generate profound resentment among many voters in the countryside and rendered Thailand all the more polarized along the putative urban–rural lines. The vengeful rural-based voters, now organized in a new populist countermovement, the United Front for Democracy against Dictatorship, have carried out nationwide "red-shirt" protests against the ruling Democrat Party and even against the Privy Council's involvement in politics. In April 2009, one of those protests forced the cancellation of the summit meeting of the Association of Southeast Asian Nations. Deeply embarrassed, Abhisit declared a state of emergency and used military force to quell the demonstrations; at least two people were killed during the crackdown. The red shirts retaliated by carrying out an assassination attempt on yellow-shirt leader Sondhi. Meanwhile, the abruptly ousted provincial-populist MPs, including Thaksin and Banharn, have simply had their proxies—wives, sons, daughters, relatives, friends, and the like—run for office on their behalf, and their constituents have eagerly voted them into office. The yellow-shirt royal-nationalists are running an endless, futile race. It is as if they were trying to eliminate cockroaches: the minute they kill one, another one appears out of nowhere.

For "yellow shirts," these developments only confirm their "rural-people-are-stupid" thesis. The solution proposed to this "problem" concerning allegedly ignorant rural masses has been predictably simple (and hackneyed): educate them about the "true" meaning of democracy. In the words of Sondhi, leader of the 2006 coup, "… it is important to educate the people about true democratic rule. It is a challenge to enable all sixty million Thais to gain an in-depth understanding of democracy … Democracy will thrive once the people learn its true meaning."[130] The elderly man in Bangkok quoted above concurs, saying, "Thailand has democracy,

---

[128] *The Nation*, October 26, 2006, cited in Andrew Walker, "The Rural Constitution and the Everyday Politics of Elections in Northern Thailand," *Journal of Contemporary Asia* 38,1 (2008): 84.

[129] Duncan McCargo, "Network Monarchy and Legitimacy Crises in Thailand," *Pacific Review* 18,4 (2005): 499–519.

[130] *The Nation*, October 26, 2006, cited in Andrew Walker, "The Rural Constitution and the Everyday Politics of Elections in Northern Thailand," p. 84.

but some people say that the grassroots are not qualified to take part [in] that. Thailand should spend time educating people about democracy before applying democratic rule."[131] These views echo the advice proffered by many academics. As one prominent Thai political scientist put it, "political education [must] be given to rural voters ... to provide them with a proper understanding of the objects of elections and their mechanisms, as well as to arouse political awareness."[132] Plainly stated, rural Thais are not ready for democracy, according to these views. Therefore, they need to be taught, reformed, and guided. These proposed educational campaigns constitute what Michael Connors refers to in his insightful study as the ideological "democrasubjection" project of hegemony and governmentality, a project that has been pursued by the ruling Thai elite in order to mold ordinary people into subjects and objects of proper democratic education.[133]

In this discursive context, many Suphanburians' support for Banharn would be regarded by well-educated, reformist Bangkokians as just another piece of evidence confirming rural voters' political naïveté that stems from their lack of education. Residents of Suphanburi would be viewed as gullible dupes, easily misled or fooled into trusting and even admiring an essentially debased politician who lacks public probity. Is such a view valid?

My answer is "no." Drawing on social identity theory, we can and should actually see Suphanburians as perfectly *normal* human beings who have a fundamental desire or need to belong to a well-respected social group and who subjectively evaluate what they see and hear to meet that desire or need. They support Banharn for the simple and sensible reason that they (want to) think he has refashioned formerly backward Suphanburi into a uniquely developed province. If it is true that the overwhelming majority of human beings share the same desire for a positive social identity, then we can conclude that Suphanburians' support for Banharn has little to do with their lack of education—it is, instead, a product of their characteristic human qualities. They are little different from the people in Trang and other southern provinces, who support Chuan Leekpai for having built up regional pride around the romanticized notion of "southern virtuosity."[134] Similarly, the Suphanburians who think of Banharn as their good leader are no less "stupid" than well-educated Americans who regarded President George W. Bush as a great leader who was building a strong America and a free democratic world. These seemingly different cases are essentially of the same kind. Laid bare, they are all based on human beings' quintessential quest for a positive social identity. I do not deny that the level of Suphanburians' educational attainment is relatively low, but we cannot use this sociological feature to explain (away) their support for Banharn. Even much better educated and allegedly rational people are perfectly capable of (unknowingly)

---

[131] BBC News, http://news.bbc.co.uk/1/hi/world/asia-pacific/4751407.stm, accessed on October 16, 2006.

[132] Suchit Bunbongkarn, "Elections and Democratization in Thailand," in *The Politics of Elections in Southeast Asia*, ed. Robert Taylor (New York, NY: Woodrow Wilson Center Press, 1996), p. 200. See also Anek Laothamatas, "A Tale of Two Democracies: Conflicting Perceptions of Elections and Democracy in Thailand," in Taylor, *The Politics of Elections in Southeast Asia*, p. 222.

[133] Michael Connors, *Democracy and National Identity in Thailand* (Copenhagen: Nordic Institute of Asian Studies Press, 2007), pp. 21–27.

[134] Askew, *Performing Political Identity.*

embracing a social order that makes them feel proud of their social group.[135] The Suphanburians who support Banharn should be seen in the same light.

To the extent that my argument is valid, it calls for a further critical reappraisal of the dominant urban-based discourse that ascribes rural voters' thoughts and behavior to their putative ignorance.[136] The vast number of people who use the powers of pens, computers, and microphones to propagate this discourse—scholars, intellectuals, politicians, bureaucrats, journalists, soldiers, ordinary voters, and so on —are all (unknowingly) complicit in waging a morally condescending, dogmatic offensive.[137] Their opinion or analysis, no matter how "objective" they may claim it to be, constitutes nothing less than ideology in a broadly construed sense.[138] They are, in effect, implicated, if unintentionally, in constructing and perpetuating a huge ideological edifice that serves to reproduce the superior position of Bangkok—an edifice manifested in the value-ridden and oppressive binary opposition between the politically sophisticated and progressive citizens of Bangkok, on one hand, and unsophisticated, backward "country bumpkins," on the other. This discursively constructed edifice does not simply represent a gross misconception that needs to be rectified; it has also become a convenient ideological tool that the ruling elites in Bangkok can deploy at will to maintain the urban-centric pattern of political, economic, and social development.

It is actually these well-educated elites, not uneducated rural-based voters, who have impeded Thailand's democratization by employing the anti-rural and royal-nationalist populist discourse to discredit any rural-based politician they dislike. If they disapprove of the likes of Banharn and Thaksin, they should try to beat them at the polls by coming up with policies that would appeal to the rural masses, instead of resorting to coups and crude legal maneuverings. Through such a process, all parties and their candidates (including the most despicable) would be forced to become more and more competitive by adopting policies that address the multiple and divergent needs of voters. That would help expand the range of Thailand's political audience and thereby widen the scope of healthy political conflicts—an essential condition for a well-functioning, vibrant democracy.[139] In this respect, the coup of 2006 and a series of subsequent court rulings were regressive acts that obstructed the process of democratization by arbitrarily restricting political competition to those who supposedly know what "democracy" is.

In making these arguments, I do not mean to claim that the rural voters' discourse is somehow "better" or "more authentic" than the urban-based discourse. Neither am I taking a purely relativist position and arguing that it would be all right

---

[135] One pathological manifestation of this phenomenon is the Holocaust perpetrated by ordinary Germans. See Daniel Goldhagen, *Hitler's Willing Executioners: Ordinary Germans and the Holocaust* (New York, NY: Abacus, 1997).

[136] For a similar critique, see Walker, "The Rural Constitution and the Everyday Politics of Elections in Northern Thailand." See also http://asiapacific.anu.edu.au/newmandala/2007/12/11/interview-with-professor-charles-keyes/, accessed on June 30, 2008.

[137] See also Thongchai Winichakul, "Toppling Democracy," *Journal of Contemporary Asia* 38,1 (2008): 26.

[138] Michel Foucault, *The Archaeology of Knowledge*, trans. Sheridan Smith (New York, NY: Pantheon, 1972); and Karl Mannheim, *Ideology and Utopia: An Introduction to the Sociology of Knowledge* (London: Routledge, 1991).

[139] See Elmer E. Schattschneider's classic book, *The Semisovereign People: A Realist's View of Democracy in America* (New York, NY: Holt, Rinehart, and Winston, 1960).

for both warring sides—the rural and urban voters—to keep on believing what they want to believe.[140] Instead, I am only disputing the widely held assumption that there is an inherently unbridgeable urban–rural divide. This is the spurious divide—just another kind of social geography—that numerous urban-based agents of ideological production have created by turning the countryside into what it is not: an undifferentiated physical mass inhabited by a huge number of poor, uneducated, and venal voters who cannot tell "good" politicians from "bad" ones. Contrary to the picture conjured up by this barbarously simplistic and condescending analysis, Thailand is not made up of two mutually antagonistic peoples with hopelessly irreconcilable interests, needs, and expectations. Depending on their different interests, needs, and expectations, urban and rural voters may support different types of politicians at times, but that is perfectly *normal* in any society. Once we see rural voters for what they are—as rational people who have their own legitimate reasons for supporting the politicians they do, just like their counterparts anywhere—the artificially constructed urban–rural divide will begin to collapse; the divide is just as arbitrary as the much-touted "clash of civilizations" pitting the West against the Islamic world.[141] The "threat" posed by rural voters to urban voters would then begin to disappear.

This is admittedly much easier said than done, given all the persistent biases that urban Thais in general hold against the countryside and its people. I humbly hope, nonetheless, that this case study will assist, albeit in a very small way, in the deconstruction of the vast and redoubtable ideological edifice that stigmatizes rural voters as the inferior "others" in Thailand. If the case of Banharn contains any lesson that might be applied to other places and peoples, it could be summed up in one phrase: human beings' willingness or eagerness to follow a ruler who enhances their collective pride. This human propensity makes us all potentially vulnerable to the type of political authority that Banharn has constructed in Suphanburi. There is no reason to assume that a politician like Banharn will not appear in places inhabited by "well-educated" people. It would be a serious mistake, then, to write off Banharn's domination as an anomalous phenomenon in the "far-off" traditional agrarian province of Thailand. It may be closer to all of us than we care to think.

---

[140] I thank one of my reviewers for raising these provocative points.

[141] Edward Said, "The Clash of Ignorance," *The Nation* (US), October 22, 2001.

SELECT BIBLIOGRAPHY

NEWSPAPERS AND PERIODICALS

Bangkok Post. Bangkok
Chart Thai Samphan (Chart Thai Relations). Bangkok
Isara (Free). Suphanburi
Khon Suphan (Suphan People). Suphanburi
Krungthep Thurakij Sutsabda (Bangkok Business Weekly). Bangkok
Nation Sutsabda (Nation Weekly). Bangkok
Suphan. Suphanburi
Suphan Post. Suphanburi
Suphanburi Sarn (Suphanburi News). Suphanburi
Thai Rath. Bangkok
The Nation. Bangkok
Thin Thai (*Thai Land*). Suphanburi
Withayu-sarn Prachamwan (Daily Radio News). Bangkok

PRIMARY AND SECONDARY SOURCES

Akhraphon and Rut Manthira. *Senthang suu Nayok Ratamontrii khong Tueng Siao Harn Banharn Silpa-archa* (Banharn Silpa-archa's Road to Premiership). Bangkok: Nam Fon, 1995.

Anant Sanokhan. *Thammai Phom Tong Than Banharn* (Why I Must Resist Banharn). Bangkok: Klet Thai, 1988.

Anderson, Benedict. "Murder and Progress in Modern Siam." *New Left Review* 181 (1990): 33–48.

—— *Imagined Communities: Reflections on the Origin and the Spread of Nationalism*. London: Verso, 1991.

Anek Laothamatas. "A Tale of Two Democracies: Conflicting Perceptions of Elections and Democracy in Thailand," in *The Politics of Elections in Southeast Asia*, ed. Robert Taylor. New York, NY: Woodrow Wilson Center Press, 1996, pp. 201–23.

Arghiros, Daniel. *Democracy, Development, and Decentralization in Provincial Thailand*. Richmond, UK: Curzon, 2001.

Askew, Marc. *Performing Political Identity: The Democrat Party in Southern Thailand*. Chiang Mai: Silkworm, 2008.

Association of Suphanburians. *Hoksip Pii Samakhom Chao Suphanburi* (Sixty Years of the Association of Suphanburians). Suphanburi: Association of Suphanburians, 1996.

Banharn–Jaemsai School I. *Phithi Morp Thun Kan Sueksa Munnithi Banharn-Jaemsai Prachampii 2538* (Ceremony for Handing Out Banharn–Jaemsai Foundation Scholarships 1995). Suphanburi: Banharn–Jaemsai School I, 1995.

Banharn–Jaemsai School IV. *Ekasarn Naenam Rongrian nai Phithi Morp Thun Kan Sueksa Munnithi Banharn-Jaemsai* (Guide to School on the Occasion of Banharn–Jaemsai Foundation Scholarship-Awarding Ceremony). Suphanburi: Banharn–Jaemsai School IV, 1995.

Banharn–Jaemsai Polytechnic College. *Ekasarn Naenam Withayalai Saraphat Chang Banharn-Jaemsai Changwat Suphanburi* (Guide to Banharn–Jaemsai Polytechnic College, Suphanburi Province). Suphanburi: Banharn–Jaemsai Polytechnic College, n.d.

Bowie, Katherine. "Vote Buying and Village Outrage in an Election in Northern Thailand: Recent Legal Reforms in Historical Context." *Journal of Asian Studies* 67,2 (2008): 469–511.

Budget Bureau. *Ekasarn Ngop-pramarn* (*Budget Document*), various years (1960–72, 1974–80, 1984–2001), various volume and issue numbers.

Callahan, William. "The Discourse of Vote Buying and Political Reform in Thailand." *Pacific Affairs* 78,1 (2005): 95–113.

Callahan, William, and Duncan McCargo. "Vote-buying in Thailand's Northeast: The July 1995 General Election." *Asian Survey* 36,4 (1996): 376–92.

Chaisit Phuwaphiromkhwan. *Ekasarn Laktharn Kham Aphiprai Mai Wai Wangjai Ratamontrii Khomanakhom, 21 Tulakhom 2530* (Documents on No-Confidence Motion against Minister of Transport and Communications, October 21, 1987). Bangkok: n.p., 1987.

Chaophraya Yommarat Hospital. *Thiraluek Phithi Perd Tuek Khon Khai Phiset Banharn-Jaemsai Silpa-archa 3* (Commemorating the Opening Ceremony for Banharn–Jaemsai Patients' Ward 3). Suphanburi: Chaophraya Yommarat Hospital, 1997.

Chatthip Nartsupha. *The Thai Village Economy in the Past.* Chiang Mai: Silkworm, 1997.

College of Physical Education of Suphanburi. *Nangsue Anuson Phu Samred Kan Sueksa 2541* (Yearbook for Graduates 1998). Suphanburi: College of Physical Education, 1998.

—— *Khu Mue Naksueksa Pii Kan Sueksa 2541 Withayalai Phala Sueksa Changwat Suphanburi 2541* (Handbook for Students, Academic Year 1998, College of Physical Education of Suphanburi 1998). Suphanburi: College of Physical Education, 1998.

Connors, Michael. *Democracy and National Identity in Thailand.* Copenhagen: Nordic Institute of Asian Studies Press, 2007.

Department of Business Development, Ministry of Commerce. Bangkok Company File no. 61 (Ban Muang Kan Phim).

—— Bangkok Company File no. 243/2512 (Siam City Cement).

—— Bangkok Company File no. 330/2513 (B.S. International).

—— Bangkok Company File no. 362 and no. 2635 (Thai Yong Phanit).

—— Bangkok Company File no. 364/2518 (Rajadamri Vachaki).

—— Bangkok Company File no. 1319/2510 (Si Saeng Kan Yotha).

—— Bangkok Company File no. 2070 (Bangkok Metropolitan Bank).

—— Bangkok Company File no. 2164/2523 (Saha Srichai Chemical).

—— Bangkok Company File no. 2975 (Ayutthaya Life Insurance).

—— Bangkok Company File no. 3893 (Saha Srichai Construction).

—— Bangkok Company File no. 7508/2533 (Siam Occidental Electrochemical).

—— Bangkok Limited Partnership File no. 527/05 (Nathee Thong).

—— Buriram Company File no. 0315534000071 (Silachai Buriram).

—— Chiang Mai Company File no. 0505522000347 (Chiang Mai Construction).

—— Chiang Mai Company File no. 0505508000084 (Siam Tobacco Export Corporation).

—— Chiang Mai Company File no. 0505513000208 (Thai Tobacco Industrial).

—— Chiang Mai Company File no. 0545517000024 (General Tobacco).

—— Chiang Rai Company File no. 0525492000034 (Thepawong).

—— Chiang Rai Company File no. 0575503000019 (Chiang Rai Borikan).

—— Suphanburi Limited Partnership File no. 60 (Sai Samphan).

—— Suphanburi Limited Partnership File no. 120/2505 (Suphan U-Thong Phanit).

—— Suphanburi Limited Partnership File no. 198 (Thawon Suphanburi).

—— Suphanburi Limited Partnership File no. 414 (Matrasri Jakrakon).

—— Suphanburi Limited Partnership File no. 443 (Sri Somboon Suwattana).

—— Suphanburi Limited Partnership File no. 1027 (Sin Somboon Kan Yotha).

—— Suphanburi Company File no. 177 (Nakphanit).

—— Suphanburi Company File no. 685/2514 (Ruam Mitr Muang Rae).

—— Suphanburi Company File no. 3195/2530 (Prasong Phon).

Department of Highways. *Rai-ngan Prachampii 2497* (Annual Report 1954). Bangkok: Department of Highways, various years (1955–56, 1977, 1981–84, 1986, and 2000).

——. *Kaosip Pii Krom Thang Luang* (Ninety Years of Highways Department). Bangkok: 2002.

Dore, R. P. "The Prestige Factor in International Affairs." *International Affairs* 51,2 (1975): 190–207.

Edelman, Murray. *The Symbolic Uses of Politics.* Urbana, IL: University of Illinois Press, 1976.

—— *Constructing the Political Spectacle.* Chicago, IL: University of Chicago Press, 1988.

Election Commission, *Khomun Sathiti lae Phon Kan Lueak Tang Sammachik Sapha Phu Thaen Ratsadon* (Statistical Data and the Results of the House of Representatives Election), various years (2001, 2005, 2007).

Escobar, Arturo. *Encountering Development: The Making and Unmaking of the Third World.* Princeton, NJ: Princeton University Press, 1995.

Foucault, Michel. *Power/Knowledge,* ed. and trans. Colin Gordon. New York, NY: Pantheon, 1980.

—— *Discipline and Punish: The Birth of the Prison.* Trans. Alan Sheridan. New York, NY: Vintage Books, 1995.

Geertz, Clifford. *The Interpretation of Cultures*. New York, NY: Basic Books, 1973.

—— *Negara: The Theater State in Nineteenth-Century Bali*. Princeton, NJ: Princeton University Press, 1980.

Goffman, Erving. *The Presentation of Self in Everyday Life*. New York, NY: Anchor Books, 1959.

Gupta, Akhil. "Blurred Boundaries: The Discourse of Corruption, the Culture of Politics, and the Imagined State." *American Ethnologist* 22,2 (1995): 375–402.

Handley, Paul. *The King Never Smiles: A Biography of Thailand's Bhumibol Adulyadej*. New Haven, CT: Yale University Press, 2006.

Hechter, Michael. *Internal Colonialism: The Celtic Fringe in British National Development, 1536–1966*. Berkeley, CA: University of California Press, 1975.

Herbst, Jeffrey. *States and Power in Africa: Comparative Lessons in Authority and Control*. Princeton, NJ: Princeton University Press, 2000.

Hewison, Kevin. "Resisting Globalization: A Study of Localism in Thailand." *Pacific Review* 13,2 (2000): 279–96.

Hirsch, Philip. "What is the Thai Village?" in *National Identity and its Defenders, 1939–1989*, ed. Craig Reynolds. Clayton, Australia: Monash University Center of Southeast Asian Studies, 1991, pp. 323–40.

Hobsbawm, Eric. *Bandits*. Harmondsworth, UK: Penguin, 1972.

Hoksip pii Bodi Chunnanond (Sixty years of Bodi Chunnanond). Bangkok: Bophit, 1995.

Ileto, Reynaldo. *Knowing America's Colony: A Hundred Years from the Philippine War*. Honolulu, HI: University of Hawaii, Center for Philippine Studies, 1999.

Johnston, David. "Bandit, Nakleng, and Peasant in Rural Thai Society." *Contributions to Asian Studies* 15 (1980): 90–101.

Jost, John, and Mahzarin Banaji. "The Role of Stereotyping in System-Justification and the Production of False-consciousness." *British Journal of Social Psychology* 33 (1994): 1–27.

Kane, John. *The Politics of Moral Capital*. New York, NY: Cambridge University Press, 2001.

Kerkvliet, Benedict. "Toward a More Comprehensive Analysis of Philippine Politics: Beyond the Patron–Client, Factional Framework." *Journal of Southeast Asian Studies* 26,2 (1995): 401–19.

Keyes, Charles F. *Isan: Regionalism in Northeastern Thailand*. Ithaca, NY: Cornell University Southeast Asia Program, 1967.

Khomduean Choetcharatfa. *Cheewa Prawat lae Thasana Banharn Silpa-archa Nayol Ratamontri Khon thi 21 khong Thai* (The Life and Viewpoint of Banharn Silpa-archa, Thailand's 21st Prime Minister). Bangkok: Soi Thong, 1995.

Kulik, James. "Confirmatory Attribution and the Perpetuation of Social Beliefs." *Journal of Personality and Social Psychology* 44,6 (1983): 1171–81.

Kulik, James, Paul Sledge, and Heike Mahler. "Self-Confirmatory Attribution and the Perpetuation of Self-Beliefs." *Journal of Personality and Social Psychology* 50,3 (1986): 587–94.

Lagos, Gustavo. *International Stratification and Underdeveloped Countries*. Chapel Hill, NC: University of North Carolina Press, 1963.

Lewis, Michael. *Becoming Apart: National Power and Local Politics in Toyama, 1868–1945*. Cambridge, MA: Harvard East Asian Studies, 2000.

LoGerfo, Jim. "Attitudes toward Democracy among Bangkok and Rural Northern Thais: The Great Divide." *Asian Survey* 36,9 (1996): 904–23.

Lord, Charles, Lee Ross, and Mark Lepper. "Biased Assimilation and Attitude Polarization: The Effects of Prior Theories on Subsequently Considered Evidence." *Journal of Personality and Social Psychology* 37,11 (1979): 2098–2109.

McCargo, Duncan, ed. *Reforming Thai Politics.* Copenhagen: Nordic Institute of Asian Studies, 2002.

—— "Network Monarchy and Legitimacy Crises in Thailand." *Pacific Review* 18,4 (2005): 499–519.

McCoy, Alfred, ed. *An Anarchy of Families: State and Family in the Philippines.* Madison, WI: University of Wisconsin Press, 1993.

McVey, Ruth. "Introduction: Local Voices, Central Power," in *Southeast Asian Transitions: Approaches through Local History*, ed. Ruth McVey. New Haven, CT: Yale University Press, 1978, pp. 1–31.

—— ed. *Money and Power in Provincial Thailand.* Honolulu, HI: University of Hawaii Press, 2000.

Migdal, Joel. *State in Society: Studying How States and Societies Transform and Constitute One Another.* Cambridge, NY: Cambridge University Press, 2001.

Ministry of Interior. *Phon Kan Lueak Tang Sammachik Sapha Phu Thaen Ratsadon* (Results of the House of Representatives Election, 1992). Bangkok: Ministry of Interior), various years (1992 and 1995).

National Archives. *Phra Rachakaraniyakit 2502* (Royal Activities 1959), jo/2502/3.

—— *Phithi Yok Phum Khaobin Yord Phra Monthop lae Sompjol Roi Phra Phuthabat thi Wat Khao Dee Salak Changwat Suphanburi* (Ceremony for Raising Offerings of Rice Wrapped up in Banana Leaves onto the Top of Monthop and for Commemorating Buddha's Footprints, Khao Dee Salak Temple, Suphanburi), Jo/2543/3, Files no. 4–5.

National Counter Corruption Committee, MP File no. 25 (Kanlaya Sophonpanich).

—— MP File no. 343 (Banharn Silpa-archa).

—— Party List MP File no. 431 (Newin Chidchob).

—— Minister File no. 41 (Chai Chidchob).

National Economic and Social Development Board. *Phalitaphan Phak lae Changwat 2521* (Gross Regional and Provincial Product 1978). Bangkok: NESDB, 1979.

National Economic Development Board. *The National Economic Development Plan, 1961–1966: Second Phase, 1964–1966.* Bangkok: NEDB, 1964.

—— *Performance Evaluation of Development in Thailand for 1965 under National Economic Development Plan, 1961–1966.* Bangkok: 1966.

—— *The Second National Economic and Social Development Plan 1967–1971.* Bangkok: 1967.

—— *Development Projects Requiring Financial Assistance under the Second Plan (1967–1971).* Bangkok: 1968.

National Statistical Office. *Statistical Yearbook Thailand 1963.* Bangkok: NSO, 1964.

—— *Statistical Yearbook Thailand 1964.* Bangkok: NSO, 1965.

—— *Statistical Yearbook Thailand 1970–1971.* Bangkok: NSO, 1972.

—— *Statistical Yearbook Thailand 1974–1975.* Bangkok: NSO, 1976.

Nelson, Michael. *Central Authority and Local Administration in Thailand*. Bangkok: White Lotus, 1998.

Nikhon Chamnong. *Boriharn Ngan Satai Banharn* (Banharn-style Management). Bangkok: Mathichon, 2000.

Nishizaki, Yoshinori. "Provincializing Thai Politics." *Kyoto Review of Southeast Asia* 1 (2002). Published online at http://kyotoreview.cseas.kyoto-u.ac.jp/issue/issue0/article_31.html, accessed October 17, 2010.

—— "The Gargantuan Project and Modernity in Provincial Thailand." *Asia Pacific Journal of Anthropology* 8,3 (2007): 217–33.

—— "Suphanburi in the Fast Lane: Roads, Prestige, and Domination in Provincial Thailand." *Journal of Asian Studies* 67,2 (2008): 433–67.

Oakes, Penelope, Katherine Reynolds, Alexander Haslam, and John Turner. "Part of Life's Rich Tapestry: Stereotyping and the Politics of Intergroup Relations." *Advances in Group Processes* 16 (1999): 125–60.

Ockey, James. "Business Leaders, Gangsters, and the Middle Class: Social Groups and Civilian Rule in Thailand." PhD Dissertation, Cornell University, 1992.

—— "Thai Society and Patterns of Political Leadership." *Asian Survey* 36,4 (1996): 345–60.

—— *Making Democracy: Leadership, Class, Gender, and Political Participation in Thailand*. Honolulu, HI: University of Hawaii Press, 2004.

Paige, Jeffery. *Coffee and Power: Revolution and the Rise of Democracy in Central America*. Cambridge, MA: Harvard University Press, 1997.

Pasuk Phongpaichit and Sungsidh Piriyarangsan. *Corruption and Democracy in Thailand*. Chiang Mai: Silkworm, 1996.

Phillips, Herbert. "The Election Ritual in a Thai Village." *Journal of Social Issues* 14,4 (1958): 36–50.

Provincial Office of Fine Arts. *Kan Buruna Boran Sathan lae Kan Jatsang Monthop Khao Dee Salak* (The Renovation of Ancient Relics and the Building of Monthop of Khao Dee Salak). Suphanburi: Provincial Office of Fine Arts, 1999.

Provincial Office of Suphanburi. *Thiraluek Phithi Perd Phraborom Rachanusawri Phrabat Somdet Phra Junla Jom Klao Chaoyuhua lae Sala Klang Changwat Suphanburi* (Commemorating the Opening of King Chulalongkorn Monument and the Provincial Hall of Suphanburi). Suphanburi: Provincial Office, 2000.

Provincial Statistical Office of Suphanburi. *Samut Rai-ngan Sathiti Changwat: Suphanburi 2539* (Statistical Report of Provinces: Suphanburi 1996). Suphanburi: Provincial Statistical Office, 1997.

Ratana Boonmathya. "Contested Concepts of Development in Rural Northeastern Thailand." PhD dissertation, University of Washington, 1997.

Regional Office of Highways Department (Suphanburi branch). *Sarup Phon-ngan Prachampii 2544* (Summary of Works 2001). Suphanburi: Regional Office of Highways Department, 2002.

Reynolds, Craig. "The Plot of Thai History: Theory and Practice," in *Patterns and Illusions: Thai History and Thought*, ed. Gehan Wijeyewardene and E. C. Chapman. Canberra: Richard Davis Fund and Department of Anthropology, Australian National University, 1992, pp. 313–32.

Rhum, Michael. "'Modernity' and 'Tradition' in 'Thailand.'" *Modern Asian Studies.* 30,2 (1996): 325–55.

Rigg, Jonathan, Anna Allott, Rachel Harrison, and Ulrich Kratz. "Understanding Languages of Modernization: A Southeast Asian View." *Modern Asian Studies* 33,3 (1999): 581–602.

Robertson, Jr., Philip. "The Rise of the Rural Network Politician: Will Thailand's New Elite Endure?" *Asian Survey* 36,9 (1996): 924–41.

Said, Edward. *Orientalism.* New York, NY: Vintage Books, 1979.

—— "The Clash of Ignorance," *The Nation* (US) 273,12 (October 22, 2001): 11-14.

Sarthit Winurat. *Ke Roi Nak Kan Muang* (Tracing the Footsteps of Politicians). Bangkok: Wisurut, 1996.

Schattschneider, Elmer E. *The Semisovereign People: A Realist's View of Democracy in America.* New York, NY: Holt, Rinehart, and Winston, 1960.

Schlesinger, Jacob. *Shadow Shoguns: The Rise and Fall of Japan's Postwar Political Machine.* New York, NY: Simon & Schuster, 1997.

Scott, James C. *Weapons of the Weak: Everyday Forms of Peasant Resistance.* New Haven, CT: Yale University Press, 1985.

—— *Domination and the Arts of Resistance: Hidden Transcripts.* New Haven, CT: Yale University Press, 1990.

—— *Seeing like a State: How Certain Schemes to Improve the Human Conditions Have Failed.* New Haven, CT: Yale University Press, 1998.

Searle, John. *The Construction of Social Reality.* New York, NY: Free Press, 1995.

Sewell, William. "Introduction: Narratives and Social Identities." *Social Science History* 16,3 (1992): 479–88.

Shao, Qin. *Culturing Modernity: The Nantong Model, 1890–1930.* Stanford, CA: Stanford University Press, 2004.

Smail, John. "On the Possibility of an Autonomous History of Southeast Asia." *Journal of Southeast Asian History* 1,2 (1961): 72–102.

Snyder, Mark, Elizabeth Decker Tanke, and Ellen Berscheid. "Social Perception and Interpersonal Behavior: On the Self-Fulfilling Nature of Social Stereotypes." *Journal of Personality and Social Psychology* 35,9 (1977): 656–66.

Somrudee Nicro. "Thailand's NIC Democracy: Studying from General Elections." *Pacific Affairs* 66,2 (1993): 167–82.

Sonn, Hochul. "Regional Cleavage in Korean Politics and Elections." *Korea Journal* 43,2 (2003): 32–54.

Sports Association of Suphanburi. *Chomrom Basketball Changwat Suphanburi* (Basketball Club of Suphanburi). Suphanburi: Sports Association, 1994.

—— *Khrop Rorp Haa Pii Samakhom Kiilaa Changwat Suphanburi* (The Fifth Anniversary of the Sports Association of Suphanburi). Suphanburi: Sports Association, 1997.

—— *Thiraluek Phithi Wang Silarert Arkhan Thi Phak Nakkiilaa Khanat 200 Tiang Changwat Suphanburi* (Commemorating the Cornerstone-laying Ceremony for Athletes' Hotel with 200 Beds, Suphanburi). Suphanburi: Sports Association, 1998.

—— *13th Asian Games Suphanburi.* Suphanburi: Sports Association, 1998.

Sports School of Suphanburi. *Khu Mue Nakrian lae Phuu Pok Khrong* (Guidebook for Students and Administrators). Suphanburi: Sports School, 1997.

—— *Kan Khaeng Khan Kiilaa Rawang Rongrian Kiilaa Thua Prathet Khrang Thi Song* (The Second National Sports Competition among Sports Schools). Suphanburi: Sports School, 1998.

—— *Pratheep haeng Kan Kiilaa* (The Light of Sports). Suphanburi: Sports School, 2000.

Steinmetz, George. "Reflections on the Role of Social Narratives in Working Class Formation: Narrative Theory in the Social Sciences." *Social Science History* 16,3 (1992): 489–516.

Tajfel, Henri. *Social Identity and Intergroup Relations.* New York, NY: Cambridge University Press, 1982.

Taylor, Donald, and Fathali Moghaddam. *Theories of Intergroup Relations: International Social Psychological Perspectives.* New York, NY: Praeger, 1994.

Thawnghmung, Ardeth Maung. *Behind the Teak Curtain: Authoritarianism, Agricultural Policies, and Political Legitimacy in Rural Burma.* London: Kegan & Paul, 2003.

Thongchai Winichakul. *Siam Mapped: A History of the Geo-Body of Siam.* Honolulu, HI: University of Hawaii Press, 1994.

—— "The Quest for 'Siwilai': A Geographical Discourse of Civilizational Thinking in the Late Nineteenth and Early Twentieth-Century Siam." *Journal of Asian Studies* 59,3 (2000): 528–49.

Turits, Richard. *Foundations of Despotism: Peasants, the Trujillo Regime, and Modernity in Dominican History.* Stanford, CA: Stanford University Press, 2003.

Turton, Andrew, ed. *Civility and Savagery: Social Identity in Tai State.* Richmond, UK: Curzon, 2000.

Verdery, Katherine. *The Political Lives of Dead Bodies: Reburial and Postsocialist Change.* New York, NY: Columbia University Press, 1999.

Walker, Andrew. "The Rural Constitution and the Everyday Politics of Elections in Northern Thailand." *Journal of Contemporary Asia* 38,1 (2008): 84–105.

Waruni Osatharom. *Muang Suphan bon Sen Thang kan Plian Plaeng Thang Prawatisat: Phuthasatawat thi 8—Ton Phuthasatawat thi 25* (The City of Suphanburi on the Path of Historical Change: 8th Buddhist c.—25th Buddhist c.). Bangkok: Thammasat University Press, 2004.

Wedeen, Lisa. *Ambiguities of Domination: Politics, Rhetoric, and Symbols in Contemporary Syria.* Chicago, IL: University of Chicago Press, 1999.

White, Hayden. *Tropics of Discourse: Essays in Cultural Criticism.* Baltimore, MD: Johns Hopkins University Press, 1978.

—— *The Content of the Form: Narrative Discourse and Historical Representation.* Baltimore, MD: Johns Hopkins University Press, 1987.

Wolters, Oliver W. *History, Culture, and Region in Southeast Asian Perspectives.* Ithaca, NY: Cornell University Southeast Asia Studies Program, 1999.

Woodall, Brian. *Japan under Construction: Corruption, Politics, and Public Works.* Berkeley, CA: University of California Press, 1996.

Yea, Sallie. "Regionalism and Political-Economic Differentiation in Korean Development: Power Maintenance and the State as Hegemonic Power Bloc." *Korea Journal* 34,2 (1994): 5–29.

—— "The Culture and Politics of Resistance in South Korea." *Futures* 31 (1999): 221–34.

—— "Maps of Resistance and Geographies of Dissent in the Cholla Region of South Korea." *Korean Studies* 24 (2000): 69–93.

Zialcita, Fernando. "Perspectives on Legitimacy in Ilocos Norte," in *From Marcos to Aquino: Local Perspectives on Political Transition in the Philippines,* ed. Benedict Kerkvliet and Resil Mojares. Manila: Ateneo de Manila University Press, 1991, pp. 266–85.

INDEX

SOUTHEAST ASIA PROGRAM PUBLICATIONS
Cornell University

Studies on Southeast Asia

Number 53   *Political Authority and Provincial Identity in Thailand: The Making of Banharn-Buri*, Yoshinori Nishizaki. 2011. ISBN 978-087727-753-8

Number 52   *Vietnam and the West: New Approaches*, ed. Wynn Wilcox. 2010. ISBN 978-087727-752-1 (pb.)

Number 51   *Cultures at War: The Cold War and Cultural Expression in Southeast Asia*, ed. Tony Day and Maya H. T. Liem. 2010. ISBN 978-087727-751-4 (pb.)

Number 50   *State of Authority: The State in Society in Indonesia*, ed. Gerry van Klinken and Joshua Barker. 2009. ISBN 978-087727-750-7 (pb.)

Number 49   *Phan Châu Trinh and His Political Writings*, Phan Châu Trinh, ed. and trans. Vinh Sinh. 2009. ISBN 978-0-87727-749-1 (pb.)

Number 48   *Dependent Communities: Aid and Politics in Cambodia and East Timor*, Caroline Hughes. 2009. ISBN 978-0-87727-748-4 (pb.)

Number 47   *A Man Like Him: Portrait of the Burmese Journalist, Journal Kyaw U Chit Maung*, Journal Kyaw Ma Ma Lay, trans. Ma Thanegi, 2008. ISBN 978-0-87727-747-7 (pb.)

Number 46   *At the Edge of the Forest: Essays on Cambodia, History, and Narrative in Honor of David Chandler*, ed. Anne Ruth Hansen and Judy Ledgerwood. 2008. ISBN 978-0-87727-746-0 (pb)

Number 45   *Conflict, Violence, and Displacement in Indonesia*, ed. Eva-Lotta E. Hedman. 2008. ISBN 978-0-87727-745-3 (pb).

Number 44   *Friends and Exiles: A Memoir of the Nutmeg Isles and the Indonesian Nationalist Movement*, Des Alwi, ed. Barbara S. Harvey. 2008. ISBN 978-0-877277-44-6 (pb).

Number 43   *Early Southeast Asia: Selected Essays*, O. W. Wolters, ed. Craig J. Reynolds. 2008. 255 pp. ISBN 978-0-877277-43-9 (pb).

Number 42   *Thailand: The Politics of Despotic Paternalism* (revised edition), Thak Chaloemtiarana. 2007. 284 pp. ISBN 0-8772-7742-7 (pb).

Number 41   *Views of Seventeenth-Century Vietnam: Christoforo Borri on Cochinchina and Samuel Baron on Tonkin*, ed. Olga Dror and K. W. Taylor. 2006. 290 pp. ISBN 0-8772-7741-9 (pb).

Number 40   *Laskar Jihad: Islam, Militancy, and the Quest for Identity in Post-New Order Indonesia*, Noorhaidi Hasan. 2006. 266 pp. ISBN 0-877277-40-0 (pb).

Number 39   *The Indonesian Supreme Court: A Study of Institutional Collapse*, Sebastiaan Pompe. 2005. 494 pp. ISBN 0-877277-38-9 (pb).

Number 38   *Spirited Politics: Religion and Public Life in Contemporary Southeast Asia*, ed. Andrew C. Willford and Kenneth M. George. 2005. 210 pp. ISBN 0-87727-737-0.

Number 37   *Sumatran Sultanate and Colonial State: Jambi and the Rise of Dutch Imperialism, 1830-1907*, Elsbeth Locher-Scholten, trans. Beverley Jackson. 2004. 332 pp. ISBN 0-87727-736-2.

Number 36   *Southeast Asia over Three Generations: Essays Presented to Benedict R. O'G. Anderson*, ed. James T. Siegel and Audrey R. Kahin. 2003. 398 pp. ISBN 0-87727-735-4.

Number 16   *The Nan Chronicle,* trans., ed. David K. Wyatt. 1994. 158 pp.
ISBN 0-87727-715-X.

Number 15   *Selective Judicial Competence: The Cirebon-Priangan Legal Administration,
1680–1792,* Mason C. Hoadley. 1994. 185 pp. ISBN 0-87727-714-1.

Number 14   *Sjahrir: Politics and Exile in Indonesia,* Rudolf Mrázek. 1994. 536 pp.
ISBN 0-87727-713-3.

Number 13   *Fair Land Sarawak: Some Recollections of an Expatriate Officer,* Alastair
Morrison. 1993. 196 pp. ISBN 0-87727-712-5.

Number 12   *Fields from the Sea: Chinese Junk Trade with Siam during the Late
Eighteenth and Early Nineteenth Centuries,* Jennifer Cushman. 1993.
206 pp. ISBN 0-87727-711-7.

Number 11   *Money, Markets, and Trade in Early Southeast Asia: The Development of
Indigenous Monetary Systems to AD 1400,* Robert S. Wicks. 1992. 2nd
printing 1996. 354 pp., 78 tables, illus., maps. ISBN 0-87727-710-9.

Number 10   *Tai Ahoms and the Stars: Three Ritual Texts to Ward Off Danger,* trans., ed.
B. J. Terwiel, Ranoo Wichasin. 1992. 170 pp. ISBN 0-87727-709-5.

Number 9   *Southeast Asian Capitalists,* ed. Ruth McVey. 1992. 2nd printing 1993.
220 pp. ISBN 0-87727-708-7.

Number 8   *The Politics of Colonial Exploitation: Java, the Dutch, and the Cultivation
System,* Cornelis Fasseur, ed. R. E. Elson, trans. R. E. Elson, Ary Kraal.
1992. 2nd printing 1994. 266 pp. ISBN 0-87727-707-9.

Number 7   *A Malay Frontier: Unity and Duality in a Sumatran Kingdom,* Jane
Drakard. 1990. 2nd printing 2003. 215 pp. ISBN 0-87727-706-0.

Number 6   *Trends in Khmer Art,* Jean Boisselier, ed. Natasha Eilenberg, trans.
Natasha Eilenberg, Melvin Elliott. 1989. 124 pp., 24 plates.
ISBN 0-87727-705-2.

Number 5   *Southeast Asian Ephemeris: Solar and Planetary Positions, A.D. 638–2000,*
J. C. Eade. 1989. 175 pp. ISBN 0-87727-704-4.

Number 3   *Thai Radical Discourse: The Real Face of Thai Feudalism Today,* Craig J.
Reynolds. 1987. 2nd printing 1994. 186 pp. ISBN 0-87727-702-8.

Number 1   *The Symbolism of the Stupa,* Adrian Snodgrass. 1985. Revised with
index, 1988. 3rd printing 1998. 469 pp. ISBN 0-87727-700-1.

SEAP Series

Number 23   *Possessed by the Spirits: Mediumship in Contemporary Vietnamese
Communities.* 2006. 186 pp. ISBN 0-877271-41-0 (pb).

Number 22   *The Industry of Marrying Europeans,* Vũ Trọng Phụng, trans. Thúy
Tranviet. 2006. 66 pp. ISBN 0-877271-40-2 (pb).

Number 21   *Securing a Place: Small-Scale Artisans in Modern Indonesia,* Elizabeth
Morrell. 2005. 220 pp. ISBN 0-877271-39-9.

Number 20   *Southern Vietnam under the Reign of Minh Mạng (1820-1841): Central
Policies and Local Response,* Choi Byung Wook. 2004. 226pp. ISBN 0-0-
877271-40-2.

Number 19   *Gender, Household, State: Đổi Mới in Việt Nam,* ed. Jayne Werner and
Danièle Bélanger. 2002. 151 pp. ISBN 0-87727-137-2.

Number 18   *Culture and Power in Traditional Siamese Government*, Neil A. Englehart. 2001. 130 pp. ISBN 0-87727-135-6.

Number 17   *Gangsters, Democracy, and the State*, ed. Carl A. Trocki. 1998. Second printing, 2002. 94 pp. ISBN 0-87727-134-8.

Number 16   *Cutting across the Lands: An Annotated Bibliography on Natural Resource Management and Community Development in Indonesia, the Philippines, and Malaysia*, ed. Eveline Ferretti. 1997. 329 pp. ISBN 0-87727-133-X.

Number 15   *The Revolution Falters: The Left in Philippine Politics after 1986*, ed. Patricio N. Abinales. 1996. Second printing, 2002. 182 pp. ISBN 0-87727-132-1.

Number 14   *Being Kammu: My Village, My Life*, Damrong Tayanin. 1994. 138 pp., 22 tables, illus., maps. ISBN 0-87727-130-5.

Number 13   *The American War in Vietnam*, ed. Jayne Werner, David Hunt. 1993. 132 pp. ISBN 0-87727-131-3.

Number 12   *The Voice of Young Burma*, Aye Kyaw. 1993. 92 pp. ISBN 0-87727-129-1.

Number 11   *The Political Legacy of Aung San*, ed. Josef Silverstein. Revised edition 1993. 169 pp. ISBN 0-87727-128-3.

Number 10   *Studies on Vietnamese Language and Literature: A Preliminary Bibliography*, Nguyen Dinh Tham. 1992. 227 pp. ISBN 0-87727-127-5.

Number 8   *From PKI to the Comintern, 1924–1941: The Apprenticeship of the Malayan Communist Party*, Cheah Boon Kheng. 1992. 147 pp. ISBN 0-87727-125-9.

Number 7   *Intellectual Property and US Relations with Indonesia, Malaysia, Singapore, and Thailand*, Elisabeth Uphoff. 1991. 67 pp. ISBN 0-87727-124-0.

Number 6   *The Rise and Fall of the Communist Party of Burma (CPB)*, Bertil Lintner. 1990. 124 pp. 26 illus., 14 maps. ISBN 0-87727-123-2.

Number 5   *Japanese Relations with Vietnam: 1951–1987*, Masaya Shiraishi. 1990. 174 pp. ISBN 0-87727-122-4.

Number 3   *Postwar Vietnam: Dilemmas in Socialist Development*, ed. Christine White, David Marr. 1988. 2nd printing 1993. 260 pp. ISBN 0-87727-120-8.

Number 2   *The Dobama Movement in Burma (1930–1938)*, Khin Yi. 1988. 160 pp. ISBN 0-87727-118-6.

Copublished Titles

The Ambiguous Allure of the West: Traces of the Colonial in Thailand, ed. Rachel V. Harrison and Peter A. Jackson. Copublished with Hong Kong University Press. 2010. ISBN 978-0-87727-608-1 (pb.)

The Many Ways of Being Muslim: Fiction by Muslim Filipinos, ed. Coeli Barry. Copublished with Anvil Publishing, Inc., the Philippines. 2008. ISBN 978-08772-605-0 (pb.)

Cornell Modern Indonesia Project Publications
available at http://cmip.library.cornell.edu/

Number 75   *A Tour of Duty: Changing Patterns of Military Politics in Indonesia in the 1990s*. Douglas Kammen and Siddharth Chandra. 1999. 99 pp. ISBN 0-87763-049-6.

Number 74   *The Roots of Acehnese Rebellion 1989–1992*, Tim Kell. 1995. 103 pp.
ISBN 0-87763-040-2.

Number 73   *"White Book" on the 1992 General Election in Indonesia,* trans. Dwight
King. 1994. 72 pp. ISBN 0-87763-039-9.

Number 72   *Popular Indonesian Literature of the Qur'an*, Howard M. Federspiel. 1994.
170 pp. ISBN 0-87763-038-0.

Number 71   *A Javanese Memoir of Sumatra, 1945–1946: Love and Hatred in the
Liberation War*, Takao Fusayama. 1993. 150 pp. ISBN 0-87763-037-2.

Number 70   *East Kalimantan: The Decline of a Commercial Aristocracy*, Burhan
Magenda. 1991. 120 pp. ISBN 0-87763-036-4.

Number 69   *The Road to Madiun: The Indonesian Communist Uprising of 1948*,
Elizabeth Ann Swift. 1989. 120 pp. ISBN 0-87763-035-6.

Number 68   *Intellectuals and Nationalism in Indonesia: A Study of the Following
Recruited by Sutan Sjahrir in Occupation Jakarta*, J. D. Legge. 1988.
159 pp. ISBN 0-87763-034-8.

Number 67   *Indonesia Free: A Biography of Mohammad Hatta*, Mavis Rose. 1987.
252 pp. ISBN 0-87763-033-X.

Number 66   *Prisoners at Kota Cane*, Leon Salim, trans. Audrey Kahin. 1986. 112 pp.
ISBN 0-87763-032-1.

Number 65   *The Kenpeitai in Java and Sumatra*, trans. Barbara G. Shimer, Guy Hobbs,
intro. Theodore Friend. 1986. 80 pp. ISBN 0-87763-031-3.

Number 64   *Suharto and His Generals: Indonesia's Military Politics, 1975–1983*, David
Jenkins. 1984. 4th printing 1997. 300 pp. ISBN 0-87763-030-5.

Number 62   *Interpreting Indonesian Politics: Thirteen Contributions to the Debate, 1964–
1981*, ed. Benedict Anderson, Audrey Kahin, intro. Daniel S. Lev. 1982.
3rd printing 1991. 172 pp. ISBN 0-87763-028-3.

Number 60   *The Minangkabau Response to Dutch Colonial Rule in the Nineteenth
Century*, Elizabeth E. Graves. 1981. 157 pp. ISBN 0-87763-000-3.

Number 59   *Breaking the Chains of Oppression of the Indonesian People: Defense
Statement at His Trial on Charges of Insulting the Head of State, Bandung,
June 7–10, 1979*, Heri Akhmadi. 1981. 201 pp. ISBN 0-87763-001-1.

Number 57   *Permesta: Half a Rebellion*, Barbara S. Harvey. 1977. 174 pp.
ISBN 0-87763-003-8.

Number 55   *Report from Banaran: The Story of the Experiences of a Soldier during the
War of Independence*, Maj. Gen. T. B. Simatupang. 1972. 186 pp.
ISBN 0-87763-005-4.

Number 52   *A Preliminary Analysis of the October 1 1965, Coup in Indonesia (Prepared
in January 1966)*, Benedict R. Anderson, Ruth T. McVey, assist.
Frederick P. Bunnell. 1971. 3rd printing 1990. 174 pp.
ISBN 0-87763-008-9.

Number 51   *The Putera Reports: Problems in Indonesian-Japanese War-Time
Cooperation*, Mohammad Hatta, trans., intro. William H. Frederick.
1971. 114 pp. ISBN 0-87763-009-7.

Number 50   *Schools and Politics: The Kaum Muda Movement in West Sumatra (1927–
1933)*, Taufik Abdullah. 1971. 257 pp. ISBN 0-87763-010-0.

Number 49 *The Foundation of the Partai Muslimin Indonesia*, K. E. Ward. 1970. 75 pp. ISBN 0-87763-011-9.

Number 48 *Nationalism, Islam and Marxism*, Soekarno, intro. Ruth T. McVey. 1970. 2nd printing 1984. 62 pp. ISBN 0-87763-012-7.

Number 43 *State and Statecraft in Old Java: A Study of the Later Mataram Period, 16th to 19th Century*, Soemarsaid Moertono. Revised edition 1981. 180 pp. ISBN 0-87763-017-8.

Number 39 Preliminary Checklist of Indonesian Imprints (1945-1949), John M. Echols. 186 pp. ISBN 0-87763-025-9.

Number 37 *Mythology and the Tolerance of the Javanese*, Benedict R. O'G. Anderson. 2nd edition, 1996. Reprinted 2004. 104 pp., 65 illus. ISBN 0-87763-041-0.

Number 25 *The Communist Uprisings of 1926–1927 in Indonesia: Key Documents*, ed., intro. Harry J. Benda, Ruth T. McVey. 1960. 2nd printing 1969. 177 pp. ISBN 0-87763-024-0.

Translation Series

Volume 4 *Approaching Suharto's Indonesia from the Margins*, ed. Takashi Shiraishi. 1994. 153 pp. ISBN 0-87727-403-7.

Volume 3 *The Japanese in Colonial Southeast Asia*, ed. Saya Shiraishi, Takashi Shiraishi. 1993. 172 pp. ISBN 0-87727-402-9.

Volume 2 *Indochina in the 1940s and 1950s*, ed. Takashi Shiraishi, Motoo Furuta. 1992. 196 pp. ISBN 0-87727-401-0.

Volume 1 *Reading Southeast Asia*, ed. Takashi Shiraishi. 1990. 188 pp.
ISBN 0-87727-400-2.

Language Texts

INDONESIAN

Beginning Indonesian through Self-Instruction, John U. Wolff, Dédé Oetomo, Daniel Fietkiewicz. 3rd revised edition 1992. Vol. 1. 115 pp. ISBN 0-87727-529-7. Vol. 2. 434 pp. ISBN 0-87727-530-0. Vol. 3. 473 pp. ISBN 0-87727-531-9.

Indonesian Readings, John U. Wolff. 1978. 4th printing 1992. 480 pp.
ISBN 0-87727-517-3

Indonesian Conversations, John U. Wolff. 1978. 3rd printing 1991. 297 pp.
ISBN 0-87727-516-5

Formal Indonesian, John U. Wolff. 2nd revised edition 1986. 446 pp.
ISBN 0-87727-515-7

TAGALOG

Pilipino through Self-Instruction, John U. Wolff, Maria Theresa C. Centeno, Der-Hwa V. Rau. 1991. Vol. 1. 342 pp. ISBN 0-87727—525-4. Vol. 2., revised 2005, 378 pp. ISBN 0-87727-526-2. Vol 3., revised 2005, 431 pp. ISBN 0-87727-527-0. Vol. 4. 306 pp. ISBN 0-87727-528-9.

THAI

A. U. A. Language Center Thai Course, J. Marvin Brown. Originally published by the American University Alumni Association Language Center, 1974. Reissued by Cornell Southeast Asia Program, 1991, 1992. Book 1. 267 pp. ISBN 0-87727-506-8. Book 2. 288 pp. ISBN 0-87727-507-6. Book 3. 247 pp. ISBN 0-87727-508-4.

A. U. A. Language Center Thai Course, Reading and Writing Text (mostly reading), 1979. Reissued 1997. 164 pp. ISBN 0-87727-511-4.

A. U. A. Language Center Thai Course, Reading and Writing Workbook (mostly writing), 1979. Reissued 1997. 99 pp. ISBN 0-87727-512-2.

KHMER

Cambodian System of Writing and Beginning Reader, Franklin E. Huffman. Originally published by Yale University Press, 1970. Reissued by Cornell Southeast Asia Program, 4th printing 2002. 365 pp. ISBN 0-300-01314-0.

Modern Spoken Cambodian, Franklin E. Huffman, assist. Charan Promchan, Chhom-Rak Thong Lambert. Originally published by Yale University Press, 1970. Reissued by Cornell Southeast Asia Program, 3rd printing 1991. 451 pp. ISBN 0-300-01316-7.

Intermediate Cambodian Reader, ed. Franklin E. Huffman, assist. Im Proum. Originally published by Yale University Press, 1972. Reissued by Cornell Southeast Asia Program, 1988. 499 pp. ISBN 0-300-01552-6.

Cambodian Literary Reader and Glossary, Franklin E. Huffman, Im Proum. Originally published by Yale University Press, 1977. Reissued by Cornell Southeast Asia Program, 1988. 494 pp. ISBN 0-300-02069-4.

HMONG

White Hmong-English Dictionary, Ernest E. Heimbach. 1969. 8th printing, 2002. 523 pp. ISBN 0-87727-075-9.

VIETNAMESE

Intermediate Spoken Vietnamese, Franklin E. Huffman, Tran Trong Hai. 1980. 3rd printing 1994. ISBN 0-87727-500-9.

* * *

Javanese Literature in Surakarta Manuscripts, Nancy K. Florida. Vol. 1, *Introduction and Manuscripts of the Karaton Surakarta*. 1993. 410 pp. Frontispiece, illustrations. Hard cover, ISBN 0-87727-602-1, Paperback, ISBN 0-87727-603-X. Vol. 2, *Manuscripts of the Mangkunagaran Palace*. 2000. 576 pp. Frontispiece, illustrations. Paperback, ISBN 0-87727-604-8.

In the Mirror: Literature and Politics in Siam in the American Era, ed. Benedict R. O'G. Anderson, trans. Benedict R. O'G. Anderson, Ruchira Mendiones. 1985. 2nd printing 1991. 303 pp. Paperback. ISBN 974-210-380-1.

TO ORDER, PLEASE CONTACT:
Mail:
Cornell University Press Services
750 Cascadilla Street
PO Box 6525
Ithaca, NY 14851 USA

E-mail: orderbook@cupserv.org
Phone/Fax, Monday–Friday, 8 am – 5 pm (Eastern US):
Phone: 607 277 2211 or 800 666 2211 (US, Canada)
Fax: 607 277 6292 or 800 688 2877 (US, Canada)
Order through our online bookstore:
www.einaudi.cornell.edu/southeastasia/publications/

Lightning Source UK Ltd.
Milton Keynes UK
UKHW031929060922
408432UK00007B/1566